Middle and High School Teaching

Methods, Standards, and Best Practices

JAMES A. DUPLASS

University of South Florida

Houghton Mifflin Company

Boston   New York

Dedicated to All My Teachers

In particular:

Al Murphy; Louis Levy; Sister Mary Alice, O.P.; Br. Gerard;
Br. Amedy Long; Br. Adrian; Br. Alton; Jeffrey Callagan, F.S.C.;
Howard Jenkins, F.S.C.; Karl Hangartner, S.J.; Frank Brennan, S.J.;
and Barry McGannon, S.J.

Editor-in-Chief: Patricia Coryell
Senior Sponsoring Editor: Sue Pulvermacher-Alt
Senior Development Editor: Lisa Mafrici
Editorial Assistant: Dayna Pell
Project Editor: Reba Libby
Editorial Assistant: Deborah Berkman
Senior Art and Design Coordinator: Jill Haber Atkins
Senior Photo Editor: Jennifer Meyer Dare
Manufacturing Director: Priscilla Manchester
Executive Marketing Manager: Nicola Poser

Cover images: (Image # AA038768: yellow green abstract background) Cover image credit: © Jason Reed/Getty Images;
(Image # dv590063a: kids at computer) Cover image credit: © Getty Images.

Text credits are on p. 369, which constitutes a continuation of the copyright page.

Printed in the U.S.A.

Library of Congress Catalog Card Number: 2005927890

ISBN: 0-618-43575-1

123456789-QUE-09 08 07 06 05

Contents

Unit 6 **Methods**   **201**

Unit 7 **Assessing Student Learning**   **261**

Unit 8 **Content Area Trends, Standards, and Teaching Methods**   **283**

Professor's Preface

Dear Colleague:

Middle and High School Teaching: Methods, Standards, and Best Practices is intended to meet the needs of full- and part-time professors who teach future middle and high school teachers in initial certification programs.

What courses is this book suited for?

This textbook is intended for:

1. General methods courses for future middle and high school teachers
2. Curriculum and instruction (C & I) courses for future middle and high school teachers
3. Introduction to education courses for future middle and high school teachers
4. The first specific methods courses in programs with two methods courses in the discipline, but no general methods or C & I courses

Why is a new approach needed?

This book and its ancillary materials (websites, PowerPoint presentations, subject matter basal text materials, etc.) were developed in response to a number of recent and significant changes that affect teacher education. These include the following:

1. The Interstate New Teacher Assessment and Support Consortium (INTASC) standards
2. The National Council for Accreditation of Teacher Education (NCATE) standards
3. The Goals 2000 legislation
4. The No Child Left Behind legislation and the High Objective Uniform State Standard of Evaluation (HOUSSE)
5. The content standards defined by the professional organizations (also referred to as **learned societies** in this text)
6. The abundant and growing Internet resources to support teachers
7. Pressures for course consolidations because of greater demands for efficiency in colleges and universities

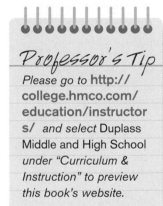

Professor's Tip

Please go to http://college.hmco.com/education/instructors/ *and select* Duplass Middle and High School *under "Curriculum & Instruction" to preview this book's website.*

How does this book uniquely respond to these changes?

This book is distinct in that it:

1. **Covers the typical topics of a methods text** (although we believe in a more engaging style) in a way that is research-based, precisely presented, and easy to read.
2. **Includes authentic assignments** that are necessary (but not overly burdensome from a grading perspective) for the kind of substantial performance-based proof of competence required of accredited teacher education programs using the INTASC/NCATE standards framework.
3. **Uniquely covers the teaching fields'** content and methods with an introduc-

tion and detailed treatment of the standards, content, and methods of the major subject fields (see Unit 8) so as to allow you to:
   a. Introduce students early in their training to their teaching field.
   b. Provide a bridge from general pedagogical knowledge to content-specific pedagogical knowledge.
4. **Promotes basic skills and critical thinking** instruction across the curriculum in response to the demands of high-stakes testing.
5. **Includes basal text materials** from the middle/high school publisher McDougal Littell or the Internet (see the ***Bonus Course Materials*** at the accompanying textbook website) for each of the teaching fields so that students can complete authentic assignments using textbooks used in classrooms today.
6. **Makes extensive use of the Internet** to create assignments on the content and pedagogical knowledge in students' teaching fields and on knowledge about middle and high schools and the education profession.
7. **Employs a scaffolding approach** through the sequence of Units and Topics.

Why will this book make my teaching more effective?

This text and the extensive website resources for use by the professor and students will facilitate your teaching because:

1. Through strategic use of posed questions, online resources, assignments, and text boxes of teacher's tips and key ideas, students are called upon to reflect and be actively engaged in the construction of their knowledge.
2. This book has more topics than can be covered in a traditional three-credit course. This allows you to:
   a. Pick and choose the topics you wish to cover in class and to the depth you feel is appropriate.
   b. Rely on students being able to read this book to acquire the breadth of topics appropriate for a secondary school teacher.
3. Individual teaching fields are discussed in enough depth to provide adequate information to professors who may only have a cursory understanding of them.
4. The professor's website has a complete set of PowerPoint slides for each topic that you can download to your computer. You can use these in class to engage students with a mixture of discussion, lecture, demonstration, out-of-class assignments, and in-class activities.
5. The straightforward, easily readable, concise text is organized into compact Topics (rather than dense chapters of text), with the result that students are more inclined to actually read their textbook.
6. Through this book's website you can access continuously updated practical and scholarly resources from ERIC, GEM, and the What Works Clearinghouse.
7. There are more assignments than can possibly be completed in a semester-long class. The intent is to provide a menu from which you can select and modify those that will be most beneficial to your students. Each assignment is tied to an INTASC standard. Table P.1 (see below) aligns the ten INTASC standards with the three primary NCATE accreditation standards. Only the INTASC standards are attached to assignments because they are more discrete than the three NCATE standards and thus lend themselves to more specific documentation. However, with Table P.1 you can also determine which NCATE standards apply.

Professor's Tip

WebCT and **BlackBoard Users:** The PDF versions of chapters from secondary-level textbooks in each of the subject fields, as well as Internet links, assignments, grade book, sample syllabus, and other **Bonus Course Materials,** may be downloaded and transferred to WebCT or BlackBoard (or another comparable system) during the semesters in which you adopt the book.

How does this book support standards-based teacher education?

The Interstate New Teacher Assessment and Support Consortium (INTASC) is an association organized by chief state school officers (at http://www.ccsso.org) from nearly forty states and professional organizations that sets standards for **initial licensure** of teachers for member states. The National Council for Accreditation of Teacher Education (NCATE, at http://www.ncate.org/) is the professional accrediting body for teacher education programs and sets standards for its voluntary member colleges for **Certification**. About 500 of the 1,200 teacher education programs are seeking NCATE accreditation. In addition, and although not the focus of this text, the National Board of Professional Teacher Standards (NBPTS, at http://www.nbpts.org/) has identified standards for in-service teachers' professional development.

INTASC (at http://www.ccsso.org/content/pdfs/corestrd.pdf) and NCATE (at http://www.ncate.org/standard/m_stds.htm) share a common construct (see Table P.1 and Topic 2, Table 2.1) that is being adopted by teacher education programs to qualify their students for certification and licensure through their states. Through the No Child Left Behind legislation, states are required to adopt a standard under what is known as the High Objective Uniform State Standard of Evaluation (HOUSSE) so that teachers can demonstrate competency in content areas.

The assignments included in *Middle and High School Teaching: Methods, Standards, and Best Practices* were developed to help professors and teacher education programs demonstrate their compliance with the NCATE and INTASC

Table P.1 | **NCATE AND INTASC STANDARDS**

NCATE Standards for Accreditation/Certification	INTASC Core Standards for Licensing *(Also see Topic 2 and Table of Assignments*)*
Content Knowledge for Teacher Candidates. Teacher candidates have in-depth knowledge of the subject matter that they plan to teach as described in professional, state, and institutional standards. They demonstrate their knowledge through inquiry, critical analysis, and synthesis of the subject. All program completers pass the academic content examinations in states that require examinations for licensure.	**Principle 1: Subject Matter Expertise.** The teacher understands the central concepts, tools of inquiry, and structures of the discipline(s) he or she teaches and can create learning experiences that make these aspects of subject matter meaningful for students.
Pedagogical Content Knowledge for Teacher Candidates. Teacher candidates reflect a thorough understanding of pedagogical content knowledge delineated in professional, state, and institutional standards. They have in-depth understanding of the subject matter that they plan to teach, allowing them to provide multiple explanations and instructional strategies so that all students learn. They present the content to students in challenging, clear, and compelling ways and integrate technology appropriately.	**Principle 4: Multiple Instructional Strategies.** The teacher understands and uses a variety of instructional strategies to encourage students' development of critical-thinking, problem-solving, and performance skills. **Principle 6: Communication Skills.** The teacher uses knowledge of effective verbal, nonverbal, and media communication techniques to foster active inquiry, collaboration, and supportive interaction in the classroom.

Table P.1 continued

NCATE Standards for Accreditation/Certification	INTASC Core Standards for Licensing
Pedagogical Content Knowledge for Teacher Candidates	**Principle 7: Instructional Planning.** The teacher plans instruction based upon knowledge of subject matter, students, the community, and curriculum goals. **Principle 8: Assessment.** The teacher understands and uses formal and informal assessment strategies to evaluate and ensure the continuous intellectual, social, and physical development of the learner.
Professional and Pedagogical Knowledge and Skills for Teacher Candidates. Teacher candidates reflect a thorough understanding of professional and pedagogical knowledge and skills delineated in professional, state, and institutional standards. They develop meaningful learning experiences to facilitate learning for all students. They reflect on their practice and make necessary adjustments to enhance student learning. They know how students learn and how to make ideas accessible to them. They consider school, family, and community contexts in connecting concepts to students' prior experience and applying the ideas to real-world problems.	**Principle 2: Learning and Development.** The teacher understands how children learn and develop, and can provide learning opportunities that support their intellectual, social, and personal development. **Principle 3: Diverse Learners.** The teacher understands how students differ in their approaches to learning and creates instructional opportunities that are adapted to diverse learners. **Principle 5: Motivation and Classroom Management.** The teacher uses an understanding of individual and group motivation and behavior to create a learning environment that encourages positive social interaction, active engagement in learning, and self-motivation. **Principle 9: Professional Commitment and Responsibility.** The teacher is a reflective practitioner who continually evaluates the effects of his or her choices and actions on others (students, parents, and other professionals in the learning community) and who actively seeks out opportunities to grow professionally. **Principle 10: Partnerships.** The teacher fosters relationships with school colleagues, parents, and agencies in the larger community to support students' learning and well-being.

*Can be downloaded from **http://college.hmco.com/education/instructors/**.

standards. Each assignment in this textbook identifies which INTASC standard(s) can be met by completing the assignment. In addition, you can download a Table of Assignments and their INTASC standards at this book's preview website at **http://college.hmco.com/education/instructors/** in an MS Word format for modification and inclusion in your syllabus or posting at a university resource like BlackBoard.

How do I access this book's website, and what kind of instructor support is available?

As an alternative to a traditional instructor's manual, this text is supported by extensive online media resources at its website. You can go to the website to preview some of the PowerPoint presentations, the Instructor's Guide, Internet links, and the Assignments.

Upon adopting this textbook, you can obtain a **CONFIDENTIAL** password to access the entire website by contacting your sales representative or the faculty service center at 1–800–733–1717. The Instructor's website includes:

1. **PowerPoint files** for each Topic. You can download these files to your hard drive and modify them to meet your needs for use in the classroom. The PowerPoint files incorporate content from the text, placeholders, Internet links, and prompts for assignments. One feature, as an example, is that each Topic starts with—as Madeline Hunter (1982) put it—an "Anticipatory Set." For this text, it is typically a "Question of the Day" taken from the book's *Questions*.

   Students should have considered the *Teacher's Tips* or *For the Reflective Practitioner* features during their reading of the Topic. The PowerPoint files are for classroom use only: That is, they are not to be made available to students via the Internet or a system like BlackBoard.

2. At the **Bonus Course Materials** link, materials you (and your students) can download are:
   a. *Middle and high school basal textbook chapters* from the publisher McDougal Littell in PDF format for each of the subject fields (mathematics, French, etc.), along with some other Internet-based resources that are provided for use with the authentic assignments in Topic 13 and Unit 8. Please go to Assignment 13.1 for a list of the available text materials.
   b. An *example/template* of a Unit Plan's Statement of Goals (see Topic 19, Assignment 19.1) and teacher's Class Notes (see Topic 20, Assignment 20.1).
   c. *Employment Portfolio Templates* for Topic 18: Preparing for the First Day of Class.
   d. *Authentic Lesson Planning Assignments* for each of the teaching fields in Unit 8.
3. **Instructor's Guide** with suggestions for using and integrating various elements of the book and website resources.
4. **Final Exam Item Databank** that contains true/false and multiple-choice questions should you use this kind of final exam in addition to the other assignments available in the book.
5. **Sample Syllabus** for a 16-week, one-day-a-week class.
6. **Sample Grade Book** in Microsoft Excel format.
7. **Assignments** copied from the text in a Microsoft Word format for your editing and revision and a table showing how each assignment meets at least

> **Professor's Tip**
> In addition to material from the textbook, the PowerPoint files will contain supplemental content. As an example, Assignment 9.1 in Topic 9 has one chart in the textbook, but three additional charts are available in PowerPoint to enhance the classroom experience.

> **Professor's Tip**
> In most cases the assignments are very specific. This is not because I believe my ideas are best, but because I believe it is easier for you to modify detailed assignments than assignments that are too generic.

one of the INTASC standards. Many assignments can be restructured for discussions and group activities during class or posted to BlackBoard or WebCT as assignments or for online discussion boards.

8. The **Authentic Unit and Daily Lesson Planning Assignments** for each subject field in *Unit 8: Content Area Trends, Standards & Teaching Methods* appear *ONLY* at the website.

9. **Links to websites** in the order of appearance in the book, as well as **Bonus Links** to useful websites too numerous to include in the text. All the links will be maintained and updated to ensure that Internet resources are current. The links are available to the professor and students at their respective websites.

10. **Links to Full-Text online ERIC** documents in the order of appearance in the book as well as **Bonus Links** to other online ERIC documents that are too numerous to include in the text. All of these ERIC documents will be periodically reviewed and new ones added to ensure a current research base. These are also available to the professor and students at their respective websites.

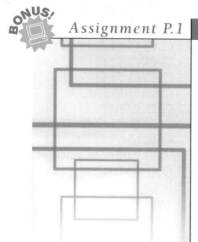

BONUS!

Assignment P.1 | **CROSSWORD PUZZLES**

INTASC STANDARDS 2–5, 7, 8

The following is the first assignment you might decide to use. **Product Assignments** in this text are used primarily to help students demonstrate synthesis of concepts and apply the concepts. The **final exam** (if you decide to use one) is intended to be used to demonstrate the professional level of literacy necessary to work in a community of practice and to remain a lifelong learner. The idea of Assignment P.1 is to facilitate a review for the final exam by having students create crossword puzzles as a study aid. Of equal importance, it is intended to encourage your students to consider assessment approaches that differ from traditional tests.

Here is the assignment: Go to the website http://www.Puzzlemaker.com or http://www.varietygames.com/CW/ (or a comparable website) or a software package that can be used to create a crossword puzzle based on one of the Topics assigned by your professor. Create a crossword puzzle of no less than fifteen items. Select the most important vocabulary and concepts, and be creative when making up the clues. Prepare one copy of the puzzle and clues for each student and the professor, as well as an answer sheet for the professor.

OnLine Resources | **PASSWORD PROTECTION**

You can preview the material on the Instructor's website without a password at http://college.hmco.com/education/instructors/. Under "Curriculum & Instruction," select "Duplass, Middle and High School Teaching" to access the Instructor's website.

Upon adoption of the text, you will receive a password to access the entire website. You can call the HMCO Faculty Service Center at 1-800-733-1717 (or contact your HMCO local representative) to adopt the text and receive a password to the instructor's website. HMCO will first verify that you are an instructor and not a student.

In addition, you can follow the directions in the "Student's Introduction" of this book to preview the student's website, using the password that is provided for students in that section.

Acknowledgments

I would like to acknowledge the support of my colleagues, especially the following specialists who read the manuscript and offered excellent suggestions: Professor J. Howard Johnston, Middle School Education and School Reform; Professor Carine Feyten, World Language Education; Associate Professor Gladys Kursant, Mathematics Education; Professor Dana Zeidler, Science Education; Professor Barbara Cruz, Social Studies Education; and Aimee Fogelman and Tom Murray, doctoral students. Grateful acknowledgment goes to the many reviewers who made constructive suggestions and provided thoughtful reactions during the development of the manuscript. They include: Paul D. Bland, Emporia State University; Nathan Bond, Texas State University; Timothy J. Duggan, University of South Dakota; W. Patrick Durow, Creighton University; Charles E. Hanus, University of Texas at San Antonio; Irvin Howard, California State University, San Bernardino; Julie H. Lester, Southeastern Louisiana University; Stephen D. McGalla III, California University of Pennsylvania; Eunice M. Merideth, Drake University; Scott Page, Minnesota State University, Mankato; Joe Parks, California State University, Fresno; Martha H. Rader, Arizona State University; Anthony M. Roselli, Merrimack College; and Marsha K. Savage, Santa Clara University.

In addition, I would like to thank Houghton Mifflin's Sue Pulvermacher-Alt, Senior Sponsoring Editor, who believed and supported this new kind of text from the beginning, and Lisa Mafrici, Senior Development Editor, for providing insightful editorial guidance throughout the development process. I also wish to thank the publisher McDougal Littell for granting permission to reprint many excerpts from their texts on the accompanying textbook website.

Student's Introduction

Your college, as part of its accreditation or certification agreement with your state, is required to demonstrate that you have a set of **dispositions, knowledge,** and **skills** related to the practice of teaching prior to completion of your teacher education program.

Universities **certify** students as having completed an **Accredited** and/or **State-Approved** program, and states **license** teachers. Many colleges will require a portfolio based on state standards as a prerequisite to graduation, or the teacher education program will tie these standards to assignments in courses so that a student's program of coursework (the **curriculum**) can be used to demonstrate that it is graduating students that are prepared for **Initial Certification** based on state standards.

Standards-Based Teacher Training

Standards-Based Teacher Training is a relatively new, nationwide movement that has come to the forefront during the last ten years at the same time as standards-based education for the K–12 system. The **Interstate New Teacher Assessment and Support Consortium** (INTASC) and the **National Council for Accreditation of Teacher Education** (NCATE) are the national organizations that, in consultation with colleges, have established the commonly used standards for teacher preparation programs. The ten INTASC standards are listed in Topic 2 (see Table 2.1), and you should review them so that you better understand what is expected of novice teachers. You can learn more about these organizations by going to their websites:

- INTASC at **http://www.ccsso.org/Projects/interstate_new_teacher_assessment_and_support_consortium/780.cfm** and a PDF file of the standards at **http://www.ccsso.org/content/pdfs/corestrd.pdf**
- NCATE at **http://www.ncate.org/**

For the Reflective Practitioner

One of the similarities between teaching at the college level and at the secondary school level is that we are both expected to address state standards.

How to Use This Textbook and Its Website

Unlike traditional textbooks, which may require only a passive reading prior to class, this book expects you to *interact* with the text, the Internet, the professor, clinical faculty members (practicing middle and high school teachers), and your fellow students as you construct your knowledge about teaching at the secondary level. *Middle and High School Teaching: Methods, Standards, and Best Practices* achieves this with a number of strategies.

Assignments

The purpose of the assignments in this textbook is for you to think about a concept, reconstruct your understanding of it, and apply your knowledge. Many of the assignments are practical and pragmatic (referred to in the professional literature as **Authentic Assessments**) like lesson plans that will be expected of you as a teacher. Some of the assignments create opportunities for you to interact with clinical faculty in what are known as **"early field"** or **"clinical experiences"** as part of **"field-based teacher preparation programs,"** and others are designed to have you reflect on your future practices as a teacher.

TEACHER STANDARDS: A CONTRARY VIEW   *Assignment S.1*

INTASC STANDARDS 9, 10

As a teacher, you have a duty to exercise your freedom of thought and speech. Now that you have learned a little more about Certification and Licensure, you should know that there is significant disagreement among educators as to the role that colleges of education should play in these systems, as well as concerns about their impact on the teaching profession (Labaree 1999/ 2000). Go to the Abell Foundation for their critique of teacher certification and licensure, "Teacher Certification Reconsidered: Stumbling for Quality." Although it specifically critiques the state of Maryland licensure practices, Maryland's policies are typical of many states. Go to http://www.abell.org/ publications/detail.asp?ID=62. Then read the rejoinder by Linda Darling-Hammond at http://www.abell.org/publications/detail.asp?ID=61. Be prepared to have a dialogue on this topic and share your opinions in class.

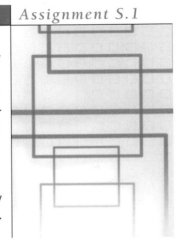

Each assignment is tied to an **INTASC standard** (see Topic 2) so that it can be demonstrated by your college that you have met a specific standard.

Many of the assignments, like Assignment S.1, are to be completed prior to the class session in which the professor plans to cover the topic. Their purpose is to create a **baseline of information** upon which the professor will develop concepts in a dialogue with the class. You should be able to successfully complete these assignments based on prior general knowledge, close reading of the book, and reflection. Other assignments are to be completed after presentations or discussions as homework or as class activities during class. Check your syllabus to determine which assignments are required, and ask your professor if there are any modifications to the submission criteria.

Questions

> *What do you think would be the advantages and impediments to creating a baseline of information in a middle or high school setting?*

Questions like this one will appear throughout the text to help you reflect on what you are learning. This question mark symbol will be your cue to consider the idea that is presented and develop an answer to a question. You should be prepared to respond to these **"Grounded"** questions during class (see Topic 28 for explanations of "baseline of information" and "grounded questions").

Teacher's Tips

In addition to the narrative, you will periodically see a Teacher's Tip—a practical idea that you can use in the classroom.

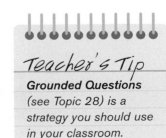

Teacher's Tip

Grounded Questions *(see Topic 28) is a strategy you should use in your classroom.*

For the Reflective Practitioner

Notable quotes, key concepts, or a thought-provoking idea will be highlighted by being presented in text boxes labeled "For the Reflective Practitioner." They are intended to give you insights that you might not easily recognize about a topic. You should be prepared to discuss the ideas in class.

References

Traditional references (in contrast to on-line "Full-Text" Internet sources) appear as citations in the text and are listed in the "References" section at the end of the book so that you can further investigate the topics covered in this textbook.

Internet Resources

Internet sites are an essential component of the text and should be as indispensable to your participation in the profession and teaching as paper and pencil. The websites that are cited are for your benefit both as a student, today, and as a soon-to-be full-time teacher. Internet sites appear in the text and as clickable URLs (website addresses) at this book's website at **http://education.college .hmco.com/students**.

Use of the Internet

Because the Internet is now an essential tool for teachers, its use has been integrated into this text. You will use the Internet in five ways.

1. **Internet searches.** Searches for content and lesson plan ideas can be conducted using any browser, like Google, Look Smart, Copernic, or Lycos. The Internet has made an enormous number of resources related to middle and high school teaching available to teachers: These include more general information about schools, motivation, and other topics as well as pedagogical and content knowledge about the individual disciplines.

2. **ERIC (Educational Resources Information Center).** No textbook can cover the vast array of educational research studies, ideas, and strategies about teaching. With over 1 million documents, ERIC is the academic index used by most educators to locate current research on education topics. It has a degree of credibility that is not true of the Internet in general because most entries are reprinted from academic journals, conference presentations, and national reports. Many of ERIC's documents are **"Full-Text"** documents, which means the entire document can be retrieved online as a **PDF** (portable document format). The goal is to eventually have all documents available as full-text, online PDF files. In the past, teachers were forced to spend endless hours in the library and at a microfilm machine to find current and classic ideas on how to teach in new ways; now we have the Internet.

 In what ways can you envision using the Internet in your middle or high school class? How will you help your students locate credible sources?

This textbook makes special use of full-text documents. Throughout this book (and through links at the Houghton Mifflin (HMCO) website for this book), you will find ERIC downloadable, full-text articles identified by a number like "ED426985." Go to http://www.eric.ed.gov, select "ERIC #" from the pull-down menu in the first "Search" box; then enter ED426985 in the second box. A page will be displayed showing you the title of the article and below that, information such as the author and the date. At the bottom will be a short abstract, or summary, of the article. Then if you click "View Full-Text," you can download the article in its entirety. With the full-text service, you should be able to print out the full text of a document in a PDF format. If you return to the main page and select "Advanced Search," you will see that, when searching for documents based on a title, author, or keyword, you can request to view only those documents that are full text. Keep in mind that many of the best articles are not yet available online.

3. **The Gateway to Educational Materials**^{SM} **(GEM)** is a federally sponsored consortium effort to provide educators with quick and easy access to the substantial, but uncataloged, collections of educational materials (primarily lesson plans and teaching materials) found on various federal, state, university, nonprofit, and commercial Internet sites. For searches, go to http://www.thegateway.org/browse.

4. **What Works Clearinghouse.** A new initiative being implemented as a result of the No Child Left Behind legislation (see Topic 3) is the What Works Clearinghouse (WWC) at http://www.whatworks.ed.gov/. The What Works Clearinghouse was established by the U.S. Department of Education's Institute of Education Sciences to provide educators, policymakers, and the public with a central source of scientific evidence of what works in education. Like ERIC, it houses publications about education; however, a major difference is that it limits its publications to reviews of scientific evidence of the effectiveness of replicable educational interventions (for example, programs, practices, products, or policies) that promise to improve student outcomes.

5. **The HMCO College Division Website** at http://education.college.hmco.com/students (under "Curriculum & Instruction," select "Duplass, Middle and High School Teaching") has all the websites and ERIC documents listed in this textbook as clickable links, as well as additional resources, such as chapters from middle and high school textbooks in your teaching field (textbooks are usually referred to as **"basal texts"**) and lesson-planning templates that may be downloaded and that your professor will likely have you use for your assignments for Topic 13 and Unit 8.

Criteria for Selection of Websites

The websites in this textbook were selected on the basis of their quality, credibility, and durability. In addition to the links in the text, there are **Bonus Links** (websites and ERIC Full Text documents) that are too numerous to include in the textbook but are included in each Topic following the links that appear in the text.

1. **Quality:** Each site was reviewed for the quality of the website and the relevance or significance of the information.

2. **Credibility:** There are no guarantees that content on the Internet is accurate. For Internet sites, like any information medium, the source is a major consideration. An emphasis was placed on sites whose sponsors have reputations for service to the public good, like the NCSS, MiddleWeb at http://www.middleweb.com/, the Smithsonian, other government organizations, and well-known organizations like universities.

3. **Durability:** Content on the Internet is fluid. Because you will need to rely on specific sites for your work as a teacher, websites that are likely to be around for a long time and that are regularly updated were given priority. You can also expect to see periodic substitutions on this when websites cease operation.

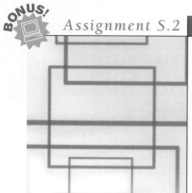

Assignment S.2

GEM SEARCH

INTASC STANDARDS 1, 2, 4, 7

Go to this book's website (see directions in OnLine Resources box below) or access the GEM website directly at http://www.thegateway.org/. Click "Browse" in the Navigation box and then click "Browse the Gateway by Subject." Select your domain/discipline, such as "mathematics," and then under "level" select a grade level for middle or high school. Review a number of lesson plans, select one, print it out, bring it to class, and be prepared to share your ideas about the document with the class and to turn in the assignment to your professor.

Editorial: Become an Independent Thinker

To greater or lesser degrees, all books reflect an author's experiences and opinions. In many cases, I raise issues for your consideration, and in others I make specific recommendations. Professors are expected to "profess" what they believe to be the wisest approach to their field of study. Not all professors will agree with my opinions. However, there is nothing more important to academia, a free society, and the education of the students you will teach than the free exchange of ideas. If you read something in this book that you don't agree with, I suspect nothing would please your professor more than for you to raise the topic in class and provide a thoughtful analysis and some good examples of why you disagree.

We wish you the very best and the greatest success as a teacher.

OnLine Resources **PASSWORD TO STUDENT'S HMCO WEBSITE**

You can enter this book's website for students at http://education.college.hmco.com/students, and under "Curriculum & Instruction," select "Duplass, Middle and High School Teaching." On the homepage, you will need to enter the username *secondary* and the password *methods*. Be sure to save this page as one of your favorites because you will be using it frequently in this class and, in all likelihood, during the remainder of your education.

UNIT ONE

The Teacher's Role and Context

http://cagle.slate.msn.com/news/education/main.asp. © Bruce Plante, Chattanooa Times Free Press.

The Teaching Profession and Craft

So, you want to be a middle or high school teacher! Great, and welcome aboard!

A recent graduate was asked what surprised her most upon becoming a teacher. Her answer bears repeating:

"I was surprised at how easy it is to get by as a mediocre teacher and how hard the job is if you want to be a really great teacher."

Education differs from other professions in that everyone entering the field knows how school works, even if only as a consumer. Changing from this common understanding to a professional orientation requires reflection and a willingness to transcend persistent beliefs (Lortie, 1975/2002). Prospective teachers bring intuition and a commonsense understanding to their training based on a lifetime of observing the **pedagogy** (the art and science of teaching) as practiced by others. A teacher education program hopes to provide the empirical, commonsense, and theoretical underpinnings of the teaching craft as well as opportunities to practice it.

David Labaree (2000) points out that teaching is a markedly complex and intricate form of professional practice because it requires one to motivate, in a group setting, individuals on a cognitive, moral, and behavioral level who are often resistant and not there voluntarily. Preparing well before beginning your career can make a significant difference in your success and professional development as a teacher.

For the Reflective Practitioner

Genius is 99 percent perspiration and 1 percent inspiration.

THOMAS EDISON

For the Reflective Practitioner

Teaching is not a lost art, but the regard for it is a lost tradition.

JACQUES BARZUN

Teaching as a Craft

I have used the word *craft* in describing teaching because it brings to my mind the fine craftsmen of the Middle Ages. These highly professional artisans merged their scientific knowledge and practical skills with individual imagination and a work ethic that produced the great cathedrals, frescoes, paintings, and sculptures that Americans flock to in their summer European travels. The **Teaching Craft** is the actual teaching part of the **Teaching Profession.** David Moore (1995, p. 1) described a teacher as a person "who knows exactly what she must do, brings the tools she needs, does the work with straightforward competence, and takes pleasure in a job well done." Kulik and McKeachie (1975) define three crucial aspects of the teaching craft:

1. Instructional skill
2. Organization ability
3. Respect for and rapport with students

Which of the preceding aspects do you think can be taught? Which do you think can be learned? Which do you think you have the most of?

Knowledge About Teaching

Individuals who are successfully working at the craft of teaching acquire four kinds of knowledge that are commonly mentioned in the academic literature:

- **Curriculum Knowledge (CUK)** is the ability to select, comprehend, transform, and implement goals and standards from a specific field of content into meaningful lessons for students (Ennis, 1994).
- **Content Knowledge (COK)** is what the teacher understands about the subject matter (see Knowledge in Topic 11) and is typically acquired in courses in his or her discipline, such as history, baseball, physics, or watercolors. Although these terms are not uniformly used in the professional education literature, Content Knowledge is divided into **Domains,** which are the broad areas of subject matter, such as social studies and science, and **Disciplines,** which are the specific subject areas, such as geography and physics.
- **General Pedagogical Knowledge (GPK)** is the understanding of the principles and strategies that can be effectively used to teach any content (Shulman, 1987).
- **Pedagogical Content Knowledge (PCK)** is the "ways of representing and formulating the subject that make it comprehensible to others" (Shulman, 1986, p. 9). It requires General Pedagogical Knowledge as a foundation, and it integrates Curriculum Knowledge and Content Knowledge from a particular domain. To have PCK, a teacher must know the instructional strategies unique to a discipline as well as any apprehensions, understandings, and misunderstandings students might have of the domain (see Brandt & Perkins, 2000).

Both GPK and PCK tend to improve with experience (Berliner, 1988; Housner & Griffey, 1985).

Teaching as a Moral Activity

The cathedral craftsmen of the Middle Ages saw their task as a moral imperative; in the same sense, teaching is also a **moral activity** (Goodlad, Soder, & Sirotnik, 1990).

For the Reflective Practitioner

Goodness without knowledge is blind. Knowledge without goodness is dangerous.

INSCRIPTION ABOVE THE ENTRY
TO PHILLIPS ACADEMY

For the Reflective Practitioner

Never mind, I leave you what is of far more value than earthly riches, the example of a virtuous life.

SENECA, JUST BEFORE HIS DEATH
AT THE HANDS OF NERO

Individuals who enter the profession because they can't figure out what else they can do or because "it's a job with summers off and good fringe benefits" do the profession a great disservice and likely end up as inadequate craftspeople, if they remain as teachers at all. Twenty to 30 percent of new teachers quit after their first year (DePaul, 2000), and after five years about 50 percent have left the profession (Anderson, 2000). To overcome the potential exhaustion, disillusionment, frustration, and inadequate support one experiences as a teacher, one must find a compelling reason to persist and excel.

It was Socrates (ca. 469–399 B.C.) who said that the overriding concern of the teacher must be the promotion of the "good life." Seneca, a Roman, said much the same thing. By **good life,** Socrates was not referring to cars, riches, and a wonderful family and job, but a satisfying state of mind and being that is based on the enlightened self-awareness that one is fulfilling one's potential as an honest human being. Almost every action taken by a teacher expresses a moral perspective. Because teaching is a caring profession that involves much more than just teaching one's subject matter, it presents middle and high school teachers with unique challenges and great opportunities to make a difference in the lives of their students. Few professions have such a moral calling.

Teaching as Enculturation

Middle and high school students are in the midst of what anthropologists call **Enculturation**: the process by which humans learn their culture. If education is thought of in this larger context, the individual teacher is but one, albeit potentially influential, person in a student's progression toward adulthood. As members of the profession to which our complex culture has assigned the task of enculturating the young, we have been asked to replace the tribal elders of preliterate societies who explained and modeled for the next generation their societies' ways of thinking and knowing, social norms, and social virtues. Although you are hired as a teacher of mathematics, health, physical education, history, science, art, or English—whatever your teaching field is—you are also called to be a model of virtuous behavior, intellectual curiosity, divergent thinking, and objectivity. In a democratic state, you are also preparing students to become productive citizens.

> **For the Reflective Practitioner**
>
> *What we do to our children our children will do to our society.*
> PLINY THE ELDER OF ROME

Teaching as a Profession

The Teaching Profession has evolved into something much more complex and larger than the Teaching Craft. Showing up for class prepared to teach about *Macbeth,* the Associative Property, drug abuse, the American Revolution, or ionization is not sufficient. Schools are multifaceted institutions where parents, students, teachers, other educational professionals, and staff converge with different histories, circumstances, ideas, and values. The ecology of a school is complex, and the school exists as part of a larger community. As members of school organizations, teachers are socialized into a school culture. Waller's *The Sociology of Teaching* (1932) and Lortie's *Schoolteacher* (1975/2002) are considered classics on this topic, and their themes of isolation, bureaucratic impediments, and other problems are still seen in the literature today (Johnson et al., 1990; Stone, 2002b).

The Socialization of Teachers into the Profession

There is considerable research about the evolution of teachers in the roles they are expected to fill in schools (Staton & Hunt, 1992). One approach to defining the professional life of a teacher is called **stage theory** (Case, 1988; Goldsmith & Shifter, 1994).

For example, Berliner (1994) describes five stages through which a teacher can pass during a career: novice, advanced beginner, competent, proficient, and expert. Although your immediate goal may be just to get through this course, to finish your internship, to graduate, or to survive your first year as a teacher, it is not too early to begin thinking about what your long-term goal should be, hopefully to reach the expert status as soon as possible.

> **For the Reflective Practitioner**
>
> *A positive attitude may not solve all your problems, but it will annoy enough people to make it worth the effort.*
> HERM ALBRIGHT

Although every teacher's development is unique, it is generally influenced by three key factors (Ball & Goodson, 1985):

1. **Individual beliefs.** A belief is an **idea** or **concept** that has been transformed because you have embraced it, made it your own, and value it; because it defines you as a person; and because you believe the idea or concept to be correct (Fenstermacher, 1994). Your **behaviors**, when they conform to your beliefs, provide a source of satisfaction and **efficacy:** you believe in your own ability to think, feel, self-motivate, and react in a proactive way to life's challenges.

   You will enter the profession with a unique disposition and set of beliefs that will shape your life's work.

2. **Change.** Change can be externally induced ("Are they changing the standards again?" or "I am being reassigned to World History—what a surprise, but that will give me a chance to try some new ideas!") or internally produced ("Half the students failed the test again; I need to try group learning, and I am not using enough questions during my lectures" or "There is a new school opening up with Internet connections in each classroom; I might transfer there just to begin using the new technology"). Your openness to new ideas and enthusiasm for change will be key variables in your evolution as a teacher (Smylie, 1988).

3. **Reflective practice.** The idea of reflecting on one's dispositions, beliefs, and practices as a teacher was initially advanced by Schön (1983). Reflection is the precursor to change and growth as a teacher (Risko, Vukelich, & Roskos, 2002; Smith, 2002).

For the Reflective Practitioner

The unexamined life is not worth living.

SOCRATES

Teacher's Tip

Joining a professional organization is an important step to remaining current in your profession. You should join the NEA or your discipline's professional organization; see Unit 8.

Assignment 1.1

CODE OF ETHICS

INTASC STANDARDS 9, 10

Retrieve a copy of the National Education Association (NEA) code of ethics at http://www.nea.org/code.html. Note the frequent use of the terms *reasonable* and *unreasonably*.

With a classmate, discuss the eight expectations under Principle I and develop two questions or scenarios that could be used in a whole-class discussion with your professor to further clarify the expectations. Be prepared to turn it in to your professor. As an alternative, your professor may want you to go to your state's department of education website and print out the department's code of ethics.

Resources	THE TEACHING PROFESSION
National Education Association	Click on teaching issues at the NEA website http://www.nea.org/search/.
ERIC OnLine ED474348	*Teaching from the Deep End: Succeeding with Today's Classroom Challenges,* by Belmonte, Dominic, 2003.
ERIC OnLine ED471195	*What! Another New Mandate? What Award-Winning Teachers Do When School Rules Change,* by Stone, Randi, 2002.

Check this textbook's website at http://education.college.hmco.com/students **for additional links.**

Challenges for a New Teacher

The current reform movements of the **K–12 education** level (kindergarten through twelfth grade) create a context in which you will carry out the daily work of teaching. However, middle and high school reform efforts are not the only changes that will affect your training and career. The INTASC standards listed in Table 2.1 are part of the current reform movement of **Teacher Education Programs** and are intended to give you a solid idea of what to expect as a teacher and what is expected of a new teacher.

For the Reflective Practitioner

May my teaching drop like the rain, my speech condense like the dew; like gentle rain on grass, like showers on new growth.

DEUTERONOMY 32:2, HEBREW BIBLE

Your teacher education program should provide opportunities to practice and develop the kinds of competency depicted in the ten INTASC standards (Danielson, 1996; Wilson & Floden, 2003):

- Your education courses will give you the opportunity to develop **knowledge** about teaching practices and the vocabulary needed to communicate in the language of the profession (referred to in the literature as a **"community of practice"**).
- Your content courses (mathematics, history, etc.) should provide the body of **information knowledge** (see Topic 11) that you will teach.
- Your **clinical experiences** (referred to as **early field experiences** and **internship**) should give you opportunities to practice and perfect your craft.

On the basis of Table 2.1, what do you feel will be your strengths as a teacher, and what weaknesses will you need the most help with?

After reading over the standards in Table 2.1, you may now have a greater sense of why teachers, particularly novice teachers, leave school exhausted at the end of the day. The work is physically, emotionally, and intellectually demanding.

So, why do you think teachers stay in the profession?

Table 2.1 | **INTASC STANDARDS**

1. Subject Matter Expertise

The teacher understands the central concepts, tools of inquiry, and structures of the discipline(s) he or she teaches and can create learning experiences that make these aspects of subject matter meaningful for students. Go to http://www.ccsso.org/projects/Interstate_New_Teacher_Assessment_and_Support_Consortium/Projects/Standards_Development/ for the content standards developed for each discipline.

2. Learning and Development

The teacher understands how children learn and develop, and can provide learning opportunities that support their intellectual, social, and personal development.

3. Diverse Learners

The teacher understands how students differ in their approaches to learning and creates instructional opportunities that are adapted to diverse learners.

4. Multiple Instructional Strategies

The teacher understands and uses a variety of instructional strategies to encourage students' development of critical thinking, problem solving, and performance skills.

5. Motivation and Classroom Management

The teacher uses an understanding of individual and group motivation and behavior to create a learning environment that encourages positive social interaction, active engagement in learning, and self-motivation.

6. Communication Skills

The teacher uses knowledge of effective verbal, nonverbal, and media communication techniques to foster active inquiry, collaboration, and supportive interaction in the classroom.

7. Instructional Planning

The teacher plans instruction based upon knowledge of subject matter, students, the community, and curriculum goals.

8. Assessment

The teacher understands and uses formal and informal assessment strategies to evaluate and ensure the continuous intellectual, social, and physical development of the learner.

9. Professional Commitment and Responsibility

The teacher is a reflective practitioner who continually evaluates the effects of his or her choices and actions on others (students, parents, and other professionals in the learning community) and who actively seeks out opportunities to grow professionally.

10. Partnership

The teacher fosters relationships with school colleagues, parents, and agencies in the larger community to support students' learning and well-being.

Source: The Interstate New Teacher Assessment and Support Consortium (INTASC) standards were developed by the Council of Chief State School Officers and member states. Copies may be downloaded from the Council's website at http://www.ccsso.org.

What Novice Teachers Need IMMEDIATE Help With

The type of help a new teacher needs to be successful ranges from converting theory into practice to the overtly practical tasks of teaching. The following is a list of activities that novice teachers need help with, based on research by Brewster and Railsback (2001):

1. Setting up a classroom for the first time
2. Learning school routines
3. Teaching with less than adequate resources
4. Learning where to find supplies
5. Involving parents
6. Developing time management skills
7. Understanding policies and procedures
8. Motivating students
9. Responding to behavior problems
10. Developing classroom management skills

In this textbook, we address all of these issues.

Teacher's Tip

Plan on finding a **mentor** soon after you accept a job by asking your department chair for the name of someone he or she would recommend. The kinds of activities found in this section can often be discussed with a mentor.

INTERVIEW WITH A PRACTICING TEACHER INTASC STANDARDS 1–10 *Assignment 2.1*

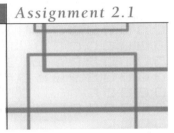

Using the information about new teachers and the INTASC standards as a starting point (Table 2.1), develop no less than ten questions that you might not feel comfortable asking during your interviews for teaching positions but that you would like to ask an experienced teacher. Arrange an interview with a practicing middle or high school teacher in your teaching field. Be prepared to summarize the comments, turn the assignment in to your professor, and discuss your results in class.

The Teacher's Ten Roles

In addition to the kinds of expectations delineated by INTASC, you will be expected to fill multiple roles as a teacher, roles that may or may not appear in the job description. The following are the most common roles that teachers must fill.

For the Reflective Practitioner

The mediocre teacher tells.
The good teacher explains.
The superior teacher demonstrates.
The great teacher inspires.

WILLIAM ARTHUR WARD

These roles are not listed in a particular order. After reading about them, can you rank them based on which ones you think are most important and explain the criteria you used?

1. Instructor

Most students can rattle off the attributes of teachers they "liked the most." But this is very different from remembering those teachers who were excellent instructors. Excellent instruction is hard to define, but most of us know it when we see it. And inevitably teaching comes from the hard work of seeking out new ways to teach, always being on the lookout for new materials, experimenting, and making adjustments to your lesson plans: Never being totally satisfied with the way a class went is the key to becoming an excellent instructor. With this kind of diligence, your personal ingenuity, inventiveness, and cleverness can turn good instruction into excellent instruction.

"Teaching is both art and science" is one of the truisms of the craft. Theories bolstered by research inform us about what works in the classroom and what doesn't, and for this reason the latest research is presented in ERIC documents at this book's website. Assignment 2.2 at the end of this Topic will provide you with an opportunity to draw on this research base and begin the integration of theory into your practice.

In the instructor role, one of the key questions you will need to ask yourself is, "Do I teach students or do I teach subjects?" When friends and family ask you what you are "studying to be," do you say "a middle school teacher" or "a science teacher"? Your answer may reveal something about your perception of your role. Generally, elementary school teachers are generalists in the sense that they don't typically have a compelling interest in one academic discipline. Middle and high school teachers tend to have a strong interest in some subject, such as mathematics or science, and want to teach their favorite subject. In spite of that difference, I believe the answer to the questions is that you teach BOTH students and subjects, and herein lies one of the great challenges of teaching.

Because you will teach students about subjects, you will have loyalties (sometimes conflicting) to your students and your academic discipline. As an analogy, camp counselors have a duty to supervise students but do not have an obligation to teach them a specific body of knowledge or expect them to meet a specific set of standards. The camp counselor's responsibility is to keep things orderly, create a climate of civility, and let the students have fun. A teacher also has a duty to supervise students, but he or she must also instruct them in a specific body of knowledge by the end of the school year. In addition, a teacher must inform the student, parents, school, and sometimes the state how much of the subject, in the teacher's opinion, the student understands. Saying, "Well, I taught them—I didn't say they learned it" is not an acceptable response, if you want to keep your job! You are expected to make sure they learned the subject—or at least that you did everything reasonably possible for your students to be both motivated to learn and to acquire the knowledge. The tensions between what you expect a student to know for a passing or superior grade and the unique and individual circumstances of a student can produce a gut-wrenching conundrum for a teacher. You, perhaps at the age of only twenty-two, will be only four years older than some of your students, and yet you will have to make judgments about their performance that can have far-reaching consequences.

 What should you do about a student who is homeless and has not been doing his or her work and is failing based on your course requirements?

Many middle and high school teachers enter the profession because they love their subject field and have developed an extensive understanding of the content. And, certainly, knowledge of your discipline and enthusiasm for it are expected and necessary for your success as a teacher. But knowing something and knowing how to teach it are two very different things. If our job as teachers were only to communicate what we know about a topic, teaching would be easy.

2. Performer

It cannot be denied that there is a theatrical aspect to instruction. Sometimes individuals mistakenly think they should be comics or they are there to put on a show.

Using humor strategically, managing the stage and props, exaggerating emotions for effect, structuring phrases to catch the learner's attention, and changing voice cadence and volume are crucial to communicating ideas. Some individuals seem to instinctively have a grasp of the performance aspect of teaching but are poor planners and fail to stay abreast of the developments in their teaching field. They mistakenly think they can adlib and be successful. Others will develop a stage presence only with practice.

When you observe excellent teachers as part of a clinical experience, it is important to remember that they have probably acted out their "play" over a number of years, have fine-tuned the presentation based on the "audience" reaction, have a wealth of props that a new teacher has yet to gather, and have rewritten their script to improve the conclusion. To overcome the shortcomings of being a new teacher, it is crucial to your early success to plan, rehearse, and be confident in your content.

For the Reflective Practitioner

Acting is the most minor of gifts and not a very high-class way to earn a living. After all, Shirley Temple could do it at the age of four. KATHARINE HEPBURN

3. Planner

It would be so simple if you only had to plan what you were going to tell the students about your content: Your career would be like writing a speech, walking into the classroom, delivering it like the *Gettysburg Address*, and moving on to the next class.

But that would mean you do not have to take into consideration the mandated standards from your state's department of education, time constraints, best instructional practices like the use of images, the Socratic method, or group activities, or your audience's age, attention span, interest, inclinations, and mood (especially if it is the Friday of the "big" football game).

You cannot plan enough! And planning is not limited to your course, term, unit, weekly plans, lessons, and class notes (see Topics 19 and 20). You need to plan your transparencies, rubrics, didactic materials, tests, floor plan, bulletin boards, classroom rules, grading practices, procedures, parent notices, professional development, and more. It will be overwhelming for you, rather than just daunting, if you do not segment the task and use the resources and ideas available in this and other textbooks, the Internet, and other resources.

Each school will have different planning expectations for new teachers and different types of forms and procedures. Managing the documentation in the approved format can be as much of a challenge as the creative endeavor to produce the actual materials to manage your courses, the students, and their parents.

For the Reflective Practitioner

You got to be careful. If you don't know where you're going, you might not get there. YOGI BERRA

Teacher's Tip

AppleWorks *and* MSWorks *are both inexpensive software packages that include a word processor, database, and spreadsheet that can ease the burden of record keeping and correspondence with students, parents, and school officers.*

4. Course Manager

The planning and management roles go hand in hand. A middle or high school teacher must manage approximately 150 students (and their parents) through a series of lessons and documentation of their progress. Schools may require filings of lesson plans, reports of conferences with parents, and detailed record keeping of grades, attendance, and referrals to counselors.

Grading of papers, exams, and portfolios can be overwhelming unless it is structured to minimize the clerical effort and strategically included in your syllabus to provide the feedback needed by your students for their success in your classes. Preparing, cataloging, and organizing course materials from transparencies to supplemental readings is essential so that they can be reused in multiple sections over numerous semesters (see Topic 20).

5. Stakeholder and Change Agent

A teacher's interest extends beyond his or her classes and students. National, state, school district, school, and department policies, the workplace environment, and extracurricular activities require your attention and participation.

Teachers have options as to what professional organizations they belong to, what extracurricular activities they participate in, and what departmental and schoolwide initiatives and changes they wish to support, lead, or be involved in. Participation in curriculum development, textbook selection, and annual assignments should be a collaborative effort by members of the department, but it will vary according to tradition. Faculty members, to varying degrees, are involved in developing and revising school policies on attendance, open house and parent-teacher conference formats, and assigned duties like supervising the lunchroom, chaperoning school dances, serving as moderator of clubs, and coaching.

Your active involvement as a stakeholder can greatly influence the quality of the environment in which you perform the core duties of instructing and managing your courses: It can make the working conditions more enjoyable and add a great deal of satisfaction to a career in public service. A teacher's union may be a part of what defines your role and can also provide a venue for you to diversify your contributions to education.

6. Advisor and Role Model

Teachers are advisors, but advisors are not counselors. School psychologists and guidance counselors are licensed professionals because they have advanced special training and serve a very specific role in school settings. Sometimes you will find it necessary to refer students and parents to a school counselor and seek a psychologist's advice about how to motivate or just work with a student.

Teacher's Tip

It is almost never wise to be alone in a classroom or office with a student. If a student wants to meet with you or you need to meet with a student, have another student stay in another section of the classroom while you talk with the student. Why do you think this advice is given?

In your advising role, students will seek your counsel on matters related to the course you are teaching but also on issues not directly tied to the course, often of a personal nature. Former students will seek you out when they need an opinion. At other times you will initiate an individual conversation with a student about his or her priorities and conduct that you feel are adversely affecting his or her performance in your class, or you may take a more proactive approach with a student who is doing well but who you would like to see capitalize more on his or her talents. This kind of continuous and often spontaneous interaction with students requires thoughtfulness, caution, and judgment, but it is crucial to the kind of human connection that allows you to succeed in your other roles and often can make a significant difference in a student's life and future.

If you are in your early twenties, you can find yourself advising the parents of one of your students who are twice your age. These advising interactions with parents are frequently formalized into parent-teacher conferences by phone and in person. Ongoing professional development, a positive attitude, active planning to involve parents, collaboration, and personal competence are all cited as teacher attributes that are highly related to successful interaction with parents (Epstein, 1984; Epstein & Dauber, 1991; Swick, 1991).

> *A high school student enrolled in one of your classes decides to talk to you about someone he or she is dating: Do you think you should discuss such things with your students? What would you do if a middle school student walked up to you at the end of class and said, "You have to promise that you won't tell anyone, but I need to tell you something"?*

7. Coach or Moderator

Providing "out-of-class" opportunities has evolved into an essential part of middle and high schools. Most agree that the additional financial compensation for the teacher is rarely worth the commitment and is rarely the motivation for taking on such assignments. Of course, you may have extensive experience in sports or activities like acting or debating, and it may be one of your motivations for becoming a teacher.

Whether you have experience or not with an extracurricular activity, it will add significant additional time to your already busy first year of teaching. Still, choosing to get more involved as a coach or moderator has an advantage: The students in the activity will get to know you outside the classroom and see you in a totally different, less formal light. The more relaxed atmosphere of extracurricular activities, in which both students and moderator/coach elect to participate, allows for more casual interactions during which students get to know you as a person outside the instructor role, and this information makes it through the student "grapevine." An extracurricular assignment gives you a chance to let students see a more well rounded version of the teacher than the one they see in the classroom.

Teacher's Tip

When applying for a job, your willingness to serve as moderator of Mu Alpha Theta, student government, or the science club or to coach a sport may be a significant factor in the school's decision. So you may want to express interest in an extracurricular assignment during your interview.

8. Colleague

You will be joining a complex organization and will likely share hallways and a teacher's lounge with teachers in your department and from other fields who are nearing retirement, in midcareer, and also just starting their career.

You may make lifelong friends in your workplace and find individuals willing to help you make the transition into the profession. As a new teacher, you will have great enthusiasm (and some apprehension), and you will want to share what you have just learned in your college education with colleagues. You will want all the friends you can get among the faculty and staff, and the best way to do that is to become a good listener.

For the Reflective Practitioner

Be courteous to all, but intimate with few, and let those few be well tried before you give them your confidence. True friendship is a plant of slow growth, and must undergo and withstand the shocks of adversity before it is entitled to the appellation.

GEORGE WASHINGTON

9. Scholar and Lifelong Learner

Just because you graduated doesn't mean you stop learning. And even though the grade-appropriate content at the middle and high school levels doesn't change by leaps and bounds, all content changes over time, and you need to stay abreast of it. Instructional approaches also change over time and are heavily impacted by changes in technology. Few saw the current digital technological changes coming or the standards movement and how both would begin to change the teaching craft.

You might consider a master's degree as a formalized way of keeping up with your teaching field and educational practices. Join your regional and national professional organization (these are listed in Unit 8), which usually comes with a journal subscription. Attend regional and national conferences; better yet,

For the Reflective Practitioner

Jails and prisons are the complement of schools; so many less as you have of the latter, so many more must you have of the former.

HORACE MANN

present at a conference or write an article on one of the lessons that you do particularly well. The Association for Supervision and Curriculum Development (ASCD) at **www.ascd.org** is one of a number of organizations that you can join. It has over 160,000 members, from teachers to superintendents, and its website includes position papers and research on most topics that would be of interest to a new teacher.

10. Classroom Manager

You can have all kinds of great ideas on how to teach and you can love your subject matter, but your first priority is to manage your students' behaviors. If you don't, you will not get to teach the subject matter that you so dearly love or try out your great ideas on how to teach it. For this reason, Topic 16 is dedicated to **Classroom Management**.

As a new teacher, you will not have a "reputation" that precedes you. Students will not have passed on information about your personality quirks, standards, approaches, or flexibility. As a result, students in your classes will test you; it seems to be part of the natural give and take between human beings who may have different roles, expectations, and agendas.

One of your most important tasks will be to make sure students understand that you are in charge and to convey that message with a demeanor that doesn't provoke animosity. This will depend on the communication style you use as you are explaining your expectations and begin to carry them out (see Topic 9). A classroom, although it can be enjoyable and everyone can have a good laugh from time to time, is a place where serious work gets done by serious-minded people who are building their futures.

> **For the Reflective Practitioner**
>
> *I not only use all the brains that I have, but all that I can borrow.*
>
> WOODROW WILSON

Assignment 2.2 **NEW TEACHER EXPECTATIONS**

INTASC STANDARDS 1–10
At this book's website, listed under Topic 2, Assignment 2.2, you will find over fifteen online ERIC documents published since 2000 that provide insights related to topics that will affect your first year of teaching. Your professor may assign one of the readings, or have you choose one on your own. Create a synopsis of the key ideas and how they should guide a new teacher, and then author a couple of teacher's tips based on the reading. Be prepared to turn the assignment in to your professor and share your tips with the class.

Assignment 2.3 **WHAT ARE MIDDLE AND HIGH SCHOOL STUDENTS THINKING?**

INTASC STANDARDS 2, 3, 5, 6, 10
Table 2.2 provides information on high school students based on a nationwide survey in 2002–2003. Please record what you think the results are and be prepared to defend your answers in class.

Table 2.2 | **2002–2003 STUDENT SURVEY**

1. How do today's middle and high school students define success in life? Rank the following, with 1 being the most frequent answer given by students and 8 being the least frequent.	
A. Being attractive or popular	___
B. Being famous or respected in your field	___
C. Being satisfied with what you are doing	___
D. Having an active religious or spiritual life	___
E. Having a close group of friends	___
F. Having close family relationships	___
G. Making a contribution to society	___
H. Making a lot of money	___
2. What are high school students' plans after high school? Indicate a percentage for each; percentages should add up to 100.	
A. College or university	___ %
B. Two-year college	___ %
C. Community college	___ %
D. Vocational or technical training	___ %
E. Don't plan on college	___ %
F. Don't know	___ %
(Note to Professor: see PowerPoint presentation for source and responses.)	

OnLine Resources

Check this textbook's website at http://education.college.hmco.com/students for online links that are periodically updated to reflect new resources as they become available.

Standards-Based Education

In virtually every decade since its formation, secondary education has been "reformed" by political, social, demographic, technological, economic, philosophical, and pedagogical professional forces. Secondary education has been taken apart (junior highs and high schools), put back together (a contemporary resurgence of K–12 and 7–12 schools in urban areas), and moved out of schools entirely (through distributed/distance learning, home-schooling and business-education partnerships). [Schools] have been assaulted by universities in 1900s, Progressives in the 1920s and 30s, civil rights activists in the 50s, Conant-Rickover in the 60s, de-schoolers in the 70s, *A Nation at Risk* in the 80s, and uncountable commissions, committees, candidates, and pundits since the early 1990s. They have been virtual battlegrounds for integration, free speech, student rights, religion, sexual orientation, military recruitment, gender equity, and dozens of other issues arising in the larger culture surrounding the school. Sometimes, they have been actual battlegrounds—with real weapons and all-too-real casualties—for wars fueled by drugs, anger, hatred, and bigotry.

— *J. Howard Johnston, Recipient of the NASSP Distinguished Service Award,*
the Gruhn-Long-Melton Award, the NMSA John Lounsbury Award,
and the Presidential Award for Excellence (2004)

? *Given this observation by Professor Johnston, what reforms do you think are necessary in schools in light of the strengths and weaknesses of your own secondary education experiences? What are your perceptions of schools today, and was your education a typical middle and high school experience? Can you convert these observations into ideas for reform?*

Reform at the Turn of the Twenty-first Century

Students may obtain a degree of general literacy (see Units 3 and 8) by the end of elementary school; then, beginning with middle school, they are expected to further develop their general literacy and also develop literacy in the various disciplines (mathematics, history, art, etc.). As early as 1983, Sewall pointed out that students have traditionally been able to largely escape literacy in the disciplines through watered-down courses, grade inflation, fewer required courses, and more electives. Remedial, general, honors, and AP (Advanced Placement) courses in the disciplines effectively create variations in the degree of emersion into the subject field, and thus literacy. Electives provide the opportunity to avoid a domain altogether, and the curriculum reflects fads and the influences of special interest groups (Evers, 2001).

The 1983 report of the National Commission on Excellence in Education labeled the American middle and high school curriculum and its lack of rigor as "the rising tide of mediocrity" and expressed concern about the adverse impact it was having on general and domain literacy. And the 1998 *Nation Still at Risk: An Educational Manifesto* by the Center for Educational Reform found no improvement in the twenty-five years since 1983. Hirsch (1996, 2001), an advocate of a more uniform curriculum, or "Core Knowledge," believes that the current standards-based reform movement is a response to the curricular chaos that has existed in schools, particularly since the "child-centered progressive movement" of the sixties.

> *Do you think everyone who graduates from high school should know Algebra 2? The Canterbury Tales? The cell structure of plants? The names of the fifty states and their capitals? Physics? Why or why not?*

The Nation's Report Card at **http://nces.ed.gov/nationsreportcard/** (see Figure 3.1 for the homepage) provides national and comparative assessment data on students' knowledge. The Organization for Economic Co-operation and Development (OECD) Programme for International Student Assessment at **http://www.pisa.oecd.org/knowledge/home/intro.htm** provides comparative data on high school students' performance from an international perspective. You should take the opportunity to review each to learn more about how well Americans are doing in general and how well they are doing in your teaching field.

Figure 3.1 | **THE NATION'S REPORT CARD**

![The Nation's Report Card website screenshot in Microsoft Internet Explorer showing the NCES National Center for Education Statistics homepage with "THE NATION'S REPORT CARD" and "2003 Mathematics and Reading Assessment Results NOW AVAILABLE"]

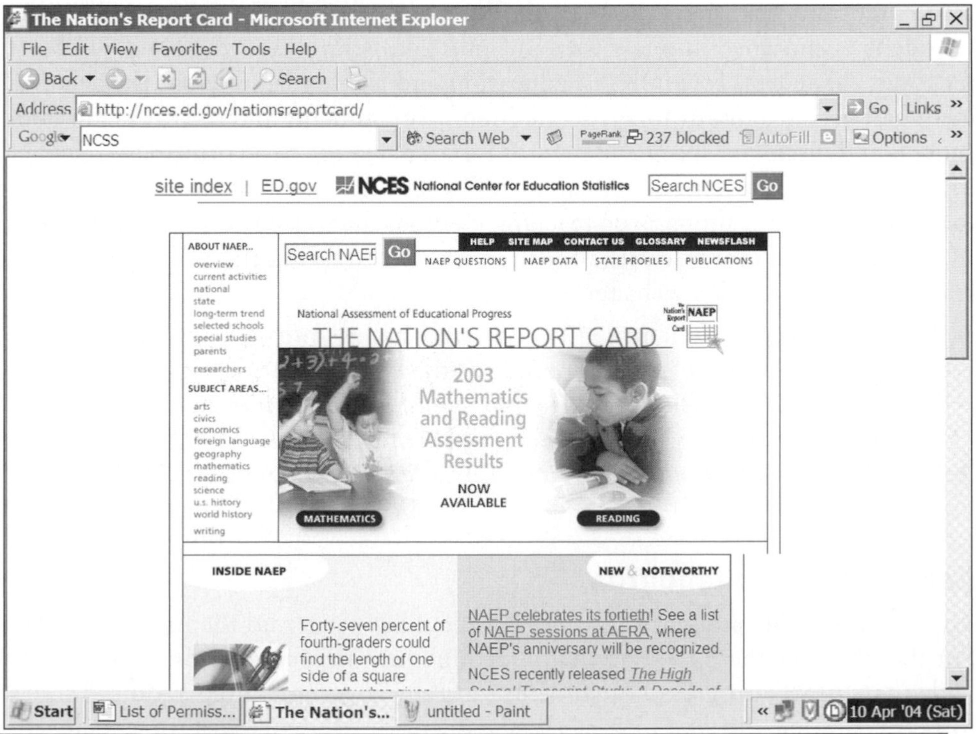

Figure 3.2 | **THE ED.GOV WEBSITE FOR NO CHILD LEFT BEHIND**

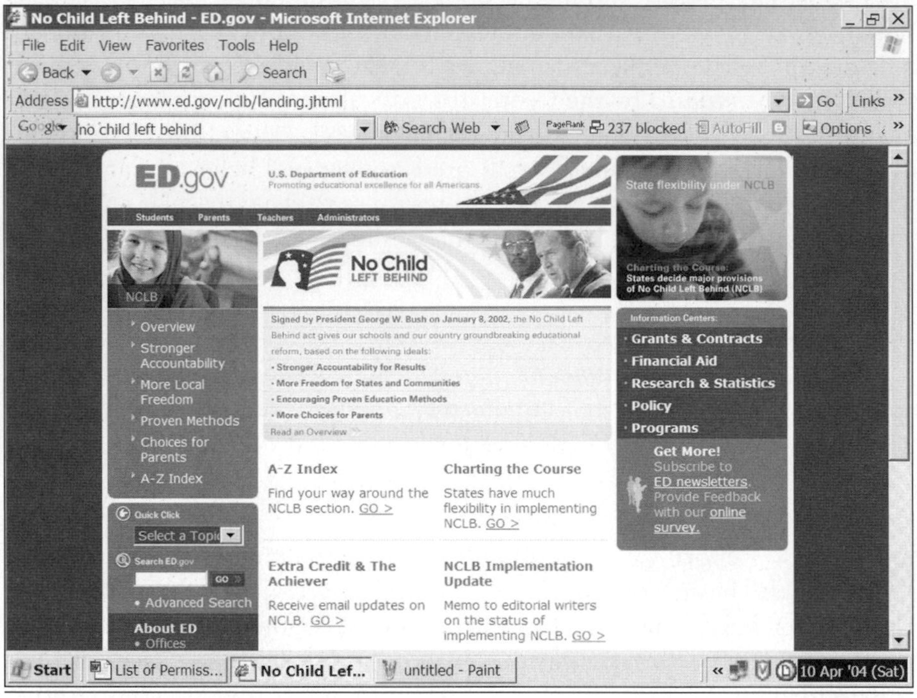

Developing National Standards

The long-standing dissatisfaction with public education because of the significant variations between schools in quality, opportunity, and expectations has led to various federal government initiatives, like the 1964 Head Start program, the Individuals with Disabilities Act of 1975, and the landmark desegregation ruling *Brown v. Board of Education* of 1954. The most recent significant effort to create more consistent and high-quality educational opportunity is currently being implemented and will shape your experience as a teacher. On January 8, 2002, President Bush signed into law the No Child Left Behind Act of 2001 (NCLB). It redefines the federal role in K–12 education and is intended to close the achievement gap between disadvantaged and "minority" students and their peers in both general and discipline-specific literacy. It is based on four basic principles: stronger accountability for results, increased flexibility and local control, expanded options for parents, and an emphasis on teaching methods that have been proven to work.

You can learn more details about the act by reviewing the following online resources at this book's website:

- The federal government's ED.gov website at http://www.ed.gov/nclb/landing.jhtml?src=mr (see Figure 3.2 for the homepage)
- ED477723, *Implications of the No Child Left Behind Act of 2001 for Teacher Education*, by Trahan, Christopher; ERIC Digest, 2002
- ED478248, *The Mandate to Help Low-Performing Schools*, by Lashway, Larry; ERIC Digest, 2003

Accountability Standards

The **accountability standards** of the NCLB act have received the most attention. For the first time there is a nationwide requirement that states must demonstrate "adequate yearly progress" of students, and the government has required states to report students in five major ethnic categories, students with low socioeconomic status (SES), disabled students, and students of limited English proficiency

(LEP) in order to comply and maintain their federal funding. The mandate to report disaggregated data, as opposed to reporting only overall averages (as has been done traditionally), focuses the standards on the students who have usually been left behind. Most of the states are adopting **high-stakes testing** (typically a point-in-time, paper-pencil test given to all students in a school district or the state) as the primary assessment tool of progress (Van Patten, 2002). The purpose of these tests is to demonstrate compliance with the act with comparative and longitudinal data by student, NCLB categories, school, district, and state. Each state can set its own standards, but it must report progress toward those standards. Some states are setting lower standards than others because NCLB penalizes states with high standards that don't achieve them (The Education Trust, 2003). Florida and California are among the most populated and ethnically diverse states in the union. Florida, whose high-stakes testing preceded NCLB, in 2002 reported half of its 2,933 schools as receiving an A by its existing state standards. However, if the standards set in Florida remain the same, only 14 percent, or 408 of Florida's schools, will have even a passing grade based on NCLB criteria, which measures PROGRESS (Jones & Brown, 2003). California has set a lower standard by which all schools will probably be considered as having made adequate progress under the new mandates (Will, 2004).

For the Reflective Practitioner

As a new teacher, you will have the opportunity to lead our education system and advocate the kinds of changes that you think can make a difference for American students.

The consequences for failing to meet the NCLB progress standards are significant. Students in failing schools are granted the right to transfer, and the schools must provide transportation. After three years, schools must offer free tutoring. After four years of failing to make the passing grade, schools could be forced to close and reopen with completely new staff. As a consequence of these standards, you will find a new focus on basic skills (see Topics, 12, 13, and 14) in the schools and a need to be more attentive to students and their families to keep them from being "left behind" (Linn, 2002). Reading, writing, and math skills are the focus of accountability, and thus all teachers—regardless of subject matter—will be expected to support the schoolwide goal of meeting the new standards by including more instruction and practice of basic skills in their classes.

For pragmatic, academic, philosophical, and ideological reasons, this NCLB legislation has both supporters and opponents. How would you analyze the issues as a teacher, student, parent, and citizen?

Other Reforms

In addition to this national legislation on accountability, there are ongoing reforms of curriculum and schools promoted by organizations of parents, teachers, principals, scholars, school districts, and states. These reforms range from home schooling to new school structures (see Topics 4 and 5) and from a new emphasis on basic skills (see Topics 12, 13, and 14) to standards for each subject field (see Unit 8) that are intended to increase discipline-specific literacy.

In the next two topics on middle and high schools, you will have the opportunity to learn about a number of school-based reforms.

OnLine Resources

Check this textbook's website at http://education.college.hmco.com/students for online links that are periodically updated to reflect new resources as they become available.

The Middle School Environment

This Topic, and the following Topic on high schools, is intended to provide an overview of the history, current issues, and culture of secondary schools. Both types of schools share common attributes, but the differences are not just based on the age of the student population. So as not to be redundant, some issues are covered only once in one of the two topics, even though they are relevant to both settings.

The National Middle School Association (NMSA) at **http://www.nmsa.org/** offers extensive resources about middle school education and is worth visiting for policy statements, research, reports, and news about regional and national meetings focused on middle-level education.

NATIONAL MIDDLE SCHOOL ASSOCIATION HOMEPAGE

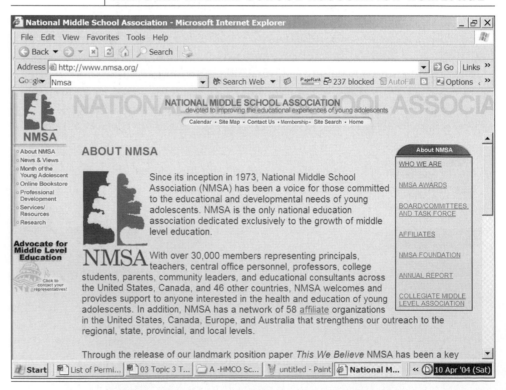

Source: *Reprinted with permission of the National Middle School Association.*

Junior High Schools

The history of junior high and middle schools reflects the emergence of educational philosophies and socioeconomic forces that resulted in over 14,000 schools that are classified as middle or junior high schools as of 2004. At the beginning of the twentieth century, schools were typically organized as either 6-6 systems, meaning six years of elementary school and six years of high school, or 8-4 systems, meaning 8 years of grammar school and 4 years of high school. At that time, the last four years of the systems were relatively rigorous and heavily focused on content because students who progressed that far were few and typically college bound. The recommended curriculum included Latin, Greek, a modern foreign language, English and mathematics every year, history, government, economics, geography, physics, astronomy, chemistry, and biology (National Education Association, 1893). But with a major increase in population and growing concern about the changing developmental differences between students in seventh and eighth grades and their elementary or senior high school "peers," the seventh- and eighth-grade years became viewed as wastelands for the students, who were neither "fish nor fowl," neither children nor young adults.

> **For the Reflective Practitioner**
>
> *Welcome to seventh grade—middle school—that shaky, hellish bridge that all of you must cross before you become members of the undying, enviable high school elite.*
>
> MR. SIMANETTI, IN THE FILM *PAY IT FORWARD*

Combined with a movement toward **"tracking"** (see later section in this Topic) into either precollege or vocational training, recommendations by three commissions would shape American education for a century: the **Committee of Ten** (National Education Association, 1892); the **Committee of Fifteen** (National Education Association, 1895); and the **Committee on the Economy of Time** (Baker, 1913).

The recommendations of these committees led to the creation of an "intermediate" school with grades 7 and 8 and a separate high school made up of grades 9–12 in Richmond, Indiana, in 1896. In 1909, the first "junior high" schools of grades 7, 8, and 9 were established in Columbus, Ohio, and in 1910, Berkeley, California, adopted the approach for its district (Melton, 1984; Popper, 1967). The purposes of the junior high by the 1920s were being attentive to the nature of young adolescents, providing for individual differences, increasing retention, starting vocational training and guidance, and exposing children to departmentalized subject matter as in high schools and colleges (Briggs, 1920; Koos, 1920).

This approach continued until the 1960s, when the "middle school movement" began, in part because many educators believed the junior highs were little more than watered-down high schools with a lack of commitment to the "in-betweenager."

Middle Schools

Because of dissatisfaction with the junior high culture, economic concerns about accommodating the 1960s baby boomers on the horizon, and the onset of puberty having declined by almost one year since the turn of the century (Tanner, 1961), advocates began to promote moving sixth grade to a "middle school" and moving ninth grade to high school. Figure 4.1 depicts the growth of middle schools since the late 1960s.

Figure 4.1 | MIDDLE SCHOOL GROWTH

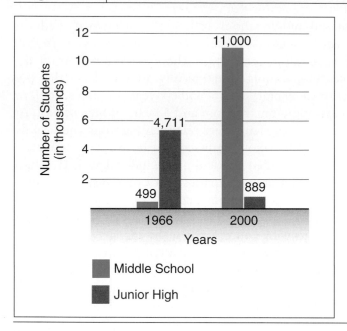

Sources: Cuff, 1966; "Number of Middle Schools" at http://www.nmsa.org/.

But the changes are not just limited to a shifting of grade levels (see Lounsbury & Clark, 1990). For many, the new structure renewed the hope that many of the original goals of the junior high might now come to fruition: a unique school culture, organization, and curriculum for these early teens. Table 4.1 depicts some of the differences between middle and junior/senior high schools.

Table 4.1 | MIDDLE SCHOOL VERSUS JUNIOR AND SENIOR HIGH SCHOOL

Middle School	Junior and Senior High School
1. Focuses on exploration in the disciplines and domains.	1. Focuses on mastery of concepts and skills in disciplines and domains.
2. Homeroom is typically an advising period with a set curriculum.	2. Homeroom is used for a range of school management issues: announcements, study hall, etc.
3. Flexible scheduling is used to support teams and thematic teaching.	3. Flexible scheduling, if used, is focused on greater mastery of content.
4. Organizes teachers in interdisciplinary teams with a common planning period.	4. Organizes teachers in departments by disciplines with no common planning period.
5. Arranges workspaces of teamed teachers adjacent to one another.	5. Arranges workspaces of teachers according to disciplines taught.
6. Emphasizes both affective and cognitive development of student.	6. Emphasizes primarily cognitive development of student.
Source: Adapted from Forte and Schurr (1993).	

The seminal statements of the philosophy of middle schools are found in the documents *This We Believe* (NMSA, 1982) and *This We Believe: Successful Schools for Young Adolescents* (NMSA, 2003). The NMSA philosophy characterizes successful middle schools as having:

1. **A curriculum that is relevant, challenging, integrative, and exploratory.** An effective curriculum is based on criteria of high quality and includes learning activities that create opportunities for students to pose and answer questions that are important to them. Such a curriculum provides direction for what young adolescents should know and be able to do and helps them achieve the attitudes and behaviors needed for a full, productive, and satisfying life.

2. **Multiple learning and teaching approaches that respond to students' diversity.** Since young adolescents learn best through engagement and interaction, learning strategies involve students in dialogue with teachers and with one another. Teaching approaches should enhance and accommodate the diverse skills, abilities, and prior knowledge of young adolescents and should draw upon students' individual learning styles.

3. **Assessment and evaluation programs that promote quality learning.** Continuous, authentic, and appropriate assessment and evaluation measures provide evidence about every student's learning progress. Grades alone are inadequate expressions for assessing the many goals of middle-level education.

4. **Organizational structures that support meaningful relationships and learning.** The interdisciplinary team of two to four teachers working with a common group of students is the building block for a strong learning community with a sense of family, where students and teachers know one another well, feel safe and supported, and are encouraged to take intellectual risks.

5. **Schoolwide efforts and policies that foster health, wellness, and safety.** A school that fosters physical and psychological safety strives to build resiliency in young people by maintaining an environment in which peaceful and safe interactions are expected and supported by written policies, scheduled professional development, and student-focused activities.

6. **Multifaceted guidance and support services.** Developmentally responsive middle-level schools provide both teachers and specialized professionals who are readily available to offer the assistance many students need in negotiating their lives both in and out of school.

Arguably, many of these characteristics and components could be equally valid goals for high schools.

The Middle School Student

The problem with defining how teachers should interact with middle school students as opposed to high school students is that it requires generalizations—stereotypical generalities about middle school students—when, in fact, each student is an individual and presents a unique disposition and unique circumstances. That being said, developmental psychology has identified a number of traits of young adolescents. The following generalizations are drawn from Gilstrap, Bierman, and McKnight (1992); Hudley et al. (2002); and Slater (1990). Young teenagers tend to be:

1. Egocentric and thus think their problems, experiences, feelings, and thoughts are unique to them.
2. Focused on acceptance by peers.

For the Reflective Practitioner

Children today are tyrants. They contradict their parents, gobble their food, and tyrannize their teachers.
SOCRATES

3. Intensely curious and vulnerable to naïve and often one-sided opinions.
4. Physically awkward and excessively concerned with physical appearance.
5. Easily offended, sensitive to criticism, moody, and restless.
6. Inclined to act out, overdramatize, rebel against parents, and test the limits of acceptable behavior.
7. Idealistic, prone to ask broad questions about ethical issues.
8. Focused on social interaction.
9. Interested in exploring values, making decisions, and learning concepts after exposure to concrete experiences.

 How do you think the above attributes should affect your teaching style, class-room management practices, and interpersonal relationships with students?

While such generalizations are helpful and, perhaps, bring back memories of our own experiences as preteens and teenagers, what is more important is how teachers respond to students progressing through this self-absorbed stage in life and how we help them move through this stage to become autonomous, thoughtful, mature human beings. Rather than encouraging their egocentrism, we need to give these students meaningful challenges that place their physical, emotional, and mental concerns in the developmental context of the human life cycle as seen through an adult's more experienced eyes (Peck, 1997). They need to be supported with routine, limits, and structure while other parts of their world change dramatically; given physical activity to exhaust the newfound energy; and offered meaningful experiences in school that challenge them to move beyond their self-absorption.

Assignment 4.1

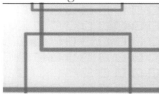

PREPARATION FOR AN INTERVIEW WITH A MIDDLE SCHOOL STUDENT

INTASC STANDARDS 2, 3, 5, 7, 9, 10
At this book's website, listed under Topic 4, Assignment 4.1, you will find a number of ERIC online articles worth reading that might be assigned by your teacher as a prerequisite to interviewing a middle school student. Prepare a summary of the key points for your professor and be prepared to share your ideas with the class.

Assignment 4.2

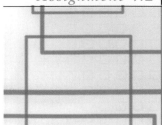

INTERVIEW A MIDDLE SCHOOL STUDENT

INTASC STANDARDS 1–9
An interview of a middle school student can be enlightening. Prior to the interview, you will likely be asked to work in a group to come up with a series of questions. You may want to develop at least one question based on each of the "Teacher's Ten Roles" from Topic 2. After completing the interview, prepare a summary of the student's responses and the insights you gained from the interview for your professor, and be prepared to share your ideas with the class.

The Middle School Context

Middle schools vary greatly based on a significant number of attributes, making generalizations about middle schools potentially misleading. The following overview should be considered in this context, beginning with the following characteristics (Peterson, 2001):

1. Seven-hour days for students
2. Seven or eight periods a day (depending on how lunch is handled), with periods lasting 40 to 50 minutes (see also Block Scheduling in Topic 5 and at NMSA at **http://www.nmsa.org/research/ressum17.htm** for a summary of this popular alternative)
3. Use of **Teams**, with a member of the team serving as a student's advisor
4. Frequent use of tracking, especially in mathematics and language arts

Teams

One of the most obvious characteristics of middle schools brought about by the reform agenda has been the emphasis on organizing teachers and students into **Teams** as a way of supporting students through shared information and targeted strategies based on individual students' needs, forging a more integrative curriculum (see later section in this Topic on thematic teaching), fostering more teacher collegiality, and establishing more uniform practices (Dickinson & Erb, 1997). *Teaming* refers to assembling a group of teachers from different disciplines to work together as a group with a shared planning period; each team is responsible for teaching a subset of the school's population. For example, a team of four teachers representing math, science, language arts, and social studies would be responsible for a "pod" of 125 students, with each teacher teaching five classes of 25 students in a seven-period day. This arrangement encourages middle school teachers to plan and think of students as more than just people learning certain subjects; the teachers' offices may even be organized by team, rather than by discipline. Planning periods can be used to focus on students who are at risk or need special opportunities, and each student's advisor (one of the teachers from the team) takes responsibility for his or her student. Often teachers develop common grading approaches, arrange a calendar of major assignments and test dates to minimize conflicts, or agree to a common writing rubric for all writing assignments. The shared planning time supports the creation of thematic and problem-centered units of study. Research on interdisciplinary teaching and thematic teaching (George & Shewey, 1994; Vars, 1996) indicates that teachers believe that teams add to the effectiveness of their middle schools and that students do at least as well as in other arrangements, if not better, when the curriculum is integrated through teams.

Two ERIC online documents that address the work of teams are:

- ED449148, *Camel-Makers: Building Effective Teacher Teams Together. A Modern Fable for Educators for Tips on How to Make a Team Better,* by Kain, Daniel L., 1998
- ED414084, *We Gain More Than We Give: Teaming in Middle Schools,* edited by Dickinson, Thomas S., 1997, a 555-page document issued by the National Middle School Association on the use and practices of teams in middle schools

In summary, since the team concept was introduced as part of the middle school reform movement, a number of positive outcomes have been reported:

1. A more coherent and relevant curriculum
2. Improved attendance
3. More consistent messages and expectations for students
4. Fewer discipline problems
5. Earlier intervention with at-risk students

Teacher's Tip

Team effectiveness is related to common planning time for teachers, team stability, and systematic staff development. Teams can be a disaster if they are allowed to evolve into gripe or gossip sessions. Staying focused on curriculum and students' individual needs requires leadership and self-discipline.

6. Greater teacher satisfaction
7. Reduced failure rate
8. Improved instruction, as well as participation in and identification with the school

Curriculum

The *what* and *when* of teaching have traditionally been referred to as the **Curriculum, Scope** and **Sequence,** or the **Framework.** The past decade has also seen increased use of the word **Standards** to refer to the curriculum. The *how* of teaching is usually referred to as **Approaches, Methods, Strategies,** or **Instruction.**

Unlike many nations, the United States does not have a nationally mandated scope and sequence. In the Constitution, the Founders delegated such matters to the individual states. However, thanks to national commissions, federal funding regulations, national learned societies, and textbook publishers, there is a great deal of uniformity and a de facto national curriculum and uniform content in courses. With the creation of the **Carnegie Unit** by the Carnegie Foundation for the Advancement of Teaching in 1906, the universal measure of a high school and middle school course was established. Subsequently, school districts and states defined course content in terms of units. For example, one unit was a total of 120 hours in one subject that met four or five times a week for 40 to 60 minutes for 36 to 40 weeks each. Fourteen units were defined as constituting the minimum amount of preparation for college and became the norm for what constituted a minimum academic education at the end of twelve grades. At the same time, national publishers, using consultants from the different disciplines, developed a relatively consistent body of content through the national sales of textbooks to school districts.

? *What are the advantages and disadvantages of a national curriculum? What are the advantages and disadvantages of a national curriculum the way it is defined in the United States?*

However, this does not mean that every student who completes middle and high school has the same education. Each state, and in some cases each school district, decides on what should be the required courses and electives in those fourteen units. Variations also result from intuitional and sociological patterns, in spite of the uniformity of the content and number of units. As an example, a ½-unit trigonometry course or a 1-unit American history course in one school may vary by degree of rigor from the same course in another school because of local or teacher expectations. Other variables are when the courses are offered and in what sequence. As an example, some states teach their state history, American history, and world geography in the middle school, whereas others teach state history, world history, and world geography at middle school or both middle and high school levels. Table 4.2 identifies the courses that might be typical of a number of sixth-, seventh-, and eighth-grade middle schools.

Table 4.2 | **TYPICAL MIDDLE SCHOOL COURSES**

Domain	Course
Mathematics	General Math 1 General Math 2 Algebra 1 Geometry 1
Language Arts	Literature/Composition 1 Literature/Composition 2 Literature/Composition 3
Social Studies	American History World Geography State History
Science	General Science: Physical Science and Astronomy General Science: Biology and Life Science General Science: Chemistry and Physics
Health and Physical Education	Health Education PE activity class each year
Exploratory Program	Technology 1, 2, and 3; World Languages, Art Appreciation; Music Appreciation; Band; Chorus; Careers and Family; Teen Life, etc.

STATE MIDDLE SCHOOL AND HIGH SCHOOL CURRICULUM

Assignment 4.3

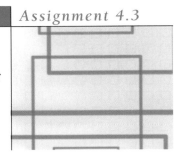

INTASC STANDARDS 1, 7–9

Visit a middle school and obtain a copy of the student handbook or another document that explains the curriculum and course options. Be prepared to compare your middle school with Table 4.2 in a discussion with your colleagues and to turn in a comparison to your professor. What do you see as the significant differences, and how would the differences affect the students and your decision about teaching in a middle school?

Thematic Teaching

Since the creation of the junior high in the early 1900s, there have been calls for a curriculum that is not based on the separate subject approach (Weilbacher, 2002). One goal is to make the content more relevant to the concerns of middle school students by addressing students' own questions with topics that connect ideas from the different subject fields through problem-centered instruction (Carnegie Council on Adolescent Development, 1989; National Middle School Association, 1995). **Thematic Teaching** (also frequently referred to as **interdisciplinary teaching**) appears to be the primary vehicle for adapting the curriculum to achieve this goal (Caskey, 2002).

To date, thematic teaching has arguably been the most enduring and widespread approach to the separate subject problem. As

For the Reflective Practitioner

The division into subjects and periods encourages a segmented rather than an integrated view of knowledge. Consequently, what students are asked to relate to in schooling becomes increasingly artificial, cut off from the human experiences subject matter is supposed to reflect.

JOHN I. GOODLAD

Topic 4: **The Middle School Environment**

an example, a team will agree on a theme like technology, the rain forests, or Australia, and all of the teachers will develop their lessons in a way that draws upon the theme. For the theme of "Australia," the science teacher might examine Australian plant life and animals, social studies would cover Australian history and geography, literature would be drawn from the same region, and math problems would have word problems using Australian themes. Research indicates that students exposed to thematic teaching learn more, have better attitudes toward school, and are more motivated (Lawton, 1994; Schubert & Melnick, 1997; Yorks & Follo, 1993). Thematic teaching's success, however, is also due to the fact that it can be implemented through teachers' initiative and collaboration within the existing organizational structure of the team and school. When attempted in teams, thematic teaching minimizes inertia and teacher concerns about loyalty and familiarity with a subject field, appropriate release time for planning, and teacher autonomy (Weilbacher, 2002).

In many cases, thematic teaching is used for a period of time, say a week or two, and at other times each team member uses the more traditional single-content teaching method. Schools that attempt whole-school thematic teaching as the only approach encounter difficulties (Johnson, Charner, & White, 2003; Powell et al., 1996), including concerns about being "too different" from the other middle schools and a deemphasis on the content knowledge needed for high school. Thematic teaching for a specified period as one of several teaching approaches used in a team environment seems to be the easiest if not most realistic approach to creating a more integrated curriculum for middle school students.

However, thematic teaching as it is often practiced is not sufficient to reach a higher goal of **curriculum integration** (Beane, 1997). For students to see their life in school as a whole, rather than as a number of discrete parts, the entire schoolday experience must be integrated in a more comprehensive and meaningful way. While thematic units are used as an organizing structure, an integrated curriculum also emphasizes projects, technology, multiple sources beyond textbooks, flexible class periods, and a variety of student grouping across and within classes and grade levels (Lake, 1994; Smith & Karr-Kidwell, 2000).

Teacher's Tip

The Internet is a great source for lesson plans, but they should not be viewed and implemented right "off the shelf." No matter how comprehensive, Internet lesson plans need to be modified to meet your students' needs and state standards.

Assignment 4.4

THEMATIC TEACHING

INTASC STANDARDS 1–4, 7–9

Read the following ERIC online article: ED448455, *Redefining Thematic Teaching*, by Johannessen, Larry R., 2000. Then search GEMS or the Internet for a thematic lesson plan on a topic in your subject field. Print out the thematic unit that you select and bring a copy of the thematic lesson to class to turn in to your professor. Be prepared to share your critique of the Internet lesson plan with the class.

Exploratory Courses

An exploratory program of courses enables middle school students to (1) discover their particular interests, abilities, talents, values, and preferences; (2) prepare for adult life, not only in terms of a vocation, but also as family members and citizens; and (3) experience leisure-time pursuits, such as the arts and physical activities (National Middle School Association, 1995). Exploratory programs often offer a set of separate, elective, "exploratory" ½-unit courses and mini-courses in a discipline-based topic like art, music, or technology; offer interdisciplinary thematic topics like the family; or formalize club experiences or activities such as dance or band into a time period (George, 2000/2001).

EXPLORATORY COURSES

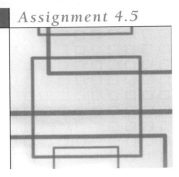

INTASC STANDARDS 1–4, 7, 9

Go to ERIC ED447970, *Exploratory Curriculum in the Middle School,* by Brazee, Ed, 2000, for more information about exploratory programs. Assume your middle school principal has asked each teacher to propose an exploratory course for next year and there are summer stipends to develop the course. Prepare a proposal for the course. Include the course, title, goal(s), why it would be relevant to and benefit middle school students, a content outline (an outline of topics), the instructional approach, and any special resources that would be needed.

Instructional Approaches

Another plank of the middle school reform platform has been to use a variety of instructional approaches. This aspect of middle school reform has had a positive effect on both middle and high school instruction. The evidence of improved achievement is compelling when hands-on experiences, group work (see Topic 31), authentic assessment (see Topic 38), individualized projects (see Topic 33), and discussions (see Topic 32) are used (Blumefeld, Soloway, & Marx, 1991; Cawetli, 1995; Johnson & Johnson, 1989; Newman & Associates, 1996; Russell, 1997). Regrettably, research also indicates that middle school and high school instruction is still dominated by passive, teacher-centered, lecture-type approaches that fall short of the engaging approaches envisioned by the middle school reform effort (Johnston, 1984; Lounsbury & Johnston, 1988; McEwing, Dickinson, & Jenkins, 1996).

Tracking and Ability Grouping

Two methods by which we accommodate individual differences based on ability or prior performance at the secondary level are **tracking** and **ability grouping,** and they begin in the middle school:

1. **Tracking** involves grouping students into paths like vocational, basic, general or standard, and college preparatory and within these tracks into sections like honors and Advanced Placement (AP) courses and the Middle Years Programme (the middle school version of the International Baccalaureate Program; see next Topic).
2. **Within-Class Ability Grouping** refers to grouping students within classes based on ability. However, the term *ability grouping* is sometimes used in the academic literature to refer to both tracking and grouping within classes.

Both tracking and ability grouping grew out of a desire and need to better accommodate individual differences.

Tracking

Turning Points, the text by the Carnegie Council on Adolescent Development (1989), referred to tracking as one of the most divisive and destructive school practices in existence and recommended eliminating all tracking of young adolescents with others of similar ability. This view is held, in part, because tracking is believed to perpetuate social inequalities for students of diverse cultural backgrounds and socioeconomic status, who have traditionally been placed in less demanding courses and tracks (Massachusetts Advocacy Center, 1990). However, many people believe tracking is necessary, and, in fact, tracking is widely used because it is almost impossible to teach or do justice to students in classes with TOO wide a range of skills and aptitudes (Loveless, 2003).

At the middle school, tracking is most frequently used in mathematics and English, whereas social studies and science tend to have mixed-ability groups; by eighth grade 73 percent of all students are tracked in some or all subjects (Loveless, 2003). At the high school level, almost everyone is tracked through a hierarchy of vocational education, general, honors, and Advanced Placement (AP) courses. To mitigate the downside of tracking in both middle and high school, academic performance based on grades and teachers' recommendations—not just scores on standardized tests—is used to determine most placements. And parents or students are typically given the opportunity to negotiate into a more demanding course if they are willing to accept a more demanding workload and potentially lower grade and to make up for projected deficiencies (Loveless, 2003).

The research on the success and failure of tracking is mixed and may have something to do with researchers' ideological perspectives. You can go to ERIC Online for ED419631, *Grouping Students for Instruction in Middle Schools*, by Mills, Rebecca, 1998, for a historical account of the research on the effects of tracking and ability grouping.

Related to tracking is multi-age grouping, where students are grouped together regardless of age in the hope of creating a greater sense of community and resiliency (Eichhorn, 1966). For a review of literature on this topic, go to the National Middle School Association's website for their research summary No. 15 at **http://www.nmsa.org/research/ressum15.htm**.

For the Reflective Practitioner

 In classes limited to high-ability students: Teachers spend less time on classroom management, more on content, cover the material at a faster pace, and have higher expectations. Students spend more time on homework, have higher self-confidence, and are more respected by teachers.

HALLINAN (2000) AND HALLINAN & KUBITSCHEK (1999)

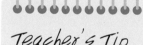

? *What is your view of tracking and multi-age grouping? What do you see as the disadvantages and advantages?*

Many parents (and students) are unaware of the implications of deciding what courses to take as early as middle school. For example, in mathematics, students who do not take the courses in middle school that will allow them to complete calculus by their senior year of high school effectively take themselves out of the running for most of the science- and technically based professions like engineering and medicine (Rosenbaum, 2001). And, in any case, parents find it difficult to "push" middle school students into more challenging courses because of their psychosocial temperament and fear of failure.

Within-Class Ability Grouping

Ability Grouping is widely used to differentiate instruction within a classroom based on students' abilities; students are placed in groups of threes, fours, or fives according to their ability. Even though tracking may present a teacher with a relatively homogeneous group of twenty-five students, the variances within the twenty-five will require **differentiated instruction** (see Topic 8). Unlike tracking, ability grouping occurs at a teacher's discretion within his or her class and is part of a repertoire of approaches used to deliver instruction. As an example, in social studies, where there is a distinct advantage to having a mixture of students discuss social issues, whole-class and group discussions of heterogeneous students would be desirable to ensure a wide variety of viewpoints and perspectives. In math, on the other hand, it is a common practice for teachers to use heterogeneous **Breakout Groups** (see Topic 31) where stronger students explain, demon-

Teacher's Tip
The NMSA's website at http://www.nmsa.org/research/research.html offers a large number of documents addressing current issues in middle schools.

strate, or solve problems with weaker students. At other times, putting students in homogeneous groups can allow a teacher to provide additional "over-the-shoulder instruction" for weaker students while stronger students tackle additional or more challenging problems.

In 1997, one of the most extensive analyses and presentations of research-based strategies on middle schools' best practices appeared in the 361-page work *What Current Research Says to the Middle Level Practitioner*. This document is the focus of Assignment 4.6.

EXPERT OPINIONS ON MIDDLE SCHOOL

Assignment 4.6

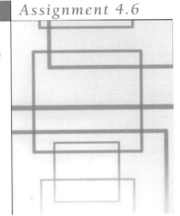

INTASC STANDARDS 1–10

At this book's website under Topic 4, Assignment 4.6, you will find most of the titles of the thirty chapters of the online ERIC document ED427847, *What Current Research Says to the Middle Level Practitioner*, edited by Irvin, Judith L., 1997. These chapters represent the authoritative work of leading middle school scholars and practitioners on such topics as ability grouping, multicultural education, and motivation. Your professor will assign you one of the chapters. Prepare a handout focusing on the Big Ideas (see Topic 11 for an explanation of "Big Ideas") in the chapter you are assigned, and be prepared to distribute and explain the handout to your classmates (as well as the professor).

OnLine Resources

Check this textbook's website at http://education.college.hmco.com/students for online links that are periodically updated to reflect new resources as they become available.

The High School Environment

There isn't a comparable national organization for the high school like the NMSA, but the American Association of School Administrators (AASA) at **http://www.aasa.org/** and the National Association of Secondary School Principals (NASSP) at **http://www.nassp.org/** provide leadership on the high school environment in much the same way and offer a website with a number of resources.

High Schools

The first senior high school was established in 1821, but it wasn't until the 1874 landmark case of *Stuart v. School District #1 of the Village of Kalamazoo* that state legislatures were enabled to levy taxes to support secondary as well as elementary schools. As of 2000, there are approximately 14,000 high schools, compared to about 15,000 middle/junior high schools (see The National Center

NATIONAL ASSOCIATION OF SECONDARY SCHOOL PRINCIPALS

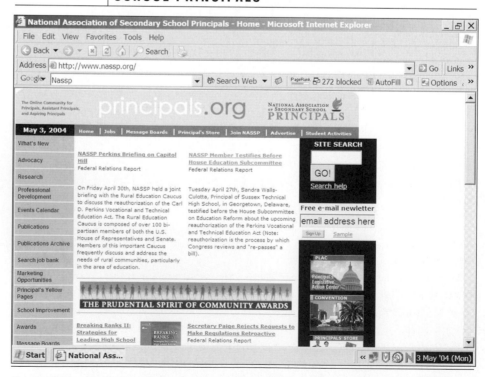

Source: *Reprinted with permission of the National Association of Secondary School Principals. For more information concerning NASSP services and/or programs, please call (703) 860-0200, or visit* **www.principals.org**.

for Educational Statistics, http://nces.ed.gov//pubs2002/digest2001/tables/dt095.asp). A critical report prepared for the National Alliance on the American High School (Martinez & Brady, 2002, p. 1) found that there has been little change in twenty years in American high schools: "If students show up, can pass their courses, and cause little trouble, they will graduate. The most significant difference is that today, many students will also have to pass a state examination to receive a diploma."

The High School Student

Although still in a pre-adult part of the life cycle, high school students have different developmental needs than middle school students. In America, the end of high school marks a major juncture for students' entry into postsecondary education, military service, or the world of work. Combined with increasing immersion in the disciplines, this becomes a growing concern for students during the latter years of high school and forces new responses to late adolescence and the onset of adulthood. Although such generalizations border on being stereotypical, developmentally by the end of high school, students should be:

1. Less egocentric than middle school students.
2. More independent than middle school students.
3. More confident than middle school students.
4. Still idealistic like middle school students.
5. Anxious to reach a more stable physical appearance.
6. Less easily discouraged.
7. Less indifferent to adults.
8. Apprehensive about their future after high school.

For the Reflective Practitioner

You don't have to suffer to be a poet; adolescence is enough suffering for anyone.

JOHN CIARDI

The good news is that more students are staying in school than in the past twenty years, and they are enrolling in more programs leading to post K–12 education, completing high school requirements, and attending some form of college (Codding & Rothman, 1999; Resnick, 1999). However, many students' weak basic skills and preparation in the disciplines will make their postsecondary education experience short-lived (see Rosenbaum, 2001). In a national survey of over 1,300 high school students (Public Agenda, 1997), teenagers were asked what they wanted from their schools. Three of the most compelling observations on what students desired from their high school teachers were:

- **Order.** Teachers were often cited for lax instruction and unenforced rules.
- **Higher expectations.** Teachers expected too little; the students said they would work harder if more were required of them.
- **Moral inspiration.** Teachers needed to promote virtues like hard work and honesty.

INTERVIEW A HIGH SCHOOL STUDENT

Assignment 5.1

INTASC STANDARDS 2, 3, 6, 9, 10

The transition from middle school to high school can be challenging. At this book's website is a link to the online document ERIC ED432411, *Helping Middle School Students Make the Transition into High School,* by Mizelle, Nancy B., 1999. After reading the brief paper, develop a series of questions for a high school student about the transition and arrange an interview with a student at an area high school. Prepare and submit a paper indicating the results of your interview as compared to the suggestions in the article; list actions a teacher can take to assist students in this important move; and be prepared to share your ideas with your professor.

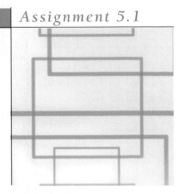

The High School Context

By temperament (see Topic 7), some people are better suited to be a teacher in the middle school culture and student age group than in the high school environment. In my experiences, too many potential teachers give too little thought to their "best fit," and because high school was their last stop on their progression to college, they think they would like to teach high school students—often in the idealized high school Advanced Placement (AP) course. Having taught at both levels, I encourage you to take a closer look at who you are and what would be the best environment for you.

Like middle schools, most high schools have seven-period days made up of 40- to 50-minute periods. Some educators feel high school students suffer from many of the same problems that have been identified in the middle school reform movement and have called for, as an example, teams to be used in high schools. You can go to ERIC ED394709, *Turning the Tables: The Growing Need for High Schools to Follow the Lead of Middle Level Reform Through Interdisciplinary Teaming*, by Spies, Paul, 1995, for a rationale for this change at the high school level.

Teacher's Tip

Although presented in this topic on high schools, types of schools, school size, and scheduling also apply to middle schools and should be considered in this light.

School Size

Public, private, church-related, magnet, vocational, urban, suburban, rural, and small and large schools are just some of the ways that we identify high schools, and each presents unique opportunities and challenges. Large schools have come under greater scrutiny by school reformers in the last two decades. In 1950, there were approximately 117,000 school districts and approximately 60,000 one-room schoolhouses. Only 14 percent of the high schools had enrollments of more than 500 students. As a result, the "small" high schools were the focus of criticism. In the 1950s, two primary justifications evolved to support larger "comprehensive" high schools: (a) cost effectiveness and (b) the opportunity with a critical mass of teachers and students to efficiently offer a more diversified curriculum. James Conant (1959), the leading advocate of the comprehensive high school, called for 100 students per grade level as the minimum critical mass appropriate for all high schools.

Through consolidations, the number of school districts has dropped to below 16,000, an 87 percent decline over approximately fifty years. America's population has increased by nearly 70 percent over the same period (Hampel, 2002; Moore, 2002). As a result, the AVERAGE high school size in America has grown to 752 students, and only six states have averages below 400 students (see NCES at **http://nces.ed.gov/pubs2001/overview/table05.asp**). However, with an average of 752 students, many high schools have well over 1,500 students.

 What is the average class size for middle and high schools of your state? What was your high school's size, and how do you think class size affected your education?

During the late 1970s and early 1980s, a movement began that called for reform of America's "large" high schools (1,200 and larger). Research shows that student achievement is adversely impacted by large schools (Fowler, 1995; Howley, 1996). Cotton's (2001) review of research conducted over fifteen years identified a number of advantages of smaller high schools. Smaller schools have been documented to improve the following:

1. Attendance rates of ethnic minority and low-SES students
2. Participation in extracurricular activities
3. Academic achievement (equal to or better than achievement at larger schools)
4. Graduation rates
5. Higher performance of minority and lower-SES students than of white and affluent students
6. Pro-social behavior of ethnic minority and low-SES students
7. Students' sense of belonging and community

Few believe that facilities can be dramatically reshaped to create more intimate learning communities. **Schools within a school (SWAS)** is a strategy by which distinct school staffs and schools are created within one facility in the hope that a greater sense of community will be fostered (go to ERIC ED461915, *Schools Within Schools*, by McAndrews and Anderson, 2002, for a summary of this movement). Some high schools have adopted teams, similar to those in middle school, to create more of a connection with students. However, the prevailing practice, regardless of the high school's size, is to have teachers organized in a **department** based on academic disciplines and students assigned a **homeroom,** with the homeroom teacher accepting a greater responsibility for his or her thirty homeroom students' general welfare than the students' other teachers.

Departments

You will likely be assigned to a department (such as a science or foreign language department), and your department chair will be your immediate supervisor. Within departments and depending on the traditions and administrative style of the chair, faculty course assignments are determined from year to year in a consultative process. For a new teacher, however, the first year's course assignments are usually determined during the hiring process. A **Course Load** is the total number of courses you will teach, and **Course Preps** are the number of preparations you will have to make (two physics courses and three chemistry courses means two preps).

Teacher's Tip

Regrettably, because seniority plays a role in assignments, new teachers are often assigned too many preps and the most challenging classes.

For the teacher, a course load of five classes, one duty period, and one planning period is typical in a seven-period day of 50-minute classes. Some teachers like having only one prep because it allows them to develop one course really well. Others prefer two preps because it gives more variety to the teaching day. Few, if any, request four or five preps because of the amount of out-of-class preparation required. Selecting textbooks, designing courses, and structuring the curriculum are also part of the departmental agenda at middle and high schools and are usually worked out collaboratively.

Orientation programs (sometimes referred to in the literature as **transition programs**) for new teachers may be district, school, and/or department based and vary greatly in quality. **Mentoring** (assigning a senior faculty member or the chair to a new faculty member to assist him or her during the first year) has become more commonplace and can be very beneficial.

There are two primary aspects to mentoring. First, you want someone to help you navigate the procedures and policies and give you general advice about your roles as a teacher. Second, you want someone to share with you the classroom materials (syllabi, handouts, classroom rules, etc.) of other teachers for the courses you will teach so you don't reinvent the wheel. I recommend that you solicit a mentor if your school does not have a formalized program. You can go

Teacher's Tip

When interviewing for positions, the quality of the transition program should be one of your considerations, and the chair should be in a position to talk about the school's, department's, and his or her support for new teachers.

to ERIC ED447104, *Lifelines to the Classroom: Designing Support for Beginning Teachers,* by Stansbury, Kendyll, Zimmerman, and Joy, 2000, for attributes of a strong new teacher support program.

Curriculum Structure

High schools typically offer ½ Carnegie unit courses, such as a semester-long trigonometry course, and whole-unit courses, like a yearlong American history course.

Requirements

Usually, state boards of education mandate a minimum number of units by discipline for graduation, and school districts or schools have some flexibility in designing the courses based on those standards. As an example, a state might mandate the following graduation requirements:

Language arts: 4 units
Mathematics: 3 units
Science: 3 units
Social studies: 3 units

Health: 1/2 unit
Physical education: 1/2 unit
Fine/performing arts appreciation: 1 unit
Electives: 7 units

For the Reflective Practitioner

Although the number of students aspiring to postsecondary education has increased, 86 percent of college-bound students with Cs or lower and 62 percent of those averaging Bs did not get even an Associate's degree.

J. E. ROSENBAUM (2001)

? *What are your state's high school graduation requirements?*

Curriculum

Students continue to be tracked into vocational, general education, and college prep curricula. Until the 1960s, each track had a much more rigid set of course requirements with very limited electives or options within the track, and students tended not to cross over between the tracks. Today, high schools, much like universities, provide a "cafeteria-style" curriculum of required and elective courses at different degrees of difficulty (see Table 5.1), and students can assert their right to more or less challenging opportunities regardless of their track. As a result, students taking a calculus sequence may be enrolled with students from a general math course in an elective course or required English course. Table 5.1 presents a sample of the mix of courses and requirements one might find in a high school.

Conant's (1959) proposition that larger high schools would provide more opportunities has resulted in the wide variety of curricular offerings, extracurricular opportunities, and support services that are the hallmark of today's American high school. The elective system was introduced to make the curriculum more interesting in hopes of retaining students. However, some argue that the reduction in specific required courses, the wide variety of elective offerings, and the segmentation of courses (as an example, one school may offer world geography or geography of the Western Hemisphere) at the high school level have come at the expense of a common body of knowledge (Powell, Farrar, & Cohen, 1985) and of what E. D. Hirsh (1987) calls **Cultural Literacy.** Advocates of Cultural Literacy have been in

Table 5.1 | **HIGH SCHOOL COURSES**

Domain	Courses
English	English (combined Composition and Literature: American and British), with general, honors, and Advanced Placement options. Reading Skills, Speech, Creative Writing, Journalism, etc.
Social Studies	American Government, American History, World History, Economics, with general, honors, and Advanced Placement options. Psychology, Philosophy, Sociology, Current Events, World Geography, African American History, Legal Education, etc.
World Languages	French, Spanish, German, Latin, etc., with general, honors, and Advanced Placement options.
Fine & Performing Arts	Drawing, painting, ceramics, pottery, print making, theatre, band, chorus, dance, etc.
Mathematics	Pre-Algebra, Vocational Math, Algebra I, Algebra II, Geometry, Intermediate Math, Analysis of Function, Pre-Calculus, Trigonometry/Analytic Geometry, Calculus, Business Math, Computer courses, etc., with general, honors, and Advanced Placement options.
Science	Biology, Chemistry, Physics, with general, honors, and Advanced Placement options. Earth Science, Ecology, Anatomy, Physiology, etc.
Health & PE	Personal fitness, team sports, aerobics, weight training, individual sports (tennis, basketball, etc.), Nutrition and Wellness, etc.

the forefront of the movement to have a uniform and well-defined body of knowledge (**Core Knowledge**) that all students should know by the end of high school so that our society gives all its members an equal opportunity (see the article "Fairness" at **http://www.coreknowledge.org/CKproto2/about/artcls.htm**).

Tiered Courses

High school course offerings (see Table 5.1), in spite of local jurisdictions, sizes, and locations, all tend to offer remedial, general, honors, and Advanced Placement options (vocational and technical education are not within the scope of this textbook, but they are a crucial component of the educational system). Students are advised or segregated into tracks or courses based on some combination of national, standardized test scores, interest, prior grades, and courses. At one end of the spectrum of requirements is a minimum math standard. In Florida, for example, state law requires that all students complete at least Algebra 1 to receive a high school diploma. As a consequence, middle and high schools offer algebra in different versions, and students in remedial sections spend more time per unit in class than other students and have laboratories and/or employ self-paced computer-based technology as a supplement to instruction. In Hillsborough County in Florida, the tenth-largest school district in the country, as many as 20 percent of the students fail Algebra 1 in the fall, and as many as 50 percent in the spring (these students take it in spring after a pre-algebra course or because they have failed the algebra course in the fall).

For the Reflective Practitioner

Mathematics is essential. Almost 80 percent of students who take calculus get a postsecondary education degree. Only about 23 percent of students who complete only algebra I and geometry earn even an Associate's degree.

J. E. ROSENBAUM (2001)

Topic 5: **The High School Environment**

At the other end of the spectrum is the Advanced Placement program. The **Advanced Placement (AP) program** of the College Board (see **http://www. collegeboard.com/ap/students/**) offers over thirty-five subjects in over 11,000 high schools, and the credit is accepted at over 2,900 universities. The AP program provides teaching materials and course descriptions, but schools select the teachers and textbooks and set the criteria for students to take an AP course. Examinations are administered in May, scored in June, and reported in July of each year.

Scheduling

One modification to the traditional scheduling pattern has been the practice of **rotating periods**. For example, on one day the first class, which normally would meet in the first time period of the day, may be in the second time period on the second day of the week. With this arrangement, students' attention spans are not affected by the time of day of one particular course, and all courses are affected equally, or at least randomly, by schedule modifications for shortened days, pep rallies, student trips to performances, and so on. Changes to the daily schedule (shortened classes, dropped periods, etc.) are one of the more problematic patterns in schools because they disrupt the well-made plans of teachers, and they seem to be on the rise (Smith, 2000).

Another change has been to provide **year-round schooling** to maximize facilities. According to the National Association for Year-Round Education (go to **http://www.nayre.org/**), in 1999 over 2 million students were enrolled in more than 2,900 year-round schools in forty-three states, a fivefold increase in the last decade. Go to ERIC ED449123, *Teaching in Year-Round Schools,* by Kneese, Carolyn, 2000, for a description of the different models and the advantages and disadvantages of the year-round school.

Block Scheduling, or using 90-minute class periods, has gained a greater foothold in many schools, and there are at least four different varieties based on this construct. The four most common models are known as the **Copernican Plan** (Carroll, 1994), the **4x4 Schedule** (Schoenstein, 1995), the **Alternate Day Block Schedule** (Canady & Rettig, 1995), and the **Trimester Plan** (Geismar & Pullease, 1996). You can go to the University of Minnesota at **http:// education.umn.edu/carei/Blockscheduling/default.html** for a detailed explanation of block scheduling. Research indicates that students prefer block scheduling because the longer time period offers more variety of teaching methods and more concentrated, individual attention by teachers. In general, teachers also favor block scheduling, believing it is better for their students than the traditional seven-period day (Pisapia & Westfall, 1997; Stanley & Gifford, 1998).

Do you think block scheduling of 90-minute periods rather than 60-minute periods may be more effective for some subject fields than others? What would you prefer?

Diverse and Specialized Programs

Middle and high schools have many shared qualities, but recent experimentation has produced a new diversity of approaches to their focus and organization. The following schools are representative of this trend.

KIPP schools (Knowledge Is Power Program; see Wingert (2004) and KIPP schools at **http://www.kipp.org/**) represent a reform movement to reshape inner-city schools that enroll primarily black and low-SES students. KIPP schools have produced impressive results by extending school hours (7:30 A.M. to 5:00 P.M.), giving Saturday classes, offering summer school for all students, requiring two to three hours of homework each night, creating a rigorous curriculum, and using contracts requiring excellence (and commitment) between teachers, parents, and students.

Charter Schools (go to **http://www.cacharterschools.org/**) have greater autonomy in terms of curriculum and staffing than the typical school district. For information, see the theme issue of *Phi Delta Kappan,* March 1998, **The Charter School Movement,** and the Charter Schools website at **http://www.uscharterschools.org/pub/uscs_docs/index.htm.**

International Baccalaureate Programs (go to **http://www.ibo.org/**) often exist as schools within a school and offer a rigorous academic track for college-bound students with a history of high academic performance. Students usually have to go through an application process that emphasizes an excellent prior academic record.

Magnet Schools (go to **http://www.magnet.edu/**) traditionally have had two purposes: (1) They desegregate public schools by using subject field specialization to attract diverse students to one setting; and (2) they assemble resources like faculty and equipment for domains like fine arts, sciences, and technology into one facility to offer a higher degree of concentration for a student with a particular interest. Students in magnet programs are not typically relieved of state curriculum requirements, and a fine arts magnet school, for example, will still have departments of math and science, but students can use electives to focus on one area of study. Originally developed in the arts, magnet schools have also evolved for fields like science and technology.

Participation in the Life of the School

Extracurricular activities have long been a hallmark of middle and high schools. This **"supplementary education"** (Gordon, 1999) is a vital part of school culture and a crucial part of the development of teenagers (Coleman et al., 1966; Comer, 1997; Holloway, 2002). Schools provide supervised opportunities which serve as what Bourdieu (1986) called **"cultural capital."** When not found at home or in the community, this "capital" can come in the form of extracurricular activities sponsored by schools (and through partnerships with community organizations and families), like sports, clubs, scouts, school theatrical and musical productions, travel, and summer camps. And in the academic realm it includes the more obvious resources such as books, computers, academic role models, and a quiet place to study. We know that this capital is less available to students from low-SES groups and that many students have to choose between working after school and participating in what capital is available to them in their school and community. In other cases, school- and community-sponsored supplemental education partially fills the void left by families without such capital (Brown & Evans, 2002). We know that more successful students are immersed in family, school, and community supplemental education activities (McCarthy, 2000) and that involvement in supplemental education facilitates moral, social, and intellectual development (Nettles, 1989). Students who spend more time in structured activities, religious organizations, and interactions with

Teacher's Tip
Before starting your first year of teaching, consider ALL your responsibilities. Don't overextend and overcommit yourself by volunteering for too many extracurricular activities.

adults (as opposed to time spent alone or "hanging out" with peers) have a more positive view of their chances for life. Conversely, students who spend little time in meaningful and structured supplemental education activities are more prone to develop maladaptive behaviors (Jordon & Nettles, 1999). Every teacher should encourage students to become participants in school-sponsored activities.

The National Federation of State High School Associations at **http://www. nfhs.org/prof_assoc.htm** is the organization that facilitates many school organizations that direct and support extracurricular activities.

Assignment 5.2

CURRENT SCHOLARSHIP ON SCHOOLWIDE TOPICS

INTASC STANDARDS 1–10

Being informed about current policies and trends in middle and high schools is crucial to your role as a teacher. At this book's website, listed under Topic 5, Assignment 5.2, are thirty recently published ERIC online documents covering topics such as drug testing, school uniforms, teacher unions, and so on. Your professor will likely assign you a topic. Read the article (and additional articles, or visit a related website) and prepare a document to submit to your instructor; also, make copies for each class member. In the paper, persuade your colleagues that your topic is important by summarizing the topic, citing key facts in a few paragraphs, and then making five specific suggestions on what a teacher should consider or do as a consequence of this information.

OnLine Resources

Check this textbook's website at **http://education.college.hmco.com/students** for online links that are periodically updated to reflect new resources as they become available.

UNIT TWO

The Effective Teacher

© Dan Reynolds.

Learning Theories and Principles

This topic focuses on a number of general instructional principles based on the most commonly accepted learning theories, which you may have learned about in an educational psychology course. At the heart of teaching is the ability of the teacher—through astute lesson planning—to place the student at what Vygotsky (1978) defined as the **zone of proximal development** (ZPD). Basically, ZPD is what a student is capable of learning—the space between the student's current academic ability and potential ability. Assuming that the teacher can create the "right" environment based on his or her understanding of the students and of the pedagogical and content knowledge, the communication and learning equation becomes the focus of the classroom experience.

Historical Perspective

The early 1900s launched an industrialization movement that instigated a more scientific analysis by psychologists of how tasks are achieved in both factories and schools (Kliebard, 1995). In factories, seamstresses were turned into buttonhole makers and former carriage makers were turned into axle assemblers in the Ford Motor Company assembly line, all in the name of efficiency and basically converting the creativity of their crafts into discrete tasks that became jobs. The focus of individual creativity was shifted to analyzing and engineering efficient assembly lines composed of repetitive tasks.

For the Reflective Practitioner

Nothing is particularly hard if you divide it into small jobs.

HENRY FORD

In education, a similar phenomenon occurred when psychologists began to analyze the steps in the learning process with an eye to greater efficiency and improved outcomes (see Brandt & Perkins, 2000). This more scientific approach to learning and teaching led to the introduction of reading materials that were crafted according to readability scales and processes such as the Madeline Hunter method (see Topic 20). It also led to two schools of learning theory: the Associationist/Behaviorist model and the Constructivist/Cognitive model.

The Associationist/Behaviorist Model

Thorndike (1922), Skinner (1954), and Gagne (1965) were among the key leaders of the **Associationist/Behaviorist** schools of learning theories, which focused on the basic tasks and the process of learning. The theories are based on a number of concepts:

1. Learning is sequential.
2. Learning is hierarchical.
3. Learning is the accumulation of bits of knowledge.
4. Proceeding to the next bit of knowledge should begin only after assessment.
5. Assessment should be used to assess and reinforce learning.
6. External motivations should be as positive as possible.

This movement still has a profound effect on teaching today, and it is based on the principle that knowledge acquisition is best learned if it is divided into a logical, sequential set of steps with reinforcement based on the accomplishment of each task assigned to each step. By the 1960s, this approach led to the widespread adoption of Behavioral Objectives, which define what is to be learned. Behavioral objectives are still in use in many schools and teacher education programs.

In the search for precision, words like *know* and *understand,* which had been commonly used by teachers to define what their goals were, became unacceptable for defining and assessing students' knowledge. More specific words like *write, identify,* and *list* were adopted to define and assess the behaviors that would demonstrate knowledge. In his *Taxonomy of Educational Objectives,* Bloom (1956) categorized cognitive behaviors into *Knowledge, Comprehension, Application, Analysis, Synthesis,* and *Evaluation* and developed the words used to describe these behaviors (see Teacherworld's listing of "Action Verbs" at http://teacherworld.com/potactionverbs.html or enter "Bloom's Taxonomy" in your search engine). So rather than explaining that students will know how to divide as an objective, teachers would use, as a procedure, the **ABCD method: Audience, Behavior, Conditions, and Degree.** An example would be "(A) Fourth-grade students (B) will divide 3-digit numbers by 2-digit numbers (C) without a calculator (D) with 90 percent accuracy." You may also want to investigate Bloom's Affective and Psychomotor domains by searching for "Bloom's Taxonomy" (see **Teacherworld** at http://teacherworld.com/potslo.html).

In addition, with new copying technology and therefore greater emphasis on assessment as part of the reinforcement regime, **objective-type testing** rather than oral and written open-ended testing became dominant in the classroom. The teacher at the turn of the twentieth century, without such tools, used daily observation, demonstration by students, dialogue, drill, practice, and questioning (also referred to as the Socratic method) as part of a daily regime of assessment that was iterative, interactive, and constant. But by the 1950s, weekly and quarterly objective quizzes became the norm, which in some disciplines have had the unexpected side effect of defining knowledge more as vocabulary, facts, and mundane skills. Lost in the transition was the opportunity to assess students' ability to generalize what they had learned, or what is referred to in the literature as **Transfer.** In its simplest form, transfer is the ability to apply the concept learned with one set of information to a new set of information. It is more difficult for a teacher to construct objective tests that measure the concepts behind vocabulary and thinking skills than it is to use the more subjective Socratic method or dialectic, which requires students to explain their thinking in real time while interacting with a teacher.

Objective-type testing, with its quantitative scores, provides comparative data and excellent documentation for parents who might be concerned about teachers with bias; with subjective testing, like essays and questioning, students are more easily compelled to construct their own knowledge, a prerequisite to transfer.

The Constructivist/Cognitive Model

Constructivist learning theory is primarily based on the work of Jean Piaget (1972), Jerome Bruner (1990), Lev Vygotsky (1978), and David Ausubel (1967), to name a few notable leaders in the field. Unlike the previous associationist/

behaviorist learning theory, constructivist theory is more of an underlying set of assumptions about how the human mind acquires and maintains knowledge. This textbook, while being eclectic, is biased toward this particular view of learning, as are most current textbooks. Constructivist practices are important to concept formation, problem solving, decision making, and lifelong learning. They emphasize teaching students HOW to think about using content, rather than to think about the exact content that teachers give them during instruction. In any Internet search engine, type "Constructivist Theory" or one of the names listed above to learn more about these principles in greater depth. What follows is a brief summary of key features of the cognitive model of learning.

Piaget described **"intelligence"** as how an organism adapts to its environment. Behavior (adaptation to the environment) is controlled through **schemas** (I like to think of these as little boxes inside one's mind) that the individual uses to represent the world. As we encounter new information, we experience **disequilibrium.** The drive to adapt comes from the need to balance the schemas in our mind's eye as we encounter new information. The two processes by which individuals move from the discomfort of disequilibrium to the temporary but more comfortable equilibrium are assimilation and accommodation. **Assimilation** is the process of placing new facts, concepts, ideas, and beliefs in the preexisting schemas. **Accommodation** is the process of creating new schemas or changing existing schemas. Both processes are used simultaneously throughout life in developing cognitive as well as affective schemas.

Can you think of an example of how Piaget's model works in a classroom setting in your discipline? Be prepared to share an example in class.

The construction of knowledge includes both (a) content in the traditional sense of facts and concepts (**Information Knowledge;** see Topic 11) and (b) thinking and basic skills (**Procedural Knowledge;** see Topic 11) (Philips, 1995). This theory is supported by Bruner (1960, 1990 & 1996), who identified four major factors that the teacher must consider when planning instruction—the first and fourth related to motivation, the second to knowledge, and the third to methods and strategies:

1. Students' predisposition toward learning
2. The ways in which a body of knowledge is structured so that it can be most readily grasped by the learner
3. The most effective sequences in which to present material
4. The nature and pacing of rewards and punishments

Vygotsky (1978) focused on the capacity to independently problem-solve, that is, to use general thinking skills or procedural knowledge. The teacher finds each student at one end of the **zone of proximal development.** The other end of the expanding zone is the potential capacity for problem solving. To move students through the zone, teachers introduce increasingly sophisticated forms of procedural knowledge by (a) modeling problem solving; (b) providing opportunities for practice in which the student is guided by the teacher; and (c) engaging other students as models who have more advanced procedural knowledge skills than their peers (Wilson, 2002). As you will learn later in Topic 10 on motivation, in the end, learners must actively **self-teach** (construct) for themselves what the new information means so that they can perform the mental task (and thus produce the behaviorists' objectively measured product) on their own.

Topic 6: **Learning Theories and Principles**

Constructivist Best Practices

The following are best practices for a constructivist classroom.

1. Constructing one's own meaning out of knowledge is the essence of learning; so thoughtful discussion and time to reflect are emphasized.
2. Students are given an opportunity to think and to propose ideas and beliefs so they can test and construct their own knowledge.
3. Teachers ask open-ended questions, listen to students' ideas, and provide alternative propositions.
4. Teachers start with what students know and use metaphors and anecdotes to help them build bridges to new knowledge.
5. Big Ideas create context for facts. Learning is accomplished when parts are developed in the context of the whole.
6. Teachers set up problems, guide student inquiry, and point out and emphasize Procedural Knowledge while monitoring students' explanations.
7. Teachers use raw data, primary documents, and realia so students can construct their own meaning out of materials rather than rely on textbook explanations.
8. Students use graphic organizers in creating cognitive structures. In direct instruction, graphic organizers can create an "umbrella" for ideas.
9. The most general ideas of a subject should be presented first; then the subject should be progressively differentiated in terms of detail and specificity.
10. Organizers should attempt to integrate new material with previously presented material.

For the Reflective Practitioner

 Spoon-feeding in the long run teaches us nothing but the shape of the spoon.   E. M. FORSTER

How would you compare and contrast a teacher's role, view of students, classroom strategies, and assessment based on these two learning theory models?

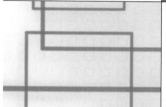

Assignment 6.1   **BEHAVIORAL OBJECTIVES**

INTASC STANDARDS 1, 7, 8
Visit **Teacherworld** at http://teacherworld.com/potslo.html and/or search the Internet for "behavioral objectives". Based on the information in this topic, construct at least three behavioral objectives using terms from Bloom's Taxonomy, and identify the A, B, C, and D of the ABCD method for each objective. Be prepared to submit this one-page assignment to your instructor and to discuss your objectives in class.

OnLine Resources	LEARNING THEORIES
University of Colorado at Denver	See the Gateway site on *models of instruction* at http://carbon.cudenver.edu/~mryder/itc_data/idmodels.html
New York Public Broadcasting	The *Concepts to Classrooms* series at http://www.thirteen.org/edonline/concept2class/ has a training seminar with streaming video on the use of constructivist theories.
ERIC OnLine ED445674	*The Legacy of Robert M. Gagne,* edited by Richey, Rita C., 2000.
ERIC OnLine ED430683	*Architects of the Intellect,* by Fogarty, Robin, 1999, presents the constructivist or brain-compatible classroom by describing classroom activities based on the work of theorists Dewey, Piaget, Vygotsky, and others.

Check this textbook's website at http://education.college.hmco.com/students **for additional links.**

Student and Teacher Dispositions to Learning

Your **disposition (temperament and learning style)** plays an important role in shaping your teaching practices and how you approach your students (Alcock & Ryan, 1999; Elias & Stewart, 1991; Foster & Horner, 1988; Garger & Guild, 1984; Kent & Fisher, 1997; Perkins, Jay, & Tishman, 1992; Richardson, 1996). In addition, it likely influenced your decision to become, for example, an English teacher as opposed to a biology teacher (**teaching field preference**). It is a truism that we prefer to teach the way we personally prefer to learn (see Carey, Fleming, & Roberts, 1989; Cuban, 1984). To be successful as an instructor, you will have to overcome your inclination to approach teaching as if all your students prefer to learn and actually learn like you and perceive your subject matter in the same way that you do. And you will need to use a repertoire of strategies that appeal to different dispositions, even though you may not personally find other approaches appealing.

Temperament

Your personal temperament influences the way you model civility, engage the students, and show your level of professionalism. It is observed by students by the way you enter the classroom, greet them, select teaching strategies, organize the instruction, react to disruptions, choose topics, and engage in all other tasks. In turn, this shapes the receptivity of the class to your motivational approaches and creates a positive or negative environment.

One of the most widely used methods to examine temperament orientation is the **Myers-Briggs model** (or **MBTI**, Myers-Briggs Type Indicator). The Myers-Briggs instrument makes it possible for a teacher to ascertain his or her dominant way of thinking, behaving, and learning. This model, although developed independently, shares a theoretical framework with Carl Jung (you can go to the Carl Jung page at **http://www.cgjungpage.org/** for more information). MBTI posits four scales of temperament (see Table 7.1). Individuals have predispositions toward one trait from each scale, and whichever combination of traits a teacher possesses provides insight into that teacher's temperament and learning and teaching style. A combination of the four predispositions, like "ISTJ," is used to define a person's temperament. Research is often conducted on pairs of letters, like NF's or SJ's, or on single letters like S's or T's. Temperament influences a teacher's selection of the topics and strategies for classroom instruction (Gordon, 1993).

The Myers-Briggs is normally administered by a licensed professional to ensure validity. However, a number of websites use a scheme similar to Myers-Briggs, so you can approximate your type and begin the reflective process of examining your temperament.

Table 7.1 | **THE FOUR MBTI SCALES**

Introverted or Extraverted (I/E)	Sensing or Intuitive (S/N)
The <u>I</u>ntroverted type (33% of the population) has a more inward-looking, reflective orientation.	The <u>S</u>ensing type (66% of the population) likes facts and details and wants directions.
The <u>E</u>xtraverted type (66% of the population) is more expressive and more sensitive to the external environment.	The I<u>n</u>tuitive type (33% of the population) looks for patterns and "Big Ideas" and relies more on imagination.
Thinking or Feeling (T/F)	**Judging or Perceiving (J/P)**
The <u>T</u>hinking type (F 33%, M 60% of the population) prefers learning that requires logic in decision making and is motivated by ideas.	The <u>J</u>udging type (55% of the population) tends to prefer analyzing, decision making, and closure.
The <u>F</u>eeling type (F 66%, M 40% of the population) prefers learning environments that are social and is motivated by interaction with peers and teachers.	The <u>P</u>erceiving type (45% of the population) is more spontaneous, prefers to keep options open, and is generally more flexible in how he or she learns.

Assignment 7.1 | **MYERS-BRIGGS PERSONALITY TYPE**

INTASC STANDARDS 2–7, 9

Go to one or more of the websites listed below (preferably the first one) to get an estimation of your Myers-Briggs type. Ask a close friend or family member if he or she believes that the description of your type is accurate. Be prepared to share your type and ideas in class.

1. **Personality Pathways** provides questions to help you identify your type, after which you can click on the types to learn more about your temperament. Go to http://www.personalitypathways.com/type_inventory.html.
2. **Interconnection** at http://www.interconnections.co.uk/Market/PCFG/learn/lrntest.htm.
3. **Humanmetrics** at http://www.humanmetrics.com/cgi-win/JTypes1.htm.

Most of your students will not be your same type. As an example, using just the I/E and S/N types, a typical class of 35 students would be divided into four types based on national averages (see Table 7.2).

So if you are an Introverted Intuitive (IN) type, the question becomes, how will you modify or alternate your instructional approaches to motivate the 31 students who are different from you? The research on trying to match teachers and students based on temperament or learning styles and its effect on student learning is mixed (Dunn & Dunn, 1987; Knight, Halpen, & Halpen, 1992). And such an approach would fail to prepare students for future encounters with employers and teachers who are different from them. One of the maxims of the Myers-Briggs model is that we all have "different gifts" and need to develop a repertoire of learning strategies that make the most of our type and that also make up for its limitations. As a teacher, we must provide opportunities for our students to learn in different ways, not just the way we prefer.

Table 7.2 | **THE TYPICAL CLASSROOM USING TWO MYERS-BRIGGS CATEGORIES**

Introverted Sensing Types (8)	Introverted Intuitive Types (4)

Desire quiet reflection.
Prefer ideas, concepts, and impressions.
Want structure and sequential, step-by-step processes.
Like hands-on activities and are fascinated
  by people.
	Desire quiet reflection.
	Prefer ideas, concepts, and impressions.
	Want inspirational teachers.
	Like individualized assignments and freedom
	  to explore and are fascinated by ideas.

Extraverted Sensing Types (15)	**Extraverted Intuitive Types (8)**

Desire thinking out loud.
Prefer working with others, discussion, etc.
Want structure and sequential, step-by-step processes.
Like hands-on activities and are fascinated
  by people.
	Desire thinking out loud.
	Prefer working with others, discussion, etc.
	Want inspirational teachers.
	Like individualized assignments and freedom
	  to explore and are fascinated by ideas.

The following are some generalizations that should guide teachers based on the research on temperament.

1. Because classrooms focus on ideas and refine concepts in an orderly sequence primarily by using the spoken word and reading material, the classroom setting and the learning experience are inherently geared to **Introverts** (33 percent of the population).

2. Activities-based learning (see Topic 21) is specifically intended to accommodate the other 66 percent of the population, **Extraverts.**

3. Questioning: **Intuitive** teachers are likely to start with higher-order questions requiring synthesis or evaluation and then solicit facts to support the hypothesis, whereas **Sensing** teachers typically request facts and then build to a concept.

4. Objectives: **Intuitive** teachers tend to select their content from their subject field and based on students needs, whereas **Sensing** teachers prefer to develop their lessons from standards, curriculum guides, and other teachers.

5. Planning: **Intuitive** teachers tend to plan in detail; **Sensing** teachers tend to plan around general themes.

6. Behavior: **Intuitive** teachers tend to feel they are successful if student involvement is high; **Sensing** teachers find success in improved grades and behavior.

7. Evaluation: **Thinking** teachers tend to give little, but objective, feedback; **Feeling** teachers are more inclined to praise and criticize.

For a more detailed article on teaching styles based on Myers-Briggs types, go to the Georgia State University Master Teacher website at **http://www.gsu.edu/ %7Edschjb/wwwmbti.html** or ERIC ED452184 *Personality Types and Teaching Efficacy as Predictors of Classroom Control Orientation in Beginning Teachers* by Chambers, Sharon M., 2001.

What do you think are the implications of your personality type for your teaching?

Myers-Briggs is presented separately from the following learning styles because it applies to the broader concept of classroom communication and also the informal interpersonal interactions that affect how a teacher "connects"

Topic 7: **Student and Teacher Dispositions to Learning**

with a student or group of students. The learning style theories in this next section are rightly the subject of in-depth courses in educational psychology. However, they are recast here to focus your attention on their corollary instructional approaches.

Learning Styles

There are a number of theories on learning and learning styles that could be presented in a methods textbook, but the following four are representative of the scholarship and should be most helpful to your practices (see also Silver, Strong, & Perini, 2000).

The Index of Learning Styles

The **Index of Learning Styles** (ILS) is an instrument used to assess preferences on four dimensions:

1. Active/reflective
2. Sensing/intuitive
3. Visual/verbal
4. Sequential/global

This learning style model was formulated by Richard M. Felder and Barbara A. Soloman. The instrument and a description of the learning styles are available at http://www.ncsu.edu/felder-public/ILSdir/styles.htm for public use at no cost for noncommercial purposes by individuals who wish to determine their own learning style profile and by educators who wish to use the instrument for teaching, advising, or research. So not only can you use the instrument to determine your personal learning style, but you can also use it with your students in your classroom.

Assignment 7.2 **LEARNING STYLES**

INTASC STANDARDS 2–9

Go to http://www.engr.ncsu.edu/learningstyles/ilsweb.html to complete the ILS instrument. At the bottom of the page of your results are links about learning styles and the implications of your scores. Bring your results to class, along with a one-page, single-spaced summary of your learning style based on the links provided with the ILS results.

Field-Dependent/Global or Field-Independent/Analytical Learning Style

Herman A. Witkin (1981) developed the theory of **field-dependent/global** and **field-independent/analytical** orientations in the 1960s. Over two decades of research have yielded considerable evidence that these orientations influence both our learning style and how we teach others (Saracho, 2003).

Field-Dependent people perceive information *globally*, make broad distinctions among concepts, adhere to structures provided by teachers, learn material best within a social context that is relevant to their own experience, have a social orientation, need organization, and are affected by criticism. The preferred teaching style involves:

1. Personalized situations that allow interaction and discussion with students.
2. Use of questions to check on student learning following instruction.
3. Student-centered activities.

4. Orientation toward facts.
5. Minimum feedback to students.
6. A warm and personal learning environment.

Field-Independent people perceive information *analytically* by viewing things in parts rather than as a whole, are verbal interactors, prefer to modify structures to meet their needs, like to categorize, have a less outwardly personal orientation, are interested in new concepts for their own sake, and tend to self-motivate. The preferred teaching style involves:

1. Impersonal teaching situations such as lectures that are focused on content or the task at hand.
2. Use of questions to introduce topics and probe student answers.
3. Teacher-centered activities.
4. Orientation toward principles.
5. Corrective feedback, even if negative.
6. Organization and guidance.

Which of the above two orientations reflects your learning, if not teaching, style?

Field-Dependent students typically perform better in school (Cross, 1977) and on standardized tests (Renniger & Snyder, 1983). Students who are matched with teachers of the same style report greater satisfaction and ease of learning (Packer & Brain, 1978; Renniger & Snyder, 1983).

Concrete or Abstract Perceiving and Sequential or Random Ordering

Anthony F. Gregorc (1979) focuses on the "Mind Styles" of individuals. These styles, which form distinctive learning patterns, are based on how we perceive and order things.

1. **Perceiving:** the way we take in information.
   a. **Concrete Perceiving** refers to the ability to register information directly through your five senses: sight, smell, touch, taste, and hearing. When you are using your concrete ability, you are dealing with the obvious, the "here and now."
   b. **Abstract Perceiving** refers to the ability to conceive ideas, to understand or believe that which you cannot actually see. When you are using your abstract quality, you are using your intuition and your imagination, and you are looking beyond "what is" to more subtle implications.
2. **Ordering:** the way we handle the information we take in.
   a. **Sequential Ordering** predisposes one to organize information in a linear, step-by-step, predetermined order and to express oneself in a precise and logical way.
   b. **Random Ordering** allows one to grasp information in a nonlinear and multifarious manner and to express oneself in a multifaceted and eclectic way.

Students who prefer sequential ordering have a stronger preference for structured teaching methods, assigned homework problems, and organized lectures. In contrast, students who prefer random ordering have a stronger preference for participating in group discussion and activities that allow for independent thought (Seidel & England, 1999). In one study, more males than females were

Topic 7: **Student and Teacher Dispositions to Learning**

found to be abstract sequential and concrete random, and more females than males were identified as abstract random (O'Brien, 1999).

Although all people are believed to use all four styles, research by Gregorc suggests that 95 percent express a preference for one or two areas. The reported distribution based on the Gregorc Style Delineator Instrument (Gregorc & Ward, 1977) appears in Table 7.3.

Table 7.3 | **GREGORC DISTRIBUTION OF PREFERENCES**

Preference	Percentage
Abstract Random	7.9
Abstract Sequential	16.8
Concrete Random	19.5
Concrete Sequential	48.9
Unresolvable	7.0

You can go to **http://www.gregorc.com/** for additional information on this learning style.

Multiple Intelligences

Howard Gardner's multiple intelligences is a departure from the IQ approach that dominated education at one time. The theory of multiple intelligences suggests that there are a number of distinct forms of intelligence and that each individual possesses them in varying degrees. Howard Gardner's Harvard University website at **http://www.pz.harvard.edu/Pls/HG.htm** provides a wealth of information on this theory.

Gardner proposes eight primary forms of intelligence. They are particularly useful for teachers who use authentic assessment (see Unit 7) and for responding to the diversity of learning styles proposed in the Myers-Briggs and by Witkin and Gregorc. The following is a list of the eight intelligences and the strategies that can be effectively used for each.

1. **Linguistic intelligence:** writing journals, making speeches, advocating, retelling, and reading
2. **Musical intelligence:** singing, performing, reading and writing poetry, and playing instruments
3. **Logical-mathematical intelligence:** outlining, calculating, analyzing statistical information, and creating timelines
4. **Visual-spatial intelligence:** drawing, using guided imagery, making mindmaps, and using graphic organizers, maps, charts, and graphs
5. **Body-kinesthetic intelligence:** role-playing, enacting simulations, playing games, and using manipulatives
6. **Intrapersonal intelligence:** doing self-reflection tasks, practicing higher-order reasoning, questioning, and taking personal inventories
7. **Interpersonal intelligence:** participating in group work, practicing cooperative learning, mentoring, tutoring, and conducting field interviews
8. **Naturalistic intelligence:** fishing, hiking, camping, farming, and investigating the natural world

Although individuals should be encouraged to use their preferred intelligences in learning, they also need to develop their less preferred intelligences.

Therefore, teachers should have multiple types of projects and assessments that allow students to demonstrate their knowledge using all the different intelligences.

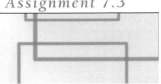

| MULTIPLE INTELLIGENCES | *Assignment 7.3* |

INTASC STANDARDS 2–8
Using the principle of multiple intelligences, write a brief description of how you could create an activity for students with each of the eight orientations as part of a lesson plan in your teaching field.

Predisposition to an Academic Discipline

How does someone come to choose physical education over mathematics or English over social studies as his or her teaching field? The reasons are numerous and complex, but one's inclinations and apprehensions about specific **Domains** (the broad areas of subject matter, such as social studies and science) and **Disciplines** (the specific subject areas, such as geography and physics) become more pronounced beginning in middle school, where education focuses more on domain/discipline-specific procedural and information knowledge. By college, preferences are even more pronounced (Kolb, 1981). To understand this phenomenon, it is helpful to think of your middle and high school students as falling into one of three categories:

- **Potential apprentices:** individuals who have *not yet decided* whether to pursue knowledge in the domain
- **Nonapprentices:** individuals with little *interest or inclination* in the field and who probably will not pursue knowledge in the domain
- **Apprentices:** individuals who are *disposed* toward the domain/discipline and are joining the community of practice through what Strife (2004) referred to as "Normation."

Students' attitudes toward one domain or discipline as opposed to another are shaped by temperament, learning style, innate ability, and a range of experiences that stem from interactions with teachers and activities involving the content and thinking skills of the domain or discipline (Becher, 1989; Howe, Davidson, & Sloboda, 1998). Early success in a domain or discipline and its unique attributes (structure, content, approaches, amount of memorization required, pace, etc.) are what MacIntryre (1981) identified as those "goods" internal to the practice of the domain or discipline that affect students' willingness to enter into it and persist (Sebart & Krek, 2002; Shulman & Quinlan, 1996; Stodolsky, 1988). Students gravitate to and self-select themselves into one domain or discipline over another, moving from potential apprentices to apprentices or nonapprentices. This sometimes subtle choice evolves over an extended period of time, but tracking and elective course requirements starting in middle school require explicit choices among courses and disciplines that greatly influence students' motivation, aspirations, and success in a domain or discipline.

The vast majority of students, except in honors and AP (Advanced Placement) courses, will be nonapprentices in your class. In honors and AP courses, many students will be nonapprentices but will be highly motivated to succeed in spite of their attitude, perhaps because of the teacher or their parents. The nonapprentice teens that teachers find in general or remedial classes often reveal themselves with statements like "Oh, I can't do mathematics," "I'm no good at language," or "History is boring." These may be students who are reasonably diligent but have already decided to opt out of one domain or discipline because of experiences that have been difficult or taxing for them. As an example, success in mathematics requires almost daily practice to succeed because of the incremental nature of the discipline, whereas with the way history is frequently taught, students can survive with more intermittent daily study. Some negative attitudes have more to do with personal circumstances (work after school, eligibility for sports, etc.) that prevent consistent and timely preparation and practice at home than with the domain or discipline itself. Except for students who are failing or excelling in all courses, domain/discipline predisposition accounts, at least in part, for students who are doing better in some courses and not others and electing out of some domains or disciplines to the extent that curriculum requirements allow.

Teaching students who have little enthusiasm for your discipline is one of the great challenges for middle and high school teachers, and this is a problem of a different order than the students who are doing poorly in general (Feldmen, 1976; Grossman, 1989; Pohlman, 1976). The ideas and strategies in this book are partly intended to help middle and high school teachers to lower the threshold for nonapprentices and potential apprentices so that they can become more motivated to acquire knowledge in a discipline that is not very appealing to them and to encourage apprentices to excel in their discipline.

OnLine Resources

Check this textbook's website at http://education.college.hmco.com/students for online links that are periodically updated to reflect new resources as they become available.

Teaching in a Diverse Classroom

In applying the principles of learning theories and dispositions to the classroom, it is important to not underestimate the implications of the diverse American classroom. This diversity was partially created by a democratic society that attracts people from around the world, by the desegregation of public schools, and by a commitment to universal access to public education. The proportion of students from diverse socioeconomic, cultural, ethnic, and religious backgrounds and with special needs will continue to grow, according to the National Center for Education Statistics (**http://nces.ed.gov/**). In addition, students with special needs disproportionately come from families with lower socioeconomic status (SES) who live in urban environments (Karlin, 2000).

Diversity and Microcultures

Students come to school from cultures shaped by their families and neighborhoods (Trumbull et al., 2001). **Microcultures** based on poverty, ethnicity, gender norms, nationality, "race," religion, socioeconomic status, place of residence (urban/suburban/rural), and language influence the way students dress, communicate, eat, maintain hygiene, respond to questions, play, organize their space, study, approach tasks, listen, and learn—and, as a consequence, how well they succeed in school. When a student's culture is similar to the larger culture, the middle and high school years are typically less taxing on the student's emotional, physical, and intellectual resources.

For others, finding personal identity and success in the foreign culture of the school can be a substantial challenge that is added on to the academic challenges of the school. What many teachers see as behavioral and academic problems are, from an anthropologist's perspective, conflicts between the teacher's or school's culture and the student's culture (Haberman, 1991).

The solution is not to identify a particular practice or strategy as most relevant to one population or another, but rather to provide excellent AND varied instructional practices that can meet the needs of ALL students. Research studies provide general guidance on how to engineer an environment that inspires students. For example, helping students feel welcome by greeting them at the door to your classroom each day should be standard operating procedure, and it can be especially meaningful to students of color where they are a minority. Encouraging divergent thinking affirms the self-esteem of gifted students and allows them to use their talents, but such an approach should be used with all students. Creating a classroom culture that supports all students, as individuals, is a first step in effective instruction.

Teacher's Tip

Cooperative Learning (see Topic 31) emphasizes interaction between students of diverse abilities and backgrounds (Nelson, Gallagher, & Coleman, 1993), and there is evidence it has a particularly positive effect on racial minority students (Massachusetts Advocacy Center, 1990).

For the Reflective Practitioner

The American Anthropological Society requires that its authors put the term "race" in quotes because there is no such thing as "race," only ethnicity. However, racism takes on many forms, see "Racism in the classroom: Case Studies" by Gwendolyn Duhon (2002). And, as the expression goes, "The best you will ever be is a recovering racist."

Best Practices for Teaching in a Diverse Classroom

Good and Brophy (2001) looked at teacher practices in high-achieving classrooms, and Ladson-Billings (1994) examined successful teachers of African American students to identify variables that positively influenced students staying in school. Their research indicates that, in successful schools, teachers:

1. Do not waste class time; students are kept busy in meaningful instructional activities.
2. Believe and expect that each and every student can succeed.
3. Have high expectations.
4. Consistently encourage students.
5. Expect students to help teach other students.
6. Have high self-esteem themselves.

In addition, research has found that a textbook-centered approach to instruction in which assigned reading is followed by a teacher-centered lecture and worksheets or end-of-chapter questions produces less-than-desirable results and can lead to classroom management problems. This kind of approach is especially ineffective with the diverse population of students who make up contemporary American classrooms. Teachers often make the mistake of assigning the most mundane seatwork to students they believe have limited abilities. In reality, the kind of stimulating and challenging learning experiences often reserved for honors and AP classes would work better with less motivated students. Some teachers use hands-on activities to reward very capable students who have mastered the content; instead, all students should receive the stimulation of hands-on activities to help them master content.

Differentiated Instruction

Differentiated Instruction, one of the primary vehicles for responding to students' various degrees of readiness, diverse interests, and diverse learning styles, adjusts learning experiences to allow for a higher likelihood of success (Smutny, 2003; Tomlinson, 1999, 2001). With tracking, differentiation takes place both within courses and between courses. For **within-course differentiation,** teachers should:

1. Give students choices about how to express what they have learned.
2. Use reading materials with different levels of readability.
3. Present ideas both visually and verbally.
4. Meet with small groups to reteach key concepts.
5. Pair students of lesser and stronger reading ability.
6. Vary the length of time for students to complete projects so struggling students can succeed.
7. Provide for individual work as well as collaborative work.
8. Tie instruction to assessment.
9. Use flexible grouping like readiness and mixed-readiness groups, same and different interest groups, and random groups.
10. Carefully organize and explain classroom routines (like where to put assignments), directions, and objectives.

Between-course differentiation is created by tracking and tiered courses like AP, honors, general, and remedial courses. In addition to having different expectations or degrees of rigor, these courses may have textbooks designed for different levels of mastery, more or fewer contact hours in class, more or fewer laboratory experiences, additional computer-assisted drill and practice,

Teacher's Tip

Within-class differentiated instruction doesn't mean you lower your standards, but rather that you provide opportunities for students to meet those standards in a variety of ways.

or after-school tutoring for some students. In honors and AP courses the teacher moves more quickly through the material and relies more on students' self-motivation—often the REAL reason why students are in the different levels, rather than innate ability. As a result, in honors courses students are required to have formulas memorized, whereas in general or remedial classes, students may be allowed to use a list of formulas. AP and honors students are assigned harder problems to solve than general class students. Also, to benefit students who take more rigorous courses, honors and AP courses typically have higher GPA values; for example, a B may be a 3.5 as opposed to a 3.0 in other courses.

For the Reflective Practitioner

The sources of inequality of educational opportunity appear to lie first in the home itself and the cultural influences immediately surrounding the home. Then they lie in the schools' ineffectiveness to free achievement from the impact of the home. JAMES S. COLEMAN

What would you do if a student didn't do any of the required homework assignments but got A's on all the tests? Does the student fail for not doing the homework?

At-Risk Students

A number of variables are involved in identifying students as being most "at risk" of failing. Poverty, ethnicity, race, gender, and language are among the most pronounced indicators (Aronson, 2001). The term *at risk* comes from a 1983 U.S. government publication, *A Nation at Risk: The Imperative for Education Reform.* Promoting academic resiliency so that students can "beat the odds" and stay in school is a primary goal for all teachers. Such terms as *at risk* are useful to the dialogue among educators seeking to reform educational institutions, but they are inherently prejudicial because they can label and stigmatize students (Haberman, 1995).

One of the continuing problems facing America is the mix of successful and unsuccessful students within a school that draws from a predominately low-SES population. Too many of our high-risk students are segregated into such schools. Haberman (1991, 1995), in describing the **"Pedagogy of Poverty,"** points out that in urban schools teaching is dominated by the practice of *giving information* (rather than trusting students to pursue knowledge), based on the false premise that students in urban schools are inferior, ill-prepared, and unwilling to pursue their education (Voelkl, 1993). He points out that these school cultures thrive on a primary mission of control and effectively set up students for failure by failing to engage them in taking on self-responsibility. This focus on imposed control is in conflict with self-control and the kind of respectful teacher-student relationships that are essential to the success of at-risk students (Ciaccio, 2000; Hixson & Tinzmann, 1991).

At-risk students create a unique set of problems for teachers that often requires a commitment by the whole school to overcome the disadvantages the students bring with them from their circumstances. KIPP (Knowledge Is Power Program) schools are one such solution that you might want to investigate at http://www.kipp.org/; for a broader perspective, go to the MDRC (Manpower Demonstration Research Corporation) site at http://www.mdrc.org/ for information on school reform initiatives.

On an individual basis, teachers are subject to a potential "blind spot" in regard to students from nondominant cultures or cultures different from their own. Low-SES students are often less familiar with the everyday workings, etiquette, interactions, types of dialogue, and traditional instruction choreography that are woven into the fabric of schools by the dominant culture. Perhaps the culture you came from was favorably aligned with the school culture, perhaps you were not from the dominant culture but were particularly intuitive and insightful and thus were able to make the transition, or perhaps you had a teacher who reached out to you and helped you make the essential adjustments.

When students begin to falter in your class or begin to share personal information because they grow concerned about their ability to make progress in your course—and certainly some will fall below and above your expectations—you will have an opportunity to extend yourself as a person by being empathetic and by further differentiating your instruction.

Students who are at risk when entering school but succeed are often characterized by the following qualities (Bernard, 1991; Wang, Haertel, & Walberg, 1995; Waxman, Gray, & Padron, 2003):

1. Self-discipline
2. High self-esteem
3. High self-efficacy
4. Autonomy
5. Strong interpersonal skills
6. Healthy expectations
7. Active engagement in school and class

For the Reflective Practitioner

> *Academic rigor (particularly mathematics) of high school courses and curriculum is the best predictor of success in college.*
>
> ALDERMAN (1999)

Best Practices for At-Risk Students

The following general practices to help at-risk students be more resilient and thrive in school can be implemented by individual teachers. These suggestions are based in part on Haberman (1995), Farner (1996), and the National Central Regional Education Laboratory recommendations at http://www.ncrel.org/sdrs/areas/issues/students/atrisk/at600.htm.

1. Help students feel welcome in your classroom and your school. Greet each student entering your room by asking questions about topics that matter in his or her life.
2. Use time outside of class to talk with students about matters unrelated to schoolwork.
3. Focus on higher-order thinking. Just because a student is at risk doesn't mean that he or she can't tackle higher-order cognition.
4. Assign projects and tasks that allow students to be successful from the beginning. This develops a sense of mastery and confidence.
5. Give students important classroom responsibilities and allow students to plan how they will complete assignments.
6. Help students reach at least one meaningful goal each day.
7. Keep learning struggles private. Encourage students to ask and answer questions and respond privately, on a one-to-one basis.
8. Use a variety of grouping approaches: by ethnicity, gender, readiness, and so on.

Students with Special Needs

Special education students have what are referred to as **Varying Exceptionalities**, based on the following categories (Kirk, Gallagher, & Anastasiow, 2003):

1. Intellectual differences: profound mental retardation, educable mental handicap, and other conditions (see the Gifted and Talented section later in this Topic)

2. Communications differences: hearing and speech disabilities
3. Sensory differences: auditory and visual impairments
4. Behavioral differences: ADHD, social maladjustment, and other conditions
5. Multiple and severe handicaps: cerebral palsy and other impairments
6. Physical differences: dwarfism, confinement to a wheelchair, and other conditions

Most of the exceptional students you will have in your classroom will have normal intellectual ability (as opposed to having Mental Retardation) but will either have **learning disabilities** indicating problems with tasks like reading, writing, and calculating (often reflected in unproductive behaviors) or **behavior disorders** that evolve out of physical or emotional problems.

This means you will customize the curriculum, environment, materials, and methods to accommodate special students and promote their development. These customizations can range from informal self-directed assignments (see Topic 33) to institutional, mandated **Individualized Education Programs** (IEPs). You can go to ERIC ED444294 *Guidance Regarding the Requirements of the Individuals with Disabilities Education Act (IDEA) on Individualized Education Programs* by Heumann, Judith E., and Warlick, Kenneth R., 2000, to learn more about IEPs.

Best Practices for Special Needs Students

The great variety of needs and of best practices for responding to those needs can be covered adequately only by a special education textbook. However, the following practices are adapted from "Attention Deficits: What Teachers Should Know" at the website of the Society for Developmental and Behavioral Pediatrics at **http://www.dbpeds.org/learning**:

1. Explain the learning and behavioral expectations in detail.
2. Use cooperative learning (see Topic 31) with heterogeneous groups, particularly for reading and composition.
3. Use peer tutoring with all students participating.
4. Use shortened assignments to accommodate the slower pace of special students.
5. Remind students how to correct their own errors.
6. Use multiple examples.
7. Refocus students who are dawdling.
8. Use one-to-one teacher-to-special-student coaching while students are in cooperative learning groups.
9. Teach a strategy's steps by using mnemonics, modeling, and choral recitation of the components.
10. Use adaptation instruction to allow special students to work on the same content but with lesser degrees of difficulty (e.g., have them list ten states, capitols, etc., while the other students list twenty).
11. Use accommodation instruction to allow special students to do the same assignment but in a different way (e.g., give a dyslexic student a verbal exam).
12. Use direct instruction for knowledge content like vocabulary and factual information.
13. Use constructivist approaches for analysis and decision making.

14. Promote independence during projects by having students maintain a folder of their work.

An exceptional website for learning more about your responsibilities and the nature of varying exceptionalities is at the National Information Center for Children and Youth with Disabilities, **http://www.nichcy.org/disabinf.asp**. At this site, you can find explanations and resources on the major categories of disabilities.

Linguistically and Culturally Diverse Students

Students with developing English-language skills and culturally diverse backgrounds come to class with the same hopes and aspirations as the more "typical" student, but with additional apprehensions and learning challenges because of their linguistic and cultural differences.

Teachers' strategies for accommodating linguistically and culturally diverse students can vary greatly depending on the makeup of the classroom. For example, you could have a classroom that is primarily populated with one dominant ethnic group (as in many schools drawing from the Hispanic communities in the Southwest or in an Inner City school with mostly African American students). You could be teaching in a suburban school with a few ethnic minority students from one culture (a relatively small number of African American or Latino students). Or, you could have a classroom with a few minority students who have diverse linguistic and ethnic backgrounds (perhaps in New York City, where you could have one Chinese, Vietnamese, Pakistani, and Haitian student in a class of thirty). In studying predominantly Mexican populations, Garcia (1991, 2001) found that successful teachers used small groups and relied heavily on informal but frequent interaction with students, created a family-type atmosphere, and favored student collaboration rather than individual worksheet tasks (see also Padron, Waxman, & Rivera, 2002).

In recent years, the acronym ELL (English Language Learners) has come to describe the population of culturally and linguistically diverse students. If you want to search the Internet for information, also try ESOL (English for Speakers of Other Languages) and ESL (English as a Second Language). Among the websites that provide strategies to use with ELL students are the Internet TESOL Journal at **http://iteslj.org** and Everything ESL at **http://www.everythingesl.net/**, both of which have tips, resources, and ELL lesson plans.

Best Practices for Communicating with Linguistically and Culturally Diverse Students

The following best practices for communicating with ELL students can be found at the Internet TESOL Journal.

1. Don't insist that students make eye contact when you are speaking to them: This is considered rude in many cultures.
2. Use drawings, dramatic gestures, actions, emotions, voice, mime, chalkboard sketches, photographs, and visual materials to provide clues to meaning.
3. Talk slowly; simplify your message (avoid passive voice and complex sentences); use short, simple sentences and no pronouns; and repeat yourself using the same grammatical form.

4. Give ELL students more time to respond; don't be impatient, and smile. Remember, they are just as bright as non-ELL students; it's the language that is the barrier.

5. Correct heavily accented speech by repeating the words correctly and asking the student if he or she would like to try.

6. Allow the use of bilingual dictionaries.

7. Use student volunteers to help new ELL students learn new phrases and pronunciations.

8. Encourage writing.

Gifted and Talented Students

The terms **gifted, talented, exceptional, high IQ,** and **creative** are frequently used to refer to students with particular talents, and these students also deserve specialized assistance in reaching their potential (Checkley, 2000). This population is as diverse as at-risk students and can include both at-risk and non-at-risk students. For example, a student may appear to be gifted in math or art but not in other subjects. Another student might seem to excel in every discipline, but this high performance could be attributable to nurture, not nature. Still another student could be inquisitive and ask many more questions than you expect, and this student may be considered a discipline problem. The student who is your greatest discipline problem may find the lessons not sufficiently challenging. Accommodating these students can be as difficult as accommodating high-risk students.

Best Practices for Talented Students

The following are some ideas on accommodating these gifted students.

1. Encourage students to share their divergent thinking.

2. Provide extra resources for independent work.

3. Promote students' suggestions on projects they would like to pursue independently.

4. Allow students to spend more time on their areas of interest.

5. Plan assignments that require more problem solving.

6. When designing learning experiences, use Gardner's Multiple Intelligences (see Topic 7) to accommodate individual talents.

7. Focus lessons on critical thinking and problem solving.

For the Reflective Practitioner

Everyone is born with genius, but most people only keep it a few minutes.   EDGARD VARESE

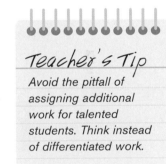

Teacher's Tip

Avoid the pitfall of assigning additional work for talented students. Think instead of differentiated work.

Gender Differences

With the onset of puberty, gender issues take on new meaning. Research by Borisoff and Arliss (2001); Chethik (1994); Dragseth, Weymouth, and Du (2003); Gilbert (1996); Hall and Sandler (1982); Karp and Yoels (1976); Sadker and Sadker (1994); Simonds and Cooper (2001); Sommers (2000); Stewart, Cooper, and Stewart (2003); and others has indicated the following:

1. Males receive lower grades than females.

2. Males are more likely to repeat grades and drop out.

3. Males are more likely to be suspended.

4. Males are outperformed by females in reading and writing.

5. Males and females perform equally well in math and sciences.

For the Reflective Practitioner

If women are expected to do the same work as men, we must teach them the same things.   PLATO

Within mixed-gender classes, teachers:

1. Make more eye contact with males.
2. Are more animated when responding to males.
3. More frequently assume an attentive posture when males speak.
4. Call on males more frequently.
5. Wait longer for males to respond.
6. Are less likely to interrupt males.
7. Accept males' ideas more readily than females'.

Males receive a disproportionate amount of teacher attention (because of both good and bad behaviors), and African American girls receive almost no attention (Sadker & Sadker, 1994). Some females are hesitant to excel in mixed-gender classrooms because of peer pressures and the competition with boys (Leslie, 1999). There appear to be few educational disadvantages with single-gender classrooms, particularly if not all classes in the school are single gender. In one study, females who were given the opportunity to participate in single-gender classes were enthusiastic about the opportunity, asked more questions in class, became more ambitious, did better in class, and were more willing to take advanced courses (Smith, 1999).

Both male and female teenagers need your support, and differentiating your communication to accommodate their perspectives will be crucial to your success. For an excellent summary of research on gender issues, go to ERIC ED441560 *Addressing Gender Differences in Young Adolescents* by Butler, Deborah A., and Manning, M. Lee, 1998, and The National Center for Educational Statistics report, *Trends in Education Equity for Girls and Women* at **http://nces.ed.gov/pubsearch/pubsinfo. asp?pubid=2000030**.

 It may surprise you to read the preceding findings. What do you think are their causes and implications?

Impressions and Dangers of Generalities

From the first day of class, teachers are, consciously and subconsciously, sizing students up or DOWN! As a result, they can develop inappropriate and lower expectations for different students (Good, 1982). Often these impressions are based on cultural, gender-related, and physical attributes that are used as indicators of ability when other information is not available (Brophy, 1986; Haberman, 1991).

First Impressions

The first encounter is crucial and lasting because impressions are difficult to dislodge once they are internalized (Friedrich & Cooper, 1990; Goza, 1993). Your first impression of a person is based on body type and appearance. Teachers who are formally dressed are viewed generally as more knowledgeable and organized, whereas less formally attired teachers are perceived as more friendly and flexible (Richmond, McCroskey, & Payne, 1987). There are three basic body types, and each has an effect on first impressions, for both the students and the teacher (Richmond et al., 1987):

- ECTOMORPHIC (tall and thin)
  Teachers are perceived as anxious, self-conscious, and intelligent.
  Students are perceived as high-strung, anxious, nervous, and competent.
- MESOMORPHIC (bony and muscular)
  Teachers are perceived as credible, dependable, likeable, and competent, but also demanding and tough.
  Students are perceived as intelligent, talkative, dependable, and athletic.
- ENDOMORPHIC (soft and round)
  Teachers are perceived as unprepared, slow, complacent, and undynamic.
  Students are perceived as lazy and lacking in intelligence, but nice and funny.

Often the next impression comes from a student's name, and even this can have deleterious effects. In a classic study, Harari and McDavid (1973) gave identical essays to elementary school teachers with authors named David, Michael, Elmer, and Herbert. The teachers consistently graded essays by Davids and Michaels higher. It is essential to reflect on your stereotypical beliefs and personal orientation toward others who are different from you because these are key determinants of your expectations, which in turn will influence your students' aspirations and behaviors.

Long-Term Impressions

Since the publication of *Pygmalion in the Classroom* (Rosenthal & Jacobson, 1968), teacher expectations have taken on more meaning. In this study, teachers were led to believe that they had a select group of "late bloomers," meaning that the students were bright but only recently motivated, when in fact they were randomly selected. These late bloomers improved their IQ scores dramatically compared to the students who were not late bloomers. The conclusion was that the teachers communicated in a manner consistent with their perceptions of the students and that the students responded based on that communication. The good news is that if a teacher has high expectations (the **"Pygmalion effect"**), students will be more likely to perform to the higher standard. The bad news is that if a teacher has low expectations (the **"Golem effect"**), the students will perform to that level as well (Rowe & O'Brien, 2002). One of the best predictors of a well-adjusted middle and high school student is a teacher's positive expectations of him or her (Murdock, Anderman, & Hodge, 2000).

As a reflective teacher, you should be aware of the following potential biases:

1. Teachers expect quiet students to do less well because they generally view them as less competent (Richmond & McGrosk, 1995).
2. Teachers give more opportunities to students they believe are more likely to learn (McCormick & Noriega, 1986).
3. The less information teachers have about a student, the more likely they are to have their grading influenced by stereotypes (Rosenthal, 1987).
4. When dealing with students they believe to be "better" students, teachers smile more, use a friendlier tone, nod approvingly more

Teacher's Tip
Alternatives to lowering expectations are to differentiate instruction, to develop "Scaffolded" lessons that require active learning, and to motivate students by being empathetic.

Teacher's Tip
When grading subjective tests and assignments, don't look at the students' names until after you have evaluated the assignment so that you can avoid bias.

For the Reflective Practitioner

Parents and teachers of Japanese and Chinese ancestry tend to believe that effort is a greater determinant of academic success than innate ability and as a result view low scores on tests as a sign of poor effort, not ability, and hold their children to that "no excuses" standard. Conversely, parents of European ancestries tend to hold the contrary view. As a result, many Americans adopt a predestination approach, writing off too many students as lacking ability when the problem is lack of sustained effort.
STEVENSON AND STIGLER (1992)

Topic 8: **Teaching in a Diverse Classroom**

often, look students in the eyes more, give them more time, teach them more difficult content, and praise them more than those they perceive to be "poorer" students (Campbell & Simpson, 1992).

5. Students fortunate enough to have one of the physically attractive face contours and body types are perceived as "better" than other students without any other data (Brylinsky & Moore, 1984; Hunsberger & Cavanagh, 1988).

6. Teachers seat students of whom they have low expectations farther away, criticize them more frequently, praise them less, and interrupt them more frequently than students of whom they have higher expectations (Good & Brophy, 1988).

7. Teachers "compromise the curriculum" (Sedlak et al., 1986) by demanding less of students in terms of content and by withholding instructional techniques like group work and independent projects from students perceived as low achievers because they are also the potential "troublemakers," when in fact these low achievers may benefit the most from more flexibility in how to learn and demonstrate their knowledge (Uguroglu & Walberg, 1979).

Assignment 8.1 | **REFLECTION ON DIVERSITY**

INTASC STANDARDS 1, 3, 5, 6, 8

As a cooperative learning activity, form a group of three or four students and reflect and discuss how the gender, culture, and physical attributes of teachers and students may positively or negatively impact students' attitudes. Imagine yourself as a teacher on the first day of school as students are entering your classroom. What do you see? What do the students look like? What biases will affect your first impressions? Have you observed overt, covert, intentional, and unintentional bias in teachers and students? Be prepared to share your ideas with the class.

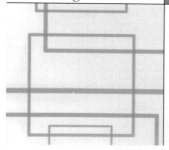

Assignment 8.2 | **STEREOTYPES AND BIAS**

INTASC STANDARDS 1, 3, 5, 6, 8

Go to the **Tolerance.org** website at http://tolerance.org/hidden_bias/index.html and read the *"Tolerance.org's tutorial"* about stereotypes and how they are formed. Then go to *"Take a test at Project Implicit's website and see what may be lingering in your psyche."* At this site you can select and take a test to assess your implicit associations on gender, "race," age, and other factors. Your professor may assign different students to take different tests and report back what they have learned from the tutorial and the test.

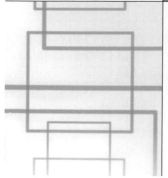

Assignment 8.3 | **CURRENT SCHOLARSHIP ON STUDENT DIVERSITY**

INTASC STANDARDS 1–10

Being informed about current scholarship on middle and high school students is crucial to your role as a teacher. At this book's website, listed under Topic 8, Assignment 8.3, are over thirty recently published online ERIC documents covering homelessness, drug abuse, truancy, and other topics. Your professor will likely assign you a topic. Read the relevant article and prepare a document for submission to your instructor; make copies for each class member. In the paper, persuade your colleagues that your topic is important by summarizing it, citing the key facts in few paragraphs, and then making five specific suggestions on what a teacher should reflect on or do as a consequence of this information.

What would you do if a student made a pejorative comment about another student's sexual orientation during a class you were teaching that was loud enough for most students to hear, including the student who was the target of the verbal assault?

OnLine Resources

Check this textbook's website at http://education.college.hmco.com/students for online links that are periodically updated to reflect new resources as they become available.

Teacher and Student Communication

ommunication between two people, much less twenty-five students and one teacher, is a complex process. In a classroom, communication includes verbal and nonverbal messages as well as the vital visual messages teachers provide in the form of transparencies, digital projections like PowerPoint, videos, board work, and the Internet. Burgoon, Stern, and Dillman (1995) describe the iterative and interactive communication process between the teacher and students as the **Interactional position.** Both parties come to the classroom with expectations of what is required, expected, and preferred. The significant difference between the two is that the teacher comes to class with the agenda and the inherent power of his or her position. The teacher's position as leader is evidenced in his or her communication (Rolle, 2002). This inherent power is known by both the teacher and the students, but if the teacher does not explicitly rely on it, the students are more likely to find the teacher credible and may be less inclined to test his or her power (Weidner, 2001).

Teacher Talk

The planned and purposeful part of a teacher's verbal communication during instruction is often referred to in the academic literature as "Teacher Talk." This talk includes (1) explanations and questions used to convey knowledge; (2) explanations and questions about tasks that students are to complete as part of the lesson plan; and (3) directives, explanations, and questions used to manage the instruction and the class. Every time a teacher communicates, there are two aspects to the message: (a) the **meaning** of the message and (b) how the teacher perceives his or her **relationship** with the listener(s), shown by the style of the communication. Having completed a series of courses in your subject field, you should be able to communicate your content fairly well. Preparing for the "relationship" part of what is communicated is, in many ways, more difficult, because your temperament and the casual and unplanned mannerisms, expressions, and traits that help shape your communication have been accumulated through interactions with friends, siblings, parents, relatives, classmates, and others over a lifetime. And while those verbal and nonverbal communications may have been acceptable in social settings or even during part-time jobs, you need to develop a repertoire of professional verbal and nonverbal communication skills specifically for the classroom (Parker, 2003). This means you will likely have to unlearn some old habits and learn some new ones.

For the Reflective Practitioner

Dang it, why didn't you warn me? Why did no one tell me that I would fall in love with those kids? I shouldn't want to keep coming to school each day looking FORWARD to interacting with my kids—MY kids, mind you, they are no one else's—and loving every crazy minute of it!!

So driving home today I was thinking about my kids. About what amazingly funny, inspiring individuals they are, even the ones that are "problems"! About how I hardly ever get my authority challenged anymore. About how I can laugh "with" them about the dopey things I do, and it's all okay. About how I hate the thought that they all won't be mine next year. . . . Who WARNS you about stuff like this?

STEVE HOGAN, NEW HIGH SCHOOL TEACHER, ST. PETERSBURG, FLORIDA

The "relationship" that is transmitted to your students in your verbal and nonverbal communication is defined by (1) what you think of yourself and (2) what you think of the students. The persona you project communicates whether you are timid, unsure of yourself, arrogant, dispassionate, confident, and so forth. Simultaneously, while explaining content, you are asking yourself: Am I speaking loud enough? Did I say that correctly? What is Anne doing? She is not paying attention. Where is the next overhead? Did I say "divide" or "multiply"? Who should I call on next? In addition, you are trying to assess how your teacher talk is affecting the students and trying to make on-the-spot adjustments. Throughout this process, you are attempting to be poised, to project confidence, and to give momentum to your lesson. Students' view of you, both individually and collectively, evolves during the daily interactions in the classroom based on this mix of planned teacher talk and spontaneous iterative communications.

Teacher's Tip

During your early field experiences or student teaching, arrange to have yourself video-taped while teaching. A videotape will help you reflect on how well you are communicating.

Researchers have identified four stages through which a class evolves into a high-quality learning environment (Education Department of South Australia, 1988):

1. **Dependence Stage.** Students start out relatively submissive and anxious, and fear of reprisal is high. Most of the communication comes from the teacher. There is little disruptive behavior, although some students will begin testing the teacher. Student motivations are mostly extrinsic.

2. **Rebellion Stage.** Students begin to test the teacher for control of the class, noise levels tend to rise, students begin to evolve into camps, and "put-downs" and adversarial comments begin to rise between students. The more rebellious groups are driven by peer acceptance and autonomy, and their behavior is moderated by apprehension of teacher reprisal for unacceptable conduct. The teacher can lose control if appropriate classroom management practices are not in place and responses to inappropriate behaviors are not immediate, appropriate, consistent, and equitable.

3. **Cohesion Stage.** Trust develops between the teacher and students and between students and students. Disruptive behavior dissipates and the atmosphere becomes more cordial. Harmony becomes more important than adversarial interactions. Peer pressure based on students' norms tends to control inappropriate behaviors, rather than direct teacher interventions.

4. **Autonomy Stage.** When students take responsibility for their learning, their statements reveal feelings as well as ideas and beliefs, disagreements are reconciled routinely by thoughtful, diplomatic responses without animosity, more flexibility in examining beliefs is exhibited, and the motivation is intrinsic because learning is seen as a source of power and autonomy.

Teacher's Tip

"Politically Correct" speech poses a challenge for teachers. Should you say, "Hispanic American," "Chicano," or "Mexican" or "girls," "females," "women," or "ladies"? For an insightful review of how this problem affects education, go to Ravitch (2003a).

What do you think a teacher can do to move students through these stages? ❓

Credibility

A teacher's credibility is crucial to reaching stage 4—and therefore to his or her success in the classroom. Teaching is not a value-neutral communication: The intent is to persuade or influence the learner to accept ideas, facts, theories, and arguments. Aristotle in his *Rhetoric* (Aristotle, trans. Roberts, 1954) argued that three factors influence the teaching act: *ethos*, meaning credibility on the part of the speaker; *pathos*, appeal to the emotions of the learner; and *logos*, appeal to reason. Teachers need to care (pathos) and at the same time establish a professional relationship (ethos) so that students learn (logos) (Cothran & Ennis, 2000; Nodding, 1992).

Topic 9: **Teacher and Student Communication**

Figure 9.1 | **CREDIBILITY PYRAMID**

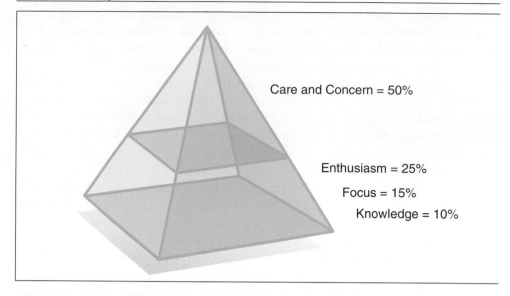

Care and Concern = 50%

Enthusiasm = 25%

Focus = 15%

Knowledge = 10%

Source: *Reprinted with permission of Graham Jones at* http://www.thecredibilitypyramid. co.uk/index.htm.

Research shows that it is not what you know, but the *way that you communicate what you know,* that contributes most to your believability, trustworthiness, and success as a teacher (Collins, 1988; Covello & McCallum, 1997; Ferreira, 2000; Tubbs & Moss, 1994). Teacher credibility is crucial to successful communication and is depicted by Graham Jones in the Credibility Pyramid, shown in Figure 9.1.

Unless your students sense your enthusiasm, care, and concern, and unless you exhibit a clear focus through well-planned lessons, they will not acquire the knowledge you are expected to transmit.

The 12 Attributes of Teacher Credibility

Frymier and Thompson (1992) have identified twelve key attributes and skills that teachers must develop to build credibility with their students:

For the Reflective Practitioner

Teacher efficacy is one of the best predictors of student success.

ASHTON (1984) AND PROCTOR (1984)

1. **Altruism** shows students that the teacher has their interests at heart.
2. **Facilitating enjoyment** makes class engaging and entertaining.
3. **A comfortable self** shows that the teacher feels at ease in the classroom and is relaxed with students.
4. **Conversational rule keeping** requires adherence to politeness and societal norms.
5. **Dynamism** is demonstrated through vocal and physical energy and enthusiasm.
6. **Eliciting others' disclosures** is genuinely seeking students' opinions and ideas.
7. **Listening** (and if necessary asking) helps ensure that what was communicated was heard correctly.
8. **Nonverbal immediacy** includes eye contact, smiles, nods, and other gestures.
9. **Optimism** is not only having an "upbeat" disposition but also being perceived as not overly negative and cynical.
10. **Presenting an interesting self** requires the teacher to reveal something of his or her person, background, and interest.

11. **Sensitivity** to students is demonstrated through empathy and interest.
12. **Trustworthiness** requires that students come to know the teacher as honest, fair, responsible, and consistent.

Teacher Communication Approaches

Your verbal and nonverbal communication approaches are equally important (Rolle, 2002). In one study, teachers who were viewed as poor communicators were labeled as not animated, inattentive to the students, too relaxed, or overly dramatic—all qualities that relate to nonverbal communication (Norton, 1983).

Verbal Communication Challenges

The listener interprets the words you use during teacher talk and develops his or her thoughts based on your words. Hopefully, the thought behind your words is the same thought developed by the students. But much can go wrong.

There are the classroom distractions and disruptions from fellow students' misbehaviors and daydreaming, and then there is the challenge of language itself. The number of **limited-English-proficient** (LEP) students has increased by more than 50 percent since 1985, primarily in the Southwest, Florida, and New York (Weaver & Padron, 1997). In addition, everyone speaks with a **dialect** (a variation of standard English that has distinct vocabulary, sounds, and grammar), all of us have **accents**, and students tend to use the slang of their peer group. *Bidialecticism* (Gollnick & Chinn, 2002) is the term used to describe the ability to switch between a dialect and a more standard, formal, workplace English. Prior education, language, culture, gender, and age are the most obvious variables that affect our verbal communication. The conscientious teacher uses repetition, examples, analogies, anecdotes, dialogue, and images to improve, but not perfect, verbal communication.

In one study, students rated a monotone voice as the most distracting feature of teacher communication because it conveyed a noncaring attitude and lack of enthusiasm (Richmond, Gorham, & McCroskey, 1986). Luckily, this can be corrected relatively easily if the teacher makes a conscious effort to listen and modify his or her voice. Good and Brophy (2001) point out the importance of using positive speech, and they offer some examples of negative versus positive phrases (see Table 9.1). If positive speech approaches are adopted, these can prevent teacher-created classroom management problems (see Topics 16 and 17).

For the Reflective Practitioner

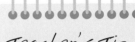

Good communication is as stimulating as black coffee and just as hard to sleep after.

ANNE MORROW LINDBERGH

Teacher's Tip

Teachers are often tempted to use the prevailing slang of the student population, thinking that this will help them "connect" with their students. But you're the role model, and you should not use slang or permit it in class. Everyone must learn to change his or her speech patterns based on the circumstances. School is where we should all learn to use the best "King's English" we can muster.

Table 9.1 | **NEGATIVE VERSUS POSITIVE TEACHER STATEMENTS**

Negative Speech	Positive Speech
Don't make so much noise.	Quiet down—you are getting too loud.
Don't cheat by copying your neighbor.	Try to work these out on your own without help.
Don't just guess.	Be ready to explain your answer—why you think it is correct.
Don't yell out your answers.	Raise your hand if you think you know the answer.
Don't slouch in your chair.	Sit up straight.

Nonverbal Communication Challenges

Both teachers and students communicate nonverbally (Canfield, 2002). Ekman and Friesen (1969) classified nonverbal communications into the following types:

1. **Adapters** are actions that reflect boredom or anxiety, like tapping a pencil or biting one's fingernails.
2. **Affect displays** are facial expressions that communicate emotions, such as confusion with a frown or happiness with a grin.
3. **Emblems** are behaviors that have direct verbal translations, such as a shrug of the shoulders for "I don't know."
4. **Illustrators** accompany verbal communication, like pointing to a map or holding up a book.
5. **Regulators** are actions that maintain or control verbal communication, like nodding or shaking one's head "no."

Effective teachers use more nonverbal communication than average teachers, and achievement is higher among students when their teachers use more movement and gestures (Wycoff, 1973).

Best Practices for Teachers' Verbal and Nonverbal Communications

Richmond and McCroskey (1999) suggest many of the following strategies for becoming a better communicator with your students:

1. **Aim to make an impression** when preparing your Class Notes (see Topic 20).
2. **Create an attractive classroom** environment that is free of clutter.
3. **Be attentive to your appearance** and posture.
4. **Smile, shake hands,** and make other warm gestures.
5. To keep students' attention, **use pace and sentence structure** to create curiosity, suspense, and surprise.
6. **Be forceful, energetic, friendly, and casual.**
7. **Change voice** intonation, rate, pitch, rhythm, cadence, and emphasis.
8. **Use gestures** (thumbs up, pat on the back, etc.), laughter, facial expressions that show pleasure, eye contact, head movement, space (move closer, etc.), and the "stage."
9. **Use humor** to reduce tension, save face, entertain, eliminate boredom, self-disclose, and minimize embarrassment.
10. **Listen authentically** (meaning with your eyes, body language, and face).
11. **Keep eye contact.**
12. **Move about the classroom.**

However, paying attention only to what you are doing or thinking is insufficient, because you must also "read your audience" and determine what they are communicating to you and fellow students both verbally and nonverbally (Gage & Berliner, 1998).

Student Communication

On any given day, a student may choose to communicate positively or negatively because of a personal issue that has nothing to do with you or the content of the class.

Nussbaum (1992) has argued that communication is really about reacting to student behaviors. Peterson and Clark (1978) found that teachers spend the

Teacher's Tip

Because you care about each student, you should feel that EVERY student's participation in class discussions and lectures is essential. To feel otherwise says you care only about the ones who come to your class highly self-motivated and prepared. Questions should be prepared in advance and allocated to ALL students on an equal basis (see Topic 28).

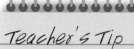

Teacher's Tip

The most obvious indicators of a failing communication process are the many classroom management problems, caused by single or multiple students, that disrupt the pace and information delivery of a class.

greatest amount of energy on the iterative, metacognitive process of assessing how well the instruction is being received, rather than on its delivery.

Students' Verbal Communication Challenges

Students choose to participate or not to participate in the verbal communication process based on their sense of personal efficacy (beliefs about their ability to succeed and exercise influence over events that affect their lives), their perceptions of the teacher, their past success or failure with the subject matter, their observations about the day's class environment, and other factors (Pines & Larkin, 2003). Hurt, Scot, and McCroskey (1981) found that quiet students do not speak much because they want to be left alone, they believe that peers do not value students who communicate with teachers, they have received previous unsatisfactory feedback from the same or other teachers, or they are afraid of being thought of as stupid or inept. The consequences of being quiet, however, are significant. Teachers can view such students as less competent and credible and may give them less attention, question them less frequently, and give them less individual assistance than they do verbal students (Mottet, 2002; Mottet et al., 2002; Richmond & McGrosk, 1995). Also, it is difficult to distinguish between genuinely quiet students and students with high communication apprehension. However, in both cases the goal is to increase their comfort level so that they verbally participate more in class, because verbal communication is essential to constructing knowledge and getting follow-up feedback from the teacher and peers. To boost participation rates, put students in groups for some discussions, give reluctant participants a "heads up" that you plan to call on them the next day, and discreetly encourage students to share their ideas.

The "too verbal" student is often highly motivated but can be a distraction to all the other students and an annoyance. Other causes of students talking too much can be low self-esteem, a desire to challenge the teacher, or simple unawareness of their own overbearing style because no one has given them feedback adequate to produce a change in behavior. If a student is dominating a class, try to elicit responses from other students. Next you might try starting the class with a general appeal for students who have been the most frequent contributors to hold back their communications to allow others to speak who have been less communicative. If the behavior persists, quietly appeal to their duty to the other students and encourage them to pay more attention to the ebb and flow of the class.

Students' Nonverbal Communication

Because you are in a class setting with twenty-five or more students, there is less opportunity for students to communicate to you verbally, so they often use nonverbal cues to express their feelings—if not their ideas and beliefs. Teachers must read and interpret these cues, just as they would respond to students' verbal statements, and then adjust how they are communicating. Responding to nonverbal cues should be viewed as a preventive classroom management practice because the negative, more explicit, and pointed verbal communication will likely soon follow if the nonverbal messages are not attended to. In a landmark study, J. F. Anderson and colleagues (1985) surveyed almost 1,000 teachers and catalogued their students' communication behaviors (see chart in Assignment 9.1). In a similar manner, you can gain a better understanding of your students by observing their nonverbal cues.

Teacher's Tip

A preventive measure for controlling dominating students is to announce at the beginning of the year that all students will be called on equally in your course for grounded questions (see Topic 28 for an explanation of grounded versus ungrounded questions).

Topic 9: **Teacher and Student Communication**

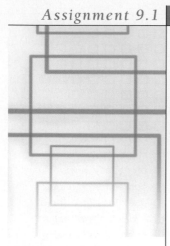

Assignment 9.1 **STUDENT NONVERBAL BEHAVIORS**

INTASC STANDARDS 2, 3, 5, 6

Complete the following chart and be prepared to share with the class the rationale for the percentages you estimated.

What percentage of students . . .	7th Graders Mean %	11th Graders Mean %
Look at you when they talk?		
Look at you when you talk?		
Flirt?		
Smile to try to get their way?		
Frown to try to get their way?		
Fidget excessively when sitting?		
Use appropriate loudness when speaking?		
Giggle excessively?		
Use an appropriate rate of speech?		
Note to Instructor: Results & Source in PowerPoint Presentation		

 Can you think of other student cues that indicate a successful or unsuccessful classroom session? How would you respond to some of these behaviors?

Listening

Listening is something we do a lot of—more than talking, reading, or writing—but few of us have ever been taught how to listen (Mead & Rubin, 1985; Strother, 1997). Listening is NOT synonymous with the sense we call HEARING: Listening is a learned behavior and involves receiving, attending, organizing, understanding, interpreting, and evaluating messages (Friedman, 1986). Listeners decide on a "real-time" basis what parts of a communication they hear that they want to listen to, convert those signals into meaning, and finally construct them into ideas or beliefs (Sacarin, 1997; Strother, 1997). Brent and Anderson (1993) define GOOD listeners as those who also ask relevant questions and make relevant comments, an essential skill to future learning.

Teachers as Listeners

Teachers can become reticent about allocating too much time to listening to students because of the demands for progress through a body of knowledge. After a number of years of teaching the same subject, teachers anticipate the questions they will receive. This can be an asset, but it can also be a curse if the teacher's demeanor reflects boredom or a "know-it-all" attitude. When listening to questions, comments, and answers from students, you need to assess both the overt and inferred message so that you can respond to the *substantive issue* (usually content or directions) and ALSO to the *process issue* (how and why the student is communicating). The process issue typically comes to the forefront of your thinking because of the student's demeanor or tone or the timing of the question or comment. You wonder why the student made the statement or needs to ask the question. Metacognitively, you ask yourself, "What did I say that confused Anne, and how can I say it differently now?" or you say to yourself, "Chris is not paying attention again!" Your response to both the substantive and process issues affects your management of the class toward the ideal autonomy stage defined earlier in this Topic.

Best Practices for Listening

Teachers need to communicate with eyes, facial expression, and body language that they are AUTHENTICALLY listening. The following are a number of ways to show that you are a caring teacher.

1. Stop what you are doing and look at the student.
2. Make eye contact.
3. Show interest by nodding or looking intently.
4. Position your arms in an open posture: not folded or on your hips, which suggests a lack of openness or impatience.
5. If it is a question, rephrase it if necessary: "Did you mean . . . ?"
6. Respond, or ask if another student would like to respond.
7. If appropriate, ask if others have additional questions.
8. Thank the student for helping clarify the information.

Teacher's Tip

The diverse American culture has made us more aware of the different listening, speaking, and responding patterns of our citizenry. Go to ERIC ED439446, Silence/Listening and Intercultural Differences, by Franks and Parthenia, 2000, for a brief description of the different listening patterns of the major ethnic groups found in America.

Students as Listeners

Poor listening skills adversely affect students' performance and are typically due to daydreaming, distractions by other students, impatience with the speaker, or disinterest in the content (Brent & Anderson, 1993; Owca, Pawlak, & Pronobis, 2003). Teachers can help students become good listeners by being one themselves and modeling thoughtfulness; they can also directly teach listening skills (see Barr et al., 2000). Finally, teachers can emphasize good listening by considering the following three aspects of listening as defined by Jalongo (1995).

1. **Physical aspect.** Part of a student's adjustment to a school setting or even the dominant culture is learning to look at you or at another student who is speaking. Encourage good posture and expect that students have only the required reading and writing materials needed for the lesson on their desk (eliminate distractions).
2. **Intrinsic motivational aspect.** Establish incentives for students to focus on learning, like structuring lessons that gain their attention; using momentum, images, breakout groups, and wit; requiring students to respond and reflect in real time; and connecting the content to their own lives.
3. **Imagery aspect.** Students must be asked, encouraged, and given time to create mental images of the content as they listen. Teachers can encourage such images by using graphic language and graphic organizers (see Topic 30) and by asking students to share their mental images that they are creating in their mind's eye. Without these mental images, students are not authentically listening and will have difficulty retaining content knowledge.

Responding

Teachers respond to students, and students respond to teachers and other students. These complex communications dart across the classroom and create a dynamic atmosphere, an atmosphere that must be encouraged but also carefully managed.

Student-to-Student Verbal Feedback

Student responses to you or to other students are, to say the least, unpredictable. Part of the classroom management process is establishing rules of civility (see Topic 16). The teacher must manage student-to-student feedback by:

1. Setting standards for the appropriate use of language.
2. Keeping everyone on track.
3. Encouraging interactions between students as well as with the teacher.
4. Managing the process of taking turns.
5. Encouraging students to elaborate on their responses.
6. Confirming or having other students confirm answers.
7. Qualifying less-than-perfect responses diplomatically.

Teacher-to-Student Verbal Feedback

Because the class activity evolves from your teacher talk, students expect your feedback to be substantive and diplomatic. Curwin and Mendler (1988) have made a number of suggestions for giving effective feedback to students:

1. Make your messages your own; say, "I think it would be best . . . ," not, "It would be best . . ."
2. Make your responses or statements complete and specific: "Your analysis should be limited to one, single-spaced page with three headings."
3. Be repetitive to make a point: "Here is another example of a protagonist."
4. Make your verbal and nonverbal messages congruent; if you say, "That is a really interesting idea," don't roll your eyes at the same time.
5. When critiquing (as opposed to criticizing), refer to what occurred, not to your judgments about the action: "Your homework does not meet the criteria stated in class," as opposed to, "Your homework is sloppy."
6. Focus on observations, not advice: "When you don't listen, you miss information," rather than, "You should pay attention."
7. Use marker expressions like "You will want to remember this," particularly when there are few questions coming from the students.
8. Ask for feedback: "Do you feel my suggestion will be helpful to you?"

Verbal Praise

Ideally, students should not desire praise, only feedback or encouragement (Dreikurs, 1998). Telling a student, "You are the best student I ever had" or "You have the highest score in the class on this exam" is praise, whereas "You seem to really enjoy learning" or "You did very well on this exam—keep up the good work" (Dreikurs et al., 1982, p. 110) is encouragement, or what Whelan (2000) defined as "effective praise." Praise should be avoided because it can undermine intrinsic motivation, create competition, encourage selfishness, and foster dependence and fear of failure (Black, 2000; Dreikurs, 1998; Kohn,

For the Reflective Practitioner

A good listener is a good talker with a sore throat.

KATHARINE WHITEHORN

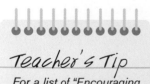

Teacher's Tip

For a list of "Encouraging Words" that teachers should use, go to http://www.noogenesis.com/malama/encouraging_words.html by Duen Hsi Yen.

1993; Taylor, 1979). There are three kinds of "effective praise" according to Whelan (2000):

1. **Recognition**, which is a straightforward acknowledgment of the student's thinking: "That was very insightful."
2. **Encouragement**: "That was very insightful—keep up the good work."
3. **Coaching**: "That was very insightful; did you also consider . . . ?"

> **Which of these three forms of effective praise do you think is most effective?** **?**

Best Practices for Using Effective Praise

The following suggestions are adapted from Good and Brophy (2001) as well as from Kohn (1993)and Black (2000):

1. Praise the work effort, not the student: "That must have taken a lot of thought."
2. Identify the specified behavior that is being praised: "You really thought that question through!"
3. Deliver praise naturally without gushing or being overly dramatic: "That was a very good question."
4. Be genuine when praising; mean what you say by combining verbal praise with nonverbal communication that indicates approval.
5. Don't praise when it is not warranted.
6. Praise students' behaviors over which they can exercise person control: "You have been paying a lot more attention in class lately."
7. Use a variety of praise statements: "thumbs up," "great idea," "that was very helpful—did everyone hear that clarification to the assignment?"

Humor

Humor is indispensable to your communication, but it can be perilous because of student sensitivities or misunderstandings (Berk, 2003; Darling & Civikly, 1987; Gurtler, 2002; Hill, 1988).

In addition, racist, sexist, or other kinds of jokes or sarcastic statements made at the expense of students or other subsets of the population will have a negative effect on the schoolroom climate (Gorham & Christophel, 1990). However, when teachers and students use appropriate humor, they create a kinship with one another, a new level of familiarity that enhances the learning process (Pollak & Freda, 1997). Humor has been shown to reduce stress and help individuals cope with external pressures (Goldman & Wong, 1997; Moran, 1996); to promote attentiveness and divergent thinking (Aria, 2002); to positively influence a reticent student's interest in learning (Pollak & Freda, 1997); and to improve students' attendance (Berk, 2003).

Teacher Humor

In addition to having the advantages just mentioned, humor can be very effective in defusing an awkward situation or a hostile student (Aria, 2002). And when teachers use self-deprecating humor, they communicate to teens that they too should not take themselves or circumstances too seriously, a potentially

For the Reflective Practitioner

Analyzing humor is like dissecting a frog. Few people are interested and the frog dies of it.

E. B. WHITE

Teacher's Tip

There will always be a student in your class who has a quicker wit and is smarter than you. You will be wise to view this as an asset and integrate the student's humor into your communication.

debitating developmental trait of adolescence. The following are suggestions for incorporating humor into your classroom:

1. Plan ahead and practice humorous stories, anecdotes, and jokes.
2. Purposefully make misstatements and joke about yourself.
3. Start class with a humorous "goofy" idea, an incorrect statement about history, a bizarre story from the news, a witty poem, a famous quote, or a cartoon.
4. Use the top ten David Letterman approach with your content.

 Can you create a top ten list for some information in your field?

Student Humor

Student humor is typically spontaneous and a reaction to something the teacher or other students have said, done, or read. Students who give presentations in class after a group activity or individual project can also see the presentation as an opportunity to add levity to the classroom. It is important for teachers to enjoy this humor along with the students, but they must make sure that the time allotted to the humor and responses does not sidetrack the class for too long from the work at hand.

Katherine Abbott of Abbott Communications tells the story of the "Lady with a Pointer" at http://www.abbottcom.com/Humor_in_the_classroom.htm:

> In a mixed class of men and women, the students were practicing using visual aids. A female student was demonstrating how to use a pointer in front of the class. Fully retracted, the pointer was the size and dimension of a pen. Fully extended, it was about 2 feet long. Never having used a pointer before, she picked it up and began extending it as she walked towards the front of the class. Without a sexualized thought in her head the woman casually said, "My, this thing gets really big!" As soon as the words were out of her mouth the class was in stitches. Recognizing the innuendo, the woman broke out in laughter with the rest of us.

Reprinted with permission of Katherine Abbott

 How do you think you should respond to this kind of "off-color" humor in your class?

CLASSROOM OBSERVATION

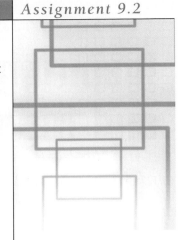

INTASC STANDARDS 2, 4, 6, 7

Brown (1975) developed some well-known abbreviations for the verbal exchanges that take place during whole-class instruction (as opposed to group activities, silent reading, or practice):

1. TL: Teacher lectures
2. TQ: Teacher questions
3. TR: Teacher responds
4. PR: Pupil responds
5. PV: Pupil volunteers
6. S: Silence
7. X: Unclassified

Visit a local middle or high school and observe a number of classrooms in your teaching field. During your observations, in 10-second intervals, tally the verbal exchanges using Brown's abbreviations and record the total number of students who participated in the lessons for each of the observed classrooms. Be prepared to turn in the assignment to your professor and to discuss your ideas in class.

OnLine Resources	COMMUNICATION
ERIC OnLine ED426929	*The Positive and Negative Effects of the Use of Humor in the Classroom Setting,* by Steele, Karen E., 1998.
ERIC OnLine ED410612	*Students' Perceptions of a Teacher's Use of Slang and Verbal Aggressiveness in a Lecture: An Experiment,* by Martin, Matthew M., et al., 1997.
Association for Career and Technical Education	Find the **ACTE OnLine** article *Using Humor in the Classroom* at http://www.acteonline.org/members/techniques/mar04_featur3.cfm.

Check this textbook's website at http://education.college.hmco.com/students **for additional links.**

Inspiring and Motivating Middle and High School Students

Teaching is not just delivering knowledge; it also requires motivating students (McCombs, 2000; McCombs & Whisler, 1997). Teenagers have a mix of aspirations and motivations that are influenced by a multitude of factors (Connell, 1991; Hidi & Harackiewicz, 2000).

It is relatively easy, when you are an adult, to identify the "right" or "smart" things that teenagers should do. But most adults admit that when they were teenagers they too did not always have the right aspirations, and, even when they did, they were not always motivated to achieve them. As a teacher, you will need to influence your students by helping them see connections between current behaviors and attitudes and short- and long-term goals and by providing learning opportunities that build their confidence to take on the escalating rigor of academic tasks (Elias, 2001; Hootstein, 1995). To understand the driving forces that shape teenagers' affective and cognitive view of the world—and ultimately their success—one needs to consider the nature of their aspirations and how students motivate themselves to take on the challenges of the teenage years (see Dekeyrel et al., 2000).

The contemporary psychological and sociological theories (see Prewitt, 2003) that shape our approaches to motivating students have their origins in classical Greek philosophy with such major figures as Socrates (469–399 B.C.), Plato (427–347 B.C.), and Aristotle (384–322 B.C.), and with such notables from the same line of philosophy as Immanuel Kant (1724–1804) and Nietzsche (1844–1900). They asked what it is to be "most" human and how humans could fulfill their potential. While it is foolhardy to attempt to condense 2,500 years of philosophical and psychological thought into a few words, the most basic premise is that humans are distinguished from other life forms by their rationality and that to fulfill their potential they must rely on their rationality and sublimate their emotions (Maulding, 2002). If they know what the "right" thing is and are motivated to do it, they can have what philosophers call the **"Good Life"**: a state of being in which we do our duty to others and ourselves and as a result enjoy intellectual, emotional, and physical well-being.

For the Reflective Practitioner

For every person who wants to teach there are approximately thirty people who don't want to learn much.

W. C. SELLAR AND R. J. YEATMAN

For the Reflective Practitioner

The mediocre teacher tells.
The good teacher explains.
The superior teacher demonstrates.
The great teacher inspires.

WILLIAM ARTHUR WARD

Psychological Constructs

Humans seek the "Good Life" by integrating their intellectual, emotional, and physical aspects (and some would argue the spiritual aspect as well). For teenagers, finding this equilibrium is particularly difficult because they have limited life experiences from which to gain perspective, and the multiple and ongoing changes in any one aspect create disequilibrium and force readjustments in the other(s). For example, teenagers have no control over their physical changes, and these changes in body chemistry affect their emotional state. At the same time, they are forced into classrooms that impose uniform and rigid intellectual standards and tasks that do not take into account these ongoing changes. Admittedly, most of us survive this developmental stage. However, the Internet, the mass media, and the "permeable family" (see later in this Topic) have created a generation of teenagers who have a wealth of ideas and behaviors that have outstripped what Coleman (2000) calls their **Emotional Intelligence,** which include self-control, zeal and persistence, and the ability to motivate oneself (Maulding, 2002). As a result, teenagers are likely to be intellectually familiar with concepts, terms, and vocabulary that are beyond their emotional intelligence; in addition, they have the physical capacity to perform as adults but lack the additional life experiences that provide a guide to that performance.

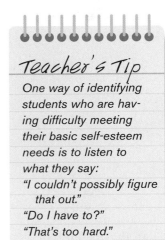

For the Reflective Practitioner

Few things are more satisfying than seeing your own children have teenagers of their own.

DOUG LARSON

Hierarchy of Needs

Abraham Maslow's (1968, 1970) classic approach to explaining motivations and aspirations is exhibited in Figure 10.1. It should be familiar to most students who have taken an educational psychology or general psychology course as part of their teacher-training program.

In brief, humans seek to meet Maslow's needs from the bottom up, and meeting these needs is necessary for **self-actualization,** which is very similar to the philosophical concept of the Good Life. Teenagers' aspirations are the same: to self-actualize by meeting their needs. As examples, eating is a **physiological need;** a future good job is a **safety need;** and peer group acceptance is a **belonging need. Esteem needs** include such things as status, attention, reputation, dignity, self-respect, and feelings of achievement, confidence, competence, independence, and freedom. Humans move through these needs during their life cycle, achieving them at different rates and to different degrees. The unique combination of physical, emotional, and intellectual challenges in the teen years adversely impacts some students' aspirations and motivation. Many teenagers "act out," make "bad choices," or do "poorly" in school because they are struggling to fulfill their needs. When needs are unmet, aspirations diminish.

Teacher's Tip

One way of identifying students who are having difficulty meeting their basic self-esteem needs is to listen to what they say:
"I couldn't possibly figure that out."
"Do I have to?"
"That's too hard."

Figure 10.1 | **MASLOW'S HIERARCHY OF NEEDS**

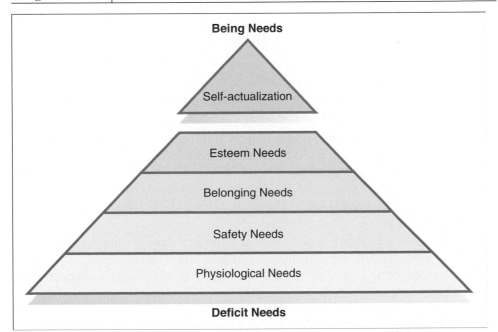

Motivation

A person's motivation to achieve is based on (a) a predisposition to achievement, (b) a perception of the value of the task, and (c) the probability of success (Atkinson & Feather, 1966). The need to succeed comes from either **intrinsic motivation** (doing an activity for no apparent reward other than the activity itself) or **extrinsic motivation** (doing an activity with an expectation of a reward) (see Atkinson, 1974; Eskeles-Gottfried, Fleming, & Gottfried, 1998; Ingram, 2000). Intrinsically motivated students compete against themselves. Extrinsically motivated students compete for rewards, weighing the value of the task against their need for an external reward. The probability of success in school for both extrinsically and intrinsically motivated students is evaluated in the framework of fear of failure (Alderman, 1999) and the public and unavoidable assessment represented by grades (Sebart & Krek, 2002). Ability AND effort are the most frequent reasons for success or failure. However, students too frequently focus on ability, rather than effort, as the major determinant of success (Alderman, 1999). As a result, they conclude that effort is useless. In addition, students may be overcome by anxiety over potential failure because of prior school experiences (Canfield & Siccone, 1993; Murphy, 1996), which limits their predisposition toward achievement and raises the threshold for a new belief about their prospects for success (Alderman, 1999; Murphy, 1996; Simon, 1988; Tracy, 1993).

The Teacher's Role

Teachers can influence these variables by creating the CONDITIONS that help students become engaged in the learning process (Deci, Koestner, & Ryan, 2001; Deci & Ryan, 1985; Ryan & Deci, 2000). In other words, they can employ instructional approaches that support self-motivation (Benson, 2003; Pastoll, 2002; Patrick, Hisley, & Kempler, 2000). This positive climate is based on three basic teacher actions (Grolnick & Ryan, 1989; Ryan & Stiller, 1991; Schommer & Dunnell, 1997):

For the Reflective Practitioner

Ability is what you're capable of doing. Motivation determines what you do. Attitude determines how well you do it.   LOU HOLTZ

- **Supporting Autonomy:** creating a structure in which students feel empowered to make decisions about their learning
- **Being Involved:** personally projecting warmth and interest
- **Providing Structure:** being well organized and consistent and planning and creating tasks that require student to reach, but that are not out of their grasp

A supportive climate can facilitate teenagers' **Locus of Control,** the internal resource mechanism that is necessary to sustain the self-motivation for academic achievement. Following are some generalizations from the literature on motivation that teachers should consider:

- Intrinsically motivated students are inclined to take on new or more demanding tasks. The challenge for the teacher is to have them overcome their fear of failure or poor performance.
- Extrinsically motivated students are more inclined to avoid even attempting new or more demanding tasks. The challenge for the teachers is to have them attempt the activity.
- When students perceive a climate that supports their autonomy, they have more confidence and self-esteem and can generate more concepts.
- Student perception of whether the teacher is controlling or supportive of autonomy is a key variable in activating intrinsic motivation.

- The success of rewards and communications is dependent on whether students interpret them as primarily informational or controlling.
- Direct rewards (like money from parents for good grades or bonus points from teachers) tend to decrease intrinsic motivation, whereas positive verbal reinforcements tend to increase intrinsic motivation.

For the Reflective Practitioner

Without a sense of caring, there can be no sense of community.

ANTHONY J. D'ANGELO

What do these psychological theories suggest that you should do as a teacher in a classroom setting? Do the opportunities or impediments differ depending on the academic discipline that is taught in middle and high schools?

Sociological Constructs

For the Reflective Practitioner

Time is a great teacher, but unfortunately it kills all its pupils.

HECTOR LOUIS BERLIOZ

In preliterate societies, children and teenagers who were not intrinsically motivated still had the advantage of knowing that the task had value because what they learned had an immediate and practical outcome. As an example, an elder of the tribe walking through the forest might say, "Always step well over a log in the woods, because there might be a snake underneath." The benefits of behaving in this way were obvious to learners, and their predisposition to learn was based on their personal connection to the respected tribe elder. For success today, knowledge must be accumulated over longer periods of time and has far fewer observable and immediate advantages; thus it requires greater acceptance of the need to persist without immediate rewards or even confidence that what is being learned is important. Explaining that to teenagers is often not enough to produce the desired intrinsic motivation, so frequently teachers and parents turn to external motivators.

Values

Today, the terms *virtues* and *values* are often used interchangeably, but they are two very different concepts. *Values* is a sociological term that has been used more frequently in recent history; it refers to a society's norms of ethical behavior, which may or may not be virtuous. *Virtues* is the older of the two terms and at the center of inquiry into motivations and aspirations as humans take on the challenges of life. Virtue is a quality of character; a virtuous person is a good person.

Values are part of the normative system of a culture that changes over time. The **normative system** of a culture includes conventions, morals, sanctions, and laws. **Conventions** (Folkways and Mores) are a society's common everyday habits, such as wearing the hairstyle of the majority of the population or one's peers. **Morals** are the generally well-known forms of acceptable behavior that are adopted by a culture; they are used to set a standard of ethical thought and conduct. If conventions and morals are not explicitly stated, teenagers decide on which conventions and morals to follow by watching the behavior of peers and adults (also by watching television and reading books). **Sanctions**, like disapproval by parents or shunning by peers and society, also promote conformity to the value system. **Laws** or **rules** are a codification of some of the preferred forms of behavior, and sanctions are used to demand a minimum standard of ethical conduct (operational values), if not belief (conceived values).

These things that hurt, instruct.

BENJAMIN FRANKLIN

Operational Values are how we act; Conceived Values are what we think to be the "right" thing to do. Teenagers may not do their homework, even though they know they should do their homework. When our operational and conceived values do not match, we form guilt; this guilt can lead to either increased self-motivation and change or to many of the dysfunctional behaviors we see in the teenage and adult population today. When operational and conceived values are in agreement, we experience a sense of well-being, the Good Life. Teachers can help students conceive the right values by communicating and modeling them, and teachers can operationalize those values by designing instruction in a way that makes self-actualization possible, if not almost painless.

Conformity

Conformity appears to be a basic drive in all humans and is essential to an orderly society and classroom; the question is: "To what do I conform?" By middle school, students to different degrees begin a rebellious stage in the life cycle during which they challenge the ideas and beliefs of their parents and the culture at large, both verbally and through behavior. This rebellious stage coincides with an increased drive to be accepted by their peers (Santor, Messervey, & Kusumakar, 2000). Visit any middle school and you will observe how the students dress alike and share many common mannerisms and language. They have decided that conforming to their peer group is more important than conforming to the larger society. But the introspection of teenagers is limited (that is why many act as if the middle school dance and senior prom are the most important events EVER in their life), and thus their ego is falsely enriched with the belief that they are nonconformist and rebelling.

The concept of conformity has both individual and communal implications. Teenagers pick and choose their peer groups (although many teenagers may feel they are being selected or shunned) and the degree to which they conform to those groups. For a summary of the criteria teenagers use in picking friends, you can go to ERIC ED467561 *Grade and Gender Differences in Adolescents' Friendship Selection Criteria*, by Zook, Joan M., and Repinski, Daniel J., 2002. Because of their "belonging needs" and "esteem needs," students may adopt nonconforming—if not disruptive—behaviors to distance themselves from teachers so as to establish independence or endear themselves to peers.

Peer Groups

If the peer culture of the school is weighted toward academics, students may conform to that norm. Conversely, if athletics are more highly prized, students may be influenced in that direction. The influence of an adolescent's **peer group** explains student behavior throughout the middle and high school years better than any other variable (Giancola, 2000). It accounts for why some students who are self-motivated and appear to have operationalized the virtue of doing well in school begin to fail, and it can also account for why some students who might be candidates for failure based on community, peers, or family circumstances begin to excel when placed with high-achieving students.

By creating an academic culture in the classroom, a teacher is socializing the individuals into a peer group that can facilitate and foster academic success. This kind of high-success peer group is forward-looking and purposeful, in contrast to some of the other peer groups teenagers find in schools. By middle school the microcultures of the student population are being reshaped based on the onset of adultlike attributes. Students find their places on the popularity hierarchy. There are the "cool kids," the "nerdy kids," the "jocks," the "weird kids," and so on. The renewed jockeying for position begins the first day of middle school as the new mix of students roll in from various elementary schools. Physical looks, attitude, body image, clothing, school supplies, and who you are seen with immediately begin to shape students' status (Adler, 1992). Becoming anorexic, taking steroids, behaving aggressively, spreading rumors, undergoing cosmetic surgery, and being sexually promiscuous are all teenage behaviors that are based on a drive to conform and to gain the "highest" rung on the popularity ladder, or at least to find their own niche. Teenagers are very aware that one wrong or right word or action in the classroom, at lunch, in a hallway, or after school can change their social status. Middle school teachers see the results as students enter their classes crying, pass notes to communicate the latest status reports of who is in and who is out, and dramatically vacillate in their participation and achievement from day to day.

By high school, students have a greater sense of who they are and where they are in the social hierarchy and have usually developed the ability to better control their outward signs of emotional distress (MacDonald, 1991). New students, even with the large number of relocations in American schools, know that the sociology of the peer groups will likely be the same at each school and find their way to their status group. In the teenage hierarchy, finding, maintaining, and moving up positions in the social strata can be a full-time job, a job many if not most will view as more important than learning. Refocusing students on the purpose of school is a full-time job for teachers. Focusing on instruction and quickly paced lesson plans sets the right priorities and redirects students from what adults know to be distractions from the real work at hand. Grouping activities to purposely mix students from what you suspect are different spots on the social spectrum can foster greater tolerance if not opportunities for new friendships.

> ### For the Reflective Practitioner
>
> *Another possible source of guidance for teenagers is television, but television's message has always been that the need for truth, wisdom, and world peace pales by comparison with the need for toothpaste that offers whiter teeth and fresher breath.* DAVE BARRY

Permeable Families

David Elkind (1994) in *Ties That Stress* has compared the **nuclear family** of the 1950s, which he characterized as having a single breadwinner, partners who have never divorced, and a full-time homemaker with a few children, to the **permeable family** of the 1990s, with a single parent or remarried parents, children, and one or two full-time working adults. He argues that the nuclear family was relatively stable: a refuge from the world's ills where more parents put their children first, set clearer boundaries and expectations, were typically available 24/7 to supervise the children, and met with their children around the dinner table each evening. Conversely, the permeable family is more of a meetingplace where as many as four parents "blend" the children into more complicated family schedules (it is estimated that teenagers have lost 12 hours a week in time with their parents since the 1960s; Hewlett, 1991), where television has a greater influence on values than conversation around the dinner table, and where the household relationships are more complex for the children to negotiate. Schools both reflect and respond to the current cultures and help shape future cultures.

Whether you agree with this assessment and its bias toward the nuclear family, the American family in the twenty-first century is certainly different from the twentieth-century family. Teachers must use approaches that are appropriate to today's clients, whose emotional intelligence may be more greatly affected by such differences than their academic intelligence. Teachers are, for many of their students, *en loco parentis* (standing in the place of the parents) and often find themselves motivating whole families, not just a student. It must also be said that because these **"blended" families** have become the norm during the last twenty years, many of your students will have exposure to only this kind of family arrangement and will have learned (along with their families) to overcome, if not make the most of, some of the differences that the former generation laments.

> **?** *Are you from a "traditional" or "permeable" family? How do you think your family structure affected your education?*

The Positive Mental Health Approach

The psychiatrist M. Scott Peck (1997), in an approach to motivation that is based in counseling theory and clinical practice, illuminates ideas that are compatible with those of Maslow, Alderman, Deci, and Ryan but in a positive mental health framework. His analysis starts with the premise that life (and thus school and being a teenager) is a series of problems that, with motivation, can be changed into challenges that can lead to fulfillment.

Problems or Challenges?

Problems have three sources. We come into the world helpless and free of any responsibility. Immediately we are forced to deal with the realties of life: parents begin to force us to sleep through the night, get into a schedule of three meals a day, and become potty-trained. Why shouldn't we sleep when we want, eat when we want, and make messes wherever we want? These kinds of problems evolve out of our existence as humans and are not of our own doing or that of others. Then there are problems that come to us from external forces: a divorce by parents, death in the family, or a girlfriend or boyfriend who "breaks up" with us. Finally, there are problems we make for ourselves: watching TV rather than doing homework, picking fights with friends, and so on.

For the Reflective Practitioner

> *When probability of success is low, as in confronting difficult tasks, there is little embarrassment in failing.* ATKINSON AND FEATHER (1966)

In addition, there are two parts to every problem: the problem itself (the **substantive problem**) and the emotional pain that accompanies every problem (the **corollary problem**). As an example, most of us have witnessed a child crying and getting "emotionally worked up," and the hysteria continues after the initial problem has disappeared. This is the classic case of how every problem or challenge has both a substantive and a corollary problem. We can avoid creating our own substantive problems, but, although we may not always have to get thoroughly "worked up," we can never avoid suffering through a problem to some extent, regardless of the source.

An Example

Remember learning to ride a two-wheel bike. First you had to delay watching TV or playing with your toys for the long-term benefits of learning to ride the bike. Then, in spite of your apprehension and fears when the training wheels were taken off, you mustered the courage to ride the two-wheeler, even though the potential pain of falling down on the pavement loomed large in your mind. Your parents, early in your life, forced choices on you, but they couldn't choose for you to have the courage to ride the bike any more than they can choose the courage for teenagers to give up TV to study. You were most probably self-motivated by a desire to do what the "big kids" or your friends were doing. You willed yourself to muster the courage to take up the problem. If you were truly fortunate, your parents helped you develop your courage by running alongside the bike, coaching and encouraging you to succeed. Teachers can do the same for their students.

Self-Discipline

Taking up the problems of school requires the virtue of courage to will oneself to suffer in the short run and to **delay gratification** for long-term gains. In **Delayed Gratification,** one decides to engage in an activity even though the rewards are not immediate. For teenagers, learning in school is the primary problem that is imposed on them. In industrialized societies, the long-term advantages of doing exceptionally well in your class may not be obvious to students, and therefore promoting delayed gratification is a challenge. This is the origin of the questions "Why do I need to know how to find the circumference of a circle (or the major battles of the Civil War, or the structure of a sonnet, or phylums and species)? I am never going to use it."

Do you have good answers to these questions? **?**

We delay gratification by exercising **self-discipline** or **self-regulation** and by finding our **locus of control.** Self-discipline is learned and requires courage. When teachers (and parents) impose discipline, students may mimick a self-disciplined behavior, but this is not self-discipline because it does not include a cognitive choice on the part of the student. Students need to learn to discipline themselves.

Habit Formation

Habits are patterns of behavior that can be formed consciously or unconsciously. Teachers should encourage habits that promote personal development but discourage destructive habits. **Serendipitous Habit Formation** occurs as a result of random, unplanned interactions with our environment. **Affirmative Habit Formation** is purposeful and planned and can be self-initiated or structured by another person when self-motivation and self-discipline are absent or not adequate to the challenge.

An Example

As early as two years of age, children and parents face the problem of getting children to begin brushing their teeth. Scenario 1 is the shared process in which children brush their teeth each day as part of a routine standing next to their parent. If articulated with enthusiasm as a shared activity, the parent often finds little resistance and the habit is formed in the child even though the child initially is not intrinsically motivated and has not made a cognitive choice to brush his or her teeth. The parent sets aside time for doing the activity with the child. This is a very different process from scenario 2, in which the parent mandates tooth brushing as a requirement, constantly badgers the child to brush his or her teeth, or gives the child rewards for doing so. In both scenarios, eventually the child will come to value clean teeth more than using the time to play or do other things and will adopt the behavior. The first scenario requires sacrifice by the parent, which is often why it is not chosen. But that sacrifice allows the child to develop a sense of self-determination, gain competence, and experience delayed gratification while being comforted through the suffering with companionship. Scenario 2 leads to confrontation and alienation, or learning to do things only if there is an external reward. This example also illustrates how to think about classroom engineering (see Topic 16) as the best, proactive approach to managing the behavior of your students.

Procrastination

By taking up the substantive problem at its onset (delaying gratification), we suffer to a lesser degree emotionally (the corollary problem) and only in the short run. But if we choose to procrastinate or avoid the substantive problem, we compound the dilemma because:

1. We will still have to eventually delay gratification and deal with the problem.
2. We lose both the short- and long-term opportunities that rely upon timely success in each of the earlier developmental challenges.
3. We will eventually have to experience the corollary emotional suffering that accompanied the initial substantive problem.
4. We have compounded our emotional trauma by creating a secondary corollary emotional problem in having "let ourselves down" the first time by procrastinating.
5. Dealing with the first substantive problem becomes more difficult because the next problem will already be upon us.

Procrastination places us in the position of having to endure more mental distress than we would have if the problems had been dealt with immediately and incrementally over a broader span of time. Figure 10.2 depicts the importance of taking up challenges and getting on with the business of life.

Figure 10.2 | **CYCLE OF CHALLENGES**

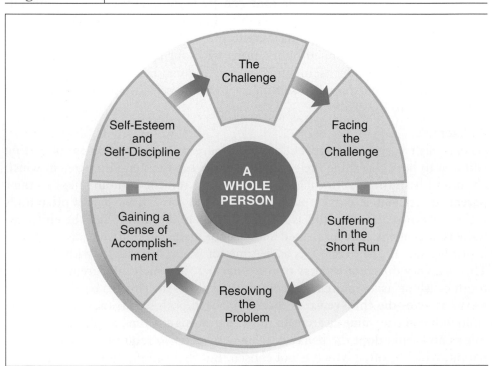

Aspirations

Aspirations are shaped by our courage and wisdom and mediate between attitudes and achievement (Abu-Hilal, 2000). When seven-year-olds say they want to grow up to be president, we encourage them and motivate them to dream. As adults, we know the odds of becoming president make it unrealistic to have such a dream, but we recognize that discouraging the dream is not in children's best interests. Parents and teachers who are focused on the long-term interests of their children would, instead of telling them to "get real," use the dream to motivate them to set goals to work harder at math, reading, and writing if they want to reach that dream AND help them develop the self-discipline that would make it possible for the dream to come true. Even if the dream stops being realistic in later years, the courage and self-esteem that comes from the diligent hard work in pursuit of the dream makes other later, more realistic dreams possible.

The Middle and High School Student's Challenges

Each middle and high school student has a unique history of dealing with problems, emotionally and substantively, and that history has shaped the teenager sitting in your classroom. The potential emotional distress of school can prevent teenagers from taking up new challenges or completing a challenge, even though success is within their reach. Their lives (as they perceive them) are complicated on an emotional level just by being a teenager, and the will to internally motivate themselves can be limited. Schoolwork, while a substantive problem, becomes just one more emotional challenge. Some teenagers will need little from you; others will need a great deal if they are to successfully negotiate the maze of middle and high school.

The mere state of being confined in school is a challenge for some teenagers. For others, school is a refuge from life's daily struggles. Apathy, poor performance, avoidance behavior, and aggression are signs of teenagers who are rebelling against the teenage years' problems that they often feel ill equipped to handle. Why some teenagers thrive, others persist, and some disintegrate through these significant challenges is subject to debate because the variables are too complex to find one explanation for all. However, there is little disagreement that students' personal aspirations and self-regulation can be positively influenced by significant others like parents and caregivers, relatives and teachers.

The period between entering middle school and exiting high school is a time when most of us "grow up." For teenagers who have had the good fortune or persisted through unfortunate circumstances to develop the habit of self-discipline, growing up requires maintaining the habits that got them to middle school with the good grades, even temper, and a healthy self-concept and making relatively minor adjustments to their expectations. For teenagers who are less fortunate, it is not too late to develop those habits—but it is more difficult and their expectations may need more significant adjustment. It is during the middle and high school years that teenagers need to develop realistic agendas, and teachers and parents must help them find their place in life and comfort them through the anguish that inevitably accompanies their ongoing challenges.

Best Practices for Helping Students Succeed

As teachers we would prefer that we simply ask and all students would comply with the challenges we put before them: If this were the case, teaching would not be OUR challenge. A textbook on methods is intended to make that task of

For the Reflective Practitioner

teaching easier by providing strategies that reduce students' inertia, make learning more pleasing to the learner, and result in self-satisfaction, high self-esteem, and confidence (Brophy, 1986).

Teachers can assess if a student is "ready," identify appropriate tasks, explain what needs to be done, encourage effort, and coach a student along the way. They cannot eliminate all anxiety from learning or failure, but they must encourage personal responsibility, even if a teenager's particular circumstances offer little support. Teachers can work together to make a difference on a schoolwide basis (Elias, Arnold, & Hussey, 2003) and as individuals. The following are steps you can take to make a difference:

1. In your own way and when the occasion permits, share the ideas in this Topic with your students. Most teenagers have never heard of Maslow, Peck, or even Socrates but would benefit from a discussion about how their ideas affect them. My experience has been that exposing teenagers to these concepts of motivation, challenges, peer pressure, and sacrifice through discussion early in the semester creates a greater understanding of the "Duty" of teachers and students, builds credibility, and encourages a positive classroom climate.

2. Turn the problems of learning into "doable" challenges. By creating lessons that are appropriate, well structured, and divided into incremental steps, you can give students a better chance of succeeding at educational challenges and the emotional reservoir that is created by success in school. They can then transfer this skill of dealing with school problems to other facets of their lives.

3. By focusing students on the challenges of school, you can diminish the exaggerated significance of dating, physical changes, peer group acceptance, and shunning and put it in the context of a life beyond the teenage years.

4. Promote education as the best opportunity for setting and realizing adult dreams or aspirations and tie it to goals.

5. Engage students in discovering the "right" priorities by asking the right questions, not by telling them the correct answers.

6. Serve as a role model of a thoughtful person by not overreacting, being analytical and logical, and organizing your thoughts.

7. Show that you care about students' long-term interests; it is OK to admit that what they are learning may not always seem particularly fun, necessary, or interesting.

8. Treat errors and mistakes as normal and part of the learning process.

9. Create thoughtful classroom management practices and demanding coursework.

Assignment 10.1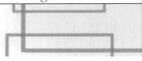

WHAT IS THE STATE OF AFFAIRS?

INTASC STANDARDS 2–8

In the following table, record what you think would be the responses to surveys taken at middle schools. Be prepared to discuss your estimates in class.

Table 10.1 | **TEACHER OBSERVATIONS OF MIDDLE SCHOOL STUDENTS**

Question	Percentage of Teachers Responding Affirmatively
Are most students motivated, as opposed to somewhat motivated or not motivated?	
Do many students have an assignment missing during a quarter grading period?	
Do many students receive comments like "inattentive in class" on a returned assignment?	
Do students who don't turn in assignments do as well on tests?	
Do you accept late assignments?	
Does a missing assignment affect a grade substantially?	
[Note to Professor, see PowerPoint Presentation for source and responses & three additional tables for use in class.]	

Reflect on your education in middle school and high school. What motivated you? What influenced you to be a low performer and a high performer at different periods? Can you recall something a teacher did that inspired you to change?

Topic 10: **Inspiring and Motivating Middle and High School Students**

UNIT THREE

Knowledge and Literacy

Defining Knowledge

As discussed in the previous Topics, a teacher's role is multifaceted, and today's schools have been called upon to provide services and activities that are far beyond what was thought to be the mission of schools not too many years ago. Because teachers and schools are **Seats of Knowledge,** their primary mission remains the transmission of knowledge. However, *learning* and *knowledge* are sometimes defined too narrowly. If *learning* is defined as teachers imparting facts and concepts, it fails to capture the essence of an education, which is the development of the more objective, reflective, analytical, and logical disposition that prepares one to be a lifelong acquirer and assessor of knowledge.

Teachers need a practical **Framework** for organizing their thoughts about what is important to teach and eventually what is the most effective way for students to learn. These decisions are made during lesson planning, when standards, goals, objectives, instructional approaches, and content are developed and choreographed. The following sections discuss a number of interrelated terms and concepts that should help you define what you will teach. Although these terms and concepts are presented as discrete categories, the nature of knowledge and the various ways in which terms are used in the professional literature make such categories somewhat artificial.

Curriculum and Knowledge

A **curriculum** is the way we define the body of knowledge that we expect students to acquire. **Knowledge,** while not fixed in time because of new discoveries and insights, is accepted as "truth" or as a proposition when it meets an evidence or analysis standard in a certain time and place (Green, 1971; Pajares, 1992). Knowledge, for purposes of this text, is subdivided into **domains** (broad fields, like social studies and science), **disciplines** (more specific subcategories, like history and geography), and **courses** (even more specific subjects, like American history and world history). *Subject Area* and *Body of Knowledge* are terms often used to refer to domains or disciplines. Every domain or discipline differs in its content, way of organizing knowledge, and approaches to examining and thinking about the content (Becher, 1989); see Topic 41. Within a domain, discipline, and course, knowledge can be further segmented into Basic Skills Knowledge, Information Knowledge, Procedural Knowledge, Ideas, and Beliefs.

For the Reflective Practitioner

The etymology of the word **Curriculum** *is the Latin word* currere, *which means "to run." It conjures up images of the hurdles students must run through as they complete the marathon.*

Basic Skills Knowledge

Basic Skills are the foundation upon which the other forms of knowledge rest; they are essential to all knowledge acquisition. Being able to do arithmetic, write, read, and speak typically constitutes the shorthand definition of Basic Skills. The contemporary technological environment has led, in recent years, to a greater awareness that some of our fellow citizens (and soon-to-be citizens) do not have the Basic Skills required to function in American society. This has led to an emphasis on high-stakes testing (see Topics 3 and 37) to identify students who need remediation and, in many school districts, a "back-to-basics" approach. The American Diploma Project (ADP) was launched in 2002 after finding that high school diplomas have lost value. ADP developed a series of **Benchmarks** in English and mathematics that, if met, would prepare students for college or good jobs in the high-performance, global workforce. In English, the benchmarks are organized into *Language, Communication, Writing, Research, Logic, Informational Texts, Media*, and *Literature*, and in mathematics they are organized into *Number Sense and Numerical Operations, Algebra, Geometry, Data Interpretation*, and *Statistics and Probability*. You can go to the American Diploma Project for the detailed Benchmarks at **http://www.achieve.org/ achieve.nsf/AmericanDiplomaProject?OpenForm.**

Middle and high school teachers will need to support their school and district's efforts to upgrade students' Basic Skills by emphasizing reading and writing in all their courses. If you are a science, math, or social studies teacher (as examples), you can no longer expect that only the English faculty will teach students how to write and read and only the English faculty will grade for spelling and punctuation. Not only will you be expected to teach students how to read and write certain content, but your grading scheme should also take into account the *quality of writing*. Furthermore, you will need to develop lesson plans to explicitly teach Basic Skills applications in your courses. In other words, you will plan some lessons to specifically teach a basic skill using your course content, rather than follow the more traditional approach of planning a lesson primarily to teach content and only incidentally a basic skill. Just as a biology teacher might plan a series of lessons focused on the parts of the human body, he or she might plan to teach how to create flow charts, perform measurements, interpret mathematical data, develop presenting skills, use reading Strategies, and so on using biology content.

Information Knowledge

Information Knowledge (sometimes referred to in the academic literature as **Propositional Knowledge, Declarative Knowledge,** or just plain **Content**) typically includes the *facts, concepts*, and *generalizations* that students acquire from the subject area that you teach. Most Information Knowledge in any given subject area is beyond the capacity of any one individual to remember. Many students remember only the drudgery of memorization or the boredom of long lectures in which a plethora of facts are delivered because the teacher failed to explicitly focus on the *Procedural Knowledge* and *Big Ideas* (see later in this Topic) or allow the students to grapple with concepts and generalizations. However, Information Knowledge is essential to literacy and the ability to communicate ideas in a concise and efficient manner. Although initially developed with social studies in mind, E. D. Hirsch's (1987, 1996) call for a **Core (of) Knowledge** is applicable to each discipline.

Facts

Facts are specific items of information: Who was Abraham Lincoln, what is an amoeba, and who is Javert from *Les Miserables*? They are important because they are crucial to the development of concepts and are necessary knowledge for participating in the **community of practice** (see later in this Topic). In teaching, facts can be used as (a) building blocks to a concept or (b) examples of a concept.

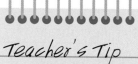
Teacher's Tip

Memorization is necessary, but it is best to study the topic before requiring students to memorize the material.

Can you give an example of each of these two important uses of facts for your content area?

Facts are often forgotten once we have internalized the concept or generalization that they supported. But facts are important to the process of securing concepts and generalizations that last a lifetime (Willingham, 2003a, 2003b). For example, we all have a conception of the solar system, but how many of us can name the planets? You may have the concept of "birthday," but it would not be wise to forget your mother's date of birth. So facts have a practical importance as well.

Teacher's Tip

When teaching, you can structure a lesson so that you ask students to apply a concept to a series of facts (**deductive reasoning**) or draw conclusions from facts (**inductive reasoning**). Both approaches are effective, and both should be used to provide variety in instruction (see Topic 23).

Concepts

Concepts are mental labels, the words that describe what a set of facts have in common. The simplest of concepts are often the ideas expressed in **terms** like *protagonist*, *prime minister*, or *exponent*. An amoeba and a protozoan are factual representations of the concept of "one-celled organisms," and Othello and Macbeth are "characters" in plays by Shakespeare. Concepts are defined by their attributes. The more attributes a concept has, the more complex and difficult it is to remember, and if a concept has affective attributes as opposed to purely cognitive attributes, it can defy objective definition. As an example, 1776 is a fact that represents the concept of "date" on a purely cognitive level. In the history community of practice these dates represent the concept of "revolution." To an American, July 4, 1776, has an affective set of attributes, perhaps about picnics, eating hotdogs, hearing *The Star-Spangled Banner*, and watching fireworks. A "revolution" to an astronomer has another meaning and other attributes.

What are the critical attributes of an island (as opposed to attributes that are common but don't define an island)? What would be some affective attributes of an island if described by an Eskimo or Tahitian Islander?

Generalizations

Generalizations express relationships between and among facts and concepts. In music, generalizations are often referred to as **principles**; in physics they are called **laws**; in history, **conclusions**; and in mathematics, **theorems**. For social studies and English teachers, generalizations can lead to the dangerous use of **stereotypes**. Carlos Cortes (2000) believes that generalizations, as opposed to stereotypical conceptions, are open to change with new information and are based on clues, rather than assumptions.

"An alligator ripped all three men apart" is a factual statement with an implicit generalization: "alligators are dangerous." This kind of statement appeals to our affective domain and creates graphic images in our "mind's eye." The less visceral approach would be an explicit generalization such as "crocodilian reptiles are carnivorous creatures." If your intent were to communicate to students a fear of alligators, the first would make the point. If you were teaching about reptiles, the latter would be more appropriate, although you might use the former if it is a headline in the newspaper and you want an attention-getter to start your Instructional Sequence (see Topic 20).

With generalizations, we convey a great deal of information in a brief, summative form. Generalizations can be dangerous, however, if the teacher

Topic 11: **Defining Knowledge**

unintentionally leaves out some information that might have been essential to the students' understanding. With generalizations, teachers should expect to also provide **Evidence** to the students by elaborating on the related concepts and their underlying facts with additional clarification that goes beyond text materials. As an example, an individual could have one bad experience with an employee of a bank's branch office and might pass on the generalization to a friend that the bank is not a very good bank without providing the basis for that generalization. Such a communication would not be in the best interest of the friend and would not be good teaching in a classroom.

Procedural Knowledge

Dewey (1916) made the distinction between the "record of knowledge" (Information Knowledge) and "knowledge" (both Information and Procedural Knowledge). In math, for example, to know what the principles of geometry are is very different from being able to do geometry. **Information Knowledge** is knowing what; **Procedural Knowledge** is knowing how.

Procedural Knowledge Across the Disciplines

The terms *Thinking Skills* and *Critical Thinking* are often used to describe general Procedural Knowledge that can be used in all disciplines, whereas **modes of reasoning** (see following section) are typically ways of thinking or working with Information Knowledge WITHIN a specific domain or discipline (Johnson, 2002). A schoolwide approach to developing thinking skills can be found at ERIC online, ED447084, *Theory into Practice: Best Practices for a School-Wide Approach to Critical Thinking Instruction*, by Kassem, 2000.

The kinds of Procedural Knowledge that cut across the domains are outlined in Bloom's *Taxonomy of Educational Objectives* (1956). *Evaluation, synthesis, analysis, application, understanding*, and *knowledge* are the six categories, with the first four being the higher-level cognitive skills. Bloom uses the term *Knowledge* to mean memory and cognition, as opposed to the way it is used in this text. Each of the six domains can be applied to a subject area. If you type "Bloom's Taxonomy" into a Web search engine, you will find a number of sites that explain the taxonomy and show how it may be applied to the subject areas.

Domain/Discipline-Based Procedural Knowledge

Thinking skills at the domain and discipline levels are often referred to as **modes of reasoning, executive processes,** and **habits of mind.** Knowing how to draw inferences and conclusions from a literary work is a mode of reasoning used by English teachers. Reading the story is a basic skill. In mathematics, we teach addition and the formula for the circumference of a circle with various combinations of numbers and examples, but we are interested in the student learning the executive processes (the concept and the mechanics) of finding the circumference—a form of Procedural Knowledge that McTighe and Wiggins (2004) call **"enduring understandings."** In science, rather than just collecting leaves and labeling them as belonging to an oak tree, maple tree, and so on, the Procedural Knowledge goal would be to have students learn to analyze the structure of a leaf and synthesize the information to find out why some trees lose their leaves in fall. In social studies, Procedural Knowledge would be knowing how to construct a timeline and draw inferences from it, rather than just learning a set of dates. Students need to be explicitly taught the Procedural Knowledge of their domains and disciplines, just as they need to learn content like the seven continents and the solar system. The focus is on transferring to students the executive processes of the discipline and having them acquire the associated skills that allow them to be lifelong learners.

Procedural Knowledge includes:

1. Deciding on the nature of the problem;
2. Creating a mental image of the problem (Grigorenko & Sternberg, 2000; Sternberg, 1992); and
3. Developing a strategy to use basic skills and executive processes.

For middle and high school content area teachers, the purpose of Procedural Knowledge is to empower people with these thinking skills in the subject area so that they can be applied to Information Knowledge. This COMBINED *Information* AND *Procedural* Knowledge cannot be separated (Resnick & Klopfer, 1989) and is what constitutes **Domain** or **Discipline Knowledge**. At the expert level, domain or discipline knowledge is utilized in the craft of the "**community of practice**," such as among physicians, engineers, mathematicians, historians, literary scholars, and so forth (Eisenhart, Finkel, & Marion, 1996; Imel, 2001; Philips, 1995; Sternberg, 1992). You, as a subject matter teacher, are part of your domain's community of practice, and it is the *Domain/Discipline Knowledge* that is the centerpiece of instruction.

Teacher's Tip

Procedural Knowledge and Big Ideas should be the focus of your teaching because they emphasize thinking skills and student autonomy. Before Procedural Knowledge was emphasized, most teachers were satisfied if students learned the facts.

What do you think made up the majority of your education, Procedural or Information Knowledge? What do you think it should be?

NATIONAL AND STATE STANDARDS

Assignment 11.1

INTASC STANDARDS 1, 7, 8

Go to your State Standards website, either at Education Standards (http://edstandards.org/Standards.html) or your Professional Association's website (see Unit 8), and review the information on their Standards. Print out at least one relevant page of your subject field Standards and identify on the pages examples of Basic Skills, Information Knowledge, and Procedural Knowledge. Be prepared to turn in your assignment to your professor and to share your examples with the class.

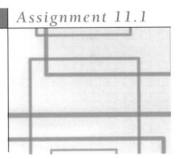

Ideas

An **Idea** is a thought or opinion that one formulates on the basis of one's unique accumulation of Information and Procedural Knowledge. The ideas may be correct or incorrect; all ideas are only partially formed and, therefore, imperfect. Adults regularly say, "The sun always rises in the east" because that's how it looks from our point of view, but at one time this was also taken as scientifically "correct." Today we "know" this idea is not "correct": the sun doesn't rise; rather, the earth rotates. Similarly, children's versions of ideas are not as well formed as adults', but that does not make them incorrect: We often refer to these as "**naïve**" **ideas** or theories. To some extent we all have naïve ideas or theories our entire lives because of our incomplete education, lack of openness to new ideas, lack of reflection, and the increasing specialization of knowledge. In addition, some ideas are wrong. The teacher, through a dialogue with students, can convert both wrong ideas and naïve ideas into more advanced, sophisticated understandings.

Ideas may be thought of as propositions communicated with the expectation that others will reflect on them and consider adopting them into their personal schemas. Our society has mandated that adolescents attend school because this is seen as the most efficient way for adults to transmit the knowledge that society has determined will be helpful to the evolution of the culture and the personal development of an individual. In a classroom, however, everyone brings his or her unique ideas based on his or her unique experiences, and students' ideas are often partially formed and based on a limited set of experiences. Part of a teacher's job is correcting and clarifying these ideas to match those of the generally accepted knowledge in the domain and discipline. Of course, if the student is an Einstein, the teacher might be the one with a limited set of experiences.

We usually assume that when students say something they believe it, but teenagers may also articulate their ideas to get attention, to challenge a teacher's authority, to persuade others to adopt the idea, or to check their own thinking about a tentative belief. Middle and high school teachers face five challenges when communicating ideas:

1. They must help students develop an ego that allows them to be open to new or more precise ideas.
2. In social studies and most literature, they must promote a virtuous and democratic ideology while also permitting undemocratic and unpopular ideas to be voiced and examined.
3. In science and math, they must help students who are anxious about their ability to develop a command of mathematical concepts.
4. They must maintain empathy for a student who resists new ideas or is slow to understand them.
5. Due to limited amounts of time for instruction, they must strive for efficiency to overcome students' attention spans and limited intellectual capacity.

Beliefs

A **Belief** is an idea that is transformed because we embrace it, value it, and believe it to be correct (Fenstermacher, 1994; Richardson, 1996). Beliefs become part of our persona and can be difficult to dislodge because we need to have an ample ego to be open to new ideas that might become new beliefs. Giving up a belief can be painful, but it is made easier if teachers can (1) provide a bridge from one belief to another potential belief by introducing alternative ideas and (2) demonstrate through their personal behavior openness to new ideas and tolerance for different beliefs and ambiguity. However, teachers are in the business of communicating well-founded ideas that they hold as beliefs based on their participation in the community of practice.

Teaching Procedural and Information Knowledge

Units 5 and 6 are dedicated to instructional approaches that allow us to change what students know and how they think. However, the following are three important considerations that apply to all the domains and disciplines.

Teaching Big Ideas

Big Ideas are powerful, long-lasting ideas, concepts, or generalizations proposed or illuminated by the teacher with the expectation that students will "think about" them (see Willingham, 2003b), examine their existing beliefs, and embrace the new ideas (McTighe & Wiggins, 2004). For example, when planning a lesson on why we experience the seasons in an earth science course, the teacher can construe his or her role narrowly and just teach the solar system and rotation of the earth, both important ideas. However, the teacher could consider an even more engaging and purposeful approach that would be more relevant to students' lives: combine the rotation of the earth, the solar system, the seasons, the impact of climate changes on humans and food production, and the link between holidays and seasonal changes into one Big Idea about the seasons' effect on our lives. Teachers who begin their lesson planning by finding the Big Ideas in their content should organize their Information and Procedural Knowledge to lead students to that idea (McTighe & Wiggins, 2004). If a lesson starts with a Big Idea phrased as a question, such as "What impact do the seasons have on our lifestyles?" students will be more interested in learning the related facts and concepts. Although Big Ideas are all around us, planning how to teach them requires insight.

Academic Disposition

If Procedural Knowledge is how to think more like an expert in a domain or discipline, an **Academic Disposition** is the *instinct* to use Procedural Knowledge and the *expertise* to use the right Procedural Knowledge. Dispositions are composed of three elements: (1) *Abilities:* the capabilities and skills required to carry through on the behavior; (2) *Sensitivities:* an alertness to appropriate occasions for exhibiting the behavior; and (3) *Inclinations:* the tendency to actually behave in a certain way (Perkins, Jay, & Tishman, 1992). We each have a **conative** style, or a preferred method of putting thought into action. Kolbe (1990) identifies four conative modes:

1. **Fact Finder:** instincts to probe, refine, and simplify
2. **Follow Through:** instincts to organize, reform, and adapt
3. **Quick Start:** instincts to improvise, revise, and stabilize
4. **Implementer:** instincts to construct, renovate, and envision

These instincts must be activated by the learner upon encountering new information. Students acquire this habit by seeing teachers model it and by doing teacher-assigned tasks. For example, you could teach students the cause-and-effect pattern (a social studies Procedural Knowledge) using the specific events of the American Revolution as factual examples. The primary purpose would be to impart the Procedural Knowledge that most immediate causes of any war can be better understood by organizing the precipitating events into a sequence. If, while reading about the Vietnam War, a student instinctively applies a cause-and-effect pattern to those facts, the student would be said to have acquired an Academic Disposition.

> ### For the Reflective Practitioner
>
> *The real voyage of discovery consists not of seeking new landscapes but of seeing through new eyes.*
> MARCEL PROUST

This Academic Disposition cuts across disciplines and becomes part of a person's temperament. The development of an Academic Disposition to employ Procedural Knowledge comes with the recognition that such tools are essential to understanding information in the domain or discipline. Part of what makes artists, biologists, and historians so good at what they do is that they have a wealth of Information Knowledge, a command of the Procedural Knowledge, and the Academic Disposition to be insightful when they apply their craft.

Explicit Teaching

One goal of education is to impart the rationality and logic needed to understand Information Knowledge when one is no longer in school and no longer

has the benefit of a teacher. Teachers must do more than hope that students will acquire an Academic Disposition in the learning process; they must be sure to teach it. One way to teach this kind of disposition is to be more explicit. **Explicit Teaching** takes place when teachers overtly plan to enculturate students into an enhanced Academic Disposition by organizing their lessons around Big Ideas and using the Information Knowledge as a foundation for teaching Procedural Knowledge.

To teach explicitly, you need to make students aware—through explanations, modeling, tasks, or active learning experiences—that they are being empowered with the skills of Procedural Knowledge and need to think critically about the content (Haberman, 1991). Your lessons will fail to resonate with students and be easily forgotten unless you find and explicitly focus on a Big Idea. In the preceding example of the lesson on the seasons, the teacher could begin by explaining what a hypothesis is; put students in groups; let them formulate why they think there are seasons; have them use their hypotheses to begin rejecting and accepting reasons with images and explanations (thus demonstrating a systematic way of analyzing a problem); and finally have them reach a conclusion. At the end, the teacher would explain that we use hypotheses to figure things out and that we have to be open to changing our minds as we gather new evidence.

Explicit teaching requires a general knowledge of pedagogy and also pedagogical content knowledge (see Unit 8). **Pedagogical content knowledge** is the knowledge about how to teach a particular domain or discipline as well as the knowledge about particular subject matter (Shulman, 1987). Successful teachers know the structure and unique executive processes of their discipline, plan to teach them to their students, and teach with an awareness of the "conceptual barriers" likely to hinder students from learning in the domain (McDonald & Naso, 1986).

Assignment 11.2

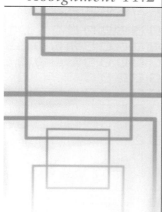

APPLICATION OF CONCEPTS

INTASC STANDARDS 7, 8

Assume you were going to teach seventh-grade students about the game of baseball or any other activity you know well. Keep in mind that you are defining what you would teach in a classroom setting, prior to actually playing the game. What are some Big Ideas that students should take away? For Information Knowledge, identify at least ten facts and concepts they need to understand the game or activity; for Procedural Knowledge, identify no less than five ways of thinking about the game or activity that you would share with your students once they had the basic facts and concepts; and for Academic Disposition, identify at least five ways of thinking that you would want your students to be able to intuitively use if they were participating in or watching the game or activity. Fill in Table 11.1 and be prepared to turn in the assignment to your professor and present your ideas to the class.

Table 11.1 | **LESSON PLAN FOR TEACHING**

Big Idea: _____ Activity_____	
Components	**Goals**
Information Knowledge (10 items)	
Procedural Knowledge (5 items)	
Academic Dispositions (5 items)	

WEB OF KNOWLEDGE

Assignment 11.3

INTASC STANDARDS 1, 4

Web Organizers, like all concept organizers, are an important part of teaching at all levels because they allow people to create mental maps. Draw a web depicting your understanding of the structure of knowledge using the major terms from this Topic. Be prepared to turn in the web and to share your ideas with the class. The web should be attractive enough to put in your teaching portfolio.

OnLine Resources

Check this textbook's website at http://education.college.hmco.com/students for online links that are periodically updated to reflect new resources as they become available.

Topic 11: **Defining Knowledge**

General and Content Area Literacy

The term *literacy* can be confusing because it is used in so many different ways. *Literacy* and *Basic Skills* are frequently used interchangeably in an effort to define what students should, at a minimum, be able to do and know, usually by a certain age or grade level. **Traditional Literacy**, in its simplest form, is defined in terms of the ability to read and write. **Basic Skills** is the broader term; it usually includes the ability to use mathematics (**"numeracy"**) and is frequently expanded to include such things as oral communication, study skills, and computer skills. **"Thoughtful literacy"** is defined by Allington and Johnston (2000, p. 1) as the "ability to read, write, and think in the complex and critical ways needed in a postindustrial democratic society." It is thoughtful literacy that is the particular interest of American society and schools (see Wood & Dickinson, 2000). Today, reading cannot be defined just in terms of books. Film-based and digital media provide alternative means of communication and also influence the page layout of books, magazines, and newspapers. Teachers must prepare students to be literate in all forms of information, including television, video, signage, computers, and the Internet (Moje et al., 2000).

The Organization for Economic Cooperation and Development (OECD) at http://www.pisa.oecd.org/, in its Programme for International Student Assessment (PISA), ranks the United States fifteenth in reading literacy, eighteenth in science literacy, and fifteenth in mathematical literacy when compared to thirty-two other industrialized nations. Unlike general literary studies and projections that compare whole populations, the PISA study collects and analyzes data on teenagers who are fifteen years old. The regions consistently surpassing the United States are the northern European countries, Japan, and South Korea.

For the Reflective Practitioner

66 *Students do not need to go to college to get a good job if they have four years of rigorous English and at least Algebra II with a B or better. Regrettably, 40 percent of high school seniors lack ninth-grade math skills and 60 percent lack ninth-grade reading skills.*

MURNANE AND LEVY (1996) AND
AMERICAN DIPLOMA PROJECT (2004)

? *Why do you think the United States is not ranked higher in this study? Can you support your hypothesis with data from the PISA website?*

Although teachers at the secondary level hope that students gain a well-developed set of **general** or **generic Basic Skills** from their elementary school experience (reading, writing, math, oral communication, etc.), they find significant variations in students' literacy (Meltzer, 2001). Middle and high school teachers also have the additional challenge of promoting domain and discipline-specific literacy. Professional organizations (or learned societies; see Unit 8 for the ones that apply to you) usually publish listings of the Basic Skills, Information

Knowledge, and Procedural Knowledge needed for their discipline, although they will not always use these specific terms and categories. These skills are more specific than the generic basic and thinking skills that one would apply to all the domains and disciplines. Virtually all learned societies, in creating their national Standards, have called for greater literacy in their domain. This Topic provides an approach to literacy education and introduces literacy approaches to all the domains.

Reading Literacy

As late as the nineteenth century, paper and pencils were the prized teaching tools because of their scarcity, and books, particularly those dealing with domain knowledge, were relatively expensive and in short supply. The middle and high school teacher was still the primary, if not only, "up-to-date" source of evolving domain knowledge. As a result, the ability to commit a large amount of knowledge by memorization was once a key indicator of "intelligence" and an absolute necessity to learning the basic knowledge required to be literate in the domain. However, the industrialization of the twentieth century brought about the mass production of teaching tools and textbooks. With a textbook for every student, the **synchronized** or **choreographed model of instruction** consisting of text and **teacher talk** (see Topic 20) became the dominant model of instruction. It is this choreographed presentation of knowledge that still dominates classroom instruction today, although copying, video, and digital technologies have also introduced a new palette of resources for the teacher.

The Nature of "Text"

"Text" should not be thought of as the narrative in a textbook, but rather any **readable asset** that a teacher may use in class, whether it is mathematics content in a textbook, a historical (**primary**) document, an excerpt from a magazine, or a novel. The Internet and compact discs (CDs) are new mediums that provide a range of text materials beyond the traditional publisher-produced **textbook.** However, textbooks continue to play a central role in general and domain literacy, and publishers also produce **ancillary materials** like teacher's editions of each basal textbook, textbook-associated websites, transparencies, worksheets, and integrated materials on a CD or a website to support their textbooks. According to the National Educational Longitudinal Study (NELS) of over 15,000 eighth-graders and 22,000 of their teachers, about 93 percent of middle and high school teachers' primary and secondary teaching resources are their textbooks (Wang, Wang, & Ye, 2002).

There is concern that the textbook can become the driving force in instruction—the outer boundary of required knowledge—rather than one of many assets that are part of choreographed instruction. In addition, in the academic community there are widespread and long-standing criticisms of textbooks' lack of rigor, readability indexes that set the bar too low, selective if not biased content, inaccuracies, superficiality, meager use of narrative, and overabundance of images (Davison & Green, 1988; Elliot & Woodward, 1990; Fitzgerald, 1979; Goodman et al., 1988; National Commission on Excellence in Education, 1983; Porter, 1989; Ravitch, 2003b; Tyson-Bernstein, 1988). Digital technology (video; the Internet; self-paced, personal computer–based

Teacher's Tip

Education Week, the weekly newspaper on education, is online at http://www.edweek.org/context/topics/issuespage.cfm?id=60 and allows you to review its articles by categories. As an example, if you select reading, you can learn about topics like the **whole-language** and **phonics** methods used to teach reading.

For the Reflective Practitioner

It is a wise man who only believes half of what he reads and hears: It is a genius who knows which half.

BENNY HILL, BRITISH COMIC

instruction; CDs with images; PowerPoint) offers a rich new medium, but even if it reaches its full potential, it is likely that it will still be integrated with textbooks as part of a publisher's package. And regardless of the medium, students will still be deciphering the meaning of words, figures, and numbers while reading text.

Differences Between General Text and Domain Text

The development of more advanced reading skills is one of the centerpieces of the No Child Left Behind legislation (North Central Regional Educational Lab, 2002). Your students' ability to read is influenced by two broad genres of text:

- **Narrative text,** which dominates elementary school reading instruction and textbooks, is used to form general knowledge from fiction and nonfiction stories (Duke, Bennett-Armistead, & Roberts, 2003). Such texts are "story driven," and as such provide a motivational element for young readers that cannot be easily achieved with expository text.
- **Expository or Informational text,** which is found in middle and secondary subject matter textbooks and ancillary materials, is used to inform the reader about knowledge in the domain (Flood & Lapp, 1986; Hoyt, 2002; Yopp & Yopp, 2000).

As a consequence of the text materials used in elementary schools, students are able to develop reading skills, a general vocabulary, and even the kind of specialized skill that is desirable for deciphering literature in the English domain; but they do not necessarily develop vocabulary or reading skills that prepare them for science, mathematics, or social studies, the domains they will encounter in middle and high school textbooks. Thus subject matter teachers can have students who are able to read but are unfamiliar with the vocabulary and structure of the reading materials for their domain (Schoenbach et al., 1999), and secondary teachers cannot assume that students understand how to read their textbooks. Regrettably, many middle and high school teachers feel inadequately prepared in the pedagogy of reading in general—or even for their content area—to be able to teach their students how to approach reading in their domain (Richards, 2001).

 Did you take a course in general reading or reading in your content area as part of your teacher preparation program?

Reading involves knowledge of (a) letters and sound correspondences, (b) words and word forms, (c) syntax (the grammatical structure of sentences), and (d) meaning and semantic relations. Teachers who encourage literacy, model and then expect students to:

1. Read strategically, reconstructing meaning as they **decode.** To some students the idea of stopping to ask a question to themselves and rereading when necessary for understanding as they process the words is a novel idea: It is part of the problem in making the transition from decoding to comprehension.
2. Preview the text for headings, pictures, graphs, and bold words, which helps them create a structure (or schema) for the reading that will follow.

For the Reflective Practitioner

There are worse crimes than burning books. One of them is not reading them. JOSEPH BRODSKY

For the Reflective Practitioner

Reading makes a full man, conference a ready man, and writing an exact man. SIR FRANCIS BACON

3. Set and adjust their personal learning goals, create cognitive associations, and assess their own understanding to prepare for their own remediation (see Greenleaf et al., 2001).

Best Practices for Reading Instruction in the Content Area

In addition to using **prereading** activities, in which background knowledge is provided or activated, and **postreading debriefings** (see Topic 13) and content presentations, subject matter teachers can use **direct reading instructional Strategies** to increase students' competency. The following are a few Strategies for reading instruction in the content area.

1. Lead students through the text organization (Berkowitz, 1986).
2. Model for students how to think about the text by reading out loud (see Topic 26 for metacognitive modeling).
3. Encourage students to reflect on text when they read (Baumann, Jones, & Siefert-Kessell, 1993).
4. Use writing to reinforce concepts (Konopak, Martin, & Martin, 1990).
5. Use graphic organizers to provide visual clues to content (Bean et al., 1986) and require students to create outlines and graphic organizers themselves.
6. Periodically revisit and remodel the direct reading Strategies (Siegel & Fonzi, 1995).

> **Teacher's Tip**
>
> **Questioning the Author** is an effective strategy with expository text. Students are required to read and then answer the following questions during a dialogue with the teacher (Beck et al., 1996):
> 1. What is the author trying to say?
> 2. What does it mean?
> 3. How does it connect with what the author already said?
> 4. Did the author explain it clearly?

The Crucial Role of Vocabulary in Literacy

Children learn their first words in the home, and these words become resources for reading. Research (see Hart & Risley, 2003) has uncovered what is known as the "30,000-word gap." By three years of age, there is a 30,000-word gap between children from professional families and children from families on welfare, with working-class families' children falling roughly in the middle. This gap becomes most evident in fourth grade, where the more sophisticated demands of the curriculum begin to require **comprehension** of the domain knowledge rather than the Basic Skills of **decoding** used in lower elementary grades (Chall, Jacobs, & Baldwin, 1990). Expository text in secondary education requires skill in both decoding and comprehending. And this comprehension is dependent on a working vocabulary and literacy in the domain.

The importance of **vocabulary** to reading comprehension cannot be overstated. Learning by reading requires:

- **Fluency:** the momentum and speed with which one reads, and
- **Automaticity:** quick and accurate recognition of words and phrases (Nagy and Scott, 2000).

Without these two acquired capabilities, the student becomes so bogged down in deciphering words and phrases that by the end of the sentence, paragraph, or page he or she has lost sight of the facts, concepts, and generalizations of the text (Willingham, 2003a, 2003b). The knowledge held in our sensory or short-term memory lapses because of what George Miller (1956) called "the magical number seven, plus or minus two." This concept states that we can only hold up to about nine bits of information at one time in our limited working memory. Therefore, we need to rely on a strong vocabulary that enables us, despite our very limited short-term memory working area, to perform feats of analysis and synthesis (Willingham, 2003a, 2003b). As an example, the vocabulary related to the *solar system* could, for a knowledge-

> **Teacher's Tip**
>
> An example of a promising literacy approach using PC-based technology is a study in which students read a passage with difficult vocabulary on a PC. Those who were given immediate online assistance (such as a pop-up definition) with the key vocabulary words that they didn't know significantly outperformed their peers on the postcomprehension test (Miller, 1997).

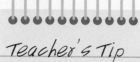

Teacher's Tip

Stopping in midsentence and looking up words in the dictionary is ineffective and not a best practice.

able person (an apprentice), contain all the names of the planets and words describing their rotation around the sun, their relative locations, the concept of gravity, and so on. All that someone with less vocabulary might know about the *solar system* would be that the earth is in it. With a strong vocabulary (even if not as sophisticated as an apprentice's), our short-term or "working" memory is freed up to capture more and more complex chunks of information.

Vocabulary Acquisition

Acquiring vocabulary, through both conversation and reading, is essential to the learning tasks required for the domain's knowledge base and is a major consideration for teachers when developing lesson plans and integrating reading into the Instructional Sequence (Texas Education Agency, 2000; see Topic 20). To be successful, students must be proficient in two sets of skills involving vocabulary: **"basic interpersonal communication skills"** (BICS) and **"cognitive academic language proficiency skills"** (CALP) (Cummins, 1999). CALP is more abstract and specific to the domain, and since it is new to middle and high school students, teachers need to provide "bridges" to the new vocabulary using Strategies like **"unpacking."**

For the Reflective Practitioner

No race can prosper till it learns that there is as much dignity in tilling a field as in writing a poem.

BOOKER T. WASHINGTON

In social studies and literature, for example, the vocabulary is thought to be more accessible than the totally new vocabulary of a foreign language or the more esoteric vocabulary of science and mathematics, or what Christie (1998) refers to as **"uncommonsense"** vocabulary. In both verbal and text-based communication, the esoteric words must be **"unpacked"** from their uncommonsense meaning to a commonsense meaning (Beck et al., 1998). For example, in physics the term *law of reflection* would become "how things reflect light," and in social studies the *Emancipation Proclamation* would become unpacked to mean "a law freeing slaves."

A primary goal of instruction is for the teacher to unpack technical terms into commonsense meanings during teacher talk. Unpacking words as part of a prereading activity can increase nonapprentices' motivation and allow them to read with greater fluency and automaticity. When left to their own devices, nonapprentices (compared to apprentices) are less likely to understand the terms in a reading assignment or be motivated to use context or ancillary resources like the Internet or an encyclopedia to find a word's meaning.

Vocabulary that is found in text is static and devoid of a conversational context (Nagy & Scott, 2000). We decipher meaning in narrative text by noticing inferences, implicit meanings, context clues, juxtapositions within a sentence, and so on, whereas in expository text we also need domain-specific knowledge and vocabulary to decipher meaning. In expository text, where domain knowledge is essential, the author often provides additional verbiage to convey the idea: perhaps a list of domain-specific vocabulary at the beginning of the section, or an organizational heading outline to give the learner structure for reconstructing the concepts.

As a middle and high school teacher, vocabulary is part of your synchronized or choreographed instruction and should be reflected in your class notes (see Topic 20). How to approach reading in your course is developed in Topic 13 (on reading) and Topic 34 (on homework). Particularly for nonapprentices, you need to plan prereading and/or postreading activities to ensure student understanding of the unpacked vocabulary in your domain. What follows are some approaches to teaching vocabulary.

Best Practices for Teaching Vocabulary

There does not appear to be a single best way to learn vocabulary. Following are some basic principles that can serve as a guide. They are based on the findings of Brett, Rothlein, and Hurley (1996), Beck, McKeown, and Omanson (1987), Teal (2003), and others.

1. Teach the concept before presenting the unknown word.
2. Realize that incidental learning of vocabulary will occur even if teaching vocabulary is not specifically part of the lesson.
3. During reading, students learn significantly more vocabulary when teachers explain new words when they are first encountered, rather than waiting until the end of the reading activity.
4. Encourage students to determine the meaning of new words by inferring the meaning from the context, using a dictionary, or using some other means.
5. Students should manipulate words by comparing them to experiences and describing how they relate to other words.
6. Make sure that discussions of words are extensive, and require that students explain their use of words.
7. Use repetition so that students encounter a new word many times.
8. Model the careful and explicit use of words.
9. Create and display a word web, matrix, or list; or use a crossword puzzle assignment to preview new vocabulary as an alternative to listing words and definitions.
10. When students are reading silently in class or during a homework reading assignment, have them record on the left column of a piece of paper the words they understand and on the right column the words they don't understand. Review both by calling on students to provide explanations prior to instruction.
11. Debrief homework reading assignments and in-class readings by referring to and using the new vocabulary.
12. Provide opportunities to decipher a word's structure (morphological knowledge), such as the roots of words like *trespass*, *overpass*, and *impasse*.
13. Require a vocabulary notebook.

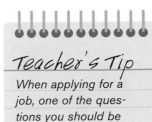

Teacher's Tip

When applying for a job, one of the questions you should be prepared to answer from your principal is, "How can you help me improve the literacy level of the school?"

The Crucial Role of Writing in Literacy

Reading is the process by which readers decipher the writer's unique mental representation that has been cast in text and then create their unique mental representation of what they deciphered (Flower 1990, 1994). Writing, for students, is casting their unique mental representation of what they have acquired through text or teacher talk into text. This creation of mental representations is the common ground of reading and writing and the reason that both are essential to literacy (Ruddell, 1997).

Teaching **Composition** or writing has long been viewed by those who are not English teachers as a "problem" for the English faculty (National Commission on Writing in America's Schools and Colleges, 2003). In addition, many teachers lack confidence in their own writing skills (Street, 2003). As a result, their willingness to engage students in writing (much less create enthusiasm for it) is a personal challenge (Draper, Barskdale-Ladd, & Radencich, 2000). However, as with reading, the development of writing skills is the responsibility of all the faculty, partly because by writing in one domain students develop general literacy skills that are transferable to writing tasks in other domains. Teachers need to use writing to help students express and solidify their conceptualization of domain knowledge and to acquire the writing conventions of their discipline. And now, with high-stakes testing, all teachers are expected to require more reading and writing in their domain because the test results may well determine the future of the school.

Writing in content areas is a higher order of thinking, requiring students to practice orchestrating conclusions, representations, evaluations, nuances, rhetoric, uncertainty, proofs, syntheses, applications, and multiple approaches (Bereiter & Scardamalia, 1986; Resnick, 1987). Flower and Hayes (1981) identified three classic stages of writing that continue to frame our way of thinking about the writing process:

1. **Planning:** generating ideas, setting goals, and organizing
2. **Translating:** converting the plans into written language
3. **Reviewing:** evaluating and revising

Applebee (1991) identified three purposes of writing for students:

1. To activate and reflect on existing knowledge before new knowledge is introduced
2. To consolidate and review new knowledge
3. To reformulate and construct new knowledge

There are a number of approaches to teaching writing (Bereiter & Scardamalia, 1986; Stephens & Brown, 2000). In English education, writing is often linked to interpretation of literature, but in other subject areas it is typically linked to reading and interpreting text to gain a greater understanding of the topic (Flower et al., 1990). Subject matter teachers, because they are primarily focused on content, tend to use **product-oriented instructional approaches** in which specific content goals are to be achieved through writing. Often they use questions posed by the author at the end of the textbook chapter, summaries of the text, or teacher-created questions, essay assignments, term papers, or the infamous **"five-paragraph essay"** (see Topic 14). Although content teachers may think of writing assignments as end products to be evaluated for their rendering of content, writing is also a process (Applebee, 1991) that—if treated as such by content teachers—will greatly enhance students' overall literacy in a domain or discipline.

Writing in a specific discipline requires that students use the discipline's vocabulary, concepts, facts, and discourse style and structure. Designing lessons in which students write something other than the standard, summative, five-paragraph essay (although this kind of task is better than no writing at all) can improve students' literacy. Topic 14 provides a number of specific projects teachers can use to integrate more writing into their courses and steps that teachers should follow to improve students' writing. The following section outlines some general best practices for developing writing skills (based on Cazden, 1993; Fitzgerald & Stamm, 1990; Flower, 1990; Flower & Hayes, 1981, 1984; Freedman, 1992; Prior, 1998; Schriver 1989; Sperling, 1996; Stephens & Brown, 2000; Zellermayer, 1989).

General Findings and Best Practices for Writing Instruction

1. Competent writers tend to spend more time thinking about how to express their ideas in rhetoric than do less skilled writers. For example, they think about what they know, their goals, and their audience. Therefore, before a writing task begins, teachers might require two- and three-student mixed-ability group discussions to help weak writers gather and organize their thoughts.

2. Competent writers make an easier transition from their individualized mental conceptions of what they want to express to the actual writing. Initially, teachers might provide goals and models of how to metacognitively plan and execute the writing process using content from their domain.

3. Novice writers often think revising their work indicates incompetence. Revising is also frustrating, particularly when they observe the person next to them spin off a more polished product as a first draft. Requiring drafting and redrafting allows students at each iteration to improve and should be promoted as an essential and normal step in the writing process.

4. Experienced writers are able to focus on argument and the needs of their audience and evaluate how their choices meet those goals, whereas inexperienced writers focus more on grammar, syntax, word choices, and other details. Therefore, in class weaker writers can read aloud in small groups or get feedback from the teacher or peers on their rhetorical choices and then spend additional time redrafting their work.

5. It is sometimes helpful to have students write for an audience other than the teacher (write an explanation for a younger student, their parents, or a magazine) to create a mentoring relationship rather than an evaluative relationship.

6. Students, if given only written feedback, tend to think it does not describe their own weaknesses but rather illustrates the teacher's inability to read "plain English." Therefore, it is good to hold conferences with students to provide both oral and written feedback.

READ ALOUD IN YOUR DISCIPLINE

Assignment 12.1

INTASC STANDARDS 1–8

Read Chapter 1 of the following online ERIC article and then read and print out the chapter for your discipline. Select a **"read-aloud"** in your chapter and prepare a typed paper that identifies its **Big Idea(s)**, its required **Information Knowledge,** and its required **Procedural Knowledge** and attach it to your chapter for submission to your instructor. Be prepared to discuss your ideas in class.

ED436716, *Read It Aloud! Using Literature in the Secondary Content Classroom*, by Richardson, Judy S., 2000

This book shows middle school and high school classroom teachers how read-aloud excerpts from a variety of genres can be used in various content areas. Each chapter begins with a brief introduction to the content area and its focus, after which three or four read-aloud and read-along selections are presented in detail, followed by some abbreviated selections. The eight chapters in the book are (1) Why Read Aloud? (2) Read-Alouds for Science; (3) Read-Alouds for Mathematics and Geography; (4) Read-Alouds for Social Studies; (5) Read-Alouds for English and Language Arts; (6) Read-Alouds for Music, Art, and Health/Physical Education; (7) Read-Alouds for Second Language Learners; and (8) Read-Alouds for Special Populations.

See Topics 13 and 14 for online resources in reading and writing.

Reading Approaches for Content Area Teachers

The goal of this Topic is to extend those principles from Topic 12 to instructional approaches that can be used by content area teachers to help students learn how to systematically analyze and interpret information in text or image form. Until the digital revolution, book-based material in the English language provided a rather straightforward approach in which words were consistently deciphered from left to right and top to bottom. Texts included relatively few images. Pictures, graphs, and other images were expensive to print. Today, information includes many more images (traditional graphics, textboxes, "pop-ups," and call-outs) that are interspersed throughout books, magazines, newspapers, electronic screens, and digital slide presentations like PowerPoint files. This array and volume of images have expanded the idea of "reading instruction" to include media of all kinds, although reading texts remains the centerpiece of school-based reading.

Internet resources present a unique challenge because, along with television, they have become primary sources of information for students. Also, a website is relatively inexpensive to produce and maintain. However, the material on websites may not be subject to review by publishing boards or experts in the field to ensure accuracy or control for bias, and the content may be totally fabricated while appearing to be legitimate. This presents a unique problem for teachers who use Internet and film resources in their instruction and who have traditionally relied on nationally recognized publishers to ensure accurate and unbiased content.

Text-Based Reading

The decision about what passages students should read in the textbook (often referred to as a **"Basal Text"**) or in other sources like the Internet should be based on a number of practical realities and strategic decisions.

First, it is highly unlikely that you will have students read an entire book in a year. In some fields like history and English, the content is too exhaustive to be entirely covered by the teacher in class. So you must decide early on (a) which parts of the text you will not develop in class but will have students read; (b) which parts of the text you will develop in class and will also have students read; and (c) which parts are not important enough for either a or b. In math and foreign language, courses are building blocks for other courses, so colleagues will rely on you to cover all the material. However, you will still have to decide which parts of the text fall into a or b above.

For the Reflective Practitioner

I took a speedreading course and read, War and Peace *in twenty minutes. It involves Russia.*

WOODY ALLEN

Teacher's Tip

Teachers often overlook introducing the text-book by teaching students what a table of contents and index are, why certain words are boldface, what the purpose of tables and callouts is, how to examine pictures, and so on. This is best done at the beginning of the year, before you start using the textbook.

Second, students in fields like history and English will not retain the voluminous facts over the long term, but they will retain concepts if they are expected to construct them on the basis of what they have read. In foreign language, mathematics, and science, vocabulary and terms need to be retained as building blocks for future learning.

Third, if you require students to master some content and then teach the same content in class, rather than spend class time giving a different perspective on it or developing related ideas, students will soon learn NOT to read because they can count on you making up for their failure to complete the reading assignment.

Fourth, some reading should take place in class and some as homework. Both approaches need to be integrated into lessons, and students need to be held accountable.

Reading at Home and at School

Students should be expected to read both at home and at school. This practice fulfills two primary goals: (a) it develops students' independent reading skills; and (b) it makes instruction efficient. By requiring students to read and holding them accountable, you create a **baseline of information** that allows you to choreograph (see Topic 20) the knowledge gained through the reading into your **Instructional Sequence** and to use the time in class to efficiently develop important ideas (particularly higher-order ideas) knowing that the students have an entry-level command of the content.

Homework Assignments

It is good practice to expect students to read grade-appropriate material before you teach it and to hold them accountable for the material before you develop the ideas associated with it. Not only does assigning reading as homework save class time for other kinds of learning, but it also encourages individual responsibility and allows the teacher to use the Information Knowledge to develop Procedural Knowledge and Big Ideas. It is a commonsense approach to have students demonstrate that they have completed the assignment by answering basic factual questions either as bell work or at the beginning of the lesson. The prereading options explained in the following section should precede the homework assignment.

Reading in Class

Having students read during class gives you an opportunity to assess their reading ability and to encourage them to improve their reading skills through the dynamic interactions afforded in a classroom setting. Because domains have **textual features** that are unique to the disciplines, reading during class allows you to instruct students on how to read content in their domain. Mathematics is considered the most difficult content to learn to read because it has "more concepts per word, per sentence, and per paragraph than any other domain" (Schell, 1982, p. 544). Social studies text is less dense but is still challenging because it is lengthy and can be presented both hierarchically, as in math and science, or as a sequential narrative, as in language arts. Figurative language in social studies and literature, unlike math or science, must be interpreted. **Images** in a domain or discipline (maps in social studies, diagrams in chemistry, graphs in math, etc.) are presented to supplement narrative or in lieu of narrative, but in both cases teachers need to teach how to read and interpret them (Duplass, 1996; Hoyt, 2002). Developing lesson plans around reading skills

Teacher's Tip

"Bell work" *is a questionnaire or paper-based activity that is to be completed individually by each student at the beginning of class and that can be used to ensure that students have read the assigned text material prior to the class session when it will be expanded upon. Teachers usually place bell work on students' desks each morning. The bell work is based on either a homework assignment or the previous day's lesson, and students complete the bell work as they arrive in the classroom. This is also a productive practice for classroom management.*

using content in your domain is just as important as developing lesson plans around content.

Three Phases of a Reading Strategy

The following three phases of reading—**prereading, reading,** and **postreading**—are adapted from Avery and Graves (1997). Because the reading should be planned as part of a lesson, these three phases would be integrated into your Instructional Sequence and may include passages from the textbook, handouts of Internet materials, primary documents, charts, and various other materials.

Prereading Options

One of the main goals of prereading is to prepare students for the reading material you have assigned. The "OK, open your books to page 73 and start reading" approach is not an acceptable strategy. You should motivate your students with an attention-getter, preview the reading to entice students, and then use one of the four Strategies listed in Table 13.1.

Table 13.1 | **PREREADING OPTIONS**

Strategy	Considerations
Preteach Vocabulary	• Ensures understanding of new terms. • Terms and definitions can be placed on the chalkboard during in-class reading.
Preteach Concepts	• Points students toward key ideas. • Can be particularly effective with a graphic organizer.
Promote Objectives	• Focuses on what you want students to get out of the reading. • Often uses questions to focus on expected outcomes.
Promote Reading Strategies	• Can be used to highlight upcoming images that are part of the reading. • Gives students a heads-up to look for figurative, biased, covert, subtle, and emotional appeals.

Reading Options

The reading Strategies listed in Table 13.2 have relative advantages and disadvantages. Assigned reading should be required so that students acquire a baseline of information that the teacher will use to examine ideas and teach Procedural Knowledge.

Postreading Options

After every reading, there needs to be a postreading activity (see Table 13.3) in which the teacher further develops some ideas from the reading or the teacher moves directly to instruction. Postreading usually precedes the instruction in which the teacher develops new but related Big Ideas or Procedural Knowledge and introduces new, related Information Knowledge. In many cases, postreading becomes a part of the content presentation.

Table 13.2 | **READING OPTIONS**

Strategy	Considerations
Reading as Homework *(Students read at home.)*	• Develops independent reading skills. • Requires students to focus on Information Knowledge. • Is effective only if the teacher has an evaluation following the reading, either as bell work or as an assessment prior to instruction. • The reading material must be at the appropriate reading level.
Reading Aloud by the Teacher *(Teacher reads the content.)*	• Models the joy and practice of reading. • Should include teacher sharing of Metacognition. The most straight-forward approach to modeling Metacognition is for the teacher to articulate his or her own thinking while reading a passage of text. This "talking out loud" approach explicitly teaches the underlying thinking process that one should use when reading. Failure to model Metacognitive processes can result in students' failing to understand and acquire the full set of skills they need to become lifelong learners. • Provides a model of correct pronunciation and how "good" reading sounds. • Students do not practice reading; they just listen. • Can be boring, so use short, interesting pieces.
Independent Silent Reading *(Students read an assigned passage in silence.)*	• Reading takes place in class, and the teacher can circulate to provide individual assistance to students with weaker reading skills. • Without an evaluation, the teacher does not know who is actually reading the material or what students' level of comprehension is, so this strategy should be paired with an activity to monitor comprehension.
Rotational or Round-Robin Reading *(Each student reads a paragraph or passage aloud.)*	• This strategy is the least efficient approach. • Weaker readers often feel embarrassed; when weaker readers' turns come up, other students may appear irritated. • Stronger readers are bored. • Better to have reading in supervised small groups.
Reading in Groups *(Each student reads a paragraph or passage aloud in a small group.)*	• Heterogeneous groups of four allow everyone to read multiple paragraphs. • Teacher can assign stronger readers to help weaker readers, or assign roles like reader, questioner, note taker, etc. • Weaker readers are not as inhibited in smaller groups. • Students can reflect and share ideas for reinforcement and uniformity of understanding. • Teacher must circulate among groups.
Student-Teacher Shared Reading *(Teacher begins to read and then asks students to read; teacher reads and asks questions to ensure comprehension; or teacher assigns short sections to be read independently and guides the discussion.)*	• Has similar shortcomings to rotational or round-robin reading, if not carefully choreographed. • Questions can be interspersed to keep everyone attentive and to ensure a baseline of content knowledge.
Choral Reading *(All students read in unison.)*	• Allows weaker readers to follow along in a large group with anonymity and little apprehension, but the teacher cannot assess individual reading ability and participation. • Often students do not participate, and their minds wander.

Topic 13: **Reading Approaches for Content Area Teachers**

Table 13.3 | **POSTREADING OPTIONS**

Strategy	Considerations
Debriefing	Debriefing (where the teacher asks questions about the reading in a whole class setting, as opposed to groups) should be applied to concepts as well as facts. The teacher should ask students to synthesize, and report their personal reconstruction of the meaning of the text material. The teacher can engage students with additional concepts.
Summarizing	Summarizing is not as effective as debriefing, and students will learn not to read because they anticipate that the teacher is going to summarize. This can be more effective if the teacher asks individual students to summarize.
Discussion	Students in groups of four or five should focus on discussion questions provided by the teacher that require predicting or analyzing, and the teacher should circulate among the groups.
Simulation	Students create a simulation (role-play) to demonstrate their understanding of the reading. Requires a debriefing by the teacher after each skit.
Project	Students are given a writing assignment, graphic organizer, or other project to demonstrate or apply their knowledge. Requires a debriefing by the teacher after the task is completed.
Basal Worksheets	Many textbook companies provide worksheets to accompany social studies textbooks. In social studies, science, and literature, these tend to be fact-based and evaluate only lower-level learning. In mathematics and sometimes in science, they often include additional examples or problems to solve. These too require a debriefing.

BONUS! *Assignment 13.1*

SUBJECT AREA READING MATERIALS AND TOPIC LESSON PLAN CONTENT

INTASC STANDARDS 1–8

At this book's website under **Bonus Course Materials** are content area readings appropriate for middle and high school students. These "Selections" from the secondary education textbook publisher McDougal Littell and from public domain websites can serve as a topic and reading content in your subject field to create textbook-based unit and lesson plans, the most common—but by no means the only or necessarily the best—approach to lesson planning by new teachers. Your professor will likely assign you one of these selections to download and use in this course, as well as in the lesson planning assignments for Unit 8 (the lesson planning assignments are not in the textbook, they are ONLY located under Bonus Course Materials on this book's website). Please print out your selection and bring the PDF or website pages to your next class meeting.

To provide you with a simulation of the real-world experience of preparing to teach, this reading material will be used in two ways, in conjunction with this textbook, for a number of assignments:

1. You will be asked to prepare a reading plan using your assigned reading material.
2. You will be asked to use your selection as the BEGINNING point—the topic—for the development of a unit and daily lesson(s). This will give you the opportunity to learn how to plan and teach a typical topic in your field.

Unit Three: *Knowledge and Literacy*

ENGLISH EDUCATION READING MATERIAL

English

The Gutenberg Project at **http://gutenberg.net/catalog/** or **http://www.gutenberg.org** has over 10,000 eBooks. Most of these are classic, older literary works that are in the public domain in the United States and can be freely downloaded and used for noncommercial purposes.

- Selection 1: *The Canterbury Tales* by Geoffrey Chaucer, for a lesson on poetry.
- Selection 2: *Four Great Americans*: *Washington, Franklin, Webster, Lincoln: A Book for Young Americans* by James Baldwin, for a biography at the middle school level.
- Selection 3: *The Gift of the Magi* by O. Henry, for a lesson on fiction.
- Selection 4: *The Raven* by Edgar Allan Poe can also be downloaded at the **Edgar Allan Poe website http://www.eapoe.org/works/poems/index.htm**, for a lesson on poetry.
- Selection 5: *Desiree's Baby* by Kate Chopin can also be downloaded at **PBS (http://www.pbs.org/katechopin/library/desireesbaby.html)**, for a lesson on short story fiction.
- Selection 6: *The Jungle* by Upton Sinclair, for a lesson on historical fiction.

Communication/Speech

- Selection 7: *The Gettysburg Address* by Abraham Lincoln is a classic for students to deliver as part of their public speaking education. It can be retrieved from the **Library of Congress** at **http://www.loc.gov/exhibits/gadd/**.

MATHEMATICS EDUCATION READING MATERIAL

- Selection 1: *Geometry Concepts and Skills* (McDougal Littell), Chapter 2: *Segments and Angles*, pages 50 to 82.
- Selection 2: *Algebra 1 Concepts and Skills* (McDougal Littell), Chapter 4: *Graphing Linear Equations and Functions*, pages 202 to 236.

SCIENCE EDUCATION READING MATERIAL

- Selection 1: *Chemistry* (McDougal Littell), Chapter 5: *Gases*, pages 189 to 212.
- Selection 2: *Earth Science* (McDougal Littell), Chapter 20: *Weather*, pages 434 to 464.

SOCIAL STUDIES EDUCATION READING MATERIAL

- Selection 1: *The Americans* (McDougal Littell), Chapter 5: *Shaping a New Nation*, pages 130 to 151 for a lesson on history.
- Selection 2: *The Americans* (McDougal Littell), Chapter 6: *Launching a New Nation*, pages 152 to 179, for a lesson on government.
- Selection 3: *World Geography* (McDougal Littell), Chapter 4: *Human Geography*, Section 1, "The Elements of Culture," pages 70 to 82, for a lesson on geography.
- Selection 4: *World Geography* (McDougal Littell), Chapter 4: *Human Geography*, Section 5, "Economic Geography," pages 91 to 98, for a lesson on economics.

WORLD/FOREIGN EDUCATION READING MATERIAL

- Selection 1: *En espanol!* (McDougal Littell), *Preliminar*, pages 2 to 22, for a lesson on Spanish.
- Selection 2: *Discovering French, Nouveau!* (McDougal Littell), *Faison Connaissance*, pages 12 to 40, for a lesson on French.

- Selection 3: *Auf Deutsch!* (McDougal Littell), *Eins Einfuhrung* (Level 1), pages 2 to 30, for a lesson on German.

ARTS EDUCATION READING MATERIAL

- Selection 1: *Fine Art, Drawing Fundamentals:* Ralph Larmann, art faculty member in the **University of Evansville Art Department** at **http://www2.evansville.edu/studiochalkboard/draw.html** has an extensive website on drawing fundamentals. Print the brief articles on Linear Perspective, Atmospheric Perspective, Shading, and Compositional Models for reading materials for students.
- Selection 2: *Dance:* **ArtsEdge** at **http://artsedge.kennedy-center.org/content/2445/** has a lesson plan for dance based on the works of Seurat and Sondheim. Print the segments of the lesson, some of which could be used as reading material for students.
- Selection 3: *Theatre:* **Cable in the Classroom** at **http://www.ciconline.com/bdp1/000_home.asp** is an online segment related to Shakespeare's Hamlet's "To be or not to be" soliloquy. You can get a copy of the soliloquy by entering "to be or not to be" in a search engine; to be used as reading material for students.
- Selection 4: *Music:* **PBS** at **http://www.pbs.org/theblues/classroom/essays.html** is a website for the Blues. Print out the two "Background Essays"; to be used as reading material for students.

HEALTH AND PHYSICAL EDUCATION READING MATERIAL

- Selection 1: *Physical Education:* **3 team basketball** at **GEM.** Go to **http://www.thegateway.org/**, enter "3 team basketball" in the full-text box, and print out a copy of the activity.
- Selection 2: *Health Education:* **Illegal Drugs. Public Agenda** at **http://www.publicagenda.org/issues/debate.cfm?issue_type=illegal_drugs** presents three perspectives on illegal drugs. Print out the three essays after clicking on "In Detail"; to be used as reading material for students.

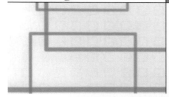

Assignment 13.2

SUBJECT AREA READING PLAN

INTASC STANDARDS 1–8

Based on your assigned reading selection from Assignment 13.1, create a detailed, step-by-step reading plan (the notes you would use in class) using the prereading, reading, and postreading approach. Be prepared to share your presentation in class and turn the assignment in to your professor.

Images

When we see an image produced by someone else, it tends to affect us all at once, as if thrust upon our consciousness. Some images, like pictures, appeal directly to our **affective domain** (our emotions). In contrast, when we read text, we create pictures out of the author's words in our "mind's eye." This process allows for a more controlled, time-delayed creation of mental images. Images like charts are powerful precisely because they capture and condense what would often take paragraphs to express in text form. A great variety of images are used in text materials, including pictures, graphs, diagrams, flow charts, and timelines, but there are common elements to teaching students how to interpret them. We will use charts to demonstrate the principle.

Teaching Students to Interpret Charts

In any chart, there is both Figurative Information and Literal Information. **Figurative Information** is deduced from the presentation of the data; it is the implied idea that the author is conveying and is effectively communicated by the type of chart chosen and the headings selected to present the **Literal Information**. Literal Information is usually the raw data or summations of raw data that appear in the cells of the chart. Teachers must emphasize the importance of both the Literal and Figurative Information contained in charts so that the author's intentions, and perhaps biases, are made obvious. One of the most important contributions a teacher can make to this process is to ensure that students understand that charts are constructed out of data collected by surveys or other techniques or found in reports, books, and other information media. The goal is for the students to capture the entire image in their "mind's eye" but also to understand the inherent messages in the image. The following steps, again using a chart as an example, show how you can model for your students the process of analyzing an image in a textbook, chalkboard display, PowerPoint presentation, or other medium (Duplass, 1996).

Instructional Process

The following steps should be used when presenting a chart for interpretation.

1. Present the chart.
   a. Define the type of chart (line chart, figure, pie chart).
   b. Identify the title and discuss facts, concepts, and generalizations related to the topic.
   c. Evaluate the reliability of the source and date.
2. Examine the categories of the Literal Information from left to right, top to bottom, and line by line to ensure a baseline of understanding of the axis titles, headings, scale, and data labels.
   a. Define the categories to reveal the assumptions being made by the reader.
   b. Explore other possible categories based on the topic.
3. Examine the Literal Information from left to right, top to bottom, and line by line to ensure a baseline of understanding.
4. Identify and discuss the Figurative Information to discover the possible inferences. Hypotheses should be tested on the basis of:
   a. The Literal Information.
   b. The Literal Information compared to the title.
   c. The Literal Information compared to the topic.
5. Extend learning by predicting future outcomes based on the Literal and Figurative Information.
6. Assess the effectiveness of the chart as a form of communication, and expose possible bias by the author in the choice of categories and chart format.

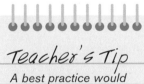

Teacher's Tip

A best practice would be, immediately after modeling how to interpret an image, to give students a second, slightly different image and have them interpret it using the same process.

INTERNET-BASED IMAGE INTEGRATION

Assignment 13.3

INTASC STANDARDS 1–8

Find a chart, graph, diagram, picture, drawing, flow chart, painting, timeline, or other visual on the Internet. Using the instructional process outlined in this section, create a set of notes that you would use to teach students how to interpret the image you found. Be prepared to share your notes in class and turn the assignment in to your professor.

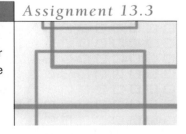

Topic 13: **Reading Approaches for Content Area Teachers**

Assignment 13.4

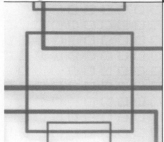

EXPERT OPINIONS ON READING

INTASC STANDARDS 1–10

At this book's website, listed under Topic 13, Assignment 13.4, is the link to the online ERIC document ED441223, *Struggling Adolescent Readers: A Collection of Teaching Strategies*, edited by Moore, David W., Alvermann, Donna E., and Hinchman, Kathleen A., 2000 (344 pages). It contains forty articles that focus specifically on teaching struggling readers in middle school and high school classrooms. Your professor will likely assign you one of the 25 listed articles on this book's website. Prepare a one-page, single-spaced handout for your classmates and the professor focusing on the "Big Ideas" of the article (see Topic 11), and plan to present these ideas to the class.

OnLine Resources	READING
ERIC OnLine ED356149	*Teaching the Reading and Study Skills Needed in Junior High School Social Studies Classes,* by Davis, E. Dale, 1992, offers detailed procedures for helping students read content in social studies and most other fields.
ERIC OnLine ED432728	*Identified Sins in Teaching Reading,* by Ediger, Marlow, 1999.
Middleweb	*Find Reading Wars at* http//www.middleweb.com/Reading.html.

Check this textbook's website at http://education.college.hmco.com/students for additional links.

Writing Approaches for Content Area Teachers

The goal of this Topic is to extend the principles explained in the section on writing in Topic 12 to instructional approaches for content area teachers. The National Commission on Writing in America's Schools and Colleges (2003) referred to the state of writing as "the neglected R" and called for the development of students' writing skills as a goal for all teachers, not just English teachers. It is assumed that English teachers should help students learn to structure their thinking and communicate ideas through writing, but this knowledge is almost exclusively learned in the context of literature instruction using just the literature genre (Hall, Morreale, & Gaudino, 1999). Writing in the content areas offers the same opportunities for students to practice and develop the sequential, analytical, and precise thinking that is part of the authoring process. However, one of the most comprehensive reports on writing instruction found that English teachers spend less than 20 percent of their time on writing instruction (Squire & Applebee, 1968). For teachers in fields other than English, high-quality and sustained writing activities can be nonexistent, even though they can be invaluable to their students' understanding of their domain/discipline. Teachers in domains other than English need to use writing to help students reconstruct and demonstrate the knowledge they have learned in the domain they need to teach both the domain's content and the executive processes of writing.

The constructivist model says that students learn to write by interacting with more experienced and supportive writers (Hester, 2001; Langer & Applebee, 1986). Students then internalize the written language structures and processes in the context of previously learned verbal language. To be successful, teachers need first to be collaborators rather than evaluators, and the learning tasks must be aligned in a sequence that is logical to the student. Whether the student is simply summarizing or making an argument during a writing task, the teacher must find a way to give the student ownership; as John Dewey (1980) said, there is "all the difference in the world between having something to say and having to say something" (p. 35). One of the advantages of being a subject field teacher is that you can energize students with something to say because you are exposing them to new ideas.

Content area teachers need to adopt the view of English teachers that writing is a dynamic and developmental process in which the teacher and student interact regarding the quality of the student's written communication as well as the ideas communicated. The following are some key points that highlight the importance of writing instruction across the curriculum.

1. The current national focus on Standards and Basic Skills makes writing assignments across the curriculum essential to your school's success.
2. As a process that differs from the verbal communication in an active learning environment, writing provides an opportunity for students who are less verbal than others to demonstrate what they know.

3. Treating writing as a process (see the section below on the **Five-Step Writing Process**) is authentic because it replicates how writing occurs in the real world (Jenks, 2003).
4. The different formats of writing (see the section below on **Writing Products**) provide variety to instruction and assessments that appeal to students' varying dispositions and abilities.
5. By focusing on teaching Genres (see section later in this Topic), students develop skills to write in different styles (Cope & Kalantzis, 1993; Devitt, 2004).
6. The use of logic that is required to write fosters critical thinking skills.

The Process of Writing

Drafts and revisions are essential parts of the writing process, as you will see in the next section. In addition, the teacher should structure the learning, researching, and writing experiences in a step-by-step process and should check on progress to ensure success. Teachers should use the following writing process when integrating writing tasks into their Instructional Sequence (the process will vary depending on the kind of writing that is assigned).

The Five-Step Writing Process

The complexity of writing tasks varies by grade level, but whether writing an essay or term paper, students should follow a consistent pattern to improve their writing. The **Process Writing Approach** that follows is adapted from Leu and Kinzer (1999) and Jenks (2003).

1. **Prewriting.** First and foremost, prewriting is an opportunity for students to gather their thoughts about the information and the organization of the topic. Writing may follow a lesson, a reading, a discussion of a reading, or the presentation of a graphic. The prewriting activity may involve creating a web of ideas, outlining, listing vocabulary, identifying headings, creating a chronology, or comparing ideas in groups. The teacher also models or presents an example of the kind of report expected.
2. **Drafting.** The purpose of drafting is to put an initial set of ideas down on paper and then receive feedback from the teacher or peers. Since this activity requires brainstorming and a degree of creativity, it is advisable to set a time limit so that students will start writing the next version of the assignment.
3. **Revising.** While revising, students have traditionally been trained to focus on the quality of their penmanship, their punctuation, and their spelling, but this is the primary focus of the fourth step, editing. During the revising stage, they should reexamine the logical progression of ideas, arguments, assumptions, headings, sentence structure, content, and word selection. Peer review is an excellent strategy for both revising and editing.
4. **Editing.** It is difficult to edit one's own work, and authentic assessment requires asking a peer to edit the revised draft. Teachers can model the following editing process:
   a. **First,** the author reads the draft aloud to the peer.
   b. **Second,** the peer reads the draft aloud to the author but pauses at each problem, explains the problem, marks the problem, and recommends a change.
   c. **Third,** the author accepts or rejects the recommended changes and rewrites the document.

Teacher's Tip

Written communication and oral communication share many attributes. The preparation process for both forces the student to conceptualize ideas, organize thoughts, and structure thoughts concisely, logically, and understandably. Whereas authoring documents may be an end in itself, most oral presentations should be preceded by some form of writing in which students organize and refine their ideas. See Topic 42 for ideas on teaching students how to make presentations.

Students should also learn the traditional editing signs for capitalizing letters, checking spelling, inserting commas, making deletions, adding insertions, starting new paragraphs, transposing letters or words, and inserting periods. The most common notations can be found at the University of Colorado website at **http://www.colorado.edu/Publications/styleguide/symbols.html**.

5. **Publishing and Sharing.** The final step is publishing the paper in its final form. The work should be shared with the class or prepared for an event such as an open house, depending on the kind of report produced.

Five Genres of Writing

Risinger (1987) and Gallagher, Knapp, and Noble (1993) identified five genres of writing that are essential to the development of meaning in the subject fields. All five can be used to give more meaning to the writing process and to allow students to be creative.

1. **Reporting.** Students are directed to compile information with a minimum of critical or original thinking. For example, they may be asked to "describe the structure of a cell."

2. **Exposition.** Students are asked to explain an idea, conduct a critical investigation, synthesize issues, or bring a fresh point of view to a problem. For example, they might answer the question "What should we learn from the Florida balloting experience in the 2000 presidential election?"

3. **Narration.** Students are asked to write a story, anecdote, tall tale, legend, drama, or vignette. The assignment might be "Pretend you are on the first space ship to Mars, and write a story that includes some facts about space flight and Mars as you are about to enter its atmosphere."

4. **Argumentation.** Students are asked to evaluate, defend, or oppose an idea or belief. For example, they might be asked to "write a letter to your fellow colonists detailing the reasons why they should not declare independence."

5. **Instruction.** Students are asked to provide directions or explain events for a broader audience: "Write a step-by-step explanation of the process of finding the area of a triangle."

Writing Products

The following product options, when combined with a process-oriented writing approach, can be effective with students in most disciplines. Some, such as the ABC report, are more effective with entry-level middle school students. On the other hand, the Take-Turns paper, which might seem more of a middle school strategy, can be used with high school students, who can turn it into an activity in which they try to outdo each other in creativity.

1. **ABC Report.** The ABC report is twenty-seven pages long, with a cover page followed by one page for each letter of the alphabet. The author of the report identifies content that can be associated with a letter. For example, if the topic is the American Revolution, A could be arms used in the revolution, B could be the Boston Massacre, and so on. The author writes multiple paragraphs for each page, accurately combining facts, conclusions, and opinions. Students could also be given the option of creating or including images. Students can be divided into three-person groups, with two group members responsible for nine letters each and one for eight letters and the cover.

Can you think of a topic in your teaching field that could be developed using the ABC report concept? Can you come up with the A through Z items?

2. **Double-Entry Note Taking.** Students take notes from the text in the left-hand column of their notebooks, and in the right-hand column they write questions about the material. After the topic has been covered, students are asked to share questions that were not answered.

3. **The Five-Paragraph Essay.** The five-paragraph essay follows a specific format.
   a. The first paragraph introduces the thesis of the essay and the three main supporting subtopics.
   b. The second through fourth paragraphs are all similar in format. They in-dividually restate the subtopics and are developed by giving supporting information.
   c. The fifth paragraph restates the main thesis idea and reminds the reader of the three main supporting ideas that were developed.

4. **Entry/Exit Freewriting.** A teacher poses a question or topic and all students are expected to respond in any way that is enlightening. It is an excellent way to start a class or end a class. It can be a question like "What did you like about last night's reading?" or something more specific about the content of a reading or video: "What surprised you most about the reproductive system?" (Elbow, 1998).

5. **Journals.** Having students keep a journal is an effective strategy that encourages reflection, writing, and dialogue with the teacher about what students are thinking, feeling, and learning (Abrams, 2001; Bromley, 1993; Simpson, 1986). An approach that is applicable to all the domains involves using five categories (Fersh, 1993):
   a. "I never knew that."
   b. "I never thought of that."
   c. "I never felt that."
   d. "I never appreciated that."
   e. "I never realized."
   The teacher can have electronic journals if technology permits, but usually teachers require students to write journal entries in a journal notebook. They then collect the notebooks, or they may have students keep the note-books in a bin in the classroom and periodically, usually on a weekly basis, respond to the students' journal entries.

6. **Magazine Report.** A magazine report involves creating a magazine-like arti-cle with photographs, drawings, and other images either created by the stu-dents or taken from published magazines.

7. **Newscaster Report.** A newscaster report is intended to emphasize public speaking and writing skills. Students can script information from newspa-pers or magazines to create a simulation of the evening news. Other students can videotape the newscast, and students can take a copy home to show their families.

8. **Note Taking.** Learning to take notes can improve students' success rate. The Cornell note-taking system is useful, even though it was designed for college students (go to the University of Santa Cruz **http://people.ucsc.edu/~mwax/ resume/write/rubric/cornellnotesys/** for more information or search for "Cornell note-taking system"). In this system, students divide a piece of paper into two columns, one about one-third page wide and the other about

two-thirds of a page wide. They write key words in the left column and notes from the lecture, video, or written material in the right column. During the early stages of learning to take notes, students are guided to identify key concepts, write brief explanations, and draw diagrams.

9. **Microthemes.** The microtheme is a short 100- to 500-word essay, usually limited to single sheet of paper, in which a great deal of thinking precedes a rather small amount of writing (Bean, Drenk, & Lee, 1982). There are four main formats, each of which cultivates writing and cognitive skills in the domain:

   a. **The Summary-Writing Microtheme.** After being given an assigned reading, students are required to condense the knowledge contained in the reading and write a summary that explains its structure (the main idea, supportive points, and connections among its parts), while retaining its hierarchy. The summary must be devoid of personal opinion and true to the author's intent.

   b. **The Thesis-Support Microtheme.** Students must take a stand and defend a hypothesis or position on a topic from a class presentation or reading using logical reasoning and argument.

   c. **The Data-Provided Microtheme.** Data are provided in the form of tables or factual statements to the class, and students must comment on their significance and make assertions by selecting, arranging, connecting, and making generalizations about the information.

   d. **The Quandary-Posing Microtheme.** Students must clearly explain the underlying principles of an occurrence or puzzling situation and suggest a solution.

10. **Outlining. Outlining** should emphasize the organization of ideas. The classic outline form uses I, A, 1, a, and so on for the various levels. When it is applied to text narrative or used to organize a lecture, outlining emphasizes the importance of sequence, hierarchy, and organization of ideas.

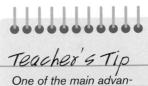

Teacher's Tip
One of the main advantages of Microthemes is that they are relatively easy to evaluate, score, and provide feedback on.

11. **Peer Letters.** Students are required to write a memo to an assigned peer in the class in which they discuss one or more concepts about a reading that they are unsure of. Students exchange the memos and respond to each other; then all four memos are turned in to the instructor for assessment and a grade.

12. **The Sentence Passage Springboard.** Students are asked to select a specific sentence or short passage from their class reading that has captured their attention and to write it across the top of the page. They should then be given time (in class or at home) to express in writing their thoughts about the sentence or passage.

13. **The Short Summary.** Students are required to come to class with a summary of the reading assignment from the night before. The summary cannot exceed fifty words.

14. **Take-Turns Paper.** This kind of paper requires students to work in pairs or foursomes and to take turns adding the next sentence to respond to a problem or topic presented by the teacher.

15. **Term Paper.** Term papers should emphasize organization and proper citation of sources. The teacher should provide an example of an end product and guide students in authoring their papers. Simple, uniform citation methods should be provided as examples.

Assessment of Student Writing

Marking writing products (see Topic 40) can become overwhelming, and those teachers without the grammar background of English teachers may feel

For the Reflective Practitioner

unprepared. Using a grading rubric can relieve some of your anxiety, and using peer reviews can significantly reduce the labor involved.

The **Northwest Regional Educational Laboratory (NWREL)** developed the Six + 1-Trait Analytical Writing Rubric, which can be downloaded at http://www.nwrel.org/eval/PDFs/6plus1traits.PDF. This useful rubric identifies and evaluates the following six characteristics of effective writing (both mechanics and content). It uses a 6-point scale, with 6 being the highest score and 1 being the lowest (see Topic 38 for a four-point rubric):

1. **Ideas/Content**
2. **Organization**
3. **Voice**
4. **Word Choice**
5. **Sentence Fluency**
6. **Conventions**
7. **Presentation**

This rubric provides an effective, consistent measure of student writing and a clear explanation of how level 6 writing differs from level 1 writing. You can download the rubric and consider giving it (or an equivalent) to your students at your first class meeting and using it during the year to give feedback. By giving this rubric to students before they write anything, you allow them to use it to assess their own writing before they turn in their assignment.

Evaluation of written drafts and final products is most effective if the student is required to follow up with corrections to the original submission. Teachers should tag questions, directions, and suggestions about content and mechanics to specific sentences. With the Six-Trait Analytical Writing Rubric categories (or any that may be used in your school) you could indicate a score for each category by attaching an **Assessment Slip** (a 3- by 4-inch piece of paper with preprinted categories and levels like "Ideas 1, 2, 3, 4, 5, 6; Organization, 1, 2," etc.) to the student's paper and circling the level of each; you would also provide a grade.

Markings on students' papers can be as detailed as an editor's notations, which give extensive feedback, or can merely inform the student that you have identified a potential problem, without stating what the exact problem is. For this latter approach, if you use the Six-Trait Analytical Writing Rubric categories, you can use just the first letter of the category as the mark, as in **I** for **Ideas**, **O** for **Organization**, and so on. When you encounter a writing element like a sentence fragment, just indicate **C** for **Convention**. This approach forces the student to take on the additional challenge of figuring out what is wrong, conferencing with you or a fellow student to analyze the problem, and then fixing the problem. It gives students more of an incentive to be attentive to their writing than if you make it easier by always informing them what needs improvement.

Best Practices for Teaching Writing

The following are some additional best practices for teaching writing in the domains.

1. When teaching students to write for their domain, provide students with a model so they can more easily conceptualize what the final product should look like and how concepts are approached in their domain.
2. Require students to write some papers on their own and other papers in collaboration with other students. Coauthoring can be particularly effective

with heterogeneous groupings when better writers understand that part of their role is to help the other students learn to write better.

3. Use peer review (students serving as reviewers and editors of one another's work) to cut down on your time spent responding to, scoring, and grading papers.
4. Have students write for imaginary, or even better, authentic audiences, rather than just you.
5. Play more of a supportive role than an evaluator role.
6. Develop writing topics that are of genuine interest or concern or that should intrigue students.

CREATE A WRITING ASSIGNMENT

Assignment 14.1

INTASC STANDARDS 1–8

This is a multistage assignment. First, develop a Microthemes writing assignment based on your assigned basal text reading from Topic 13. Second, swap assignments with a peer from your class. Third, complete the assignment you received. Fourth, turn in your submission to your peer. Fifth, score your peer's submission using the **Six-Trait Analytical Writing Rubric** and procedures described in this topic. Be prepared to share your experience with the class and turn in the products to your professor.

OnLine Resources	WRITING STRATEGIES
ERIC OnLine ED467300	*Computers in the Writing Classroom: Theory and Research into Practice,* by Moeller, D., 2002.
ERIC OnLine ED443369	*Grading Students' Classroom Writing: Issues and Strategies,* by Speck, Bruce W., 2000.
Purdue University	Website links for general writing support and support for specific issues like punctuation, grammar, etc., can be found at http://owl.english.purdue.edu/handouts/print/index.html. *These downloadable resources* can be useful to teachers in all disciplines.
GEM	At http://www.thegateway.org/ you can find over 3,000 resources on writing for the middle and high school levels. These resources can be sorted by teaching field.

Check this textbook's website at http://education.college.hmco.com/students for additional links.

UNIT FOUR

Organizing to Teach Middle and High School Students

"No, it's not for my history class...I'm wearing it when I monitor 5TH hour study hall!"

Dan Rosandich (www.danscartoons.com)

Student Behavior and Effective Learning Environments

Much of what you read about in education textbooks and articles deals with the nontypical student and the challenges of classroom management. This can lead to a pessimistic view of the teaching profession, which is not my intention. I make this point because in the vast majority of middle and high school classrooms, teachers are doing great jobs, they are optimistic about their craft and the profession, and students are being quite responsible and trying to learn. As in any profession, we have our "bad eggs" and our troublesome clients, but these are the exceptions. The purpose of the Topics in this Unit is to provide concepts and strategies to consider for creating an effective learning environment.

Middle schools and high schools are great places to make a life and a career as a teacher. The schools are full of energy, and the students—well, they are just as goofy, silly, and full of themselves with the same false airs of maturity as we had when we were their age. In my visits to middle and high schools, 90 percent of the students I see are good-natured, paying attention, doing their work, and trying to succeed, and 90 percent of the teachers are prepared, energetic, and truly concerned about their students. Hopefully, your early field experiences will give you the opportunity to observe classrooms, and I bet (and dearly hope) that your experiences will be similar to mine.

However, classroom and schoolwide lack of discipline is frequently cited as the number one problem that faces new teachers. Over the last ten years, "lack of discipline" has consistently been identified as the most serious problem facing schools in America in the annual Gallup polls. Few in the field of education would disagree. The disruptive classroom behaviors of a few students range from general verbal interplay and silliness during transitions between classes and instructional segments; to inattentiveness and passivity in class; to blatant actions like cheating, teasing, uncontrolled talking, "talking back," yelling, threatening, bullying, stealing, and fighting. Regrettably, more than 50 percent of all classroom time is taken up with noninstructional activities that deal with managing students (Cotton, 2003). If student conduct is not effectively managed by the teacher, it will undermine any efforts to teach. Civility and order are as essential to a classroom as to society, and they should be promoted through a proactive program of classroom management and engineering.

For the Reflective Practitioner

There was a time when we expected nothing of our children but obedience, as opposed to the present, when we expect everything of them but obedience.

ANATOLE BROYARD

Why Students Misbehave

Misbehavior can be perplexing to the teacher and contagious for other students. The following most common reasons for misbehavior are adapted from the

Teacher's Tip

After accepting your job, contact two other teachers in the school and ask them for a copy of their classroom **rules, penalties,** *and* **rewards;** *also ask them how frequently they refer students to the principal's office. By gathering this information, you will gain a sense of the school's norms and will have a classroom management plan that works.*

Wonder Wise Parent Resource at the University of Kansas at http://www. ksu.edu/wwparent/courses/rd/rd4.htm. Misbehaving students may be:

1. Bored.
2. Testing rules.
3. Asserting independence.
4. Seeking attention.
5. Misunderstanding teachers' expectations.
6. Emulating the behaviors of others.
7. Repeating behavior that was rewarded in the past.
8. Seeking peer approval.

These commonsense reasons for student misbehavior are supported by a more in-depth study of the problem. The **Discipline Help** website at http://www.disciplinehelp.com/ identifies 117 misbehaviors and gives a psychological explanation of each behavior, its causes, and preventive or remedial practices. The list includes behaviors such as being angry, apathetic, rude, or disrespectful; talking incessantly; and being unprepared. The Discipline Help site may also be accessed through this book's website.

Locus of Control

One of the most fundamental principles to keep in mind is that when students choose to misbehave, regardless of their rationale or justification for the inappropriate behavior, they have what in counseling is known as a **locus of control** problem. Being angry does not mean that they have to act out in response to that anger; there is a choice that is made. People with an **internal locus of control** believe they control their own destiny: They tend to be convinced that their own ability and efforts determine the bulk of their life experiences. People with an **external locus of control** believe that their lives are determined primarily by sources outside themselves, like fate, chance, luck, circumstance, or powerful others. How each of us evolves into one of these two dispositions or inclinations and why we give in to our feelings on some occasions is the subject of numerous psychological theories. But, as explained in Topic 10, most psychologists generally agree that one develops an internal locus of control by constantly facing challenges that require one to assert self-control and "stretch" oneself; by being encouraged to take up challenges; and by being supported emotionally by loved ones, parents, coaches, moderators, teachers, and others as one progresses through life's challenges (see Bowker et al., 2000; Manger, Eikeland, & Asbjornsen, 2002).

Students with an external locus of control fail to control their behavior in the classroom and, for that matter, in most of their interactions with their world. In addition, although they may have the intellectual capacity to achieve academically, they are failing in some or all school subjects because they also struggle to control their concentration or focus on schoolwork. Some students did not succeed in taking on challenges in their childhood, and the onset of adolescence makes matters worse. In these cases, the reservoir of experience and the internal locus of control are insufficient to overcome the new, more adultlike challenges. For this reason, sometimes formerly successful children lose their internal locus of control in adolescence.

Conflict

Classrooms place students and the teacher in an environment where the parties may have different agendas. Because adolescents are seeking autonomy, they have a heightened interest in achieving their own objectives and will have difficulty putting themselves in "your shoes," arguably the first step in resolving conflicts.

Teacher's Tip

If you have made a mistake or doubt your original assessment of a student's behavior that produced an infraction of your classroom rules, you need to be willing to apologize and undo the harm. Apologizing, when you are wrong, builds credibility.

Types of Conflict

Misbehavior is the symptom of conflict. Conflict emerges between teachers and their students because of differences in interpersonal styles, concepts, goals, and approaches to classroom processes.

Interpersonal style conflict is largely addressed in the earlier Topics on temperament (Topic 7) and communication (Topic 9). By being attentive to temperamental differences, teachers can often prevent interpersonal conflict from reaching a disconcerting point. However, it should be noted that interpersonal conflict is not based on a rational disagreement, such as over goals, concepts, or processes. Interpersonal conflict is the most difficult to resolve because it may be seated in temperament. Sometimes the only solution for a teacher is to negotiate a common ground whereby the teacher and student agree to minimize the aggravation for the good of the class and their individual goals.

By **conflict over concepts**, I am not referring to academic questions like whether evolution is true or what makes a "good" president, because these kinds of academic questions are excellent sources of motivation during instruction. Rather, with conceptual conflict a student has a fundamental philosophical or ethical difference with a teacher about the rightness, wrongness, or acceptability of a task, punishment, or decision the teacher has made. As an example, when a punishment is imposed on a student, the student may believe that it's unreasonable or even that the teacher is "picking on" him or her. The resolution of such differences is challenging because both the teacher and the student have different conceptions of the issue. The teacher's credibility is in question with other students if he or she changes the punishment because of the student's aggressive response, and it's in question with the punished student if the teacher does not alter the punishment. Often the best recourse is to provide examples of comparable incidents and punishments and clarify the facts or circumstances in a nonthreatening, conversational manner. But such conflicts can be minimized, if not prevented, if students perceive you as a fair-minded, reasonable, and evenhanded person—that is, if you have built up credibility by your former actions.

Conflict over goals arises out of the student's inclination to avoid delayed gratification and short-term suffering (review Topic 10 on motivation). Goals like reading a short story for homework, authoring a term paper, and creating a science project can create immediate challenges to a student's plans, but conflict can be minimized if teachers are realistic about their assignments, carefully think them through, and introduce them to students in a way that allows for student input and adequate time to complete the task. Teachers must stick to their goal, but they can minimize conflict by articulating numerous rationales for that goal, at least one of which may be sufficient for the student to adopt the goal.

Conflict over process encompasses conflict over classroom rules and academic assignments and is often the easiest to resolve because the teacher and student don't have the same degree of commitment in a process as in a goal or concept. Both parties, but particularly the teacher (who initiates the agenda), should accept that processes are meant to change with new circumstances and information. Although classroom rules and their applications, as well as classroom assignments, need to be clearly articulated, based on good reasons, and discussed openly, the teacher should be open to modifications and options that students propose to achieve the same goals. In fact, a proactive approach of asking students for suggestions on modifications that might make the process easier builds credibility.

Teacher's Tip

Take some time during the first week of class to teach appropriate behavior, just as you would content. Go to ERIC online and look up ED444089, *Improving Student Behavior by Teaching Social Skills, by Cone et al., 2000,* for approaches.

Teacher's Tip

Teenagers are infamous for shifting the burden of their problems to teachers. Barbara Coloroso (1995) recommends that when middle school students come to you and say something like "I left my homework at home," you say, "You've got a problem, and you need a solution." Let them sit down and figure out three options for your consideration, and then you tell which, if any, you will accept. Don't say, "Oh, that's terrible, what can I do to help you?" because that promotes irresponsibility.

Topic 15: **Student Behavior and Effective Learning Environments**

It is crucial for the teacher to keep in mind that conflict over assignments, homework, and learning activities creates opportunities and justifications for misbehaviors, particularly when the teacher has poorly conceived or executed those tasks. These internal reasons for misbehaving may be just as powerful as reasons external to the class. Often teachers do not recognize that their behavior is the source of student misbehavior and that they could have prevented the problem with more forethought.

Approaches to Student Behaviors

There are a number of theoretical models of classroom management to choose from when looking for general principles about discipline or specific tactics. The **Assertive Discipline Model** (Canter & Canter, 2001) and Richard Curwin and Allen Mendler's **Discipline with Dignity** model (at http://www.discipline associates.com/dwd.htm), Harry Wong's work (at http://www.harrywong.com/), Barbara Coloroso's approach (at http://www.kidsareworthit.com/), and Edmund Emmer's work (2002) all offer very practical approaches to classroom management from which you can develop your own approaches. All of these practitioners have something to offer. The Reality Therapy Model, which is widely accepted, is suggested here as a philosophical foundation for your approach to student discipline.

Reality Therapy Model

William Glasser's (1997) **Reality Therapy Model** at http://www.wglasser.com/ is presented here because it offers the psychological and philosophical construct that it is a teacher's duty to help the student make good choices, which in turn results in good behavior. If you start with this premise and the following principles, you will likely select Strategies that produce positive results.

1. Behavior is a choice. Students make choices, and unacceptable behavior is a bad choice.
2. Good choices produce good behavior, and bad choices produce bad behavior.
3. Misbehavior should always be followed with appropriate consequences.
4. Teachers who care about their students accept no excuses for unacceptable behavior.
5. Teachers should establish rules and review classroom procedures.
6. The teacher should stress personal responsibility.
7. The teacher should emphasize that students are in school to study and learn.
8. The teacher should have students make judgments about their misbehavior and require them to suggest suitable alternatives.
9. The teacher should stress the concept of "duty" to classmates as a reason to affirmatively work to make class a good experience.

Best Practices for Student Discipline

Teachers should assume that conflicts are resolvable by reasonable people and that it is their job to initiate actions to manage the resolution of conflicts. Vigilant teachers spot problems early and become more attentive to students on an emotional level by:

1. Engaging students informally and talking with them about the problem.
2. Explaining their academic understanding of the problem to students (often this is the first time students have been appealed to as autonomous persons).

3. Asking what students think about the problem and helping them sift through the options.
4. Encouraging students to believe they REALLY DO have choices.
5. Suggesting more self-awareness.
6. Helping students see long-term advantages and consequences.

SCHOLARSHIP ON STUDENT DISCIPLINE

Assignment 15.1

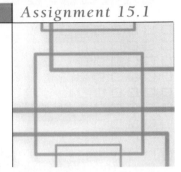

INTASC STANDARDS 2, 3, 5–7, 10

At this book's website, listed under Assignment 15.1 in Topic 15, there are over fifteen online ERIC documents published since 2000 that provide insights related to topics that will affect your classroom management. Your professor will provide details about how each topic will be assigned, but you should be prepared to author teacher's tips similar to those in this book that summarize key ideas and show how they should guide your thinking or actions as a teacher. Be prepared to turn the assignment into your professor and share your tips with the class.

OnLine Resources

Check this textbook's website at http://education.college.hmco.com/students for online links that are periodically updated to reflect new resources as they become available.

Classroom Management

Classroom management is the term used to refer to how teachers promote productive behaviors and diminish unproductive behaviors in classrooms. It is a leadership skill that some teachers come to easily. For others, leading a class of 30 fourteen- to eighteen-year-olds may be a far greater challenge than they anticipated. Classroom management requires having a philosophy, confidence, street smarts, mental toughness, a sense of humor, preparation, and, at times, acting skills—abilities that are not easily learned during a teacher education program.

Your leadership style evolves out of your disposition, and your decisions on Strategies evolve out of a set of beliefs about your duty as a teacher. There are numerous philosophies that you can draw upon for your approach to classroom management. The **Assertive Discipline model** has been developed by Lee and Marlene Canter (2001) and is presented here as an example of a perspective that is widely accepted. It proposes the following principles as the basis for a teacher's practices:

1. Teachers have the right and obligation to determine what is best for students.
2. Teachers have the right and obligation to expect compliance.
3. Students cannot be allowed to prevent teachers from teaching, or other students from learning.
4. Students must be informed of expected appropriate behaviors and the consequences should they fail.
5. Teachers must assert their leadership to ensure that these goals are met.

The Assertive Discipline model informs students of the "right" kind of behavior described in Topic 15 (see Glasser, 1997), for which they are then held responsible.

Attributes of Successful Classroom Managers

I am always struck by the different personalities, ages, cultures, and genders of the teachers I perceive as high-performing teachers **AND** how they all have something that is extremely difficult to define.

Teachers who have "IT"

Some teachers have a natural **presence** that seems to create an emotional attachment with the students and allows students to conclude that this is a person worthy of respect and cooperation. Students are able to spot "**IT**" (this vibe or presence) in these teachers even though it is sometimes camouflaged by age differences, organizational demands to take on a certain role or façade, physical appearance, and idiosyncrasies. I suspect you earn "**IT**," rather than get "**IT**," by passing through the cycle of challenges described in Topic 10. These teachers seem to have few classroom management problems and are not "pushovers," undemanding teachers, or easy graders. It is hard to tell if they started out their careers with this gift, but for most teachers, classroom management techniques are essential to managing student discipline (Jones & Jones, 2001) and can carry them through even if they don't "have IT"—or until they "get IT."

Students respond to teachers' management efforts on the basis of four kinds of teacher power (Levin & Nolan, 2000).

1. **Referent power.** Students like the teacher on a personal level because the teacher is able to communicate caring and empathy.
2. **Expert power.** Students view the teacher as knowledgeable in his or her subject field and therefore as someone who can help them learn.
3. **Legitimate power.** Students see the teacher as an authority figure who has authority and power.
4. **Reward/coercive power.** Because the teacher uses rewards and punishments in a consistent way, students see the connection between behaviors and consequences.

> *During your observations in classrooms, which kind of power do you find most dominant? How do you think students will perceive you?*

Kounin (1970), in his classic book on discipline, identified five teacher attributes that prevent and minimize problems that might require disciplinary interventions. Because of these attributes, students accept the teacher's leadership based on referent and expert power, the two power bases that facilitate student self-motivation.

Five Attributes of Effective Classroom Managers

1. **"Withitness."** Students sense that you know what is going on in their world, the school, and the classroom.
2. **Momentum.** Students sense a pace of instruction and clear direction.
3. **Alertness.** Students sense that you are keeping track of their behaviors and involving them.
4. **Multitasking or Overlapping.** Students see you attending to control, content, and time simultaneously with ease.
5. **Stimulation.** You provide students with seatwork opportunities to practice (see Topic 34) that are challenging and full of variety.

Low-Control and High-Control Teachers

Novice teachers can acquire the attributes listed in the previous section, but to do so they need to attend to the communication process and planning (Landau & Gathercoal, 2000). Teachers with different temperaments and approaches can succeed even when taking different approaches to managing students. **Low-Control Teachers** plan less, are more flexible, diverge from planned tasks, and are perceived as more outgoing and personable; **High-Control Teachers** plan more, are more structured, are more driven to complete tasks, and are perceived as more reserved (Turanli & Yldrim, 1999). While you may tend toward one inclination over the other, the following analysis points out the importance of having a repertoire of strategies that will allow you to achieve a mean between the two ends of the spectrum. Two analyses may be helpful.

Teacher's Tip

As a new teacher, your age provides a connection to the students' world that is not available for older teachers. Use it! I recently referred to Seinfeld in a college class, only to realize that most students were not that familiar with him or the show. By the time this book is published, my new Chris Rock reference may be dated as well.

Analysis A

High-control teachers tend to eliminate misbehavior by eliminating ambiguity: they plan instruction in detail and pace the instruction to keep everyone on task. They can give very detailed, structured (and potentially too long) explanations that cause boredom in some students but are appreciated by students who recognize the effort put into the lesson as a sign of caring and professionalism. Low-control teachers manage potential misbehavior by walking around the room, stopping and engaging students in questions and answers as they go, and keeping individuals on task who are known to be easily distracted by friendly communication. They are appreciated by students who understand that the individual attentiveness, in spite of the stop-and-start nature of the instruction, is a sign of caring. To be most effective, teachers should strive to use both Strategies.

Analysis B

Low-control teachers' tendency to diverge from less structured Instructional Sequences and tasks creates opportunities for disruptions, but high-control teachers' tendency to avoid off-task friendly interactions diminishes personal affinity and results in disruptions. Starting class with a brief, friendly conversation and then sticking to tasks is a good practice.

> **Do you think you are inclined to be a low- or high-control teacher? Which of Kounin's five attributes do you think will be most difficult for you to acquire?**

Teacher's Tip

You will spend 75 percent of your time motivating and managing 10 percent of your students.

For the Reflective Practitioner

> *The time has come for someone to put his foot down. And that foot is me.*
>
> DEAN VERNON WORMER FROM THE FILM *ANIMAL HOUSE*

Classroom Management Practices

Engineering your classroom practices to create a classroom environment free of behavior problems is obviously the best strategy. The term *classroom engineering* connotes plans and structures that are relatively imperceptible to the student. In a well-engineered transportation intersection, the red light doesn't last too long, one turn lane (not two) is just enough to do the job, trees don't block visibility, and the lights and roadway are maintained: things you don't notice until the light breaks, traffic dramatically increases, or there is a pothole. To engineer your classroom, the same level of thought, detail, and planning that you use to prepare your lessons should be brought to bear on your **classroom management practices.**

The following practices are drawn from recommendations by Canter, Glasser, and others (see Curwin & Mendler, 1988; Logan, 2003; Mendler, 1992), as well as from practical experience, to create a coherent Framework of best practices that can lead to your success as a classroom engineer.

Best Practice 1: Manage Your Time in Class

When I was fifteen, I took a job as a YMCA summer day camp counselor, which was my first experience in a "teaching role." At the orientation of the ten counselors who were sitting at a picnic table, the camp director, a school principal earning a little extra money during the summer, asked with great enthusiasm, "What's the purpose of day camp?" Responding with equal enthusiasm, I said, "Fun!" He responded, "No!" After we all had a good laugh, he elaborated, saying, "The reason why parents send their kids to us is so that we can send them home tired!" He then went on to explain that we can ensure both a fun time for the kids and meet their parents' goal, but only if we are organized and keep things moving at a very fast pace. He told us that we would move students quickly between each activity by jogging from one activity to the next; that each activity was to be well planned and organized with all the equipment waiting; that the start-up time had to be short; that counselors were to participate as well as supervise the activities and keep them on time; and that all students would participate in all activities—in short, NO DOWN TIME! Next, he handed out a nonstop schedule of baseball, soccer, volleyball, swimming, lunch, crafts, kickball, tag, red rover, and so on.

This story makes a most important point about classroom management: If you have meaningful, engaging, and active lessons with discussions, questions, examples, exhibits, and tasks prepared and ready to fill up every minute of every class, every day, the students will not have the time or desire to create classroom management problems. This being said, there are a number of additional practices and ideas that can serve as a guide through those moments when, in spite of your best efforts, you do have a management problem.

Best Practice 2: Establish a Set of Clear Privileges and Expectations

It is important to distinguish between classroom privileges, rules, and expectations (Queen et al., 1997). **Privileges** are not earned: Students get them just by being part of the class. Instead of "rules," talk to students about **expectations**. Privileges should be announced and planned just like your expectations, but they can be withdrawn if they are abused.

Privileges

The following are some privileges you may want to consider and announce to your students.

1. Students can decide where to sit (you might want to start that after the first two weeks).
2. Students can individually negotiate modifications to assignments.
3. Students who maintain A averages have the option to not turn in homework.
4. Students can suggest modifications to expectations.
5. In some group activities, students can choose their partners.

Can you suggest some more privileges?

Classroom Expectations

Your classroom expectations and consequences (often called "classroom rules" in the literature) should be approached like content; that is, they need to be taught and reviewed—particularly at the start of the year or semester—so that everyone is working from the same page (see Topic 18 for suggestions for the first day of class). Barbara Coloroso (2002) recommends the following first four classroom rules as the minimum. I suggest two more:

1. Show up on time.
2. Be prepared for the day's work.
3. Do all assignments on time and as required.
4. Respect others and their belongings and space.
5. Be attentive in class.
6. Ask questions when in doubt.

Students and parents should be given a copy of the expectations at the first class meeting if they are not mailed home before the start of classes.

Best Practice 3: Give Rewards and Enforce Consequences Equitably, Promptly, and Consistently

There are a number of models for consequences and interventions; Table 16.1 provides some examples. What the various models have in common is that the consequence escalates in severity (there is a hierarchy) based on the seriousness and frequency of the undesirable behavior (see Emmer, Evertson, & Worsham, 2003). I would be remiss not to provide you with this kind of list, but I would be equally remiss if I did not stress that it is better to inspire students by interacting with them and serving as a role model than to give out praise or interventions (see Topic 8).

Best Practice 4: Maintain Students' Dignity

Don't back students into a corner. Communicate your concerns about their behavior in a way that they can find a solution and positively respond with new behaviors (Curwin & Mendler, 1988; Mendler, 1992). Remember that your

Table 16.1 | **SAMPLE INTERVENTIONS AND CONSEQUENCES**

Level of Significance	Affirmations of Improved Behavior	Nonaffirming Intervention or Consequence for Misbehavior
Minor	Smile. Praise student. Give cheery note.	Make eye contact. Stop until you have student's attention and have student state the standard that was broken. Exert proximity control. Change seats. Conference with student after school. Confiscate forbidden objects or schoolwork not on task.
Moderate	Post good work. Give a positive note to student. Give student special privileges.	Require letter of apology to the teacher. Require student to stay after school. Withdraw privileges. Send note home to parents. Prohibit student from going to recess. Have student write proposals to change behavior.
Extensive	Phone parents or send them a positive note.	Have student describe occurrence and write plan for remediation. Call parents. Conference with parents. Draw up a Behavior Improvement Contract. Refer student to principal's office. Exclude student from special class event (e.g., field trip). Institute in-school detention. Institute after-school detention.

Source: Adapted from Emmer, Evertson, and Worsham (2003).

goal is to change their behavior, if not their minds, not to create another problem for them. Two ideas worth considering are the following:

- Avoid disciplining students in front of their peers. If nonverbal and casual verbal cues do not change the student, simply ask the student to meet you after class and discuss the problem at that time.
- Avoid invading a student's space. Nonverbal and mild verbal reprimands can be given from across the classroom, but more poignant reprimands should be given from 3 to 5 feet, but not closer.

Best Practice 5: Ignore Irrelevant Behaviors

You don't have the time to take on every kind of minor school and classroom infraction or aggravation. That is why it is important to have just a few expectations and concentrate on those and enforce them; and even those should have their limits. As an example, one standard is to come prepared for class. So if you see a student borrowing a pencil (because he or she is not prepared), purposely ignore it (see Good & Brophy, 2000). If it happens two days in a row, mention it to the student on the way out of class. If you adopt this kind of approach and consistently follow it for any student who forgets a pencil or makes a similar infraction, you will be treating students equitably.

Best Practice 6: Minimize Referrals to Detention or the Principal's Office

Different schools have different policies regarding **referrals,** or sending a student to the principal's office or detention. One thing is for sure: Excessive referrals tell the administration something negative about you or about the effectiveness of your classroom management plan. Therefore, keep referrals to a minimum (see, McGinnis, 1995). In one study, teachers who had the lowest referral rates ALSO were brief in their corrections of misbehavior, called misbehavior to a student's attention more frequently, used more nonverbal approaches (such as silently looking at a student), and did not threaten to punish (Roy, 1998).

Teacher's Tip

A key question to ask your colleagues before the school year begins is how many referrals they had the previous year. Their answers can serve as a gauge for how you are doing. You might also find another teacher from whom you can seek advice.

Best Practice 7: Use Effective Classroom Engineering Strategies

Disruptions and confusion arising out of poorly engineered course expectations increase the potential for misbehavior. Process decisions related to the collection of homework, entry and egress from your classroom, hall passes, assignments handed in late, how students who are absent are expected to find out what they missed and need to do, and so on—if not engineered to minimize aggravation—can be disruptive or at best take away from instructional time (Kariuki & Davis, 2000). The following examples of effective management practices should be helpful:

1. In between every class, stand in the doorway and greet the students as they come in, and make it clear that they don't leave class until you are standing at the door.
2. Have three milk crates on a table in the back of the room. One crate is the *Absent Crate* for leftover handouts and assignments for each day of the week. Students are told that, if they are absent, when they return to class they should check the box for materials distributed while they were absent; they should also be told that they have three days to turn in the missed work, for example. The *Homework Crate* is where students turn in their homework and pick up homework. The third crate is the *Journal Crate:* If you require journals, that is where students retrieve the journals and return them after the next entry is made.

3. Some schools require students to keep a **Planner** in which they note deadlines and assignments. Periodically checking the planner and making comments and notes is an effective way to communicate with students and have a record. Many schools also use it for hall passes.

4. Require that each student has one, if not two, **Homework Buddies** by the end of the first class. Students who miss class or have a question should contact their homework buddy, not you.

5. Use a **Seating Chart.** This can eliminate calling the role so that you have more time for instruction.

6. Institute **Questions of the Day.** Require students to hand in a written question about a procedure or content, and you respond to these at the beginning of class. By requiring students to write the questions, you help them be deliberate and thoughtful.

7. At the beginning of class, play classical music as students enter, take their seats, and begin their bell work. Do the same as a cue for leaving. It has a calming effect.

8. Announce homework assignments at the beginning of class and have them written on the board. Homework quickly explained at the end of class causes confusion and minimizes its importance.

9. At the end of class, have students pull together their books and materials, but leave a little time to spare. Once everything is put away, ask, "What did we learn today?" and lead a brief review; then remind students about the upcoming assignment by asking a student to explain it for everyone else.

 Can you add some additional ideas based on your experiences as a middle or high school student or your early field experiences?

Best Practices for Every Day

The following practices should be helpful to teachers who need to think through the subtle and not-so-subtle implications of their verbal and nonverbal communications. Every time you are trying to persuade a student to "do the right thing," all the other students are observing you and making judgments about your character. Therefore:

1. Overprepare and have engaging lessons.
2. Wait for a noise reduction and then quietly gain attention when beginning class.
3. Randomly call on all students to keep all students involved in the class.
4. When observing a discipline problem, be deliberate: Stop, look, listen, think, and act.
5. Use **proximity control** (walking by or standing next to disruptive or inattentive students while you conduct the lesson) and circulate around the room as you teach to keep students on task and attentive.
6. Use nonverbal clues: Stop, look, and frown to redirect behavior.
7. Use consequences only when verbal appeals to "right action," nonverbal warnings, and verbal warnings have failed.
8. Change to a firmer tone of voice when dealing with misbehavior, but never yell.
9. Combine warnings with having the student restate the standard.
10. Combine consequences with having the student restate the standard.
11. Follow through with mandated conferences or punishments.

12. Praise students who change behavior favorably, saying, "I appreciate your having stopped talking for the rest of the class; you must be very pleased with yourself."
13. Apply warnings and punishments equitably, allowing no exceptions.
14. Do nothing if you don't know what to do.
15. Admit if you made a mistake and correct it.
16. Have a quiet word with misbehaving students to appeal to their sense of duty and community.
17. Focus on what you want, not on what you don't want. "I want you to . . . " is better than "I want you to stop . . . "
18. Don't spend a long time dealing with a student; correct the misbehavior and immediately return to teaching.
19. Don't get mad, overreact, threaten, taunt, ridicule, or make idle threats.
20. Don't insist on public apologies.
21. Don't physically handle students.
22. Don't show favoritism.
23. Don't nag.
24. Don't argue with a student.
25. Never punish a group, only individuals.

Classroom Space and Organization

One of the most fundamental classroom management questions facing a teacher is how to use classroom space and resources to create a climate focused on learning (Lang, 2002).

Seating Selection

The decision as to whether students are assigned seats or choose their own seats has implications for student conduct because it deals with human territoriality and freedom of association, which for some teenagers are a significant part of their drive for autonomy. Which seats students select or that you assign them also affects learning. Students feel more relaxed if they can choose their seats based on a personal preference like a social relationship (Dykman & Reis, 1979; Totusek & Staton-Spicer, 1982) or their planned level of participation, and disrupting this feeling by assigning seats can cause a great deal of enmity in the classroom.

Teacher's Tip
Seating charts are wise because they cut down on the time taken by calling role and help you learn your students' names more quickly.

There is significant evidence that students in the back rows and to the sides participate less than those in the front and middle seats, the **"action zone."** The action zone is an area of high participation and interaction (Adams & Biddle, 1970; Delefes & Jackson, 1972; Schwebel & Cherlin, 1972). Research has linked seating positions in the action zone to higher student achievement, and high achievers prefer the center seats in a classroom (Wulf, 1977). Teachers also perceive students in the action zone more favorably (Daly & Suite, 1981).

In light of these considerations, teachers must weigh elective seating against their obligation to involve all students and their duty to encourage students to take responsibility for their own learning. Many teachers resolve this issue by starting out the year with assigned seats (often alphabetical) and a seating chart so that they get to know the students. After a few weeks, some teachers allow students to choose their seats as a classroom privilege, and others reassign seats every month to encourage greater socialization between status groups and to put students in the action zone on a regular basis. Regardless of the strategy you select, you need to make a special effort to engage all the students by paying particular attention to those on the perimeter of the classroom.

Seating Arrangements

The most traditional and common seating arrangement—students in rows of desks facing the teacher—is successful because it enables the teacher to effectively observe and communicate with individual students during the class (Rosenfeld & Civikly, 1976). However, how these desks are arranged has various effects.

Because your methods will change during class, your classroom seating arrangements should also change. For the most part, teachers use the desks-in-rows organization because it facilitates using videotapes, audiotapes, transparencies, or Internet resources along with lectures and tasks. This is often called **theater seating** or **traditional seating** (see Figure 16.1 for diagrams of each of the seating arrangements). **Modified theater seating** is more effective because you can more easily see students' faces (and eyes). In this type of seating the desks in one row are offset so they are not directly behind the desks in the row in front of them. In **round table seating,** the seats are arranged in a circular fashion around the perimeter of the room and facing a center point; the desks are offset as in the modified theater approach. Round table seating is best suited for whole-class discussions. **Group seating** usually involves having groups of four or five desks arranged in circular fashion and is used to support small-group work or discussion. **Half-circle seating** is best suited for guest speakers, demonstrations, and role-playing. **Desk Tops Together** is often used when students are working in pairs or foursomes; their desks are lined up front-to-front.

The primary goal of changing the seating arrangement is to use physical arrangements to focus students' attention. Students are also stimulated by the changes, and they get to physically move the furniture. The reorganization breaks up the monotony of class, and students develop a sense of responsibility for THEIR learning environment. It is a good idea to go through this little bit of disruption to reorganize seating based on the kind of instruction that is planned.

Teacher's Tip

Even though you may be lecturing, don't picture yourself in the front of the class. Move around the room and lecture and lead discussions from various locations.

Key Research Findings on Classroom Seating

The following is a summary of the key research on group interactions based on seating arrangements (Bonus & Riordan, 1998; Leavitt, 1951; McCrosky & McVetta, 1978; Ridling, 1994; Schofield & Sagar, 1977; Sommer, 1977).

1. Different seating arrangements affect students' efficiency, errors, comfort level, and degree of satisfaction.
2. Students can feel peripheral or unimportant with some seating arrangements and locations.
3. In round table and half-circle arrangements, the students closest to the middle participate the most.
4. In the theater seating arrangement, students in the front rows and those seated in the middle of the rows participate the most.
5. Gender and "race" are major factors in voluntary seating; students tend to sit with someone of the same gender and same "race."
6. Students prefer theater seating for required courses and half-circle arrangements for electives.
7. "Time on Task" increases when the seating arrangements match the kind of instruction.
8. Unobstructed eye contact has a major impact on participation.

Figure 16.1 | **SEATING ARRANGEMENTS**

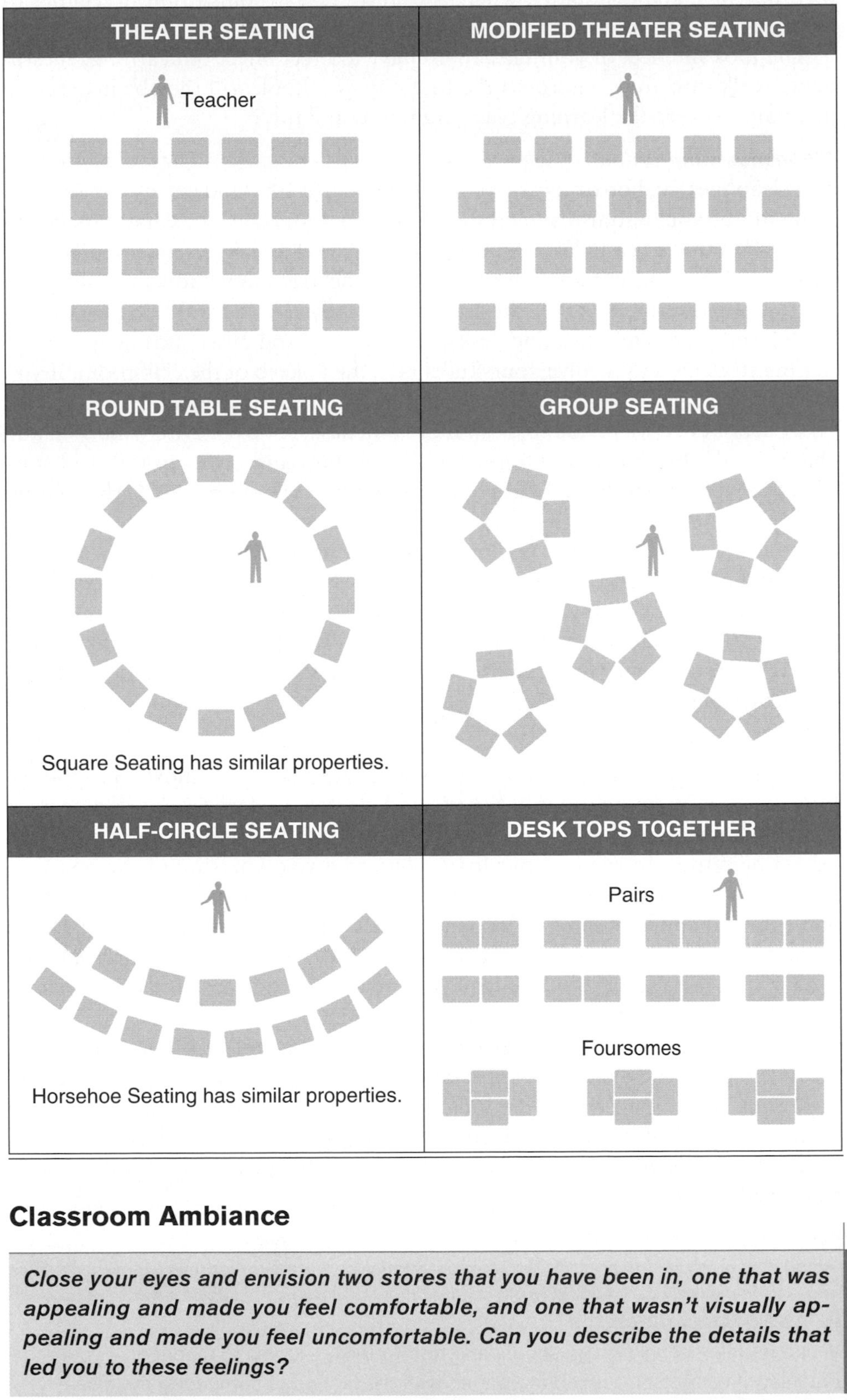

THEATER SEATING	MODIFIED THEATER SEATING

Teacher

ROUND TABLE SEATING	GROUP SEATING

Square Seating has similar properties.

HALF-CIRCLE SEATING	DESK TOPS TOGETHER

Horsehoe Seating has similar properties.

Pairs

Foursomes

Classroom Ambiance

Close your eyes and envision two stores that you have been in, one that was appealing and made you feel comfortable, and one that wasn't visually appealing and made you feel uncomfortable. Can you describe the details that led you to these feelings?

In what is considered a classic study, Maslow and Mintz (1956) compared people's interactions in so-called "ugly" versus "beautiful" spaces. They found that beautiful spaces created more feelings of energy and well-being. In a similar

Topic 16: **Classroom Management**

way, classrooms that are ugly produce monotony, fatigue, headaches, discomfort, hostility, and irritability, whereas beautiful classrooms result in feelings of comfort, enjoyment, energy, and a desire to persist.

The look and feel of your classroom have a direct effect on learning. As students walk into your classroom the first day of school, will they be inspired to learn and to keep the learning place organized and tidy?

Cleanliness and Order

The cleanliness and orderliness of your classroom tell the students not only something about you, but also something about the importance of what happens in the classroom space and how important the students are. As schools tighten budgets, housekeeping services are often one of the areas most adversely affected. Even if housekeeping may clean the floor periodically, it would be rare to find the housekeeping crew cleaning desks, bookshelves, and other such items.

One strategy is to involve your students in the upkeep of the classroom. If you are teaching five classes, each class could be assigned, once every few weeks, to take part of the class period to clean the room, desks, bookshelves, windows, and chalkboards. Bring in spray bottles of disinfectant and paper towels and start cleaning with the students. During your cleanup, pitch old materials that clutter the room and reorganize materials while wiping them down. The loss of one class period will seem minor compared to the sense of belonging and cleanliness that everyone will sense and the spirit of teamwork everyone will experience.

In between classes, always put the desks back in neat rows, and if you notice some writing on a desk, wipe it clean. Students will be more respectful of their classroom if it is kept tidy, organized, and clean and they see you being attentive to the learning space.

Bulletin Boards

Attractive, meaningful bulletin boards are expected in most classrooms. However, maintaining bulletin boards and classroom decorations can become time-consuming, and as a novice teacher, you will have your hands full with lesson planning. To reduce your load, you can give ownership of the board to students by having them bring in materials for posting that they think are relevant. Assign pairs or teams of students to find materials on the Internet for an upcoming topic. Keep clutter down to a minimum and remove materials that look tattered. Many professional organizations and textbook companies provide materials for classroom walls and bulletin boards that can be very effective. Have some space for permanent items like a collection of pennants of local college teams, classroom expectations, and so on, as well as space for temporary items to support something like national science or history week. Although you will want to keep some things posted year-round, replace them with a new version or rearrange them to create change and to attract or reattract students to them.

Assignment 16.1	**CLASSROOM TOUR**

INTASC STANDARDS 1, 2, 4

Visit a middle school or high school and tour four classrooms of teachers in your teaching field. Author a two-page paper, with the first page comparing the classroom environments and the second page identifying how you plan to organize your own classroom based on the information in this Topic; include a list of displays for the walls or bulletin boards for your first day of class. Be prepared to turn in your assignment to the instructor and to share your ideas with the class.

Schoolwide Discipline Management

Your practices in your classroom are part of what needs to be a schoolwide effort to create an environment of civility, respect, and self-control. Your commitment to fulfilling schoolwide expectations, even if you don't agree with some of them, conveys to students that teachers and students are part of a larger community.

Best Practices for Schoolwide Discipline

Kathleen Cotton's (1990) extensive review of the literature on schoolwide discipline concluded that the following elements are essential to creating an environment conducive to classroom learning:

1. Commitment and action on the part of all to establishing and requiring appropriate student behavior in and out of class.
2. Clear expectations, sanctions, and procedures that are widely disseminated and articulated.
3. A "warm" climate created by teachers and administrators taking genuine interest in students' personal goals, achievements, and problems.
4. The presence of a visible and supportive principal.
5. General agreement that teachers are responsible for and have authority to handle routine discipline problems and that the administration is responsible for serious infractions.
6. Punishments that are appropriate for the offense, perceived by the students as costly, and delivered with support like counseling, home follow-up, in-school suspension, and contingency contracts.

> ### Teacher's Tip
> There are innumerable classroom management practices you could follow. Solicit advice from the teachers in YOUR SCHOOL because they have developed practices that work in your school's unique environment. But remember that you are a new teacher and that their practices may work for them because their reputation precedes them, and they can draw on experience.

CLASSROOM EXPECTATIONS (OR RULES)   *Assignment 16.2*

INTASC STANDARDS 2, 3, 5, 6, 7, 9, 10

Interview a practicing teacher using the following questions.

1. What do you do the first hour of the first day of class to establish control?
2. What did you do your first year as opposed to what you do now?
3. What are your classroom privileges, expectations, and penalties? Can I have a copy?
4. How many times did you send a student to the principal's office last year?
5. Name three things that you definitely think a new teacher should do to establish classroom control.

Following the interview, create a handout for students and parents that includes an introductory paragraph and a list of your planned classroom privileges, expectations, and consequences. Be prepared to share your ideas with the class and submit this assignment to the professor.

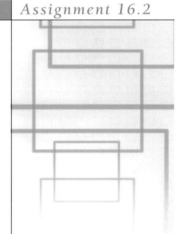

OnLine Resources	CLASSROOM MANAGEMENT
ProTeacher	Go to http://www.proteacher.com/ and look up *Discipline Plans*.
Honor Level System	Go to http://www.honorlevel.com/hls_intro.xml and look up *Discipline by Design*.
ERIC OnLine ED426985	*Good or Bad, What Teachers Expect from Students They Generally Get!* ERIC Digest, by Tauber, Robert T., 1998.

Check this textbook's website at http://education.college.hmco.com/students **for additional links.**

Home-School Relations

For some families, education is the focal point of their children's growth and development; some will hold this belief as a conceived value but not an operational value; and others will treat their children's education as an inconvenience. Regardless of the disposition of the parents (or caregivers), the teacher's duty is to forge the best possible positive relationship with the parents because the teenager's success will likely depend on it (Trumbull et al., 2001).

Parents become less involved with their children's schools as their children advance through the school system (Epstein 1984; Lucas & Lusthaus, 1978), and by high school there may be only 4 or 5 parents out of a possible 125 families to visit during parent-teacher conferences. This can be attributed, in part, to students' growing autonomy. However, stepfamilies and low-income, minority, and single-parent families have the lowest participation rates and therefore will require a special effort on your part to create the collaboration that can be crucial to a student's success (Dornbusch & Ritter, 1988; Freytag, 2001; Trumbull et al., 2001).

Teacher's Tip

Most parent operate on the principle that "No news is good news." One way to maintain positive relations with parents is to communicate good news as well as bad news.

Start the Year Off Right

Parent-teacher collaboration starts before the school year begins, and it is the teacher who must establish the foundation for the relationship (Moles, 2000). This is especially true for a new teacher because parents cannot get "the scoop" on you from other parents of previous students. Preferably, and even if it isn't your first year, you should consider sending a letter to the parents and students before the school year begins. In the letter, introduce yourself, give information about your background, and include a questionnaire for the parents and student to fill out and send back or bring to class on the first day (see Landsverk, 2000).

Assignment 17.1 | **LETTER TO PARENTS**

INTASC STANDARDS 3, 5, 7, 9, 10

Draft your introductory letter and questionnaire for parents that will be sent home at the beginning of school. Bring your letter and questionnaire to class for discussion and possible modification before it is turned in to your professor.

Open House

An **open house** or **back-to-school night** can give parents an opportunity to meet you, see your classroom, and find out what their teenager will learn by the end of the year. Long before the open house, either by mail or at the first class meeting, the student and family should receive detailed information on homework policies, class rules, and other matters.

Schools approach an open house event in different ways, and you need to organize your planned interactions during the open house to fit the required format. The following are suggestions based on the two most common approaches.

- Some schools expect you to be in your classroom for a three-hour period in the evening to informally meet with parents. Since you must be spontaneous and informal in this scenario, it is even more important to make handouts available about classroom management practices, homework policies, and other matters.
- Other schools have a modified class day schedule, with 15-minute periods in each class during which parents visit the classroom based on their student's schedule. In this scenario, you should have a short (5-minute) rehearsed statement about what the students will learn that year and then ask for questions.

Best Practices for an Open House

The following Strategies should help you prepare for open house events.

1. Weeks before the open house, start encouraging all students to have their parents attend.
2. Involve the students in planning and creating a special bulletin board to welcome parents.
3. Make sure the classroom is particularly neat and orderly.
4. Have copies of the packet you mailed to their home at the beginning of the year or that you gave to the students, and refer to it.
5. Prepare and rehearse your presentation.
6. End the question-and-answer session by thanking everyone for coming. Then walk into the seating area and begin introducing yourself to the parents, keeping the conversations brief and nonsubstantive about individual students; perhaps start with "And you are a parent of . . . ?"
7. Do not use this time for teacher-parent conferences. Ask parents who solicit individual information for their phone numbers, and call them the next weekend to talk about their questions or to arrange a meeting.

Parent-Teacher Conferences

Parent-teacher conferences can make even experienced teachers anxious, and with good reason, because they can be unpredictable. The key to successful conferences is preparation and a disposition that communicates that you and the parent are a team (Georgiady & Romano, 2002). Some schools have individual conferences after school or in the evening over a two- or three-day period. Some schools allow students to come to the conference; others prefer

Teacher's Tip

For the **open house,** have four or five important items of information on the chalkboard and have handouts for parents to take with them. Refer to both in your brief introduction and in response to questions.

Teacher's Tip

Your time and the parents' time are valuable. For your presentation at open house, be upbeat, start with a witticism, but leave out the personal history (they already know that from your letter) AND do not use the "we are going to have so much fun this year" approach. Parents want to know how their sons and daughters are going to learn, what they are going to learn, and what they need to do to help secure their children's success. Think of the event as an opportunity to sell yourself.

148

Teacher's Tip

Student-Run Conferences *are effective and encourage self-responsibility. Have each student prepare a portfolio of work for the scheduled parent-teacher conference. Expect that students will sit down with their parents and go over their prior work and grades and set two or three goals for the next grading period. You can host four or five families during one 20-minute time period while you circulate and respond to specific questions. For more on student-led conferences, see Hackmann (1997).*

Teacher's Tip

Consider buying a software package like Microsoft Works or Apple Works, both of which integrate a digital database and word processor. These are relatively inexpensive, and with them you can create a grade book and an address book. With the address book you can easily create Mail Merge documents so that each parent receives a personalized letter.

only parents. You should be prepared for parents who bring their son or daughter. In addition, be prepared to make adjustments for the myriad of unexpected possibilities.

Best Practices for Parent-Teacher Conferences

The following Strategies should help create a team approach in a parent-teacher conference.

1. Don't wait for conferences to start working with a parent if a student is struggling academically or behaviorally.
2. If possible, schedule parents in 20-minute intervals, unless you anticipate a particular problem, in which case allocate more time. If after 15 minutes you realize that more time is needed, schedule another meeting or a phone call. Whatever you do, stay on schedule.
3. Consider having parents complete a preconference survey to identify agenda items.
4. Have each student complete a self-assessment a few days before the conference.
5. When talking with a parent, make sure that no one can overhear the conversation. Reorganize the classroom so that there is a waiting area out of earshot for the next parent who is scheduled to see you.
6. Rise from your chair and greet each parent in a positive and upbeat manner.
7. Don't sit behind your desk; sit to the side, and place the parent's chair next to your chair.
8. Start the conference by asking the parent to share his or her assessment of how things are going and whether any particular topics need to be discussed.
9. Have a folder of each student's work, tests, grades, products, and homework.
10. Review each folder and prepare a set of notes on each student.
11. Be prepared to review selected items to demonstrate problems; parents want concrete information, not generalities.
12. Be prepared with three positive things to say about each student.
13. Be prepared to indicate three areas for remediation (academic or behavioral).
14. Be prepared to suggest specific remedies so that "WE can improve Johnny's performance": for example, daily reports from you, having parents check homework, or extra assignments for the student to do at home.
15. Conclude on a positive note and with a plan.
16. Make notes about the conference and about what was agreed upon.
17. If a parent becomes irritated or there is a disagreement, offer to reschedule and have a member of the administration join the next meeting.

 What special considerations and approaches do you think might be necessary to meet with parents who speak another language, who are deaf, or who have a gifted/talented or special education student?

OPEN HOUSE PRESENTATION

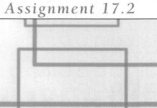

INTASC STANDARDS 3, 5, 7, 9, 10

Create an outline of an open house presentation to be turned in to your professor, and be prepared to share your ideas with the class. Be creative. For example, find a cartoon that parents can relate to that can be used as a transparency on the overhead projector.

OnLine Resources	HOME-SCHOOL RELATIONS
National Parent Teacher Association	http://www.pta.org/parentinvolvement/index.asp.
ERIC OnLine ED447961	*Reaching All Families: Creating Family-Friendly Schools. Beginning of the School Year Activities,* edited by Moles, Oliver C., 2000.
ERIC OnLine ED478537	*Positive Parent-Teacher Conferences,* Fastback 491, by Georgiady, Nicholas P, and Romano, Louis G., 2002.

Check this textbook's website at http://education.college.hmco.com/students **for additional links.**

Preparing for the First Day of Class

The transition from student to intern to first-year teacher is an exciting but demanding time because your transformation into a confident teacher is important to your initial success and that of your students. The following advice is intended to help you make the evolution smoothly.

Transition to Teaching

According to the National Education Association, over the next ten years America will need to hire more than 2.4 million teachers. The greatest teaching shortages will be in the southern parts of the United States and in special education, mathematics, science, computer science, English as a second language, and foreign languages (go to NEA's website at **http://www.nea.org/teachershortage/**). The months and weeks leading up to the all-important first day of class can be crucial, and they start with job hunting. The following brief advice is intended to help you get not only a teaching job but also a position in a school where there will be a great "fit."

Teacher's Tip

At this book's website under **Bonus Course Materials,** you will find templates for creating an **Employment Portfolio**.

Job Hunting

When job hunting, you should consider the following:

1. Your college probably offers guidance on resume writing (there are plenty of Internet sites and books on this topic) and placement services to assist you. Take advantage of these opportunities.
2. Although getting a job is your ultimate goal, it is important to approach the job hunt as a matching process between you and the school. You will not be a good fit for every school, and every school will not be a good fit for you.
3. Often students get their first job as a result of their internships. It may not necessarily be at the same school, but students who excel in their internship are often recommended through the informal grapevine for jobs within a school district.
4. Most school districts will require you to complete their formal application form. Be sure to attach a cover letter and your resume to put your best foot forward (see Close & Ramsey, 2000).

Interviewing

? **What and how should you learn about the school before your interview?**

Keep these points in mind about interviewing:

1. When called for an interview, be enthusiastic, but take the time to find out about the interview format. It is OK to ask, "Can you tell me a little bit about

the interview process and hiring timelines?" Typically, you will be invited to an interview with the department chair and assistant principal or principal. Hopefully, you will get to meet the other faculty, perhaps sit in on some classes and have a tour of the school.

2. Go to the Internet and find out about the school: its curriculum, students, extracurriculars, policies, and so on. In the current information age, you should be well informed about the school, its students, and your department for your interview.

3. Many school districts publish their fringe benefits and salary structures on the Internet, so unlike in the private sector, compensation is rarely negotiable and is public information.

4. Prior to the interview, go by the school when students are arriving or leaving and drive around the neighborhood. Such an experience can give you a much better understanding of the students and community.

5. For the interview itself, come with a portfolio and extra copies of your resume. Your portfolio should have, at a minimum, a statement of your teaching philosophy, resume, samples of lesson plans, and copies of awards.

6. Be prepared to interview with the principal or assistant principal and the chair, and perhaps you will have a group interview with faculty, so have some questions prepared.

7. Dress professionally.

8. A portfolio that you can share with your interviewers can be used to shape the conversation around what you can do for them and your approaches to teaching. However, it is most important to project that you have learned a lot but have a lot more to learn.

Can you develop a list of questions you would like to ask during an interview? What questions do you anticipate the administrators and faculty might ask?

Accepting the Job

When you receive a job offer, consider the following:

1. By the time you receive a phone call offering you a job, you should have decided whether you will accept the job. You shouldn't need to request additional time to decide; if you do ask for additional time to consider the offer, the person making the offer may conclude that you don't think it is as good a match as he or she thinks it is.

2. After the official offer, there will be the customary paperwork. When accepting the job, ask about whom you should contact and arrange to have those tasks taken care of.

From Job Offer to Official Orientation

There will probably be an official orientation at the district, school, or departmental level, but that won't take place until just before the fall term (assuming you are hired for fall).

1. Don't wait for the official orientation to start preparing. Call the person who hired you and ask him or her to give you the names of two teachers—one with several years of experience and one relatively new—that he or she thinks do a great job. Call them, take them to lunch (separately), and "pick their brains" (see Daresh, 2003). It is at this time, not during an interview, that you can ask many of the operational questions that are important to your transition.

2. Take your orientation seriously.
3. Overprepare for the first day of class.
4. Ask for copies of your textbooks and begin preparing your lesson plans.

First Day of Classes

The impact and importance of the first impression as you stand at the door greeting your students on the first day cannot be overstated. Just as crucial, your first words and body language as you stand in front of the classroom in your first class will set the tone for the year (Hayward, 2001).

An experienced teacher has a reputation that is passed on by word of mouth to students and their parents. When an experienced teacher has a reputation for being fair and friendly but no-nonsense and demanding, the students come into the class with a predisposition that will make classroom management easier. As a first-time teacher or teacher in a new school, you will not have the benefit of a reputation that precedes you. Thus, your communications to students and parents before the start of school and the impression you make on students during the first class are crucial.

The Strategy you use for the first hour of the first day has long been recognized as one of the most important preventive classroom management practices (Hudson, 2002; Waller, 1932). The teachers in your school can give you excellent advice on first-day Strategies, classroom expectations, and other matters (Moir, 2003). Effective teachers focus on classroom expectations their first class (Sanford & Evertson, 1985; Wilke, 2003). The following suggestions outline a first-day strategy that is effective for a novice teacher. Although it is specific, you can reflect on these suggestions and modify them to suit your personality.

1. Place a numbered list of class privileges on poster paper on the left side of the chalkboard.
2. On poster paper on the right side of the chalkboard place a list of your classroom expectations (rules) and consequences—no more than ten—and numbered.
3. On the board write, "Until everyone has arrived, please quietly read over the syllabus and list of privileges, expectations, and consequences that are on your desk. Thank you."
4. On each desk place a packet for students with a copy of the **Handout of Classroom Expectations** and **Syllabus**. Attach an end page with your academic honesty policy and a place for the student's signature and personal information; you will collect this last page.
5. On each desk place a tent card with a student's name (you are assigning seats for at least the beginning of the semester).
6. Stand at the door, with one foot in the hallway and one foot in the room. Shake hands with and introduce yourself to each student as he or she arrives. Make sure students cannot enter the room without meeting you. Spend no more than 30 seconds per student.
    a. Greet each student by shaking his or her hand (hold on to it firmly while you continue).

Teacher's Tip

A teacher can always move from a more "high-control" posture to a less rigid or disciplined posture, and it is easier to do so once you know the cast of characters. It is very difficult to create a more disciplined environment once you have lost control.

b. Ask his or her name.

c. Repeat the name, and say, "Welcome, Ms. Sunseri, to our classroom."

d. Add, "We are going to work really hard this year! I am looking forward to working with you!"

e. Point to the desk with the student's name card; ask the student to take his or her seat and quietly read the materials (Handout of Classroom Expectations and Syllabus) until all the students have arrived.

7. Stop and observe the students in class periodically, correcting attempts to talk or leave their desks.

8. Once all students have arrived, close the door.

9. Go over the Handout of Classroom Expectations. Cover each of the classroom privileges and expectations, referring to the posters on the wall. Call on the student who seems to be the least attentive and ask the student to read the first expectation.

10. Call on another student and ask, "Why is it a reasonable privilege or Standard?" Ask three or four students to give different reasons. Affirm each one, elaborate, and say, "Thank you."

11. Ask students for questions and comments after each privilege, Standard, and consequence is stated.

12. Go over the syllabus items one by one (see Parkes & Harris, 2002).

13. When you get to homework, tell the students that you also have a Standard for the teacher. As an example, explain to the students that they will have homework every Monday, Tuesday, Wednesday, and Thursday, and they will always receive feedback the next day after the due date. Call on a student to explain why homework is important. Ask three or four students to give different reasons. Call on a student to explain why giving feedback right away is important. Ask three or four students to give different reasons, affirm each reason, elaborate, and thank each student.

   At the end of this discussion, ask students if there are any modifications or additions to the expectations and privileges that they think would make the class go better. If you get a good idea, add it to the poster paper and tell them to add it to their documents.

14. Then give them a homework assignment due the next day and explain that your normal practice will be to give the homework assignments for the upcoming week on Friday so they will have more flexibility as to when they complete the tasks, regardless of when they must turn it in.

15. If there is any time remaining, teach something!

This approach is thoughtful, and it conveys a clear message about the importance of your students' duties and your duties as a teacher. In the following days and weeks it is essential to periodically review the expectations as a preventive measure and maintain consistency in applying them.

Teacher's Tip

Syllabi may not be required in your school, but it is a good idea to have one for each course. A syllabus, unlike the handout on classroom expectations (which would likely be the same for all your classes), details expectations for students in a particular course. It is similar to the syllabus you received in college.

How will you approach the second day? ?

Topic 18: **Preparing for the First Day of Class**

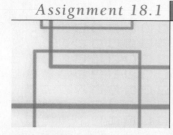

Assignment 18.1 | **CREATE A SYLLABUS**

INTASC STANDARDS 1–8

Contact a teacher in your discipline and ask the teacher to give you a copy of his or her syllabi for two different courses (for example, a biology and a chemistry course). Bring them to class and be prepared to work in a group to develop an outline for a syllabus that you would use and to evaluate how different teachers express their expectations and practices.

OnLine Resources	TRANSITION INTO TEACHING AND PREPARING FOR THE FIRST DAY OF CLASS
MiddleWeb	Go to http://www.middleweb.com/1stDResources.html and find *The First Days of School*.
ERIC OnLine ED467618	*The First Day of Class: Establishing Rapport as Well as Ground Rules,* by Hudson, Larry, 2002.
ERIC OnLine ED436487	*Beginning Teacher Induction,* ERIC Digest, by Weiss, Eileen Mary, and Weiss, Stephen Gary, 1999.

Check this textbook's website at http://education.college.hmco.com/students **for additional links.**

Planning Efficient Instruction

Planning what you intend to teach does not have to be complicated, but it does require a great deal of thought, organization, inspiration, and judgment. At first, planning to teach two or three "preparations" can seem overwhelming. There are so many ways to teach and so much content. The purpose of this Topic is to simplify the process for a new teacher with the expectation that as you mature into your role as an instructor, you will adopt planning processes that best fit your disposition and the needs of your students.

The Importance of Planning to a New Teacher

Planning requires setting priorities. Because of the various new Standards movements, you will likely be expected to define knowledge in terms of state Standards (see Unit 8). Your school may require detailed daily, weekly, monthly, semester, and yearlong planning as part of a formal monitoring and evaluation process for a new teacher.

There are two primary schools of thought about planning. Alternative 1 is deciding what the student is to know based on Standards, selecting the Strategies by which the students will learn, and deciding on the assessment. Alternative 2 is deciding what the student is to know based on Standards, designing the assessment, and selecting the strategies by which the students will learn.

Which do you prefer? Why? Do you think they are both equally effective? **?**

Planning is crucial for a novice teacher because plans:

1. Define the Big Ideas, Procedural Knowledge, Information Knowledge, tasks, strategies, and the sequence of events.
2. Require you to think through what you plan to do and have your students do, which becomes your plan of choreographed instruction.
3. Act as a road map that will keep you headed in the right direction.
4. Structure the development, selection, and organization of all your materials to support your choreographed instruction.
5. Ensure that the instructional time is meaningful, productive, and rigorous and that the teacher has made the best use of the limited amount of time spent with the students.
6. Integrate assessment into the instruction as seamlessly as possible.
7. Focus assessment on providing remediation, rather than grades.

Teacher's Tip
You can always have too much planned, but classroom management problems start when teachers underplan and find themselves without meaningful experiences for the students in the afternoon.

For the Reflective Practitioner

> *In 1999, the typical U.S. school year was 180 days long. The average in Germany was 240 and in Japan, 243. The actual number of full teaching days is far less than 180 in American schools because of special events, interruptions, and canceled school days.*
>
> U.S. NEWS ONLINE AT
> http://www.usnews.com/usnews/

Teacher's Tip

Those unexpected, periodic detours that take you away from your planned trip can often lead to excellent learning experiences if used judiciously and are what are known in the literature as "Teachable Moments."

Instructional Efficiency

As a professional, you decide how to teach and how much time to allocate to each topic in each course based on your best assessment of your students' abilities and the tasks needed for them to master the Basic Skills and Procedural and Information Knowledge dictated by your state's Standards. Accurately gauging and planning the amount of time and number of days it will take to complete a lesson is difficult at best. For that reason, it is wise to start planning by thinking in terms of taking as much time as needed for students to gain the knowledge you plan for them to learn. Lesson planning should begin after asking the question, "How do I want them to think differently at the end of the lesson?" Your lesson should then be structured to produce that result (Bearman et al., 2003).

Because the time you have to teach is limited, whether you have block scheduling or 50-minute classes, you need to be efficient during your class period (Leonard, 2001). It is easy to lose 15 minutes in the beginning of each class, stray from your class notes with unnecessary information, or allow distractions to take you off course. One of the key planning decisions that affects efficiency is determining (a) what should be "covered" in class and (b) what knowledge or tasks should be allocated to homework to create a baseline of information (see Topic 34). Once this decision is made, the efficient use of the instructional time becomes paramount and will depend on your planning skills, your classroom management skills, your instructional delivery skills, and your approach to classroom organization (seating arrangements and the aesthetics of the room) (WestEd, 2001). The physical space of the classroom, combined with how the teacher's and students' communications flow through the space, is often referred to as the "ecology" of the classroom (Shulman, 1986). With every planning decision you make, you create your own classroom ecology.

> **?** When individual students are released from your class for band, student government, athletics, or a trip to a district debating competition, you will need some creative Strategies to avoid multiple makeup tests and to ensure that all students are getting the knowledge. How do you plan to manage these kinds of approved absences?

Instructional time is the time allocated to whole-class presentations and various kinds of seatwork (see Guided and Individual Practice in Topic 20). Most current models of instructional time stem from Carroll's (1963) seminal work defining the major variables related to school learning. Carroll believed that time is the most important variable in school learning and stated that instructional time should be based on the time actually needed to learn the content.

Time on Task refers to the proportion of instructional time that INDIVIDUAL students are ACTIVELY engaged with learning. Students who are high achievers are reported to be engaged for 75 percent of the time or more, whereas low achievers are engaged less than 50 percent of the time (Everston, 1980; Frederick, 1977). Keeping high achievers on task and raising the participation levels of low achievers requires attentive communication and engaging lessons that are incrementally staged so that students feel they are succeeding.

A shortcoming of Carroll's early model is it fails to consider the influence of external factors like the family, media, and community on learning time. As a result, individuals like Proctor (1984), Cruickshank (1986), Gage and Berliner (1998), and Huitt (1995) have refined Carroll's model, and all support the belief that "Academic Learning Time" is the best predictor of academic success (Zimmerman, 2001).

Academic Learning Time

Academic Learning Time (ALT) is the amount of time students are SUCCESS-FULLY involved in the learning of content that WILL BE TESTED (Huitt, 1995). This excludes housekeeping and transitions like time spent socializing, daydreaming, engaging in antisocial behavior, and "dead time" due to poor teacher planning or delivery of the lesson (Anderson, 1981). ALT is a combination of three separate variables:

1. *Content Overlap* (Brady et al., 1977) is the percentage of the content covered on the test that is actually covered by students in the classroom; it is sometimes referred to as "time on target."
2. *Involvement* is the amount of time students are actively involved in the learning process (see Topic 21) and is the aforementioned Time on Task or Engaged Time.
3. *Success* is the extent to which students accurately complete the task they have been given.

These three components should be considered the "vital signs" of an effective and efficient classroom. In short, a high level of ALT means that (1) students are covering important content that will be tested; (2) students are "on task" most of the class period; and (3) students are successful on most of the assignments they complete. Student variables over which teachers have little or no influence, like home or community environment, attendance, and the length of the school year, can adversely affect ALT (Caldwell, Huitt, & Graeber, 1982). However, the variables that teachers do have control over, like selection of the knowledge to be taught, planning, Instructional Sequence, choreography, classroom organization, and ambiance, can definitely promote high-ALT classrooms.

Types of Lesson Plans

Expectations for the amount and detail of lesson planning vary greatly among schools and districts. Planning requires progressing from yearlong plans to semester (multiple months and weeks) plans to daily lesson plans for each one of your preparations (see Figure 19.1).

There are many kinds of lesson plan formats, and you should eventually create a format that best meets your needs. At this book's website under Bonus Course Materials, you can download a template for a Topic Lesson Plan, and Class Notes in an MSWord file format to use with this textbook, as well as a sample of each based on the U.S. history topic "The Lewis and Clark Expedition." These materials can be useful to you as a new teacher until you settle on your own preferred formats. They can also be used in Unit 8's authentic lesson planning assignments. The MSWord Calendar Wizard can be used to create your semester- and year-long plan, and an example is provided in the Bonus Course Materials.

Figure 19.1 | **LESSON PLANNING**

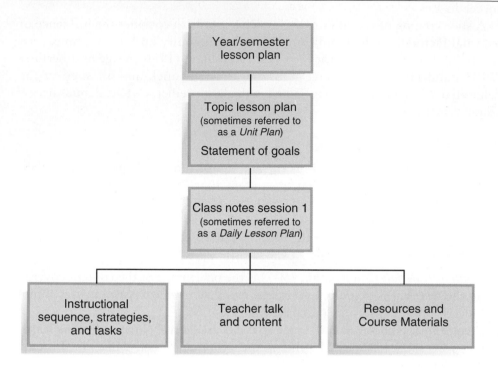

The Planning Process

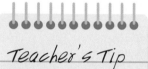
Planning a lesson is a creative endeavor that combines pedagogical knowledge with Information and Procedural Knowledge to engage students and forge new thinking on their part. There are a number of questions that you need to answer as you think about a topic that you might teach, whether it is the associative property in mathematics, the French revolution in history, or a work of poetry in English.

Key Planning Questions for the Teacher

1. What is the goal or standard? You begin by considering state or national Standards, but then you should also think about how you plan to assess the students (see Unit 7).
2. Do I have the background knowledge to teach this topic? If not, where and how can I get up to speed, fast? Today, your best resource will often be the Internet.
3. How much time am I going to have to commit to learning the content to teach it well? What resources are available to teach it well? Are there resources for the students so that this can be an active learning experience?
4. What is the Big Idea in the topic?
5. Is there Procedural Knowledge that can be the focus of the lesson? If not, are there Basic Skills that could be the focus? Are there both?
6. How can I make the topic relevant to students' lives?
7. How much time will I give to my instruction and practice (the application of concepts)?
8. What tasks can I have them complete to ensure that they reconstruct the knowledge?

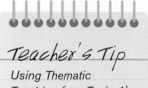

9. What instructional approaches should I use to ensure that I am accommodating individual differences among the students and using a variety of methods?
10. Will this change the way students think in the future (create a new Academic Disposition)?

Can you think of some additional questions you should ask?

The Seven-Step Lesson Planning Process

The following process model should be helpful to a first-year teacher. However, the planning process in not as linear as it appears in the following sequence: It is more interactive and divergent. For example, resources change as goals change, and goals change as you discover more resources; or you may initially think you will lecture but then change to a group activity.

Macro Planning: Year-, Semester-, and Weeklong Plans

1. *Identify the state Standards* for your course.
2. *Evaluate* the basal textbook, the publisher's ancillary materials, and other resources (like the Internet) for both background knowledge for your personal benefit and materials that you could use in class, such as graphic organizers, didactic materials, readings, primary documents, simulations, sample lesson plans, and so on.
3. *Draft a year-, semester-, and weeklong plan* (see Bonus Course Materials, Employment Portfolio Templates) based on topics you will cover to achieve the state Standards on a weekly basis. For a novice teacher, the textbook is a valuable asset because it defines the broad topics and the usual sequence of the content.

Micro Planning: Topic and Class Note Plans

4. *Conceptualize* the Big Ideas, identify Procedural and Information Knowledge related to the state Standards, and identify the basic skills and Academic Disposition that can be developed using the Information Knowledge you will teach.
5. *Identify and collect your SPECIFIC resources*, such as articles from the Internet, the textbook's ancillary materials, manipulatives, and laboratory materials. The availability of resources over the Internet has dramatically changed this step of lesson planning. Prior to the World Wide Web, material for lesson plans was limited primarily to ideas from colleagues at your school and your publisher's ancillary materials that accompanied the textbook. Now, with the kinds of lesson plans available at GEM at http://www.thegateway.org/, for example, teachers no longer have to start by conceptualizing their topic but can use field-tested lesson plans as their starting point and modify them.
6. *Create a Topic Lesson Plan,* which consists of two major components: (a) a *Statement of Goals* for the entire topic or unit and (b) *Class Notes* for each class session or period. In Topic 13, Assignment 13.1, you downloaded a PDF copy of a chapter from a basal textbook. In many cases, you would typically BASE a lesson on the topic of a chapter or unit of your textbook, which is very different from teaching the textbook. For the purposes of this textbook, a Unit Lesson Plan and a Topic Lesson Plan are synonymous. For example, a Topic Lesson Plan for a history course would be to teach the American Revolution, and for a biology course, cell division; then, depending on how

Teacher's Tip

A lesson plan from the Internet or ancillary materials should rarely, if ever, be used as is with your students. Such plans provide great ideas and resources, but they need to be modified to meet the unique needs of your students, your state or district Standards, and your style of teaching.

many class sessions you intend to dedicate to the topic, you would create Class Notes (your daily lesson plan script and materials) for each session or class period.

    a. *The Statement of Goals* would include the following for the ENTIRE plan (that is, all the class sessions):

- **Topic Lesson Plan Title** (often the same as the topic)
- **Resources**
- **Big Idea(s)**
- **Standards** (national if not state). Some professors and school districts prefer that teachers write behavioral objectives rather than goals or include behavioral objectives in the Class Notes. See Unit 8 for your teaching field's Standards.
- **Basic Skills Development**
- **Information Knowledge**
- **Procedural Knowledge**
- The **Academic Disposition** you want the students to acquire during or as an outcome of the lesson.
- **Assessment.** Decide how you will know they have learned what you have taught; that is, what the forms of Evaluation will be.

    b. **Class Notes** (see Topic 20). It is wise to complete one set of notes for each day to help you as realistically as possible distribute the lesson plan's content and tasks over the class periods (the lesson may end up taking more than one class period). The Class Notes are based on the Statement of Goals for the lesson and are sequentially organized. They link together what you will say, what the students will do, and the resources you will use by drawing on the following components of the **Instructional Sequence** (see Topic 20):

- Bell Work
- Homework Due
- Attention-Getter
- Statement of Objectives for the day
- Review
- Content Presentation(s)
- Guided Practice(s)
- Independent Practice(s) or Homework(s)
- Evaluation(s)

As you develop your thinking about the attention-getter, content presentations, practice sessions, homework assignments, and evaluations, you draw upon your pedagogical knowledge to employ a variety of methods and strategies (see Units 5 and 6) that appeal to different temperaments and that accommodate diversity.

7. Prepare the materials (graphic organizers, supplemental readings, visual images, handouts, didactic materials, quizzes, rubrics, etc.) needed to choreograph the lesson.

The lesson may take longer or shorter than you planned; this is not unusual for even experienced teachers. You should always overprepare and plan on doing the lesson "right" even if it takes a long time—but within reason!

Resources for Lesson Planning

As a novice teacher, you will not have a wealth of materials or plans from previous years to draw upon like experienced teachers. During your first year, you would be wise to find a colleague who will share resources and ideas with you.

The Internet resources identified in this book can also help make your transition into teaching easier than it was for those who came before you. Gathering information and sharing Strategies used to require staying after school, visiting libraries, or attending special training sessions. With the Internet and home connection, teachers finally have convenient access to information that can improve the quality of their teaching. For each new year, your goal should be to redevelop or replace about 20 percent of your lessons. Your students' achievement and enthusiasm will indicate which plans need replacement.

Many schools provide teachers with a copy of the students' textbook, a teacher's edition of the textbook, and the related ancillary materials (transparencies, CDs, worksheets, hand-held devices, etc.). Regrettably, many teachers believe that they should teach the textbook as is, or they plan their instruction based solely on the publisher-provided material or ideas. Others resort to teaching the textbook because the task of developing lesson plans for each preparation is daunting. But lesson plans on the Internet and publishers' lesson plans need to be recrafted to meet your goals, school-mandated expectations, state Standards, and the needs and abilities of the students. The textbook will, one hopes, provide an accurate and well-conceived presentation of content that can be used to develop Big Ideas and Procedural Knowledge. But do not assume that textbooks will provide all the materials necessary to meet your goals.

LESSON PLAN STATEMENT OF GOALS: EXAMPLE AND TEMPLATE	*Assignment 19.1*

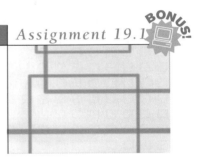

INTASC STANDARDS 1–8

Go to this book's website **Bonus Course Materials** and print out a copy of the Topic Lesson Plan Statement of Goals for a lesson on the Lewis and Clark Expedition and the Word template for the Lesson Plan Statement of Goals, and bring both to class. Be prepared to discuss how you would prepare a statement of goals for the lesson plan topic and basal text content you were assigned in Topic 13.

OnLine Resources	INSTRUCTION AND EFFICIENCY
The Institute of Learning Centered Instruction	http://www.learnercentereded.org/new/models.htm.
ERIC OnLine EJ617005	*Managing Each Minute*, by Clough, Michael P., Smasal, Randal J., and Clough, Douglas R., 2000. Discusses increasing students' time on task.
ERIC OnLine EJ619584	*Quantity Matters: Annual Instructional Time in an Urban School System*, by Smith, BetsAnn, 2000.

Check this textbook's website at http://education.college.hmco.com/students **for additional links.**

The Choreography of Daily Instruction

This topic provides an in-depth look at the choreography of daily instruction by explaining:

1. The typical components of the **Instructional Sequence**, the sequential steps of instruction that would be taken during a typical class session.

2. **Class Notes** as a strategy for organizing the lesson into a written format that a teacher would use as a script in the classroom.

Instructional Sequence

A number of psychological and practitioner-developed approaches provide a basis for the following best practices for the Instructional Sequence.

- Madeline Hunter (1982) identified key components of the instructional process that are intended to ensure **"mastery"** by students: This structured approach to the sequence and content of an effective lesson is typically referred to in the literature as **target** or **clinical teaching.**

- The pattern is often used as an organizer for the **direct instruction method,** although direct instruction is most associated with teaching skills, not content. Educators have converted Dr. Hunter's theories into a seven-step or, sometimes, ten-step direct instruction process usually referred to as the **Madeline Hunter Method** (Goldberg, 2000).

- The **Nine Events of Instruction** by psychologist Robert Gagne (Gagne, Briggs, & Wagner, 1992; Richey, 2000) has similarities to the Hunter method.

- Merrill's (2002) **First Principles of Instruction** proposes four phases to the instructional process: (1) activation of prior experience, (2) demonstration of skills, (3) application of skills, and (4) integration of these skills into real-world activities.

- The **concept attainment method** based on the work of psychologist Jerome Bruner (1960 and 1990) has a sequence similar to Hunter's direct instruction method.

- A **constructivist model** has been proposed by George Gagnon and Michelle Collay (2001). The terminology is substantially different from that of the previous models, but the concepts and steps are similar.

These five models have a number of components in common. For simplicity's sake, only the Hunter and Gagne approaches are presented in more detail here. Figure 20.1 presents the Strategies of these two approaches. The sequence shown

Figure 20.1 | **INSTRUCTIONAL SEQUENCE MODEL**

Madeline Hunter's Direct Instruction Method	Robert Gagne's Nine Events of Instruction
Anticipatory Set	**Gaining Attention**

Show an image, picture, map, or chart.
Begin with question: "What do you think . . . ?"
Show a video clip, etc.

Objectives or Purpose	**Informing Learner of Objective**

Explain lesson objectives.
Describe what students will learn.
Provide written objectives.
Demonstrate the actual performance that is expected, etc.

Review	**Stimulating Recall of Prior Learning**

Pretest for existing skills or knowledge.
Use graphic organizers to show current conceptions and misconceptions about topic.
Dialogue with students about prerequisite knowledge and skills, etc.

Content Presentation (CP)	**Presenting Stimulus**

Present the Information and Procedural Knowledge through a variety of methods:

Simulation	Problem Solving
Group Activity	Decision Making
Lecture	Cooperative Learning
Reading	Projects
Case Study, etc.	

(Since many lessons will have multiple CPs, the content can be subdivided into smaller and incremental segments.)

	Providing Learner Guidance

Model the skill or knowledge.
Describe or present a prototype product.

Checking for Understanding (CU)	**(See providing feedback, below)**

Ask questions.
Circulate among groups to give feedback.
Organize peer critiques.
Suggest alternatives.
Ask "what if?" questions.
(This kind of feedback is typically interspersed with the CPs.)

Guided Practice (GP)	**Eliciting Performance**

Students demonstrate skill or apply knowledge *during class,*
often in groups, with teacher guiding by assigning tasks.
Students create relevant graphic organizers, write essays, solve problems, calculate formulas, role-play, etc.

Figure 20.1 | **continued**

Independent Practice	
Students demonstrate skill or knowledge without assistance and independently, *frequently in a homework assignment.* Students create relevant graphic organizers, write essays, solve problems, calculate formulas, etc.	

	Providing Feedback
Ask questions. Circulate among groups to give feedback. Organize peer critiques. Suggest alternatives. Ask "what if?" questions.	

Evaluation	Assessing Performance
Observe students. Give traditional tests of new knowledge and skills. Use authentic assessment products. Students make presentations, etc.	

	Enhancing Retention and Transfer
Explain applications that generalize skill or knowledge. Summarize future applications. Identify next level of skills or knowledge.	

Missing from this Instructional Sequence model, but important to any planning, are homework, bell work, etc. (see text discussion of class notes).

in the figure underscores a basic principle in middle and high school education: It is not enough for a teacher to be able to demonstrate that something was taught; teachers are expected to have students demonstrate that they have learned the new knowledge. These models are presented here as a Framework for choreographing instruction using either direct or indirect instructional approaches. As an example, a teacher with multiple content presentations to deliver could use either lectures (direct instruction) or group activities (indirect instruction). "Content" as it is used in this Topic refers to what is being taught, so it could include Procedural and Information Knowledge as well as Basic Skills. Finally, an excellent way to start your career is to use the Madeline Hunter method with the anticipation that you will adopt various approaches as you mature as a teacher.

Gagne proposed that teachers should identify the **terminal objective** (what students should know at the end of the instruction) and the **intermediate objectives** (what students must know to reach the terminal objective), as well as the most logical way to proceed through the intermediate objectives, starting with factual representations. His **task analysis model** provides a strategy by which teachers can identify and order the objectives. This concept is supported by the model shown in Figure 20.1 and the Class Notes model discussed next.

Class Notes

A teacher's Class Notes are, as they say, "where the rubber meets the road." First and foremost, they constitute the teacher's choreographed script that he or she will use to move students through the Instructional Sequence. **Class Notes** are what you would have on your desk or in your hand as you move down the learning path. They should include:

1. What you will say (teacher talk) and do.
2. What you expect the students to do (tasks) and say.
3. All the teaching resources (images, supplemental readings, handouts, transparencies, etc.) identified that you need to teach the class; they should be part of the folder for the topic lesson.

The design of your Class Notes may vary, and you should develop one that meets your needs. The following format is suggested based on my years as a secondary teacher, and I still use it as a college professor. It is loosely based on the principles of the **Cornell Note-Taking System** (see Topic 27), a note-taking system for students. The **Duplass Class Notes System** is, in a sense, the mirror image of the Cornell system; it provides a format for incorporating and cataloging resources like websites and paper-based materials for future use using digital word-processing technology. The goal is to create a simple, straightforward document that you can refer to when you are teaching. After teaching the same course a number of years, you may not need as detailed a set of class notes as proposed here, but for a new teacher, the more detail the better. Another advantage of this format is that it helps you organize your materials. You can save your notes (particularly with embedded Web addresses) and teaching materials like handouts to your computer, and then improve upon your past lessons every time you teach them again.

With the instructional pattern providing a sequence, your Class Notes detail the choreography of the teacher talk, resources, and tasks into a plan that allows students to learn (see Figure 20.2).

Teacher's Tip

When you are a novice teacher, scripting your lesson reduces anxiety and increases the likelihood of success during your first weeks and months.

Figure 20.2 | **CHOREOGRAPHED INSTRUCTION**

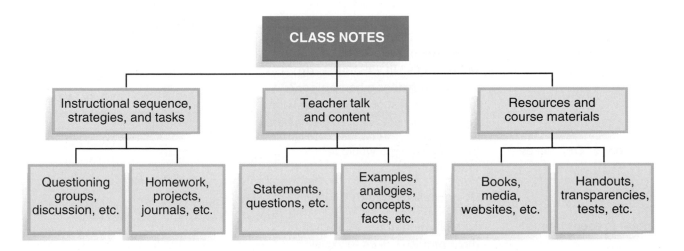

The example shown in Figure 20.3 is based on a mathematics lesson plan with the topic *Order of Operations*. This **annotated outline** includes some *examples of teacher's writing* that you can use as models to document your choreography of instruction in the authentic assignments planned in Units 5, 6, 7, and 8. For these assignments, as well as when you teach, the Class Notes would be more detailed than the example that appears in Figure 20.3.

Figure 20.3 | **CLASS NOTES SYSTEM**

Column 1: Instructional Sequence: Strategies and Tasks	Column 2: Teacher Talk and Content *Examples/Facts/Concepts/Big Ideas*	Column 3: Resources and Course Material *Texts, tests, handouts, transparencies, websites, etc.**
Under each of the **Instructional Sequence Headings,** *indicate directions to yourself, the methods you selected, and the tasks you will require of the students.*	*In this area write in key facts, concepts, Big Ideas, and things you will say that are related to the step.*	*In this area write in the name of a video, handout, test, Internet address, etc. (Use "OOO" for "order of operations" to identify documents related to the plan.)*
Day 1 of an x-day lesson		
Background Information		Background Web resource for teacher: http://www.mathgoodies.com/lessons/vol7/order_operations.html
Bell Work	Chalkboard display: **Each student write down one question about yesterday's lesson and leave it on the teacher's desk.**	
Homework Due		Rubric for homework from yesterday's lesson would be indicated here. *OOO homework rubric 1.doc*
Attention-Getter	**Have any of you worked in McDonald's? In what order do you put together a hamburger?** Indicate the rest of the dialogue with with key concepts and examples here.	
Statement of Objectives	Indicate what you would tell the students here.	
Review	Use questions from Bell Work.	
Content Presentation(s)	The following would be the first of three problems used to explain the concept for the first content presentation:	

Figure 20.3 | **continued**

Column 1: Instructional Sequence: Strategies and Tasks	Column 2: Teacher Talk and Content *Examples/Facts/Concepts/Big Ideas*	Column 3: Resources and Course Material *Texts, tests, handouts, transparencies, websites, etc.**
Day 1 of an x-day lesson		
Questioning	**Evaluate $3x^2 + 1$, when $x = 4$** $3x^2 + 1 = 3 \times 4^2 + 1$ $= 3 \times 16 + 1$ $= 48 + 1$ $= 49$	OOOProblems Transparency1.doc from page XX of the text.
Guided Practice(s) **Place in heterogeneous groups of four.**	Here would be the problems and answers for the guided practice, or you might indicate (at right) the Internet site for problem examples and a transparency you created with the problems answers.	Online game/examples: http://www.funbrain.com/algebra/ OOOGuidePractice1Answers.doc
Independent Practice	Here would be the problems and answers, or you might indicate (at right) the pages of the text or a transparency you created with the problems.	Problems 3–10, page XX OOOIndependent Practice1Answers.doc
Homework **Listed on chalkboard at beginning of class**	Due tomorrow, problems 14 and 15, page xx.	OOOhomeworkProblems Answers.doc
Assessment **Friday**		OOOquiz1.doc OOOquiz1answers.doc
Create a new set of Class Notes for day 2 of the topic lesson plan.		
Day 2		

*Because you will be saving tests, handouts, transparencies, etc., to your PC, you should develop a nomenclature using the folder and file system to keep your daily lessons and materials organized. As an example, create a folder entitled "Order of Operations" and then save files and list them in your class notes, such as *OOO Classnotes.doc*, *OOO guided practice.doc,* etc. It is also best to keep related items in each column on the same lines.

CLASS NOTES: EXAMPLE AND TEMPLATE   *Assignment 20.1*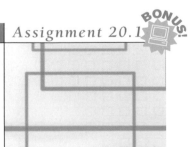

INTASC STANDARDS 1–8

Go to the **Bonus Course Materials** on this book's website and print out a copy of the Class Notes for a lesson on the Lewis and Clark expedition and the MSWord template for the Class Notes, and bring both to class. Be prepared to discuss how you would prepare Class Notes for the topic you were assigned in Topic 13, Assignment 13.1, using the mathematics and Lewis and Clark examples as models.

Instructional Sequence, Strategies and Tasks

Strategies are the instructional approaches and methods drawn from this text and the literature on instruction, in general. Tasks are what you want the students to do. They are written into the class notes in the sequence in which you will explain them during teacher talk. Tasks can be processes, like directions for students to move into certain kinds of groups, or products students are to produce, such as a timeline or a solution to a math problem (Doyle, 1992). Units 5, 6, and 7 provide several examples of tasks that would appear in Class Notes.

Teacher Talk and Content

Teacher Talk is also referred to in the literature as **instructional explanations, lesson talk, classroom talk,** and **scripts.** For the purposes of this book, **teacher talk** is the script: the planned and purposeful part of a teacher's verbal communication. It is intended to convey knowledge through a variety of verbal Strategies like explanation and questioning or to explain the tasks through which students will acquire or demonstrate their knowledge. It is YOUR script of what you will say to efficiently teach (see last section of this topic) and should be more detailed for a novice teacher than for an experienced teacher. It is not limited to what you will say, but what statements you anticipate from the students that are needed to move the lesson through the instructional sequence.

No matter how complicated we may try to make it, the craft of teaching basically involves choreographing teacher talk, reading materials, visuals and manipulatives, and tasks so that the student will internalize and then generalize content (Eisenhart et al., 1996). The teacher integrates his or her concepts and vocabulary with the text's equally important concepts and vocabulary. Prereading and postreading (see Topic 13), along with teacher talk and content presentations, provide the interactive and verbal process that should accompany a reading assignment of text and are essential to comprehension (Dole et al., 1991; Rinehart, Barksdale-Ladd, & Paterson, 1994). Unlike a static textbook read in isolation, teacher talk envelops the reading material with more examples and targeted emphasis. Teachers are viewed as redundant, if not boring, when they read or "teach the text" to students rather than creating a lesson to expand upon the text and to introduce analogies, explanations, and examples that differ from those given in the text (see Topic 27). Planned teacher talk and tasks should be linked to text (to reemphasize the point, "text" may also mean websites, multimedia presentations, primary documents, etc.) with in-class or homework reading assignments. Teacher talk is also adjustable based on, as an example, students' body language and questions during instruction.

Like a textbook, teacher talk benefits from a structured tier of Big Ideas. In textbooks, Big Ideas are often the headings for thematic sections and are shown in decreasing sizes and various typefaces (bold or italics, etc.); they thus provide a structure that supports the student reader. In class, the professor can use graphic organizers, outlines, and the logical structure of his or her lesson to provide a comparable "schema" or structure for the student to latch on to. And, like an actor, during instruction the teacher moves through the dialogue and improvises as he or she observes the students' reactions and interactions.

Resources and Course Materials

The **resources** may be background sources for you, but primarily column 3 will include **course materials** such as **videos, transparencies, "boardwork" (a layout of what you plan to write on the chalkboard), laboratory supplies, a document with a list of questions** (if not in the class notes themselves), and so on in the order of their appearance in the Instructional Sequence. **Texts** (reading materials) are primary resources for most instruction and should be integrated into the **Resources** column as well and in a number of ways:

1. To be read by students to create a **baseline of information** prior to instruction so that the teacher can use classroom time to develop ideas.
2. To be read by students for a second opinion, if you will, on the topic, since the text's examples, analogies, and arguments may appeal more to some students than the teacher's construction of the knowledge.
3. As a tool to teach reading skills in the discipline and to reinforce the structure of the domain, so that students can be lifelong, autonomous learners.
4. As a source of problems, tasks, projects, and resources.
5. As a review of content.
6. As an example of one approach to teaching the content, which might be different from the approach the teacher prefers based on his or her personal pedagogical and domain knowledge.

The teacher talk, tasks, and resources should be choreographed to make the best use of the instructional time.

There would be variations in this class notes model based on the unique demands of the subject matter. As an example, for a history lesson on Lewis and Clark (see Bonus Course Materials), a history teacher would have a large number of facts like names, dates, places, and key concepts listed in column 2 and websites and primary documents listed in the third column. For a lesson on *Macbeth* in English, the teacher might list the reading strategy from Topic 13 in column 1, or a video of parts of the play along with a handout of the main characters in column 3, and a list of questions for the debriefing in column 2. For a science lab, the teacher would list the expected conclusions based on the observations in column 2 and the tasks to be listed on the board as the word document "Boardwork 1" in column 3 along with a list of the materials for the experiment. The variations are endless, but if carefully crafted the result is a very useful tool for planning and choreographing your instruction.

Teacher's Tip

The three phases of a reading strategy (see Topic 13) would be detailed in a Content Presentation in the Instructional Sequence.

OnLine Resources

Check this textbook's website at http://education.college.hmco.com/students for online links that are periodically updated to reflect new resources as they become available.

Instructional Approaches

Randy Glasbergen (www.glasbergen.com)

Active Learning Strategies

Because teaching is both science and art, there are many "right" ways to teach that are applicable to all the domains and disciplines. The purpose of the Topics in this Unit and the next Unit is to provide a repertoire of those universal Strategies that you should draw upon, along with the specific Strategies used in each domain or discipline (see Unit 8), when teaching middle and high school students. The terms *Strategies, Instructional Approaches,* and *Methods* are frequently used interchangeably in education literature. For the purposes of this text, Instructional Approaches and Methods are both types of Strategies. **Instructional Approaches** (the focus of this Unit) are, for the most part, fundamental or underlying Strategies; they include active learning, critical thinking, and so on. **Methods,** which are presented in Unit 6, are typically *procedures* (such as lectures and cooperative learning), *tactics* (such as the use of analogies), and *tools* (such as the Internet and graphic organizers).

The Purpose of Strategies

After you decide what to teach, you need to decide how you will teach it. Each teacher's unique personality can be an asset when using some Instructional Approaches, and a limitation when using others. A Strategy can be a dismal failure when used by one teacher with one set of students and a success when used by another teacher, even with the same students. Some teachers consistently use particular Strategies that reflect the way they like to learn. The selection of Strategies should be based on the students' needs and readiness, as well as on the teacher's strengths and weaknesses. Strategies are intended to:

1. Effectively deliver Information Knowledge.
2. Provide opportunities for students to develop their Procedural Knowledge.
3. Have students consider Big Ideas and adopt new beliefs.
4. Have students learn to apply their developing Academic Disposition.

Best Practices for Selecting Strategies

The pivotal question is, what Strategies work best? The problem is that because teaching is a craft, the variables are too amorphous and the outcomes not sufficiently precise for anyone to reach a definitive conclusion.

We do know that students remember more if they are required to generate the information, rather than being given it by the teacher (Slamecka & Graf, 1978). This kind of active learning requires students to be mentally engaged in what they are learning and generating connections, that is, practicing Active Learning. This is why all lessons must move beyond "Shallow Knowledge" (Willingham, 2003a, 2003b). We know that teachers need to focus on Big Ideas in order to lead students to Procedural Knowledge and an Academic Disposition, that is, an orientation toward constructing meaning out of knowledge.

While we may be certain about some principles of learning, questions such as the impact of homework and class size on learning are still debated: In these areas research and practical experience often conflict and research results may be less than objective. If you look long enough, you can find research that claims to demonstrate that the amount of homework does not have a significant effect on students' success. Such research typically asserts that the average improvement of an experimental group was not significantly different from that of the control group. Similar studies can be found suggesting that differences in class size don't matter, either. But studies claiming that smaller classes and more homework have no significant impact on learning defy our experience; we expect that students in a class of ten taught by a highly qualified professional will learn more than students in a class of twenty-five, and we expect that students who do homework will learn more than students who do not. In fact, both have a positive effect for most students (see Cooper, 2001; National Research Center on Education in the Inner Cities, 2000). In the studies that indicate no difference, the teacher with a class of ten students may not have changed his or her methods to suit the unique opportunities of a class of ten and the homework assignments were so poorly conceived that they didn't make a difference (see Topic 34).

Teachers should select their Strategies on the basis of both research findings and common sense, and on common sense if empirical data are lacking. The Topics in this Unit and the next provide Strategies based on theory, research, and common sense. When selecting your Strategies, consider the following:

1. Use multiple Strategies so that each student has the opportunity to develop the skills to learn in different ways.
2. Use Strategies that work for you and that you are comfortable with, but develop a repertoire of Strategies that appeal to all of your students.
3. Use Strategies that research and/or common sense indicate are most likely to succeed.
4. Do not reject a method if common sense and experience indicate that it works.
5. Design all lessons (instruction, reading assignments, practice, and tests) so that students can't avoid thinking about the Big Idea and the Procedural Knowledge.

For the Reflective Practitioner

There seems to be, among students and parents alike, a perception of education as something that is "done to" you, rather than "provided for" you.

ANONYMOUS QUOTE FROM TEACHER CITED IN BROWN (2004)

One of the first decisions made in the lesson planning process, once you have decided on what you will teach, is whether you will:

1. Organize the learning process so that you *directly teach* students what you want them to know (through lectures, teacher-led discussions, etc.);
2. Organize the instructional sequence so that the students *indirectly acquire* the knowledge more independently (through discovery learning, group activities, etc.); or
3. Use a combination of both.

The following discussion should provide a background for making this pedagogical decision.

? What is your favorite way of learning: lecture, discussion, group work, or other?

Active Versus Passive Learning

Regardless of the option you select from the above three choices, what is needed for instructional approaches to be effective is Active Learning. **Active Learning** occurs in a high-energy classroom of where students are seeking to understand through both direct and indirect instructional approaches (see Topic 23 for a definition of these approaches). Active Learning requires teachers to create instructional patterns that allow students to actively construct knowledge by listening carefully, conversing, and performing meaningful tasks. The students are engaged mentally, emotionally, and sometimes physically. The term *Active Learning* can be confusing because it is mistakenly used to refer to **Activities** (as in an **"activities-based classroom"**). But there are many activities, like having students complete worksheets, that require little if any Active Learning, only a passive find-and-record procedure. In addition, activities like having Chinese food as a culminating activity for a lesson on China may or may not have any significant knowledge associated with them, depending on the teacher's choices about content.

If you are over forty years of age, you probably were exposed to an education that was primarily passive. **Passive learning** is almost exclusively teacher-centered instruction, with students seated at their desks for most of the class and with memorization, note taking, recitation, and drill as the primary instructional methodology. Group learning was almost nonexistent prior to the 1960s, except in Montessori schools. Today's students, given the contemporary culture, would find a passive learning approach a challenge to their stamina, their prior experiences in elementary classrooms, and their expectations. At the secondary level, the extent to which students are actively engaged in a thinking process is the measure of whether they are "actively learning."

The Role of Passive Learning in Student Development

Learning the virtues of patience, diligence, and persistence; embracing multiple learning strategies; employing memorization skills; and practicing note taking are vital to students' long-term success, either in college or in the world of work. From the start of their education, students should come to understand that it is their responsibility to learn, regardless of the degree of boredom, the teacher's skill (or lack thereof), or support at home, and that not all learning will be entertaining. Not all learning can be fun, but it should all be meaningful. Creative teachers can make most learning engaging. We engage students when we require that they reconstruct the knowledge that they acquire.

At the middle school, high school, and college level, as well as in the workplace, efficiency dictates less pleasurable learning Strategies with less personal attention and more self-responsibility. As students progress through the school system, the burden for motivation and learning shifts more to them; this transfer of duty is an essential part of the maturation process required by the organized school system, as well as the workplace, and it should be a goal of every teacher.

Teacher's Tip

You can minimize passive learning and emphasize Active Learning by allocating many passive activities (reading, drill, and practice) to assigned homework and using the classroom for communal and Active Learning experiences.

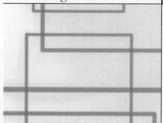

Assignment 21.1 **INTERNET SEARCH FOR IDEAS ON ACTIVE LEARNING**

INTASC STANDARDS 1–8

MiddleWeb.com at **http://www.middleweb.com/CurrStrategies.html** has an extensive listing of links that cover various aspects of teaching Strategies. Investigate one or two of the links and find two ideas that would allow you to create an Active Learning lesson for your students. Record the source and briefly summarize the ideas in a paper to be turned in to your professor, and be prepared to share your ideas with your classmates.

OnLine Resources

Check this textbook's website at http://education.college.hmco.com/students for online links that are periodically updated to reflect new resources as they become available.

Concept Formation

I n Topic 11, knowledge is organized in a hierarchical fashion, with ideas built upon generalizations that are composed of concepts and facts, in order to provide a Framework for organizing your thinking about what to teach. So, in economics we would define supply/demand theory as a concept, but the price of $25,000 for a car as a fact. However, the word *concept* as used in **"concept formation"** (also referred to as **concept attainment** in the literature) also means the process of turning what we hear and see in a classroom into **conceptualizations** within our mind's eye. That is what Piaget described as schemas (see Topic 6). So, in this construct, concept formation involves the students creating an understanding of both individual facts, concepts, and generalizations and the overall relationships among them from the most accepted formulation of the idea from the domain or discipline. All of these forms of knowledge become *conceptualizations*, the "airy" thoughts lodged in our psyches. Teachers use various Strategies to transfer their conceptualizations to students.

Is the organization of the objects in Figure 22.1 satisfactory to you? Why or why not? How would you prefer to CONCEPTUALIZE these objects?

Figure 22.1 | **CONCEPT OBJECTS**

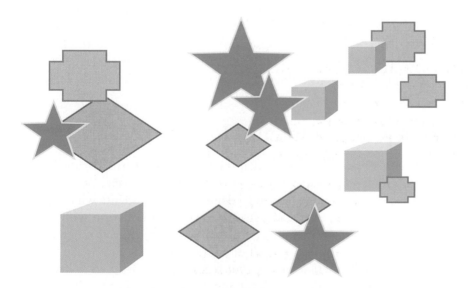

Source: Adapted *from Bernoff (1992): figure presented in a training session on how to teach critical thinking by Professor Robert Bernoff of Penn State University.*

Developing Students' Conceptualizations

We often forget what learning looks like through the eyes of novices in our domains and disciplines, and we make poor assumptions about what potential apprentices, nonapprentices, and apprentices actually know. Teachers' conceptualizations about their body of knowledge are far more complex than students' and therefore must be presented in increments of complexity for students' benefit. Teachers first introduce "foreign" information to their students and then help students make sense of it. As you are presenting your conceptualizations of knowledge, the student will either:

1. Acquire the knowledge by:
    a. Taking it into existing **schemas** (refer to Topic 6);
    b. Taking it into newly formed schemas; or
    c. Using **rote memorization** (putting it into temporary storage); **or the student will:**
2. Fail to successfully acquire the knowledge because:
    a. The existing schemas are inadequate;
    b. The teacher has given insufficient clues to place the information into the right context;
    c. The student used inadequate or incorrect schemas and thus distorted the message; or
    d. The student was not actively engaged mentally.

Revising one's **conceptions** is not just a matter of adopting the teacher's more sophisticated conceptualizations, but rather of evaluating, reorganizing, and integrating existing and new conceptions (diSessa, 1993; Duit, 1999; Posner et al., 1982; Schnotz, Vosniado, & Carretero, 1999). Essential to this process is **Metacognition** (Livingston, 2003), what Flavell (1976) defined as "one's knowledge about one's own cognitive processes and products. . . . Metacognition refers, among other things, to active monitoring and consequent regulation and orchestration of these processes in relation to cognitive processes and data on which they bear, usually in the service of some concrete goal or objective" (p. 232).

It is through metacognition that students change or **mediate** their preinstruction conceptions and modify newly acquired conceptions (Beeth, 1998; Hennessey, 1999). When students are not encouraged, prodded, or required to think about their thinking and to produce models of their conceptions, they remain reliant on their preinstruction conceptions (White & Gunstone, 1989; Yuruk, Ozdemir, & Beeth, 2003).

The Concept Attainment Model

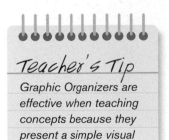

When using the concept attainment model, the teacher must initially decide on the appropriate conceptualization the students should adopt. With direct instruction, often a graphic image is used to depict for the students what knowledge is and how it should be organized. It is followed by discussion with examples and then an application. In indirect instruction, often the teacher has in mind the equivalent of the graphic image but does not share it with students and instead creates an instructional sequence that forces the students to collectively or independently create what they think the most accurate conceptualization is. Then the teacher debriefs the conceptualization of the knowledge that the students have formed (for an example of an indirect learning assignment, see Assignment 11.3).

Whether it is through direct or indirect instruction, the process of having students develop their conceptualization involves, implicitly or explicitly, defining the terms that make up the knowledge and the relationships among them.

Definitions of Terms

Students must have a command of the terms (see Topic 12 on the importance of vocabulary) to conceptualize the knowledge because a baseline of information is needed for the teacher to build upon in the classroom. Students can learn the meaning of terms by memorizing definitions, intuitively concluding what the definition is as a result of a reading assignment, reviewing the terms in class as part of pre- or postreading instructional strategy, getting the terms during a content presentation by the teacher, and/or using the terms during practice. For example, after reading the British classics about William Tell, Robin Hood, and Sir Lancelot, a student would create a conceptualization for "heroic characters." After reading about Joan of Arc, the student would enlarge this conceptualization (schema) by adding (through assimilation) this "heroine" as a new *fact* and modifying the schema (through accommodation) to create two subsets of the *concept* "hero": "male heroes" and "female heroes." More experienced readers will have multiple conceptualizations of heroes based on changes in the depiction of heroes and heroines by culture and time. However, for conceptualizations to be accurate, both novice and expert readers would also need, as an example, a separate schema for villains.

As an instructional approach in concept formation, teachers should use the **Critical Attributes** Strategy. In this approach, the teacher creates an Instructional Sequence that focuses on the essential elements of a concept so that students do not form inaccurate concepts. As an example, the critical attributes of a peninsula are that it is a body of land surrounded by water on three sides. The **Comparable Entities** Strategy is a powerful method to facilitate the definition of concepts because it allows students to learn critical attributes and Information Knowledge about two entities at one time. For example, students could compare and contrast peninsulas and islands to learn their critical attributes.

What are the critical attributes of a hero?

Conceptual Relationships

The **mental maps** we create of knowledge are the conceptualizations. Graphic Organizers (see Topic 30) are depictions of either a student's or teacher's internal mental map based on his or her understanding of the domain or discipline. We create internal, personal conceptualizations of webs, flow charts, diagrams, timelines, and other visuals. One of the most familiar, a **Hierarchy Organizer,** will be used here to develop the importance of all mental maps to conceptualization.

You probably remember from your biology class that humans are classified as *Homo* for the Genus and *sapiens* for the Species. These classifications are derived from the work of the philosopher Aristotle and later the scientist Linnaeus in *Systema Naturae* (System of Nature), which was published in 1735.

For the Reflective Practitioner

All things must be examined, all must be winnowed and sifted without exception and without sparing anyone's sensibilities.

DENIS DIDEROT

Topic 22: **Concept Formation**

Figure 22.2 | **SYSTEM OF NATURE**

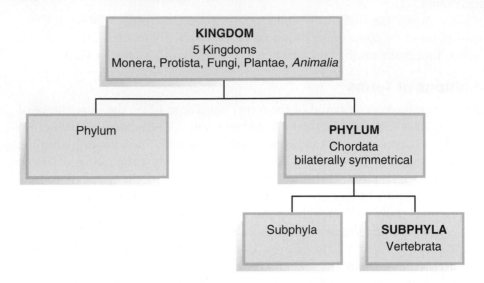

This twelve-level hierarchical classification system, starting with the five Kingdoms as the broadest categories and followed by Phylums and finally Genus and Species as the most specific classifications, is still used in biology to classify organisms, although it is not the only system. Figure 22.2 shows how this classification works on the kingdom Animalia as far as the subphylum level. As in Figure 22.2, when we teach we assist students in creating new schemas and placing facts and concepts in the correct location in a hierarchy.

In a hierarchy organizer, the relationship of a cell to other cells is defined as **superordinate, subordinate,** or **coordinate.** Superordinate ideas are higher than related subordinate ideas; the subordinate idea can be a subset of the superordinate idea, or a lesser idea because of a certain attribute. For example, in Figure 22.3 a governor has less authority than a president. Coordinate boxes represent equalities; mayors of two cities are an example. In Figure 22.3, the

Figure 22.3 | **HEADS OF GOVERNMENT**

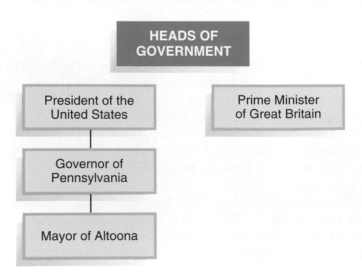

concept is "heads of government." The U.S. president is superordinate to the governor of Pennsylvania, and the mayor of Altoona is subordinate to the governor of Pennsylvania. Prime minister is coordinate to the president.

Definitions and their relationships are used to create a mental map that reflects a conceptualization. **Misconceptions** are developed when students do not focus on critical attributes and fail to identify the most accurate relational aspects of a concept. Students can be led through an inductive or deductive reasoning process to acquire the critical attributes and relational aspects of a concept so that they form the most correct and least naive conceptualization.

To do this, teachers can use prototypes, models, and examples and nonexamples (Schwarts & Resiberg, 1991; Tennyson and Cocchiarella, 1986). **Prototypes** are the "best" representation of a concept. They can be factual; for example, Tony Blair would be a prototype of a head of state of a foreign nation. They can also be abstractions; a Prime Minister is a "kind" of head of state. **Models** are typically concrete representations of things we cannot observe that help us visualize the concept. These are frequently used in science and mathematics to help students acquire a concept; a model of DNA would be an example. **Examples** and **nonexamples** are used to clarify critical attributes and to illuminate conceptual relationships. Pictures of different islands and peninsulas would provide both examples and nonexamples for learning the concepts of islands and peninsulas.

Can you devise a graphic organizer to depict the conceptual relationships of islands and peninsulas?

Best Practices for Concept Formation

There are a number of best practices for using the concept formation approach. The teacher should:

1. Assess information by having students reveal their preexisting conceptualizations of the knowledge, perhaps by asking questions or having them create a graphic organizer.
2. Expect students to generate opinions about the knowledge, explain key ideas, formulate questions, and reflect on opinions.
3. Expect students to listen to others' opinions, consider new ideas, and formulate responses.
4. Expect students to reflect on their thinking (metacognition) by having them report on key decision points, the process they used, and how they recognized that their new conceptualization was better than the old one.
5. Systematically use metaphors, models, examples and nonexamples, prototypes, images, and graphic organizers.
6. Debrief students through questions and discussions.

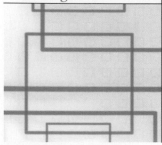

Assignment 22.1 | **DEVELOP A LESSON ON CONCEPT FORMATION**

INTASC STANDARDS 1–7

Topic 20 discussed the purpose of content presentations in the Instructional Sequence. Develop only the content presentation portion of the Instructional Sequence using the Class Notes format by selecting part of the content from your assigned topic and selection in Topic 13. Use the critical attributes and comparable entities Strategies to teach concept formation, and include at least one graphic organizer that would be used as a transparency. Be prepared to present your ideas to the class and to turn the assignment in to your professor.

OnLine Resources	CONCEPT FORMATION
ERIC OnLine ED477313	*Cognitive Conflict, Direct Teaching and Student's Academic Level*, by Zohar, Anat, and Kravetsky, Simcha-Aharon, 2003, compares the effectiveness of two teaching methods used to teach concepts.
ERIC OnLine ED474534	*The Connection Between Conversation and Conceptual Understanding*, by McDonald, James T., 2003.

Check this textbook's website at http://education.college.hmco.com/students for additional links.

Direct and Indirect Instruction

irect teaching of the whole class together does not mean a return to the formal chalk and talk approach, with the teacher talking and pupils mainly just listening. Good direct teaching is lively and stimulating. It means that teachers provide clear instruction, use effective questioning techniques and make good use of pupils' responses.

—*Numeracy Task Force (2004)*

Direct Teaching (also referred to as **direct instruction, explicit instruction, clinical teaching, target teaching, whole-class instruction, teacher-led instruction, lecture,** and **teacher-centered instruction**) is often attributed to the behaviorist school of psychology (Carnine, 1993). It has been characterized by detractors as less effective than indirect teaching (Lamber & McCombs, 1998; Shuell, 1996).

Indirect Teaching (also referred to as **indirect instruction** and **student-centered instruction**) tends to be associated with the constructivist school of psychology. In indirect teaching, the teacher creates an instructional sequence whereby students work more independently—as individuals, in pairs, or in groups—to construct knowledge rather than hear about it. The multiple terms used to describe these two approaches to instruction can be confusing. For example, when is teaching not "student-centered"? And indirect instruction is always preceded by some form of teacher talk that is "directive." Table 23.1 classifies a number of direct and indirect Strategies, all of which should be used during your instructional sequences over the span of a month, if not a week.

For the Reflective Practitioner

The whole art of teaching is only the art of awakening the natural curiosity of young minds for the purpose of satisfying it afterwards.

ANATOLE FRANCE

Table 23.1 | **DIRECT AND INDIRECT INSTRUCTION STRATEGIES**

Direct Instruction	Can Be Both Direct and Indirect Instruction	Indirect Instruction
Lecture	Concept formation	Hands-on activities
Modeling	Inductive reasoning	Individual projects
Graphic organizers	Deductive reasoning	Cooperative learning (discussions, projects, etc.)
Teacher-led discussion	Problem-based instruction	Group learning (discussions, projects, etc.)
Debriefings	Discovery learning	Peer tutoring

Direct Instruction

When using direct instruction, the teacher must explicitly plan for a high degree of Active Learning; when organized with this goal in mind, direct instruction is one of the most effective and efficient forms of teaching. In a comprehensive review spanning thirty years of research on direct instruction's effectiveness, Adams and Engelmann (1996) found that it produced far superior gains to other forms of instruction in almost all domains and for students with different abilities. Drawing partly from the research of Shuell (1996) and Eggen and Kauchak (2001), we can say that direct instruction is most effective when:

1. The content (remember when used in this context, "content" includes Big Ideas, Information Knowledge, and Procedural Knowledge) is straightforward and well defined, like the process for balancing equations or making a chronology;
2. The content needs to be mastered by all the students;
3. The content would be difficult for students to master in indirect instruction, such as when balancing an equation;
4. The goal is to integrate the facts, concepts, generalizations, and ideas of an organized body of knowledge; and/or
5. The goal is to introduce prerequisite knowledge to set up an indirect instruction approach to follow.

 What content in your domain or discipline do you think lends itself to direct instruction? Can you give a specific example?

For the Reflective Practitioner

Good teaching is one-fourth preparation and three-fourths theater.
GAIL GODWIN

Best Practices for Direct Instruction

Many of the following best practices are a restatement of the Instructional Sequence recommended for planning lessons in Topic 20. The inclusion of both guided and independent practice in that sequence, however, is a specific attempt to integrate indirect instruction with direct instruction. Additional best practices such as lecturing, modeling, and questioning can be found in direct instruction methods in the next Unit. Following are some best practices for direct instruction.

- Open lessons by reviewing prerequisite knowledge.
- Use an overview or analogy to create a context.
- Provide a short statement of goals.
- Present new material in small steps, with student practice after each step.
- Give clear and detailed instructions and explanations.
- Ask a large number of questions.
- Check for understanding.
- Guide students during practice segments of the Instructional Sequence.
- Provide systematic, immediate feedback and corrections.
- Monitor students during tasks.
- Involve all students.
- Maintain a brisk pace.
- Teach skills to the point of overlearning.
- Introduce materials.
- Praise and repeat student answers.

Indirect Instruction

Indirect instruction has been promoted as an alternative to the direct instruction method, which dominated education until the early 1960s, because (a) it appeals to different students' sensibilities; (b) students should learn to learn in many different ways; (c) it capitalizes on social interactions in ways that whole-class instruction cannot; (d) if the teacher plans astutely, students are required to not only learn the knowledge but also to initiate and manage their own learning; and (e) the burden of learning is strategically shifted to the student, whereas in direct instruction it can become a process of passively receiving information. The research on indirect instruction indicates that it too is successful when it is employed effectively (Jacques, 1992; Michaelsen, Fink, & Knight, 1997; Slavin, 1990). Unlike direct instruction, which can fail because of student passivity and boredom, indirect instruction may fail because the teacher does not define the tasks, provide adequate structure and monitoring, or hold students accountable.

Best Practices for Indirect Instruction

In addition to the following general best practices, you can find more detailed practices explained in the next Unit in the Topics on group learning, practice, homework, and other matters.

- Carefully plan the transition from direct to indirect instruction.
- Carefully define the tasks.
- Monitor the students' progress.
- Establish clear time limits and outcomes.
- Ensure equitable participation.
- Establish student-to-student communication rules for group activities.

> *Teacher's Tip*
>
> Why not form two-person teams of students to teach a topic to the class? If you assign topics in the beginning of the year and model what you want done, by the second semester your students can take charge of the learning and teach each other, with you adding expertise as needed. This approach is meant to boost students' self-interest, not to embarrass them in front of their peers.

What content in your domain or discipline do you think lends itself to indirect instruction? Can you give a specific example? **?**

Direct Versus Indirect Instruction: Three Examples

As a comparison of the two approaches, consider the following examples. Assume your goal was to teach students the differences between humans and animals.

Direct Instruction 1. The teacher lectures using a transparency with columns for humans and animals, sequentially identifying a critical attribute of each. The teacher asks students to take notes.

Direct Instruction 2. The teacher leads a discussion using a table on the chalkboard with columns for humans and animals, asking students to hypothesis the unique attributes of each and asking follow-up questions to probe individual students' thinking as they offer ideas. The teacher then adds correct conceptions, offers modifications or solicits them from students, and tactfully rejects misconceptions while completing the columns and rows on the chalkboard.

Indirect Instruction. In this indirect approach, the teacher gives students a Venn diagram, puts them in groups, and asks them to hypothesize which attributes animals and humans have in common and which they do not have in common. Students are then asked as a group to offer their ideas and rationale, while the teacher serves as an interlocutor, probing and suggesting alternatives.

Can you develop a similar set of direct and indirect instruction scenarios based on the topic you were assigned in Topic 13?

OnLine Resources	DIRECT AND INDIRECT INSTRUCTION
ERIC OnLine ED448424	*Classroom Strategies for Interactive Learning*, 2nd ed., by Buehl, Doug, 2001.
ERIC OnLine ED469734A	*A Teacher's Guide to Project-Based Learning*, by Fleming, Douglas S., 2000, introduces teachers to the ideas and methods that underpin project-based learning.
ERIC OnLine ED462729	*The Authority of the Teacher in the Student-Centered Classes*, by Hackelton, Devon, 2002, explains how teachers can assert authority without giving up the benefits of classroom interaction.

Check this textbook's website at http://education.college.hmco.com/students **for additional links.**

Critical Thinking and Reasoning

When I discovered critical thinking, my teaching changed. Instead of focusing on questions that had "right" answers, I wanted children to think through situations where the answer was in doubt. I expected them to decide which of two or more conflicting theories, procedures, beliefs, observations, actions, or expert claims made the most sense.

—Wright (2002), p. 9

Different disciplines, such as biology and literature, have specific critical thinking and reasoning processes that are unique and used only in those disciplines (see Unit 8 and Topic 7). However, these disciplines also benefit from generic critical thinking and reasoning strategies that we apply to any field of study (Toplak & Stanovich, 2002). It is this generic disposition of applying critical thinking and reasoning that is the primary focus of this Topic.

Critical Thinking

Critical thinking is the most common term used for **analytical reasoning, thinking skills, problem solving,** or **higher mental processes.** All these phrases describe the processes by which we construct a new conceptualization by applying existing concepts to solve problems and make decisions (Chance, 1986; Ennis, 1987; Scriven & Paul, 1992).

McGuinness (1999) identified the following abilities and skills of critical thinking:

- Collecting relevant information
- Sorting and analyzing information
- Drawing reasoned conclusions from information
- "Brainstorming" new ideas
- Solving problems
- Determining cause-and-effect relationships
- Evaluating options
- Planning and setting goals
- Monitoring progress
- Making decisions
- Reflecting on one's own progress

To some extent, all of us have critical thinking skills. However, superior cognitive ability is not all that sets "good thinkers" apart from noncritical thinkers. Research indicates that students often fail to use the thinking skills that they have (Perkins, Farady, & Bushey, 1991). We impart a critical thinking disposition by exposing students to the critical thinking of others, by modeling critical thinking ourselves, and by constructing lessons that explicitly require students

Teacher's Tip

The key to successfully promoting critical thinking is for you not to do the thinking for your students, but to bring just enough information and structure to a lesson so that—to use a metaphor—it puts them on the end of the diving board and requires them to jump. The Big Ideas are in the deep end, where they have to learn to swim.

Teacher's Tip

Bloom's Cognitive Comprehension, Application, Analysis, Synthesis, and Evaluation are examples of critical thinking at high levels.

to adopt the more *Academic Disposition* that was explained in Topic 11 (Brown, Collins, & Duguid, 1989; Costa, 1991; Perkins, 1992). One goal of teachers is to move students to increasingly more sophisticated ways of thinking critically in their domain and to inspire students to choose to use that disposition consistently.

The basic components of the critical thinking process are inductive and deductive reasoning, because these processes represent the most basic logical orders by which we define concepts and place them in hierarchies.

Inductive and Deductive Reasoning

All instructional approaches are based on the most fundamental process of reasoning or thinking logically. When preparing a lesson, the teacher uses reasoning to organize the lesson into a logical progression of ideas based on his or her thinking about the subject. Because reasoning is common to all people, there is a natural bridge from the teacher's logical organization of the lesson to the students' innate reasoning powers.

Reasoning can be organized as an active or passive learning experience as well as a deductive or inductive experience. The following examples use the overly simplistic concepts of island and peninsula to demonstrate the possible combinations.

Inductive Reasoning

The concepts of *island* and *peninsula* can be taught as an inductive or deductive Active Learning lesson. **Inductive reasoning** is the process of drawing conclusions from observations, or moving from the specific to the general (see Figure 24.1). It is an open-ended process in which ideas are explored.

1. The inductive approach starts with pictures of islands and peninsulas. Students might be divided into groups and asked to analyze the pictures to see if they can place them into two categories based on similarities that form a pattern.
2. When they have grouped the islands in one stack and the peninsulas in another stack, students would be asked to develop a hypothesis that would include definitions of stack X and stack Y, or their Critical Attributes.
3. Each group might present a definition, and the teacher would probe for their thinking by asking questions or showing more pictures.
4. A debriefing would include confirming the definitions, reinforcing that X is an island—a small body of land surrounded by water—and Y is a peninsula—a body of land surrounded by water on three sides.
5. Students would record the definitions.

Figure 24.1 | **INDUCTIVE REASONING**

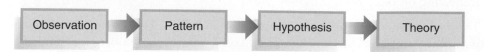

Observation → Pattern → Hypothesis → Theory

Figure 24.2 | **DEDUCTIVE REASONING**

Theory → Hypothesis → Observation → Confirmation

Deductive Reasoning

Deductive reasoning is the process of applying a generalization to an illustration, or moving from the general to the specific (see Figure 24.2). It is focused on proving a theory, rather than discovering a theory.

1. The teacher would write the definitions of *island* and *peninsula* on the board.
2. Students would be given pictures and asked to apply the definition to the illustrations.
3. When they have placed the islands in one stack and the peninsulas in another stack, students would be expected to justify their decisions.
4. A debriefing would include reinforcing the concept.
5. Students would record the definitions.

Which way do you prefer to learn—by inductive or deductive reasoning? Why?

In both cases, the teacher is promoting a correct formulation of the concepts and a mental map of the concepts' relationships by having students identify the **Critical Attributes**. Both inductive and deductive Strategies can require students to do the thinking, use their observation skills, predict, and justify. Almost anything we teach can be structured into one of these two approaches. Both involve Active Learning because the students construct knowledge.

Passive Instruction

However, this lesson could also have been delivered using a more passive approach. It is a commonplace practice and offered here only as an example of what not to do, a **nonexample**. This passive approach would entail the teacher lecturing by giving a definition of an island and peninsula, asking if everyone understands, and moving on to the next topic, leaving the students to record and memorize the definition with little or no reconstruction of knowledge. This would no doubt be followed by a quiz asking for the definition.

The Ten Academic Virtues

Perkins, Jay, and Tishman (1992) identified seven **Thinking Dispositions** that should be acquired by students. Their dispositions have been expanded into the following ten academic virtues that teachers can foster by constructing Active Learning experiences for their students.

1. **To be broad and adventurous:** The tendency to be open-minded, to explore alternative views, and to be alert to narrow thinking; the ability to generate multiple options
2. **To have sustained intellectual curiosity:** The tendency to wonder, probe, find problems, have a zest for inquiry, and be alert for anomalies; the ability to observe closely and formulate questions

Topic 24: **Critical Thinking and Reasoning**

3. **To clarify and seek understanding:** A desire to understand clearly, to seek connections and explanations, and to be alert to lack of clarity and the need for focus; the ability to build conceptualizations

4. **To be planful and strategies:** The drive to set goals, to make and execute plans, to envision outcomes, and to be alert to potential lack of direction; the ability to formulate goals and plans

5. **To be intellectually careful:** The urge for precision, organization, and thoroughness; the drive to be alert to possible error or inaccuracy; the ability to process information precisely

6. **To be respectful of evidence:** The aspiration to accept new evidence and formulations of data and concepts

7. **To seek and evaluate reasons:** The tendency to question the given and to demand justification; the ability to weigh and assess reasons

8. **To be metacognitive:** The tendency to be aware of and monitor the flow of one's own thinking and to be alert to complex thinking situations; the ability to exercise control of mental processes and to be reflective

9. **To be tolerant of ambiguity:** The ability to resist the drive to bring closure to problem solving and decision making for the sake of inquiry and thoughtfulness

10. **To be skeptical:** The inclination to require proof and logical analysis to demonstrate ideas and generalizations and to look for flaws

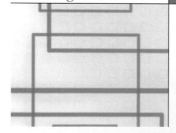

Assignment 24.1 **DEVELOP A LESSON ON INDUCTIVE AND DEDUCTIVE REASONING**

INTASC STANDARDS 1–7

Topic 20 discussed the purpose of content presentations in the Instructional Sequence. Develop only the content presentation portion of the Instructional Sequence using the Class Notes format by selecting part of the content from your assigned topic and selection in Topic 13. Develop the content presentation portion using both inductive and deductive approaches. Be prepared to present your ideas to the class and to turn the assignment in to your professor.

Assignment 24.2 **RESTRUCTURING LESSONS FOR CRITICAL THINKING**

INTASC STANDARDS 1–7

Go to the Critical Thinking Consortium at http://criticalthinking.org/resources/articles/#Teaching and select either "6-9: Remodeled Lesson Plans" or "9-12: Remodeled Lesson Plans." A "Remodeled" lesson is an "ordinary" lesson that has been turned into a lesson that focuses on developing critical thinking. Download one of the lessons for your teaching field and bring it to class. Be prepared to analyze and discuss how the lesson develops critical thinking in class.

OnLine Resources	CRITICAL THINKING
Critical Thinking on the Web	This comprehensive resource on critical thinking can be found at http://www.philosophy.unimelb.edu.au/reason/critical/. National Council for Excellence in Critical Thinking. Go to http://www.criticalthinking.org/ncect.html.
ERIC OnLine ED408570	*Cooperative Learning in the Thinking Classroom: Research and Theoretical Perspectives,* by Lee, Christine, 1997.

Check this textbook's website at http://education.college.hmco.com/students **for additional links.**

Selected Models of Instructional Approaches

Based on the fundamental instructional approaches in the previous three topics (Concept Formation, Direct and Indirect Instruction, and Critical Thinking and Reasoning), a number of models of instructional approaches have evolved that refine or revitalize these most basic approaches. The following are summaries of the main points of some classic Strategies used in secondary education instruction.

Teaching Based on Problem Solving and Inquiry

Critical thinking often begins with a question or presentation of a problem by the teacher that forces students to make an educated guess, that is, to form a hypothesis and then solve the problem. **Problem solving** is the process of seeking an explanation for observed phenomena. **Speculation** and **prediction** are essential components of problem solving and **inquiry-based teaching,** which asks students to act as experts in their field: to question the information and classify the facts and concepts that are advanced by others and the teacher. Both are crucial to developing Procedural Knowledge, which is part of acquiring a more sophisticated Academic Disposition. In science, we think in terms of testing a hypothesis in an experiment that has unequivocal results. In social studies, where conducting experiments with controlled conditions is difficult, we focus on gathering facts on phenomena that have already occurred in the real world and on making logical assertions that can be used to accept or reject a hypothesis.

Teacher's Tip

Almost everything we teach can be turned into a problem-solving or decision-making lesson. Every time you start a lesson and say to yourself, "I will tell them X," stop! Instead, ask yourself, "How can I turn this into a problem for them to solve or a decision that they have to make?"

Can you give an example from your discipline using the above descriptions? ?

When structuring the instructional pattern for a problem-solving lesson, the teacher, although interested in the content and solution, is just as interested in teaching the Procedural Knowledge of problem solving and in modeling an Academic Disposition. If instruction is teacher-centered, the focus is on questioning (see Topic 28) in a whole-class environment, or the case study method (see Topic 32) is used. If student-centered, a group activity (see Topic 31) method is used. In both cases, lessons are purposely converted into a format and sequence that require students to think about their thinking as well as to form answers.

Whimbey and Lockhead (1980) identified traits that are associated with successful and less successful problem solvers, which have been adapted to create Table 25.1. The traits of successful problem solvers should be modeled by the teacher and expected of the students.

Table 25.1 | CHARACTERISTIC OF PROBLEM SOLVERS

Characteristics of Successful Problem Solvers	Characteristics of Unsuccessful Problem Solvers
Are concerned about accuracy	Fail to observe and use all the facts
Break problems into parts	Are not systematic in their work or thinking
Avoid random guessing	Do not identify relationships fully
Have a positive attitude	Are sloppy in collecting information
Are energetic in the process	Do not reflect enough

The Five Steps in Problem Solving

There are many variations of the steps in problem solving, depending on how specific one wants to be. The following version is based on Beyer (1988) and Kalsounis (1987) and is a group activity using learning packets (see Topic 33), rather than a whole-class, teacher-centered activity.

1. **Become aware of the problem:** The teacher introduces a topic, leads an introductory discussion, and then poses the question.
2. **Gather data:** Students are given packets of information or are directed to resources for individualized collection of data.
3. **Form hypotheses:** Students are placed in groups to form a set of hypotheses about the problem.
4. **Test the hypotheses:** Students analyze, evaluate, and interpret data or facts to determine if their hypotheses are accurate or confirmed based on the evidence.
5. **Reach a conclusion:** Students report their findings and conclusions, perhaps using graphic organizers.

When the students develop their hypotheses, conclusions, and rationale, they are developing and forming schemas composed of generalizations, concepts, and facts. You should teach the problem-solving process so that students can name the problem-solving steps and apply them in sequence to a problem you present. Your success in creating problem-solving lessons depends on your ability to give students just enough information to place them in the proximity of the answers, but not so much that solutions are too obvious.

The following lesson example from an earth science class requires students to create the categories of phenomena (causes) that might affect temperature and to determine their effects. With this two-step structured approach, the teacher emphasizes problem solving as Procedural Knowledge, prompts systematic brainstorming of the possible causes (to be rejected or accepted), and asks for the effects on the temperature as a follow-up to the first decision.

A Problem-Solving Example: Juneau and Chicago

In a typical passive approach to teaching about the variables that affect climate, the teacher would list the variables on the board, give definitions of each, and explain how each affects two cases, for example, Juneau, Alaska, and Chicago, Illinois. This is efficient and orderly. But if your goal is for students to think, a more Active Learning approach should be used that encourages students to acquire the characteristics of successful problem solvers—that is, a

Table 25.2 | **HOME TEMPERATURE**

Possible Causes	Possible Effects
Thermostat	Set higher: warmer Set lower: colder
Insulation	
Number of windows	
Etc.	

more Academic Disposition. The following is a problem-solving strategy that incorporates the **Suchman Inquiry Model** (Suchman, 1977) and uses an analogy to place the students in reach of the answers. The hallmark of the Suchman approach is that the teacher presents students with a puzzling situation or event.

1. Show a map of North America on which Juneau and Chicago and their longitude and latitude are clearly labeled.
2. Explain longitude and latitude.
3. Ask students which place they think is colder. They will probably say Juneau because it is farther north than Chicago.
4. State the problem: In the month of December, the average temperature of Juneau, Alaska, is warmer than the average temperature of Chicago, Illinois. Explain "average" by having the tallest and shortest students come to the front of the class and measuring them.
5. Place students in groups, and ask them to figure out (hypothesize) why Juneau is warmer.
6. With a Cause/Effect Organizer on the board (see Table 25.2), explain that if asked what affects the temperature of your house, you would list the thermostat setting, insulation, windows, doors, appliances, and number of people in the first column. In the second column, for thermostat you would write that the higher it is set, the warmer the temperature, and the lower it is set the colder the temperature. From this analogy and with a globe and world map to consult, the students should begin brainstorming about Juneau and Chicago.
7. Once students have finished, have different groups report one item for the first column, and probe their thinking. Then have groups report the effect for each item listed in the first column, and probe their thinking. As the students report, introduce topographical maps and other additional data to demonstrate and support the correct hypothesis.
8. Probe, confirm, and elaborate for each item and effect.

WHY IS JUNEAU WARMER? A COLLABORATIVE ASSIGNMENT   *Assignment 25.1*

INTASC STANDARDS 1–7
With a colleague, create a cause-and-effect chart similar to Table 25.2 and hypothesize why Juneau is warmer. In the first column list the possible causes for Juneau's being warmer than Chicago, and in the second column list the effects.

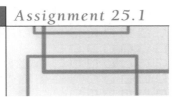

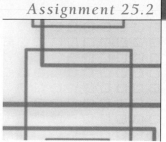

DEVELOP A LESSON USING HYPOTHESIS FORMATION

INTASC STANDARDS 1–7

Topic 20 discussed the purpose of "content presentations" in the Instructional Sequence. Develop only the content presentation portion of the Instructional Sequence using the Class Notes format by selecting part of the content from your assigned topic and selection in Topic 13. Develop the content presentation portion using the approach to teaching hypothesis formation. Be prepared to present your ideas to the class and turn the assignment in to your professor.

Decision-Making Model

The problem-solving and decision-making approaches share many of the same qualities. Scientists and mathematicians solve problems that typically do not engage people's emotions, or what we call the **affective domain**. Social studies and English also have problem-solving opportunities: But when problems have social or personal implications, decision making becomes the primary vehicle for understanding because ideology, values, and virtues come into play.

Decision making involves choosing between alternative solutions based on ideas and beliefs, in contrast to figuring out an answer from a set of possible answers. Like problem solving, decision making starts with the introduction of a problem. Sometimes getting the involved parties to reach an agreement about the problem is the problem. For example, what do you think the problem in determining the winner of the 2000 presidential election was? **Framing** the problem is a crucial aspect of decision making (see Topic 29) because it may be based on ideology, level of expertise in the domain, and/or changing circumstances. So two people may find two very different solutions to a problem that they frame differently. Furthermore, implicit in decision making is the notion that we would act on the choices, that we would promote or make some kind of a change.

Eight Steps in Decision Making

Naylor and Diem (1987) have identified eight steps in decision making. Note that step 2 includes the five steps in problem solving. A social studies lesson on homelessness illustrates the process.

1. **Recognize the situation as one in which a decision needs to be made:** People are homeless, and we need to solve the problem.
2. **Clarify the problem:** Follow the problem-solving steps.
3. **Identify relevant values:** Put students in groups to discuss their feelings and attitudes about people who are homeless.
4. **Indicate the desired outcome (goal):** Have the groups indicate what they think should happen to homeless people.
5. **Propose and consider a range of potential alternatives:** Expect the groups to come up with solutions, such as more low-income housing, jobs, and orphanages.
6. **Project the likely consequences for each alternative (both positive and negative):** Expect the groups to identify higher taxes and other consequences.
7. **Choose the best alternative,** or rank the alternatives based on an analysis of projected consequences and their consistency with the stated goal and one's values: Have the students forge a consensus.

8. **Apply the decision and assess the consequences:** Have the groups report their decisions. The teacher should emphasize that following deliberate steps is a crucial form of Procedural Knowledge.

Like problem solving, decision making can be used in direct or indirect instruction. The following questions by Riecken and Miller (1990) provide a Procedural Knowledge approach. Using the case study method (see Topic 32), a social studies teacher presenting the bombing of Hiroshima, an English teacher following a dramatic reading of "Desiree's Baby" (see Topic 42), or a health teacher introducing the topic of sexually transmitted diseases could use many of these questions for either whole-class or group discussion.

1. What is the problem?
2. Why is it a problem?
3. What might have been done to prevent the problem?
4. What has to be decided?
5. What are the options?
6. Does a decision have to be made at this point?
7. Did the character's solution work?
8. What can the character do now?
9. What would you do if you were in this situation?
10. Given the situation, what are three different things the character can do?
11. Are some options better than others?
12. What do you think might happen if the character did X?
13. What might happen to the other characters if the main character did Y?
14. How could the character decide what he or she should do?
15. What do you think the character will do?
16. Have you ever had to make a similar decision?
17. How was your experience different from this story?
18. How was your experience the same as this story?

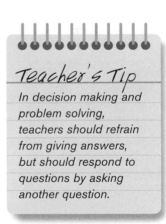

Lessons constructed using these processes allow students to acquire the academic inclinations to objectively analyze problems and issues. The emphasis in the instruction is on framing the "right" questions. This kind of systematic approach creates a Framework students can use to think critically about issues and to reflect on their biases and thinking processes. Teachers should teach the steps using content, as well as teach content using the steps. Just as students should be able to recite the seven continents, so they should be able to recite the eight decision-making steps. The teacher, in decision making, is not a provider of answers, but rather a "provocateur" who forces students to consider alternative positions by posing alternative perspectives.

Teacher's Tip

In decision making and problem solving, teachers should refrain from giving answers, but should respond to questions by asking another question.

DEVELOP A LESSON USING DECISION MAKING

Assignment 25.3

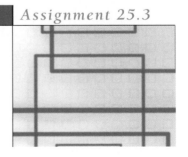

INTASC STANDARDS 1–7

The purpose of "content presentations" in the Instructional Sequence was explained in Topic 20. Develop only the content presentation portion of the Instructional Sequence using the Class Notes format by selecting part of the content from your assigned topic and selection in Topic 13. Develop the content presentation portion using a decision-making approach. Be prepared to present your ideas to the class and to turn the assignment in to your professor.

Advance Organizer Model

An **advance organizer** is a cognitive Strategy proposed by Ausubel (1968) in his **Subsumption Theory,** which emphasizes that learners recall their prior knowledge and transfer it to the new information being presented. The advance organizer is a brief, general introduction (typically accompanied by a graphic organizer of some kind) that the teacher gives before presenting the new knowledge. The advance organizer should provide a bridge that links the known to the unknown. Using Figure 22.3: Heads of Government, as an example, there would be at least three steps.

1. **Advance Organizer.** The teacher would start the lesson by asking if the president of the United States is a "head of state," what is a head of state, and so on and providing a definition along the way. The graphic organizer (Figure 22.3) would be introduced to graphically depict some examples. At this point, this strategy provides a frame of reference, a link to prior knowledge (or at least something familiar, that is, president of the United States), and creates a context, a conceptualization for the new learning.
2. **Progressive Differentiation.** The teacher begins examining and defining each of the cells in the graphic organizer so that they can be understood independently.
3. **Integrative Reconciliation.** The teacher begins examining the relationships between the cells.

This approach is a highly interactive process, very conversational, focused on concept formation, and based on well-planned questions (Taricani, 2000; Walberg, 1991).

Assignment 25.4 | **DEVELOP A LESSON USING ADVANCE ORGANIZERS**

INTASC STANDARDS 1–7
Topic 20 discussed the purpose of content presentations in the Instructional Sequence. Develop only the content presentation portion of the Instructional Sequence using the Class Notes format by selecting part of the content from your assigned topic and selection in Topic 13. Develop the content presentation portion using an advance organizer approach. Be prepared to present your ideas to the class and to turn the assignment in to your professor.

List, Group, and Label Model

Hilda Taba et al.'s (1971) **List, Group, and Label Model** is considered a best practice because it is an Active Learning experience in which students "construct" information by appropriately juxtaposing concepts and facts (Costa & Loveall, 2002). While interacting with the students, the teacher ensures that the students' construction matches the dominant model in the community of practice. This approach relies on students to provide ideas, which the teacher must adroitly work into his or her prepared construction of the knowledge. The process is as follows:

1. The teacher asks the students to come up with examples of well-known artists, which the teacher, using a whole-class discussion Strategy, *lists* on the chalkboard as the responses are given and as the teacher asks questions and probes students' thinking.

2. The teacher asks the students if there are some ways to organize the items on the list into logical *groups*. The teacher then either organizes the students into **quick groups** (with each student working with the student in front of him or her or behind or to the side) or continues with whole-class instruction.

   a. If whole-class instruction is continued, the teacher reorganizes the list on the board into a table with *labels* for columns and possibly rows by calling on students to propose the reorganization and placements. The teacher probes their logic, presents alternative possibilities, and ultimately introduces the most appropriate organization from the domain by integrating the students' correct conceptions (those that support the community of practices conception) and tactfully rejecting misconceptions and naïve conceptions.

   b. If the teacher uses quick groups, when the students finish, he or she then calls on students in the quick groups to record their categories on the chalkboard, with each category labeled. Once the groups have placed their ideas on the chalkboard, the teacher debriefs the students, having them critique each other's renditions, and uses the opportunity to introduce the most appropriate organization from the domain.

How do you think the product of this List, Group, and Label Strategy would look using the term artists *(as in the example), and what would the teacher add to it if the students were suggesting too narrow or too exhaustive a definition?*

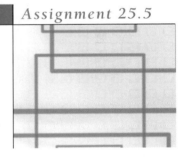

DEVELOP A LIST, GROUP, AND LABEL LESSON   *Assignment 25.5*

INTASC STANDARDS 1–7

The purpose of content presentations in the Instructional Sequence was explained in Topic 20. Develop only the content presentation portion of the Instructional Sequence using the Class Notes format by selecting part of the content from your assigned topic and selection in Topic 13. Develop the content presentation portion using the Hilda Taba List, Group, and Label approach. Be prepared to present your ideas to the class and to turn the assignment in to your professor.

Scaffolding

Scaffolding supports students' quest to acquire the critical thinking skills needed to reach their potential (Wood, Bruner, & Ross, 1976). Scaffolding instruction moves students carefully from what they know to what they don't know: It helps learners develop their independence, fluency, and range of performance as they move from novice to expert learner (Meyer, 1993; Stone, 1993). It is based on the theories of Lev Vygotsky (1978) and entails the teacher doing the following as part of the lesson (Larkin, 2002):

1. The teacher starts with something that is familiar and within the students' capacity. In English class this might mean asking students who the good and bad guys were in the movie *Gladiator*.

2. The teacher relates this knowledge to new knowledge by using metaphors, examples, and demonstration. In this case, the English teacher draws an analogy to characters in *Macbeth*.

3. The teacher marks critical features of the ideas presented by students and models the comparison process.
4. The teacher then shifts the burden for learning to the students by asking them to compare the characteristics and motives of characters from *Gladiator* and *Macbeth*, allowing the students to direct the discussion.

The purpose is for students to master the concepts, not just the routines and bits of information by repetition and rote memorization. Scaffolding has many of the same attributes as the List, Group, and Label model and the Advance Organizer model.

Instructional Conversations

Tharp (1997) proposed **Instructional Conversations** as a kind of informal, conversational teaching that motivates students. Such conversations rely heavily on dialogue or dialectic (the Socratic method). This kind of planned dialogue, combined with the kind of questioning recommended in Topic 28, can create a classroom culture that encourages all students to reconstruct and transfer knowledge. It also minimizes classroom management problems because it becomes the social norm of the class (Hogan & Pressley, 1997).

Teachers can create instructional conversations by adopting the following practices:

1. Model the characteristics of a thoughtful person by showing interest in students' ideas and their suggestions for solving problems.
2. Model problem-solving processes rather than just giving answers.
3. Ensure that classroom interactions focus on a sustained examination of a few topics rather than a superficial coverage of many.
4. Acknowledge the difficulties involved in gaining a clear understanding of problematic topics.
5. Segment the knowledge into chunks with clear objectives.
6. Pose questions rather than promote answers.
7. Press students to clarify or justify their assertions rather than merely accepting and reinforcing them indiscriminately.
8. Give students sufficient time to think before being required to answer questions.
9. Encourage students to generate original, unpopular, and unconventional ideas in the course of the interaction.
10. Involve all students in the class dialogue, not just the volunteers.
11. Make preparation for class and class participation a significant part of the grading scheme.

The Great Books Method

The phrase "**The Great Books**" usually refers to a curriculum that focuses on students reading and sharing ideas derived from the classics: well-respected philosophers, playwrights, historians, economists, and others. However, it is presented here as an instructional approach for a content presentation or as a debriefing (see Topic 13) following the reading of text material. It places students in the position of having to construct meaning out of a work while the teacher provides insights, background, and supervision. It can be used in any discipline and typically proceeds as follows:

1. The teacher selects an article, set of problems, section of a book, primary document, short story, or other such work.
2. The students are required to read the material prior to class and come to class prepared to reconstruct their knowledge.
3. Groups of three or four discuss the meaning of the material over a period of time that the teacher considers feasible, based on the length of the material or the teacher's judgment of how much time the groups need to reconstruct the information.
4. Using poster paper, each group is to:
   a. List key points.
   b. Create arguments that validate or invalidate the key points.
   c. Explain how the work is relevant.
5. Sometimes the teacher joins a group and asks questions to engage students' thinking and to check for understanding.
6. Grading is based on the teacher's observations of each student's contribution to the group process.
7. The teacher serves as a resource to clarify concepts, add background, and so forth based on students' requests.

This approach shifts the burden of learning to students and focuses on the kind of dialogue that requires reconstruction of knowledge both before class and during class.

OnLine Resources	MODELS OF INSTRUCTIONAL APPROACHES
University of Colorado at Denver	For this gateway site on models of instruction, go to http://carbon.cudenver.edu/~mryder/itc_data/idmodels.html.
ERIC OnLine ED379303	*Teaching Thinking Across the Curriculum with the Concept Attainment Model*, by Pritchard, Florence Fay, 1994.
ERIC OnLine ED465995	*Scaffolding in a Learning Community of Practice: A Case Study of a Gradual Release of Responsibility from the Teacher to the Students*, by Kong, Ailing, 2002.

Check this textbook's website at http://education.college.hmco.com/students for additional links.

Methods

Schoolies © 2000 by John P. Wood

Modeling and Metacognition

Before we begin this Topic, let me share an uncomplicated example of modeling. One day, my daughter-in-law, Tina, was growing exasperated at her two-and-a-half-year-old daughter, Lizzie, and said, "You're not listening, and I have had enough!" A little later, when Lizzie was playing "family" with her stuffed bears, she copied her mother by shaking her finger at the baby bear and saying, "I have had enough!"

Modeling is one of the most powerful ways to transmit an Academic Disposition, reasoning skills, and the Procedural Information of your domain to students, because students learn by observing and emulating the teacher and the other students (Bandura, 1986, 1997; Nauta & Kokaly, 2001). Teachers also play a crucial role in shaping students' decisions to become an apprentice or nonapprentice in a particular subject.

Modeling should not be confused with the use of models when demonstrating and lecturing. Models can be physical equipment (apparatuses, didactic materials, manipulatives), examples (an ideal essay, Realia), or depictions (graphic organizers, etc.; see Topic 30). Models are integrated into the choreography of the lesson plan and are used by teachers to clarify concepts: They might demonstrate with a model during a content presentation or have students manipulate or create models as a task or during practice. Although models should be used in all domains, the types of models and the degree to which they are used vary greatly based on the discipline. Their effectiveness is undisputed and is linked to their appeal to the senses of sight and touch as opposed to just the hearing sense used in lectures.

Types of Modeling

There are a number of ways to think about the types of modeling that can be used in the classroom setting.

Disposition Modeling

In **disposition modeling** teachers (and frequently students) transmit a set of personal values or ways of thinking in a domain or discipline. How we are thinking unfolds before others by what we say and what we do. This kind of modeling reflects, negatively or positively, on our approach to others, on learning, and on our academic disciplines. Students are always assessing and considering whether they should adopt the thinking and values that lie behind our words and actions.

Teacher Modeling

Students are constantly making judgments about a teacher's character and drawing inferences about the domain based on the teacher's disposition.

Teacher's Tip

Whether it is equipment like hand-held devices or models such as a human skeleton or a replica of a Civil War musket (**Realia** in social studies), if it will be used in a classroom during instruction, the teacher should rehearse its use before demonstrating it to the whole class, make sure there are sufficient numbers or copies for everyone if that is the Strategy, and also make sure that the equipment is in good working order.

A teacher's integrity, empathy for students, and high expectations are communicated to students whether planned or not. Teachers who are creative, diligent, well prepared, and organized model the kinds of Strategies needed to succeed in the workforce. This personal modeling occurs not only during instructional events, but also during transitions in a classroom, when there is a less formal, free flow of ideas and interactions. A teacher cannot stop being a teacher, even in those less formal moments. In both instructional and noninstructional interactions, teachers need to carefully choose the words they use, the ideas they articulate, and the actions they take.

Student Modeling

Unlike the teacher, students do not generally plan their modeling, and therefore they exhibit both productive and unproductive thinking and behaving when they serve as models for other students. Teachers can expand productive modeling beyond themselves by identifying students who model appropriate behaviors and strategies so that other students might choose to adopt similar approaches and ideas. When students exhibit unproductive thinking, teachers must help them acquire a more Academic Disposition. As an example, a student who reaches a faulty conclusion and proclaims in a discussion on poverty, "All poor people are lazy" has articulated a conclusion that is based on an inadequate analysis. When something like this happens, the teacher's first consideration should be to focus on the thought process rather than the conclusion. By having the student who made the statement reconsider his or her thought process—usually by questioning the logic and examples used to reach the decision—the teacher can guide the student through a more precise or detached analysis that might lead to a different conclusion and a new disposition.

Task and Performance Modeling

Task modeling (also called performance modeling) takes place when the teacher demonstrates a task that students will be expected to complete. It almost always precedes some form of practice that is planned as part of the Instructional Sequence. Laboratory classes in science and physical education courses are replete with this kind of modeling. Other examples include foreign language teachers who model communication in the target language, the foreign language students are learning, and social studies teachers who model the task of developing a historical timeline. The teacher can perform an identical or similar activity to the task that will be asked of the students so that students can observe the process. Or the teacher can provide a sample of an end product and describe the process that led to its creation. If students are expected to create a map, complete a chemistry experiment, or write a poem, the teacher should present and explain a model as part of a content presentation so that students have a clear understanding of the task.

Often, students can be called upon to show and explain their work as a way of modeling the task for other students so that there is less teacher-centered instruction. A teacher may be aware of an apprentice's particular interest or ability and will ask the student to model a task. For example, a student who is particularly poised and articulate could model making a presentation. The teacher always works with the student before the modeling takes place.

Metacognition

Metacognition includes both knowledge about cognition and regulation of cognition (Everson, 1997). It is defined as "thinking about thinking" and involves the ability to monitor, evaluate, and make plans for one's learning (Wilson, 1997; Schunk, 1996). It is essential to the maturation process of teenagers to employ metacognition in their learning (El-Hindi, 1996). It is one of the critical elements that distinguishes successful from unsuccessful students (Kuhn & Dean, 2003; Puntambekar & duBoulay, 1997), and, for many students, teachers are their only models of both general and domain-specific metacognition. Teachers at the secondary level serve as models for their disciplines by the way they:

1. Articulate Information Knowledge from the domain.
2. Use and employ the executive processes of the domain.
3. Conduct discussions.
4. Share ideas.
5. Organize the classroom.
6. Structure the learning experience.

Teacher's Tip

Most teachers find it a little odd to share their thinking the first time they use the metacognitive modeling process, but this will pass and the students will benefit from this Strategy.

Metacognitive Modeling

Every discipline requires thoughtfulness and enthusiasm for the ideas of the domain. Students who see this in their teachers develop the general and domain-specific Academic Disposition important to their success. **Metacognitive modeling,** or modeling how to think, is required whenever Procedural Knowledge or Big Ideas are the focus of instruction (Beeth, Ozdemir, & Yuruk, 2003). It is particularly necessary when the lesson focuses on deciphering information, interpreting data, analyzing assertions, or drawing conclusions.

The need for metacognitive modeling becomes clearer when one thinks about watching a math teacher, for example, solve a problem at a chalkboard in anticipation of students solving a similar problem. Typically, the math teacher proceeds through a series of steps to model how to solve the problem, listing each change on the next line on the chalkboard. The teacher talk can often be little more than a verbal statement of the results or recitation of the steps seen on the board. For metacognitive modeling, the teacher talk must also deliberately include his or her thinking—the **"inner speech"** that reveals the executive processes of the domain; this is called the **Thinking-out-loud approach.** Even if the mathematics teacher has a destination and a road map in mind, failure to articulate the inner speech leaves the students with no understanding of the Procedural Knowledge needed to succeed. As a consequence, students will memorize the steps learned from the lesson, but they will not understand how the teacher made the decisions to move from one step to the next.

Metacognitive modeling is intended to make up for the all-too-common instructional shortcomings of teachers who are experts in their domain. This kind of instructional deficiency is at least partially attributable to teachers having almost always been apprentices in their domain, which hinders them from communicating the knowledge in a way that allows the nonapprentice student to reconstruct it. The instructor may skip over steps based on inflated beliefs of what the student should already know or be able to intuitively figure out.

The *thinking-out-loud approach*, in which the teacher plans and then explicitly articulates the underlying thinking process he or she goes through, should be the focus of teacher talk. A teacher can implement metacognitive modeling in a number of ways:

• **In decision making and problem solving:** Just providing students with the decision-making or problem-solving steps is not enough. Unless the teacher also models how to think during the process of working through the sequence of steps, students will not learn the metacognitive process of applying the steps. As an example, in a lesson on continuous quantity, the teacher might show two containers with water, one that has half the diameter of the other and twice the height. The teacher would share his or her thinking in the form of a statement such as "I wonder if they have the same amount of water" and then pour the water in the taller container into the shorter container.

- **In reading:** During shared reading with students, the teacher asks rhetorical questions or makes comments to demonstrate the kinds of questions and thoughts that students should process while reading. For example, while reading about the Lincoln assassination, the teacher might say, "I am wondering what impact this will have on how the North and South reconcile." The teacher would then ask a student what he or she is thinking. This metacognitive process can be used not only with content, but also with procedures: "I need to look up that word" or "What word do I want to use to label this row (of a data retrieval chart)?"

- **In questioning:** The teacher asks a question and then explains how he or she would think about answering it. The teacher shares not the answer, but the thinking process. As an example, after students have read the Bishop's tale from *Les Miserables*, a teacher would share his or her thinking in a question such as "I am wondering what impact this will have on Jean Valjean" and then would explain how he or she analyzed the story line.

Teachers should not assume that their students have been exposed to thinking about thinking. Consistent use of metacognitive modeling techniques will help students understand the important role they play in reasoning and understanding.

 In your observations of teachers, how frequently have you seen them using metacognitive modeling? Can you think of a specific example from your current experience as a student?

OnLine Resources	MODELING AND METACOGNITION
ERIC OnLine ED457222	*Students Reflecting on What They Know*, by Gil, A., Osiecki, N., and Juarez, A., 2001, focuses on metacognition in reading.
ERIC OnLine ED477315	*The Role of Metacognition in Facilitating Conceptual Change*, by Yuruk, N., Ozdemir, O., and Beeth, Michael E., 2003, has activities that are likely to change students' conceptions.
ERIC OnLine ED468203	*Virtual Manipulatives in the K–12 Classroom*, by Spikell, Mark A., Bolyard, Johnna J., and Moyer, Patricia S., 2001, discusses the unique properties of virtual manipulatives and their usefulness in the K–12 classroom.

Check this textbook's website at http://education.college.hmco.com/students for additional links.

Lecturing and Note Taking

Instruction by lecturing is often associated with the terms *direct instruction* and *teacher-centered instruction*. For the purpose of this Topic, we will use the term *lecture* to describe those occasions when the teacher is THE primary communicator of knowledge and directly manages the pace and sequence of the instruction through his or her communications. This would be in contrast to group activities or primarily discussion-based classes.

Lectures can be an efficient way to convey information. However, at the end of a lecture a teacher may be able to say, "I taught them," but that does not mean the students have necessarily learned what was taught. Hearing information, even when enhanced with visuals or models, does not guarantee that students have reconstructed the new knowledge or developed a new Academic Disposition. This is one of many reasons why extensive use of questioning (see Topic 28), group activities (Topic 31), and practice (Topic 34) needs to be integrated with lectures into the Instructional Sequence.

Because of Standards-based education and time constraints in your classroom, you will find it necessary to lecture at times to achieve your school's goals. And in fact, students need to learn how to persist through lectures, how to take notes, and how to reconstruct the knowledge based on a lecture, because this approach will be needed in post K–12 education and the world of work. However, you will be most effective when you (a) conduct lectures more as discussions; (b) purposefully integrate different types of lectures and organizing patterns into the content presentations of your Instructional Sequence; and (c) integrate visuals and manipulatives into the lecture (see Cusik, 2002).

Types of Lectures

The types of lectures presented in Table 27.1 offer several approaches to varying your lectures. One attribute common to these lecture types is that they are purposefully interrupted with breakout groups (see Topic 31) and/or individual tasks. Because middle and high school students have limited attention spans, this Strategy usually increases the likelihood that they will reconstruct the knowledge (Ruhl, Hughes, & Schloss, 1987). Dividing up the content into lecture "chunks" of about 15 to 20 minutes each is also a sound planning strategy. But the best way to know when you have lectured too long is to observe the students. An individual student can be brought back into the lecture by using proximity control and asking questions, but when the whole class begins to exhibit signs of tiring (talking, dazed looks, no spontaneous questions), it is time to stop and shift gears to a more active segment of the instruction. The lectures in Table 27.1 include activities in their organization.

Teacher's Tip

If the traditional lecture method of "chalk and talk" with the teacher talking and pupils taking notes is your idea of teaching, you will find yourself with an inordinate amount of classroom management problems.

Teacher's Tip

When lecturing, do not spend all your time at the chalkboard or overhead projector. Assign a student to record information on the board or display transparencies. You should be walking around the classroom monitoring and engaging all the students.

Table 27.1 | TYPES OF LECTURES

Lecture Type	Process
Feedback Lecture	*Lecture:* 10 to 15 minutes. Students are given an outline of the lecture beforehand. The teacher lectures from the outline (Class Notes), with students taking notes. *Breakout group:* 15 to 20 minutes. Students are given questions to answer based on the lecture and their notes. *Debriefing:* 10 to 15 minutes. The Socratic method is used and is structured around the questions given to the students. The teacher uses a list of Big Ideas, key concepts, and facts to ensure understanding.
Guided Lecture	*Lecture:* 10 to 15 minutes. Students are given a list of objectives. The teacher lectures from Class Notes. Students are asked to listen (no writing) and are expected to be able to recall the information. *Individual assignment:* 5 to 10 minutes. Students are to write down all the information they can recall. *Breakout group:* 10 to 15 minutes. Students work in groups to reconstruct the Big Ideas, concepts, and facts. *Debriefing:* 5 to 10 minutes. Students ask questions to fill in and expand on missing information. The teacher calls on other students to respond and uses a list of Big Ideas, key concepts, and facts to ensure understanding.
Responsive Lecture	*Breakout group:* 15 to 20 minutes. The teacher, perhaps once a week, sets aside time for questions on material covered during the week. Students develop and rank open-ended questions for a recent or upcoming topic for the teacher to answer, with at least one question from each student. Or, when they arrive for class, students drop off a question in a box for the teacher to respond to. *Lecture:* 15 to 20 minutes. The teacher asks why each question is important and answers it. Student volunteers should also be called on to answer the questions.
Demonstration Lecture	*Lecture:* 15 to 30 minutes. The teacher lectures from Class Notes. At points during the lecture, the teacher stops to demonstrate a procedure or process. The demonstration is laced with questions to draw out of the students the next steps in the demonstration. *Demonstration:* 15 to 20 minutes. The demonstration can occur anytime during the lecture. *Debriefing:* 5 to 10 minutes. Teacher calls on students to explain or demonstrate the process or procedure.
Pause Procedure Lecture	*Lecture:* 15 to 20 minutes. The teacher lectures from Class Notes with students taking notes. *Breakout pairs:* Every 5 minutes. The teacher pauses to allow pairs of students to share notes to correct and collect missing information. *Debriefing:* 5 to 10 minutes. The teacher calls on students to respond to prepared questions to summarize the Big Ideas, key concepts, and facts.
Think/Write/Discuss Lecture	*Lecture:* 15 to 20 minutes. The teacher lectures from Class Notes. At least four key questions are planned at pivotal points in the lecture. *Student response:* 2 to 3 minutes. The teacher pauses after each question for students to write answers to the question. *Debriefing:* 5 to 10 minutes. The teacher calls on students to recite their written answers to the questions. The teacher repeats and summarizes Big Ideas and concepts.

Table 27.1 | **continued**

Lecture Type	Process
Lecture with Graphic Organizer	*Lecture:* 15 to 20 minutes. Rather than taking notes, students are provided a handout of a graphic organizer (web, Venn diagram, etc.), map, or other visual to complete while the teacher lectures. The teacher completes the same organizer on the chalkboard or a transparency on the overhead projection. *Debriefing:* 15 to 20 minutes. The teacher circulates during the lecture, making sure students are completing the organizer and probing for concepts through the Socratic method.
Socratic Method Lecture (named after Socrates for his persistent questioning; see Topic 28)	*Lecture:* 15 to 30 minutes. The lecture is structured on a series of carefully sequenced questions. This kind of lecture usually follows a reading assignment so that students have a baseline of knowledge, although many questions require students to use logic and inference skills. This lecture can be longer because the number of questions increases students' engagement in the class.
Traditional Lecture	*Lecture:* The teacher has a set of Class Notes that are similar to the notes that the students are expected to record and primarily reports information so students can record their notes (see discussion of note taking below). Such lectures today should be rare in middle and high schools and are presented here more as a nonexample. They should be converted into one of the other types of lectures.

Adapted from Bonwell and Eison (1991).

CREATE LECTURES BASED ON TYPES   *Assignment 27.1*

INTASC STANDARDS 1–7

Write a description of how you would employ each of the types of lecture from Table 27.1 using the topic and selection you were assigned from Topic 13. Expect to share your ideas with the class and submit your typed assignment to your professor.

Organization of Lectures

The way a lecture is organized will also determine its effectiveness. The lecture-organizing schemes in Table 27.2 are adapted from the University of Pittsburgh website at **http://www.pitt.edu/~ciddeweb/FACULTY-DEVELOPMENT/FDS/lectmeth.html** and the University of Illinois website at **http://www.oir.uiuc.edu/Did/docs/LECTURE/Lecture2.htm**. The organization of a lecture should be based primarily on the nature of the content; therefore, each organization type may not work equally well in all teaching fields. As an example, the rule-example organization is frequently used in mathematics, chronological lectures are common to history, and cause-and-effect lectures are used in both science and social studies.

Table 27.2 | **ORGANIZATION OF LECTURES**

Lecture Organization	Definition
Cause-and-effect	Focuses on cause-and-effect relationships
Chronological and flow chart	Demonstrates the order of events
Compare-and-contrast	Identifies significant differences and similarities
Conflicting generalities	Poses one principle, then forces the examination of a counter principle
Part-to-whole	Emphasizes how a Big Idea is composed of several concepts
What-why	Emphasizes application of a concept
Parallel elements	Compares two events or ideas based on a set of common elements
Problem-solution	Identifies a problem and then identifies solutions
Ascending-descending order	Arranges topics according to their importance or complexity
Rule-example	Either begins with a rule, followed by examples and then restatement of the rule; or begins with examples, followed by analysis of the rule

Best Practices for a Good Lecture

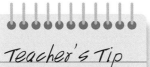

Teacher's Tip

Images, and even sounds, are so readily available on the Internet that no teacher should consider lecturing without the use of visuals, such as transparencies, to enrich the classroom experience.

There are a number of practices teachers should use when lecturing. Lectures can be successful when the teacher:

1. Presents the content in small steps.
2. Focuses on a single Big Idea.
3. Plans and asks many questions.
4. Plans and gives many examples and analogies.
5. Interrupts the lecture with individual or group activities.
6. Constantly checks for student understanding.
7. Doesn't talk too fast.
8. Changes inflection, volume, and pitch.
9. Uses eye contact to keep everyone involved.
10. Holds students responsible for the content.
11. Employs concept-related humor.
12. Shows enthusiasm about the subject.
13. Promotes note taking by speaking slowly and repeating important information.
14. Gives motivational cues such as "On Friday you will need to create a legend for a map of Florida."

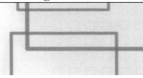

Assignment 27.2 | **CREATE LECTURES USING DIFFERENT ORGANIZATIONS**

INTASC STANDARDS 1–7

Write a description of how you would employ *each* of the lecture organizations from Table 27.2 using the topic and selection you were assigned from Topic 13. Expect to share your ideas with the class and submit your typed assignment to your professor.

Note Taking

Taking notes is a skill that can improve students' success when you lecture. While there are a number of note-taking approaches, the **Cornell Note-Taking System**—although designed for the college level—is one of the best known and can be used at the middle and high school levels.

Students should be taught to divide their paper into two vertical columns. A vertical line drawn about $2^1/2$ inches from the left side will create the *Recall Column* on the left for key words and concepts. This will leave about 6 inches on the right for the *Notes Column*. During a lecture, the student records thorough notes in the Notes Column, using abbreviations if necessary. After the lecture, the student reads through the Notes Column and extracts key words and concepts from it to put in the Recall Column. The student can then cover up the right-hand column and drill the words in the Recall Column for review. In addition, there is a row at the bottom where the Big Ideas are summarized. An example of this method is available at Bucks County Community College at **http://www.bucks.edu/~specpop/Cornl-ex.htm** and at the University of Santa Cruz at **http://people.ucsc.edu/~mwax/resume/write/rubric/cornellnotesys/**.

It would be well worth your while, during the first week of classes, to teach your students how to take notes using the Cornell system or another approach. The best practice would be to model how to take notes by explaining the system, lecturing about it, having students compare their notes, and then showing them your version of what it should look like. By creating a structured note-taking approach, students are:

1. Compelled to be engaged in the class.
2. Creating a written record for study and review.
3. Required to be organized.
4. Forced to condense and rephrase the lecture (a form of reconstructing knowledge), which leads to understanding.

Teacher's Tip

Memorizing is not the same as understanding, but it is often a prerequisite and necessary to learning. Only have students memorize what is essential, use mnemonics when possible, and try to construct a context for the material to be memorized before the memorization is to take place.

Six Steps in Note Taking

The six steps in the Cornell note-taking system can be found at many websites by searching for "Cornell note taking." Part of your instruction on how to take notes should include the following information (adapted from the Brigham Young University website at **http://www.byu.edu/stlife/cdc/learning/note-tak.php**):

1. **Record.** Record as many facts and ideas as you can in the 6-inch column. Do not be concerned with getting every word down that the lecturer says or with making sure your notes are grammatically correct. To ensure that your notes make sense weeks later, after the lecture is over, fill in blanks or make incomplete sentences complete.
2. **Reduce or Question.** After you read through your notes, reduce important facts and ideas to key words or phrases or formulate questions based on the facts and ideas. Key words, phrases, and questions are written in the narrow column on the left of the 6-inch column.
3. **Recite.** Recitation is a very powerful process in the retention of information. When reciting, cover up your notes in the 6-inch column, while leaving the cue words and questions uncovered and readily accessible. Next, read each key word or question, then recite and state aloud, in your own words, the information.
4. **Reflect.** Reflection is pondering or thinking about the information you have learned. Reflecting is a step beyond learning note content. It reinforces deeper learning by relating facts and ideas to other learning and knowledge.

5. **Review.** Review notes nightly or several times during the week by reciting, not rereading.

6. **Recapitulate.** The recapitulation or summary of your notes goes at the bottom of the note page. The summary should not be a word-for-word rewriting of your notes. It should be in your own words and reflect the main points you want to remember from your notes: the Big Ideas and key concepts. Reading through your summary(ies) in preparation for an exam is a good way to review.

OnLine Resources	LECTURING
Indiana University	*Improving Lecturing Skills* at http://www.indiana.edu/~teaching/lectskills.html.
ERIC OnLine ED445728	*Know Your Student's Learning Style: The Missing Link in the Lecture v. Active Learning Issue*, by Crowe, Richard, 2000, discusses how David R. Kolb's methodology of identifying four types of student learning styles can be helpful in teaching.
ERIC OnLine ED424103	*The Effectiveness of Teaching Mnemonics in the Study of the Solar System*, by Pickens, Teresa Lynn, 1998, describes the effectiveness of a mnemonic approach in a lecture.

Check this textbook's website at http://education.college.hmco.com/students for additional links.

Questioning

uestioning students while teaching ensures that all students participate in class and are active learners. Questioning students has its origin in the **Socratic Method,** a specific kind of instruction used by Socrates that depends entirely on asking students questions (see the *Meno* at **http://classics.mit.edu/Plato/meno.html** for what most philosophers would agree is an excellent example of the Socratic Method). Well-formed questions are essential to teachers who believe that their primary focus should be having students develop their critical thinking skills and learn the executive processes of the domain (Brogan & Brogan, 1995). Unlike when they provide written answers to written questions, with verbal questioning students have an opportunity to elaborate and adjust their responses based on their interaction with the teacher and other students, as well as to put forth unique insights. Questioning is one of the easiest ways to convert instruction from a passive to active learning experience, but it must be planned and purposeful (Schurr, 2000).

For the Reflective Practitioner

The problem today isn't that we don't have the answers, but that we don't have the questions.

MARSHALL McLUHAN

A former student told me that one of her students complained to a parent that she was asking her too many questions, and the parent complained to the teacher that it was "cruel to put students on the spot." How would you respond to this parent and student?

Some teachers call on the same relatively small group of students and "shop" around the classroom until someone has an answer. This is a common mistake. All students should be required to answer questions. Teachers need to think of questioning as a tool to ensure that all students are attentive, thinking, and reflecting.

Uses of Questions

Questions can be used to:

1. **Evaluate students' preparation and comprehension.** For example, when students read a passage assigned from their basal text, the teacher should question them about it to ensure a baseline of information before developing the Big Ideas.
2. **Diagnose the strengths and weaknesses of students' thinking skills.** As an example, a teacher might ask a student to list and categorize material from the basal text in order to determine the student's ability to categorize. The teacher would then ask additional questions of students who were having difficulty with that task.
3. **Develop, review, and/or summarize content.** It is better to organize the questions you will ask students than to organize what you will tell students.

Teacher's Tip

To integrate homework reading assignments and questioning, have students come to class with questions based on their reading.

In other words, rather than telling students what is in the basal text reading, ask them to explain it to you.

4. **Develop higher-order thinking.** With modeling from students or the teacher, mundane facts can be turned into Big Ideas and Procedural Knowledge. After stating a principle gleaned from the text, students might be asked to apply the information to a new set of circumstances.

A Protocol for Questioning

The following protocol can positively influence how your students feel about questions and reduce the anxiety that some students experience even when they know the answers. The first task in this process is to create a thoughtful atmosphere.

Creating an Environment Conducive to Questioning

Creating an environment conducive to questioning or discourse is essential. Newmann (1988) identified a number of indicators of a "thoughtful classroom":

1. Classroom interaction focuses on sustained examination of a few topics rather than superficial coverage of many. That is, Big Ideas and Procedural Knowledge are emphasized.
2. Students are given sufficient time to think before being required to answer questions.
3. The teacher presses students to clarify or justify their assertions (rather than merely accepting and reinforcing them indiscriminately).
4. The teacher models the characteristics of a thoughtful person. The teacher shows interest in students' ideas and their suggestions for solving problems, models problem-solving processes rather than just giving answers, and acknowledges the difficulties involved in gaining a clear understanding of problematic topics.
5. Students are encouraged to generate original and unconventional ideas in the course of the interaction.

Choosing Grounded and Ungrounded Questions

To organize your questions, you need a Strategy that takes into account different types of questions. There are a number of ways to think about the questions you will pose during the content presentations. One way is to divide your questions into those that are grounded and those that are ungrounded.

Grounded Questions

Grounded questions are those that students should know the answers to because they have been taught the information or were expected to acquire it, perhaps in a homework assignment.

As an example (and admittedly a simplistic one), if you just taught that Columbus's three ships were the *Nina, Pinta,* and *Santa Maria* or if you required students to read a paragraph with that information, they should know the answers to questions about the names of the ships because the information is **"grounded"** in content that has been assigned. During verbal questioning of grounded information, students need to be held accountable through an evaluation and grading system in which the answers to the questions have the same importance as a test. If not, they will soon learn they do not have to read or pay attention during class.

Teacher's Tip

All students should be required to prepare for questioning, and their **answers need to be part of your evaluation scheme.** When a student fails to answer a grounded question, the teacher can indicate verbally, by facial expression, or by body language that an answer is expected. Students have a duty to study and assist other students by answering their fair share of questions. If you don't want to have your grade book open during questioning to record scores for answering and correct answers, make mental notes and record scores at a later time. In either case, your grade reports should include a category for "Answering Questions," just as you have a category for "Tests." Problems of inattention or not completing assignments will dissipate if questioning is elevated to the level of a performance evaluation.

Grounded questions are not limited to simple recall of facts. Students should also be held accountable when they are unwilling or fail to infer, predict, or deduce an answer appropriate to their maturation level. For example, if, after reading about the circumstances of Columbus's first voyage, a teacher were to ask, "What do you think the natives in the Caribbean might have thought about Columbus when they first saw him?" the student should be expected to respond with a thoughtful answer even though the teacher did not explicitly teach the answer or it did not explicitly appear in the text.

Ungrounded Questions

Ungrounded questions are asked as part of an attention-getter or content presentation because they rely on common knowledge. Students may not know the answer through no fault of their own. "Can someone tell me what they already know about Shakespeare?" is an example of a question that might be asked before teaching about sonnets. Students cannot be held accountable if they do not volunteer an answer or if they give a wrong answer.

Structuring Effective and Efficient Questions

Bloom's *Taxonomy of Educational Objectives* (1956) offers a format for structuring effective and efficient questions. Successful teachers take care to craft questions that force students to think at higher levels. The following examples of different levels of questions should help you prepare lesson plans.

1. **Knowledge questions** check only memory: Students show that they have previously learned the material by recalling facts, terms, basic concepts, and answers. A knowledge question should have a follow-up question or should be framed to access both knowledge and a higher-order thinking skill.
   a. *Base question:* What is an amoeba?
   b. *Follow-up question:* What are some of its critical attributes?
   c. *Combined question:* What is an amoeba, and what are some of its critical attributes?
2. **Comprehension questions** check memory and comprehension: The student demonstrates understanding of facts and ideas by organizing, comparing, translating, interpreting, giving descriptions, and stating main ideas. A comprehension question should have a follow-up question or should be framed to access both comprehension and a higher-order thinking skill. Comprehension questions usually require the student to explain the answer in his or her own words.
   a. *Base question:* Please explain supply and demand.
   b. *Follow-up question:* Please give the class an example.
   c. *Combined question:* Please give the class an example of supply and demand and explain the difference.
3. **Application questions** require students to apply their acquired knowledge and comprehension of facts, techniques, rules, and concepts to a new situation or a new problem.
   a. *Question:* So how do the concepts of protagonist and antagonist apply to *Macbeth*?
4. **Analysis questions** require the student to scrutinize Information Knowledge and explain its significance by breaking it into parts, identifying motives or causes, making inferences, or finding evidence to support generalizations.
   a. *Question:* What conclusions did you draw from the evaporation of the water?
5. **Synthesis questions** require the student to combine Information Knowledge to form a new idea based on relationships. The student compiles information

together in a different way, combines elements in a new pattern, or proposes alternative solutions.

   a. *Question:* If you know the longitude and latitude of a place, what other things can you hypothesize about its location?

6. **Evaluation questions** require the student to use a set of criteria to make a reasoned judgment. The student presents and defends opinions and makes judgments about information, the validity of an idea, or the quality of a work.

   a. *Question:* What are the most important criteria for selecting a president of the United States?

The process of questioning is as important as the questions themselves, as we will see in the next sections.

Wait Time Approach

The wait time approach is based in part on the research and principles of **wait time** (Rowe, 1972, 1987) and **think time** (Stahl, 1980). For a synthesis of studies on this topic, see Tobin (1987) and Tobin and Capie (1980). The most basic principle of wait time is that a question is followed by a minimum of 3 seconds of silence so that every student has time to collect his or her thoughts and devise an answer. Then a student is selected, and that student is given as long a time as it takes to collect his or her thoughts prior to answering. By waiting for as long as it takes the student to answer, the teacher conveys an unequivocal message that he or she cares about the individual and that the student must take responsibility for learning. After only a week of consistent use, you should see a change in your students' approach to questions and their preparation for class.

Some of the positive aspects of this strategy are:

1. All students are motivated to develop answers.
2. The length and correctness of students' responses increase.
3. Silence and the number of "I don't know" responses diminish.
4. The number of volunteered answers to ungrounded questions increases.
5. Scores on academic achievement tests increase.
6. Teachers tend to increase the number of higher-level questions.
7. The classroom becomes a quieter and more civil community of learners.
8. Students become more active agents in their own learning.

Teacher's Tip
Students from diverse cultural backgrounds should not be exempted from the questioning process, but they deserve nuanced approaches. See Topic 8 on teaching diverse students for specific recommendations.

Implementation of a Questioning Strategy

Because each teacher has a different approach to questioning, students should be briefed about your approach at the beginning of the term. On the first day of class, explain that questioning is important and how questions will be handled in class. This explanation can have a dramatic effect on the quality of the learning environment. Explain the difference between grounded and ungrounded questions, and tell students the following:

1. During grounded questions, they need not raise their hands. You care about each one of them, so you will call on all students an equal number of times during the course of a week.

2. You will always ask the question before calling on a student so that students will have plenty of time to think about the answer.

3. You will keep track of students called on and their answers because questions are evaluated like a test.

4. Each student is important and is in school to learn. You will give students time to remember what they learned and time to share it with the class. They have to think and pay attention while they are reading, while you are teaching, and while they are being questioned.

5. You will wait in silence for as long as it takes the student to answer. The student always has to answer. Correct, thoughtful answers result in better grades. Partial answers are acceptable. You will not call on another student before the student has given you an answer or has said that he or she does not know the answer.

6. If the first question required only the reporting of knowledge or comprehension, you will usually ask the same student to apply, analyze, synthesize, predict, or evaluate the reported information.

7. Students who wish to comment or expand on another student's answer may raise their hands only after there is a period of silence in which all students consider whether they want to comment.

You should be consistent in applying this framework and use it on an everyday basis if you want your students to enjoy the benefits of the question-centered classroom.

Teacher's Tip

Questions are so important to the development of thinking skills that teachers should place a sign in the back of the classroom that says,
"Ask Questions Wait for Answers"

Best Practices for Questioning

The following additional questioning practices should guide teachers in a classroom of active learners.

1. Create and announce your questioning framework at the first class.
2. Use wait time. If a student doesn't answer, then:
   a. Repeat the question.
   b. Rephrase the question.
   c. Simplify the question.
   d. Ask a student to attempt to rephrase your question.
   e. Break the question down into its component parts.
   f. Make your question more specific.
   g. Ask students what it is about the question that they are finding difficult. Try to elicit some kind of an answer; don't just move on to another student.
3. Ask all students an equal number of questions during the course of a week.
4. Prepare questions that focus on higher-order thinking.
5. Since answers to verbal questions are part of assessment, make sure they are reflected in students' grades.
6. Call on other students to repeat a particularly good answer.
7. Encourage students to answer to the class, not just to you.
8. Form questions that are precise and definite, not ambiguous.
9. Encourage students to ask qualifying questions.
10. Keep questions short and to the point.
11. Avoid fill-in-the-blank questions.
12. Do not ask for trivial information.
13. Hold students accountable by expecting, requiring, and facilitating their participation and contributions.

14. Never answer your own questions! If the students know you will give them the answers after a few seconds of silence anyway, there isn't an incentive.
15. Establish a safe atmosphere for risk taking:
    a. Praise correct answers.
    b. Always respect incorrect responses by saying something positive about students' efforts.
    c. When students make mistakes, ask follow-up questions designed to help them correct themselves.
    d. Model how to think about a question.

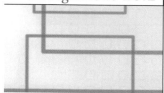

Assignment 28.1 **QUESTIONING FOR A CONTENT PRESENTATION**

INTASC STANDARDS 1–7

Create a grounded questions lecture using the Class Notes approach for the topic you were assigned in Topic 13 by listing a series of questions (followed by the expected answers in parenthesis) that will allow you to "walk" the students through to an understanding of a Big Idea or the Procedural Knowledge that you are trying to convey. Be prepared to turn the assignment in to your professor and to discuss your ideas in class.

Assignment 28.2 **QUESTIONS BASED ON BLOOM'S TAXONOMY**

INTASC STANDARDS 1–8

Using the selection you were assigned in Topic 13, create an example question for each of Bloom's six categories (followed by the expected answers in parentheses). Be prepared to turn the assignment in to your professor and to discuss your ideas in class.

OnLine Resources	QUESTIONING
Wait Time Tips	http://id-www.ucsb.edu/IC/TA/tips/wait.html.
The Socratic Method	http://www.garlikov.com/Soc_Meth.html. http://www.middleweb.com/Socratic.html.
ERIC OnLine ED383706	*Wait-Time: Effective and Trainable*, by Barnette, J. Jackson, et al., 1995, identifies variables related to the use of wait time.
ERIC OnLine ED461411	*Reformulating Useless Questions for Classroom Instructions*, by Sponder, Barry, 1988, provides examples of how to create better questions.

Check this textbook's website at http://education.college.hmco.com/students **for additional links.**

Analogies

t can be argued that all learning requires a bridge from an existing idea to a new idea (Duplass, 1996). The word *analogy* is frequently used to describe metaphors and similes. If we use the word *analogy* loosely to mean a general comparison, then we could say that an analogy happens when we compare two examples: "This is like that." "Boy is to girl as rooster is to hen" is an analogy because we generally think of boys/girls and roosters/hens as two very different things (humans and lower level animals), but they are alike in that both are male/female and animals. A new idea (gender) is formed from the one-to-one relationship by analogizing two existing distinct categories (people and chickens) but with a common attribute (male/female) (Marzano, Gaddy, & Dean, 2000; Nielsen, 1986; Ortony, 1979; Petrei, 1979; Thompson, 1986). Analogies are among the most powerful ways of creating a bridge to a new idea or concept, but they must start with something the student knows (Baldwin et al., 1982; Block, 2001; Readence et al., 1986). Analogies are effective because they create a form of tension or disequilibrium between the known and unknown and require students to "conceptualize abstractions which, in turn, serve as models for thinking" (Manhood, 1987, p. 286).

Analogies are most frequently thought of as based in verbal or written words, but models, simulations, films, and musical compositions are, in a larger sense, also analogies. Analogies of this kind tend to appeal to the affective (emotional) domain to convey an idea. For example, the scene of soldiers landing on D-day in the film *Saving Private Ryan* is an analogy to what combat is like, and, by all accounts, it successfully taps into the viewer's emotions. However, verbal similes and metaphors can also touch our emotions in a powerful way. Expressions like "I was a morsel for a monarch" from Shakespeare's *Anthony and Cleopatra* and "there is a cancer growing on the presidency" by John Dean of Watergate fame are two examples.

Teacher's Tip

If Earth were 24 hours old, dinosaurs would have existed about 1 hour ago, and humans began about 5 seconds ago.

> *Consider these two commonplace analogies: "She is a real prima donna!" and "He is a real Don Juan!" Would you like someone to say this about you? If it were said about someone else, would the impressions you formed about the person stay with you longer than if an analogy had not been used?* **?**

We speak in analogies so frequently that we take them for granted, but excellent teaching requires careful construction of analogies.

Types of Analogies

Analogies can take a number of forms. **Public analogies** can be found in resources like text materials, literature, and periodicals and are incorporated into instruction by teachers. **Teacher-created analogies** are the invention of a teacher, usually created while developing his or her Class Notes. Selecting the examples like roosters/hens and boys/girls to compare in the analogy can involve identifying both **examples** and **nonexamples** that allow the student to easily identify the common attributes of the concept you are trying to teach. They can be provided verbally and by graphic images such as models, pictures, films, and Venn diagrams (see Topic 30).

Similes

Similes are explicit comparisons of two unlike things, usually using *like* or *as*. "Reason is to faith as the eye is to the telescope" by the philosopher David Hume is an example. This kind of analogy draws direct connections from one idea to another, usually by saying, "It is like . . . " For example, when using the term *prime minister* (from the example in Topic 22) for the first time, a teacher can quickly and efficiently create a bridge to the new concept by saying, "It is like the president of the United States." The teacher's analogy can be further developed with additional examples and by dissecting the attributes that are the same and those that are different.

Metaphors

Metaphors are implied comparisons of two unlike things in which *like* and *as* are not typically used. The earlier "I was a morsel for a monarch" is a good example. Here a woman (Cleopatra) says she is (like) a tasty bit of food to the king. Metaphors are more subtle than similes and therefore may require closer scrutiny and analysis. President Theodore Roosevelt's statement "Walk softly but carry a big stick" expresses a complex set of ideas about America's position on the world stage. If a teacher says, "I came to a fork in the road," some students may want to know if the teacher leaned down to pick up a fork unless the teacher clarifies the meaning of this metaphor.

Constructing Analogies

Analogies are made up of three parts: a topic (the main subject of the comparison), a vehicle (the thing that is compared to the topic and illuminates it), and the matching characteristics of the two (Martorella, 1988; Ortony, 1979). In Table 29.1, this has been expanded to include a **topic, topic characters,** a **vehicle,** and **vehicle characters.** Constructing the analogy includes framing the idea in relation to the vehicle and selecting its components. Teachers should plan analogies to ensure that the vehicles and characters have as accurate **parallel construction** as possible. This is known as **framing** the analogy. Table 29.1 uses a social studies example. In this analogy, the Civil War is like two brothers fighting.

Table 29.1 | **AMERICA IN 1860: A FAMILY FEUD**

Topic	Vehicle
America in 1860	Family
Topic Characters	**Vehicle Characters**
Civil War	An argument
North	One brother
South	Another brother

Pitfalls of Analogies

Whereas bias is not a significant problem when using analogies in science, foreign language, or math, a teacher of English or social studies must be acutely aware that it is exceptionally difficult to frame an analogy that is free of bias.

What are the biases in "Walk softly but carry a big stick"?

Because analogies are so powerful, they can be used to overtly or covertly mislead or misinform people. Nazis overtly compared Jews to rats. But the analogy from the Toronto newspaper, "Starbucks coffee shops are spreading through Toronto faster than head lice through a kindergarten class," may seem on the surface to be neutral because it does not state an objection or support for Starbucks. But upon reflection, the choice of lice can be judged to reflect the author's concern about the multiple locations of Starbucks in Toronto. Analogies are efficient and potent, but culture and age differences can also limit their effectiveness (Readence, Baldwin, & Rickelmanm, 1983; Tierney, 1991). As an example, in a social studies class, the teacher asked if anyone knew who Lewis and Clark were. A student whose first language was not English said that he was Superman and she was his lover in the popular 1990s *Lois and Clark* TV series. Obviously, any analogy built around these names might have a rough going with this student. A personal example from my own teaching: I recently drew on my childhood experiences and referred to my students as the "peanut gallery" when they were too talkative for me to get their attention, but because all of them were born well after the *Howdy Doody* show had left the air, they didn't know what to make of it, and some of you, as readers, may not either!

Can you frame an analogy for a topic in your domain?

OnLine Resources	ANALOGIES
ERIC OnLine ED356137	*Using Analogies in Secondary Chemistry Teaching*, by Thiele, Rodney B., and Treagust, David F., 1991, reviews recent literature and considers approaches for using analogies in chemistry.
ERIC OnLine ED378554	*Teaching Science with Analogies: A Resource for Teachers and Textbooks*, by Glynn, Shawn M., et al., 1994, describes the role of analogies in science instruction and presents research on a model for teaching with analogies.
ERIC OnLine ED414206	*Figurative Thinking and the Nature of Physics*, by Mashhadi, Azam, 1997, analyzes metaphors, analogies, and models and describes the results of an empirical investigation of students' conceptions of figurative language.
ERIC OnLine ED391504	*Scientific Thinking Is in the Mind's Eye*, by Ganguly, Indrani, 1995, is a study in which twelve different analogies were used by six teachers engaged in teaching high school science.

Check this textbook's website at http://education.college.hmco.com/students for additional links.

Graphic Organizers

Concept organizers, graphic organizers, and concept maps are terms generally used interchangeably and describe various, typically paper-based formats that assist students in developing concepts and placing information into the correct schemas (Couch, 1993; Dunston, 1992; Rumelhar, 1982).

Concept mapping has its origins in constructivist theory and the work of David Ausubel (1963) and Joseph D. Novak (1993). The goal is to move teachers away from the kind of rote learning and traditional worksheets that are still used in schools today to what Ausubel called **"Meaningful Learning."** While there are many different forms of concept maps (flow charts, Venn diagrams, etc.), the one attribute that makes these images successful is their visual simplicity (Stone, 2002a). They typically consist of nodes (points or vertices) representing concepts, and links (lines and arcs) representing either temporal or causal relationships between the nodes (Vacca & Vacca, 2001). Figure 30.1 shows an example of a concept map.

Concept maps are important tools for a number of reasons.

1. They are appropriate to almost all grade levels and domains.
2. They visually enhance learning.
3. They accommodate different learning styles.
4. They are easy to teach from and use.
5. They include both Information Knowledge and Procedural Knowledge.
6. When teachers use them, they model how to construct knowledge.
7. When students make or complete them, students must reconstruct knowledge.

The use of graphic organizers tends to follow one of two approaches, teacher-centered or student-centered, and both are best practices.

Concept Maps in Teacher-Centered Instruction

Concept maps should be integrated into the instructional pattern of lectures, discussions, question sessions, and case studies. Teachers often use graphic organizers as transparencies on the overhead projector or as boardwork. Not only is a graphic organizer a valuable visual clue about the organization of the conceptualization that is about to be taught, but the teacher is also modeling how to organize concepts, select organizers that are most informative, and analyze concepts and their relationships. In these situations, the teacher is modeling the use of graphic organizers for depicting knowledge from the domain and provides the students with a conceptual framework. The goal is for students to capture the entire image in their mind's eye while the teacher progressively differentiates the information in the organizer (Ausubel, 1963); see Topic 25.

Sometimes the teacher uses the **"reveal method,"** whereby parts of the organizer are hidden and revealed as the components are discussed and examined. In other cases the graphic map is displayed in its entirety at one time during teacher talk. Frequently, teachers create unique graphic organizers based on the specific Information and Procedural Knowledge they are teaching. Other organizers may come with the teacher materials for the textbook or from websites (see the online resources at the end of this Topic). The number and variety of graphic organizers seem infinite, but it is crucial that the teacher selects an organizer that most correctly depicts the concepts being presented and has the organizer completed in his or her Class Notes, as it should appear at the end of the lesson, before instruction begins.

Figure 30.1 shows a Hierarchy Organizer used to explain Roman Civilization. The items in boxes (*the nodes*) are **concepts** (such as "empire") or **facts** (such as "Augustus" and "7 kings"), and the terms between the boxes are **connectors** or *links* (such as "had" and "started with").

One teacher-centered approach would be to exhibit the completed Figure 30.1 as a transparency and to deliver a lecture with questions about the more detailed information on each component. A second approach would be to require students to draw an identical Hierarchy Organizer and fill in the missing concepts, facts, and connectors and take notes as instruction progresses. A third option would be to distribute copies of a blank Hierarchy Organizer, rather than have the student draw it, and have them fill it in as explained in the second approach. In all three cases, as the teacher progresses through each of the topics "framed" by the organizer, he or she would introduce images taken from the Internet that illuminate the concepts. The wealth of images about the Roman Empire on the Internet makes it possible for a teacher to provide an image for almost every example included in the concept map.

In this teacher-centered approach, the active learning is limited to looking at images, replicating or filling in the graphic organizer, and perhaps asking questions and taking notes. In spite of this shortcoming, the teacher-centered approach should be used, if for no other reason than to appeal to different students' learning styles (Taricani, 2000).

Figure 30.1 | **ROMAN CIVILIZATION CONCEPT MAP**

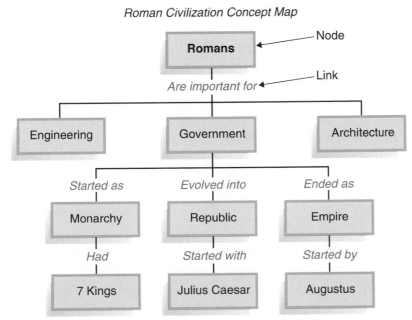

Roman Civilization Concept Map

Concept Maps in Student-Centered Instruction

Student-constructed graphic organizers appear to be more beneficial than organizers used to structure teacher talks (Bean et al., 1986; Moore & Readence, 1984; Ruiz-Primo & Shavelson, 1996). Students retain information longer (Novak, Gowin, & Johansen, 1983) and typically generate more sophisticated thinking (Jonassen, 1996) when the lesson requires them to construct a concept map out of notes or reading materials. When created by students, concept maps also serve as excellent diagnostic tools because they graphically depict students' accurate conceptions and misconceptions. Teachers can thus use them to gage the success of the lesson for all the students and to either reteach the lesson or provide feedback to individual students (Ross & Munby, 1991). Requiring students to create a graphic organizer after a lecture, discussion, or other activity (practice or homework) challenges them to be more actively involved; accommodates individual differences by allowing individuals to use different kinds of graphic images; and forces students to conceptualize their understanding of the concepts, rather than just being presented with the teacher's view.

Continuing with our social studies example of the Roman Empire, assume that you modeled the use of the graphic organizer in a lecture on the Roman Empire. Now you want students to read a passage in the basal text on the medieval period. You could use a **Timeline Organizer** (see Teacher's Tip) for the medieval period and then cover the components of the society, such as serfs, lords, and the economics of a castle and fief system, in a lecture. In your guided practice you could ask students to create a concept map of medieval civilization based on your lecture and the text. As an independent practice, students might create a **Compare and Contrast Organizer** (see Teacher's Tip) to compare the Roman and medieval civilizations.

Reading and Concept Maps

Topic 13 identified a number of prereading, reading, and postreading options that should be used each time a teacher requires students to read texts. Concept maps can be used to structure a process whereby students must reconstruct the knowledge from their reading at increasing degrees of difficulty and self-initiative.

The following **Guided Reading Escalation Model** (Duplass, 2004) is based on a number of premises and goals:

1. The priority is construction of knowledge based on reading to ensure long-lasting concept formation.
2. Students should learn to take responsibility for their reading. Prior to the teacher's instruction, students should read the material until they comprehend it at least at the recall level.
3. Students should use graphic organizers to help them form concepts and decide how to present ideas they acquired from the text.
4. Incremental increases in expectations create a scaffold for students and increase their likelihood of success.

If students are expected to create graphic organizers, the teacher should consider three questions:

1. Which type of organizer should be used? Would a Venn diagram, a data retrieval chart, a timeline, or a cause-and-effect diagram most effectively convey the ideas?

2. What type of Knowledge is to be recorded? For example, data retrieval charts lend themselves to categories, while sequences are best shown in timelines, flow charts, and escalator diagrams.

3. How should the Knowledge be organized? In the case of a data retrieval chart, decide what vertical and horizontal headings will create meaningful relationships between the data in the cells. For timelines, determine how long the time period should be and what the important benchmarks are.

Graphic organizers appeal to our inclination to visualize conceptualizations: "A picture is worth a thousand words." To translate text into a concept map, students must be given the opportunity through demonstration and practice to develop:

1. The skill of identifying and recording relevant information correctly.

2. The Procedural Knowledge of how to organize the information based on the relationships of facts and concepts and to decipher any figurative, biased, covert, or emotionally charged textual approaches.

3. The intuition that is part of an Academic Disposition to select the best graphic organizer to project their conceptualization.

Do you prefer to create concept maps or have them presented to you?

The Guided Reading Escalation Model would start with the teacher modeling different types of organizers that reflect the concepts in the reading passages selected from the textbook. With perhaps the first half-dozen or so passages assigned for students to read (either in class or as a homework assignment), the teacher might suggest the kind of organizer to use. Sometimes the students would be allowed to work in pairs or in groups, and at other times they would be required to complete the organizer on their own. In all cases, each student completes his or her own organizer. For example, completing a graphic organizer might be the **bell work** at the beginning of class (see Topics 20 and 34).

The ultimate goal of the Guided Reading Escalation Model is for each student both to decide what type of concept map will best depict the information he or she has read and to organize the knowledge in a way that reflects the best representation that is accepted by the community of practice. So after the teacher has initially modeled the process and advised students which organizer to use in the early stages of the course, the students should be expected to select the kind of organizer that is most appropriate and create the organizer so that it is complete and accurate. A box of graphic organizer forms would typically be kept at a resource table, and after reading a passage a student would be expected to select one that he or she believes will best reconstruct the passage and most clearly communicate the ideas to someone else. Having students not only read but also select the best method to visually explain the passage empowers them to be lifelong learners, fosters autonomy, and ensures the highest level of knowledge reconstruction.

Topic 30: **Graphic Organizers**

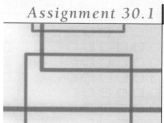

Assignment 30.1 **DEVELOP A TEACHER-CENTERED GRAPHIC ORGANIZERS LESSON**

INTASC STANDARDS 1–7

Based on the topic you were assigned from Topic 13, create a concept organizer that you would use in teacher-centered instruction and briefly explain how it would be used. Be prepared to turn the assignment in to your professor and to discuss it in class. For a selection of types of organizers, visit one of the websites cited at the end of this topic.

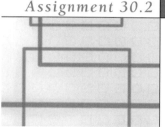

Assignment 30.2 **DEVELOP A STUDENT-CENTERED GRAPHIC ORGANIZERS LESSON**

INTASC STANDARDS 1–8

Based on the Selection you were assigned from Topic 13, create a *different* concept organizer from Assignment 30.1 that you would use in student-centered instruction based on their reading of a passage in the basal text. Be prepared to turn the assignment in to your professor and to discuss it in class. For a selection of types of organizers, visit one of the websites cited at the end of this topic.

OnLine Resources	GRAPHIC ORGANIZERS
Eduplace	Organizers can be obtained in PDF form at http://www.eduplace.com/graphicorganizer/.
California Department of Education	Organizers can be obtained at http://www.sdcoe.k12.ca.us/score/actbank/torganiz.htm.
ERIC OnLine ED471633	*Improving Tenth-Grade Students' Five-Paragraph Essay Writing Skills Using Various Writing Strategies, Guided Assignments, and Portfolios for Growth*, by Hopkins, Carolyn, 2002, explains the use of graphic organizers as part of a strategy to improve low-achieving tenth-grade students' essay-writing skills.
ERIC OnLine ED420853	*Improving Student Reading Comprehension in the Content Areas Through the Use of Visual Organizers*, by Velasco, D., Pearson, I., Jockl, P., and Agnello, C., 1998, describes a program for using graphic organizers to enhance reading comprehension in the content areas.

Check this textbook's website at http://education.college.hmco.com/students for additional links.

Group Learning

Group Learning, *Cooperative Learning,* and *Collaborative Learning* are terms used interchangeably in the academic literature because they share one attribute: Learning takes place in groups (typically no more than four students to a group), rather than through instruction delivered in a whole-class setting (Cohen, 1986). Grouping approaches allow the teacher to change the class tempo, reduce teacher-centered instruction, and increase student opportunities to construct ideas (Smith, 2000). For these reasons, learning in groups is a powerful and essential tool for the teacher and it is demonstrably effective (Elhoweris, 2001; Johnson & Johnson, 1989; Johnson et al., 1981, 1983, 1990; Sharan, 1980; Slavin, 1990a, 1990b). When compared to students in traditional whole-class or individualized learning, students who have participated in well-structured and meaningful group learning situations have been shown to develop:

- Higher-level reasoning.
- Greater empathy for fellow students.
- Enhanced social perspective taking (the ability to understand how a situation appears to another person).
- Better self-esteem.

However, there are pitfalls, particularly when teachers are not vigilant in monitoring the groups' activity. When teachers are not attentive to the activity of the groups, a few students in the group may take over and do the majority of work or monopolize the discussion; classroom management problems erupt; and the groups become unproductive, creating apathy. Middle school students typically have extensive experience working in groups from their elementary school settings and expect to find this kind of learning Strategy in the classroom; however, some of the behaviors students may have learned because of inattentive teachers will be unproductive and need to be unlearned (Tiberius, 1999).

For the purposes of this textbook, group learning is segregated into two broad categories, the less formal **Breakout Groups** and the more structured **Cooperative Learning Groups.** Tiberius (1999), Johnson and Johnson (1989), Johnson et al. (1981, 1983, 1990), Kagan (1989, 1993, 1994), Slavin (1984, 1990), and Ellsworth (2003) offer a number of principles and practices that are applicable to both breakout groups and cooperative learning groups. They provide some of the foundation and many of the strategies proposed in this Topic. The Cooperative Learning Center of the University of Minnesota at **http://www.co-operation.org/** was created by Johnson and Johnson, and Cooperative Learning at **http://www.cooperativelearning.com/** is sponsored by Kagan and associates, go to Products and then Research. Both sites are worth visiting.

Teacher's Tip

Learning alone (as opposed to in groups) is preferred more by Caucasian students than by Mexican Americans. It is also preferred more by Mexican American students than by African Americans.

See ERIC OnLine ED393607. Hispanic-American Students and Learning Style. *ERIC Digest.*

Breakout Groups

The breakout group strategy is typically used in conjunction with whole-class discussion, lecture, and reading activities, although it can be very effective as an attention-getter as well. The teacher pauses, announces the task, and assigns or allows students to organize themselves into groups of two, three, or four. Students either turn to each other in their desks or move their desks around to form groups. Typically, students are given a task (discuss, create a diagram, etc.) that can be completed in less than 15 minutes. Breakout groups can be organized around existing seating, but it is best to vary the members of the groups so that each student learns to work with all other students. Breakout groups should be formed and unformed quickly with a sense of urgency about getting down to business. They have short-term goals and typically lack the formality and structure of cooperative learning.

While the breakout groups are meeting, the teacher circulates among them to ensure that everyone is participating. For evaluation purposes, if a product such as a graphic organizer is to be created, each student should create his or her own while working with the other students. When members of the group contribute to a project by creating individual components, using a cooperative learning approach may be more effective. Participation in the discussion or activity should be observed and graded as well. Students must be held accountable, so if questioning is used during a debriefing following the breakout groups, the teacher must remember to call on different students on different days and to record their participation and questioning grades. The following are some structured grouping methods that are frequently used with pairs, one form of a breakout group.

1. **Pairs create sequences:** Students write notes on small pieces of paper. Each pair of students compares notes and puts the notes in an order that reflects the organization of the new information.
2. **Pairs compare:** Two students work independently, but are allowed to check one another's work.
3. **Pairs paraphrase:** The teacher requires one student to paraphrase the other student's statement, verbally or in writing.
4. **Pairs interview:** After a content presentation or reading assignment, two students interview each other about the information.

Cooperative Learning

Cooperative learning is an effective group learning method that is very structured compared to breakout groups. To be successful in breakout groups or cooperative learning, students must master interpersonal skills (Jacobs, Power, & Inn, 2002). However, one of the goals of cooperative learning is to develop those skills. Cooperative learning promotes thinking skills and positive interdependence among students, while holding each student accountable. The cooperative learning structure helps students develop these skills by providing specific rules and roles during the group activity.

The Key Elements of Cooperative Learning

The following describes some of the requirements for effective cooperative learning.

1. **Teacher supervision** is needed to establish the rules. The teacher should observe groups to ensure that all students are gaining from the experience.

Teacher's Tip

During group learning, teachers should never sit down. They must circulate among the groups to ensure that students stay on task. Teachers who use the time to prepare the next lesson or grade papers are setting themselves up for discipline problems and less than desirable learning outcomes.

If a student is off task or misbehaving, the teacher should join the group to reinforce the rules or answer questions about the assignment.

2. **Heterogeneous groups** are usually used to ensure that students of different abilities and backgrounds learn to work together to achieve a goal.

3. **Positive interdependence** is achieved through group goals, joint rewards, divided resources, and role assignments. Students are responsible for their own behavior in the group.

   a. Students are accountable for contributing to the assigned task.

   b. Students are expected to help any group member who wants, needs, or asks for help.

   c. Students will ask the teacher for help only when everyone in the group has the same need.

4. **Face-to-face interaction** encourages eye contact and verbal and nonverbal responses. Students explain, discuss, solve problems, and complete assignments as a team.

5. **Individual accountability** requires students to be held accountable for individual tasks that will help the group meet its overall goal. Some possible roles include:

   a. Leader.
   b. Recorder.
   c. Timer.
   d. Encourager.
   e. Reader.
   f. "Gofor."
   g. Artist.
   h. Proofreader.
   i. Checker.
   j. Observer.

6. **Social skills** are behaviors that enhance positive interaction and communication among group members. Students learn to compete at a young age, but we must continue to teach middle and high school students to collaborate and use social skills in a cooperative group as well. The teacher needs to review behaviors and establish rules. Students must:

   a. Take turns.
   b. Share information.
   c. Speak quietly.
   d. Listen to the person speaking.
   e. Use time wisely.
   f. Politely criticize ideas, but never people.

7. **Group processing** is a discussion of how well the group has functioned. Key words for this element are *participation, feedback, reinforcement, clarification,* and *refinement.* Group processing allows for closure when a cooperative assignment is completed.

8. **Evaluation** should include both an individual performance assessment and a team assessment.

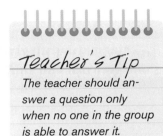

Teacher's Tip

The teacher should answer a question only when no one in the group is able to answer it.

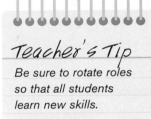

Teacher's Tip

Be sure to rotate roles so that all students learn new skills.

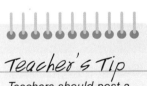

Teacher's Tip

Teachers should post a set of class rules for cooperative learning based on the principles in this Topic on a wall for continued reference during the school year.

How do you personally feel about your experiences in group learning activities? **?**

Topic 31: **Group Learning**

Primary Cooperative Learning Models

There are numerous models and types of cooperative learning to use, depending on your lesson goals. Table 31.1 provides brief descriptions of the most common models.

Table 31.1 | PRIMARY COOPERATIVE LEARNING MODELS

Name of Model	Brief Description
Co-op	Students work in teams, and each contributes to an assigned product by accepting responsibility for a part of the project.
Corners	Students form a team in each corner of the room to discuss an idea presented by the teacher. A social studies teacher might ask students to come up with stereotypes of Asian Americans, African Americans, Italian Americans, and Native Americans. Each team discusses the idea and prepares statements about its ethnic group. Each corner shares its idea, and then all four teams listen to and paraphrase each other's ideas.
Jigsaw	The number of members in a team is determined by the number of separate subtopics. Each student on the team becomes an expert on one of the subtopics by working with the experts on the same topic from the other teams. Upon returning to the primary team, the student teaches the other members about the subtopic. In a biology class, one person in the group might be assigned the heart, another the kidney, etc.
Numbered Heads Together	Every team member is numbered; for example, in a team of four, students would take numbers 1 through 4. The teacher poses questions; team members consult to make sure that everyone knows the answer; the teacher calls a number and that student responds.
Pairs Check	Students work in groups of two pairs each. One student in a pair coaches while the other student solves the problem. Then they alternate. After every two problems, the pairs check each other's answers.
Round-Robin	Each team member takes a turn to share with classmates.
Roundtable	Each team member writes one answer as a paper and pencil are passed around the group.
Student Teams Achievement Divisions (STAD)	Teams are organized following a lesson, and members help each other master the knowledge. Students take individual quizzes, and the team evaluation is based on the success of individuals.
Teams-Games-Tournament (TGT)	TGT is the same as STAD, but quizzes are replaced with a tournament in which teams compete with each other. Low achievers from one team compete with low achievers of other teams, and each member earns points.
Team-Assisted Individualization (TAI)	TAI combines group and individualized learning. Students on a team work individually on a self-paced assignment, and members check on each other and help solve problems.
Think Pair Share	Students think about a topic, pair with another student to discuss ideas, then share their revised thoughts with the class.

Source: Adapted from Kagan (1989).

Grouping Decisions and Tasks

Two key decisions for the teacher have to do with whether students can select their groups or whether the teacher assigns students to groups. The best practice is to incorporate both into your planning. As an example, in Topic 13, I suggested heterogeneous groups when the reading plan calls for students to read in class. In cooperative learning, groups are typically heterogeneous based on a number of variables like achievement and ethnicity. With few exceptions, for heterogeneous groups you need to assign the students to achieve the desired mix to support your goals. If you are using small groups (such as pairs), and if you are using quick groups (whereby students work with the person next to them or in front or behind them), it is easier to achieve your goals and convenient to let students select their partner even if they are not always heterogeneous. In classes where a small number of students might not have mastered some Procedural Knowledge but most of the other students have (such as in mathematics), it would be effective to group those students together so the teacher can reteach the procedures while the other students work on other schoolwork.

Students should be put into groups to perform a task whenever additional, more intimate student-to-student interaction might produce a better result than whole-class instruction. The kinds of "practice" activities envisioned in the Instructional Sequences explained in Topics 20 and 32 are ideal for group activities. The kinds of tasks assigned for group work are similar to those used for self-directed instruction (see Topic 33, Table 33.1) and tend to either be:

1. **Discussion Tasks,** in which students are expected to have a dialogue that results in a more detailed analysis, debate and discussion by the group, and then reports of either personal or group decisions or solutions; or
2. **Product Tasks,** in which a tangible product is produced by each individual or the group, which is facilitated by student collaboration. This would include simulations, skits, and presentations, as well as papers, charts, and results of experiments (see Table 33.1).

When defining the task that will be completed in a group, the teacher must integrate the group activity into the instructional pattern, whether it is a breakout group or a cooperative learning activity. For product tasks, the teacher should have created a model in advance of starting the lesson. For discussion tasks, the teacher should have Class Notes for the debriefing.

COOPERATIVE LEARNING LESSON   *Assignment 31.1*

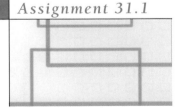

INTASC STANDARDS 1–8
Based on your assigned lesson plan topic from Topic 13, create a cooperative learning lesson and explain how it would include the eight "Key Elements" provided in this Topic. Be prepared to turn the assignment in to your professor and to discuss your ideas in class.

OnLine Resources	GROUP LEARNING
PBS's Thirteen EdOnline	The *Concept to Classroom* page at http://www.thirteen.org/edonline/concept2class/month5/index.html offers various topics on group learning.
The Jigsaw Classroom	Go to http://www.jigsaw.org/links.htm.
ERIC OnLine ED334922	*Implementing Cooperative Learning Methods*, by Lyons, Paul R., 1990, identifies the basis and rationale for the concept of cooperative learning, describes the dynamics of the cooperative learning approach, and proposes methods.
ERIC OnLine ED392100	*Dealing with Parasites in Group Projects*, by Carter, Judy H., 1995, lists eight criteria of successful groups and a number of practical suggestions.

Check this textbook's website at http://education.college.hmco.com/students for additional links.

Discussions and Case Studies

"Leading an effective discussion can be one of the most difficult tasks of teaching" (Barton, 1995, p. 346). It requires a commitment to a shared dialogue with the students and great restraint by the teacher, who naturally wants to work through his or her planned lesson. Discussions are effective and necessary because, by requiring students to think critically and logically, they force students to be active agents in their own learning (Bridges, 1979; Erskine & Tomkin, 1964; Douglas, 1970). However, since students' ideas (sometimes poorly conceived, tentative, or not well thought out) become public through their communication, discussions can be both intimidating and gratifying on a personal level for the student.

The subject of this Topic is not the serendipitous discussions that occur in the classroom, but the **planned discussions** in whole-class settings and choreographed group activities. In both cases, the teacher has knowledge that he or she has decided the students need to know, but he or she believes the best approach is to have the students come to the new understanding through a dialogue with the teacher and other students. A discussion approach can be the entire content presentation, part of a lecture, or planned as small-group activities (Muller, 2000). But in all cases, your Class Notes should clearly delineate what knowledge will be conveyed and the kinds of propositions or topics you may need to interject should the students not be as spontaneous as anticipated.

Discussions

In **whole-class discussions,** the teacher typically serves as the guide, but he or she needs to develop a communication style that is informal and conversational. The substance of discussions should be propositions delivered in a casual environment, rather than the kinds of questions used in the Socratic method. This casualness requires a high degree of self-control in the teacher, who can become impatient and too quickly bring closure to the dialogue. Teachers have been shown to wait less than a second after a student's last syllable is uttered before interjecting something (Rowe, 1974). Poorly managed discussions can take on the form of a "quiz show" characterized by the teacher as inquisitor at one end of the spectrum and the "bull session" at the other end (Roby, 1981). Therefore, even though the teacher has planned the outcome (the destination, if you will) by choosing a discussion approach, he or she must accept that the trip to the knowledge will not be the most direct route and will take longer than a traditional lecture.

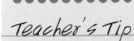

Teacher's Tip

Don't assume because it is a whole-class activity that you must lead the discussion. As an alternative, consider having one or two students lead the discussion while you join the class by taking a seat in one of the students' desks.

Best Practices for Discussions

There are a number of best practices to consider when planning and conducting discussions, some of which are drawn from Parker (2001) and Johannessen (1984, 2002):

Teacher's Tip

An excellent strategy when preparing for a discussion is to create the lecture and then convert all the statements to questions and answers and use those as your Class Notes.

1. To prepare students for general discussion, at the beginning of the year have students discuss the nature of a good discussion.
2. Create a set of guidelines or rules for discussions that ensure civility, and review those in the beginning of the year and periodically.
3. Plan the discussion. What topics do you want to cover? In what order? What will you do if nobody says anything?
4. Create a stimulus, what Larry Johannessen (1984) calls "Controversy," to begin the discussion. This is usually a provocative question, an emotionally laced statement, a proposition that on the surface appears to be a contradiction ("The sun doesn't rise in the east!"), a crux, a dilemma, a problem, a paradox, or something similar.
5. The focus is not on what you will say, but on how you will respond to students' propositions and questions. With your experience and because you are the expert, you can hypothesize the direction of the discussion just as you would anticipate the sequence of a lecture. Both should be planned.
6. Use students' comments as points at which you insert your planned agenda, rather than as in a lecture, where you lay out your agenda and then entertain questions from students.
7. Use a combination of group and whole-class discussions, even on one topic. As an example, provide the stimulus, put the students in groups, and then debrief through a whole-class discussion.
8. Guide participation by rephrasing a statement by one student into a question for another.
9. If a class discussion is not going well because of lack of energy or enthusiasm, stop and discuss the situation with the students.
10. Discussion must be based on substantial knowledge; thus the teacher needs to consistently ask the students to relate their comments to the content that was either read or viewed by them or presented in a lecture.
11. Use silence—your own! If you are silent they will speak. Studies show that teachers dominate what are characterized as discussions almost as much as lectures (Bellack et al., 1966).
12. Purposely slow the pace so that students sense they have time to reflect.
13. Remember that you are modeling for your students how to listen while being involved in a class discussion, so you are teaching both content and an Academic Disposition (Borg et al., 1970).
14. Rather than respond, ask another student what he or she thinks.

Teacher's Tip

If participation in the class is being dominated by a few students, give every student five rubber bands or paper clips. Each time a person speaks, he or she must throw a rubber band into a plastic bucket in the middle of the room. When students have used up their rubber bands, they can't talk anymore until everyone has participated.

Discussion Versus Questioning by the Teacher

The inclination of teachers is often to use questions to promote discussion. However, the kind of structured and rigorous questioning described in Topic 28 can detract from the more casual, reflective strategy of leading discussions if students sense that they are being quizzed or evaluated by the teacher. And too many questions tend to disrupt the flow of a discussion. In addition, we know that students' responses are longer and more complex when they are (1) responses to statements by the teacher, rather than to a question (Colby, 1961; Dillon, 1981a), and (2) responses to fellow students' statements or questions rather than to the teacher's questions (Mishler, 1978). You can use a number of alternatives to questions to maintain momentum in the discussion (Dillon, 1981b, 1981c):

1. Express your own thought.
2. Summarize your interpretation of what the last speaker just said.
3. If you are confused by the last statement, express your feeling and invite the student to elaborate.
4. Invite a student to comment on the last statement.
5. If a student has difficulty making him- or herself understood, suggest that he or she turn the thought into a question for the class.
6. Be silent—someone will speak.

Discussion and the Affective Domain

The **affective domain** deals with the emotions, feelings, and values that are naturally expressed by students during discussions. The content of social studies, literature, and health education, because it is subject to opinion and values more than, as an example, science or math content, lends itself to discussions that can be emotionally charged. However, in homeroom and on those occasions when topics arise serendipitously in all classrooms, teachers can find themselves dealing with controversial issues.

Developing an Academic Disposition requires the kind of thoughtfulness that allows students to reflect on the congruence or incongruence of their feelings and emotions with the more detached, logical approach that characterizes decision making. This general area of instruction is often referred to in the literature as **values analysis** and **values formation** and is usually based on the seminal work of Lawrence Kohlberg (1981, 1984, 1987). For example, in a landmark study, Blatt and Kohlberg (1975) demonstrated that students who participated in a discussion of moral dilemmas improved their moral reasoning over those who did not have such an experience. One of the key issues that teachers face is how much they should direct or attempt to shape students' thinking (which becomes perhaps most important if the student's comment seems to reflect an undemocratic notion) and how they can best do that while allowing students' autonomy. This is a major consideration for all teachers, who must balance their responsibilities to society with the rights of parents to shape their children's thinking and values and the students' right to their own thoughts.

Teacher's Tip

When students ask, "What do you think?" your response should be, "It is not important what I think; what do you think?" This gives a clear message that their ideas are important and you are there to help them think, not to pontificate.

> *In the high school homeroom, you are collecting money for the senior prom, and a student comments (loud enough for a reaction from other students) that he isn't going to the prom because some of the gay students are going as couples. How would you handle this?* **?**

Kelley (1986) described four approaches to dealing with the teacher's need in discussing controversial issues to balance **indoctrination** and **enculturation** (the passing on of the culture to the next generation): (1) Exclusive Neutrality, (2) Exclusive Partiality, (3) Neutral Impartiality, and (4) Committed Impartiality. These Strategies can be used by a teacher to deal with topics that have an affective component. Given the maturation level of middle and high school students compared to elementary students, Kelley's models of Neutral Impartiality or Committed Impartiality would be appropriate on most occasions. **Neutral Impartiality** requires that teachers withhold their perspective about their own position on a topic so that students, who do not know where the teacher stands, are forced to rely more on their own critical intelligence. **Committed Impartiality** entails two beliefs. First, teachers should state rather than conceal their own views so that students can judge if they are letting their bias interfere with the discussion of the issues. And second, teachers should encourage the pursuit of truth by ensuring that competing perspectives receive a fair hearing. In both cases, the successful values analysis discussion requires students to reflect on the inevitable conflicts between their affective and cognitive domains.

What approach do you favor when dealing with subject matter that has an affective aspect to it? Why?

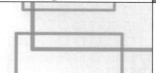

Assignment 32.1 **DEVELOP A DISCUSSION GUIDELINES LESSON**

INTASC STANDARDS 1–7

Develop a discussion lesson in the Class Notes format that results in a set of guidelines or rules for discussions that ensure civility in your classroom. Be prepared to turn the assignment in to your professor and to discuss it in class.

Assignment 32.2 **DEVELOP A DISCUSSION LESSON**

INTASC STANDARDS 1–7

Based on your assigned lesson plan topic from Topic 13, create a discussion lesson using the Class Notes format. Be prepared to turn the assignment in to your professor and to discuss it in class.

Case Studies

Case studies are a very formalized version of discussion and requires *neutral impartiality* on the part of the teacher until the end of the case. The case study method is one of the most successful instructional approaches because it effectively organizes a process that integrates new knowledge, discussion, self-examination, and reflection into a consistent approach. Fundamentally, it is a discussion-based, problem-solving instructional approach that encourages critical thinking (Wood & Anderson, 2001).

What Is a Case Study?

The case study describes a problem that the students must solve. If there is a chance that students would already know of the case or if they are likely to be familiar with the problem, it is generalized by the teacher to disguise the outcome and circumstances. The information provided in a case is ambiguous, complex, or incomplete, thus forcing students to analyze and make decisions. The typical case study is a written account, but it can also be presented verbally. It can be a homework assignment to be debriefed in class, or a short case can be a classroom reading. When the case is assigned as homework, students can be required to bring their solutions to class for discussion; that way, all students are prepared to be participants. The teacher first presents the case, and then students—in groups or as a whole class—participate in a collective analysis and decision-making discussion. The concepts and ideas emerge interactively through the case study process. At the end, the teacher debriefs the class, restating and clarifying the principles and ideas developed by the students rather than teaching the concepts directly in a lecture.

Preparing for a Case Study

Teachers need to prepare students for a case study. One of the first steps is to model how to read a case. The following suggestions are adapted from the Political Science Department at Florida Atlantic University (at http://www.fau.edu/polsci/1930/cases.html). Students should be instructed to:

1. Read the case quickly the first time to get a sense of it.
2. Identify the decisions that have to be made.
3. Reread the case, noting facts.
4. Identify and list the problems, constraints, and opportunities.
5. Identify alternative actions, as well as good and bad short-term and long-term consequences.
6. Be prepared to present their ideas forcefully, and to support them with as much care and persuasion as they can.
7. Listen to other students' ideas.
8. Ask questions and admit confusion.
9. Keep on track; do not raise another issue until the current topic is exhausted.
10. Build on the ideas of others.

Organization of Cases

There are a number of ways to organize cases to produce different effects.

1. **The Full Case:** All the narrative and background information is provided at the beginning and all at once.
2. **The Sequential Case:** The narrative and background information is given out in installments so that the case changes over time. After the discussions on the case have begun, the teacher provides additional information that creates a new challenge to the students.
3. **The Research Case:** Students are expected to research and gather information before making a decision.
4. **The Unsifted Case:** Narrative and background information is handed out, but some of the background information is irrelevant. This forces students to make a judgment about the relevance of the data.

The Advantages of Using Case Studies

There are a number of benefits to using the case study method.

1. Students are taken out of a passive role and become active agents in the learning process.
2. Students are typically required to analyze information and develop solutions to problems.
3. Students develop skills that allow them to think clearly about unstructured, ambiguous situations using incomplete information.
4. Students must decipher the underlying motivations of the characters or the causes of events or phenomena.
5. Students must deduce assumptions and principles because cases do not explicitly denote the underlying problems.
6. Some students are natural listeners and some are natural talkers; a case study, with appropriate teacher supervision, should ensure that students learn to do both, regardless of their temperaments.
7. Students develop skills in articulating ideas to influence and persuade others.

Assignment 32.3

DEVELOP A CASE STUDY LESSON

INTASC STANDARDS 1–7

For your discipline, find a case study by conducting a search of the Internet and create a lesson using the Class Notes format. Be prepared to turn in both the Internet resources and your Class Notes to your professor and to discuss them in class.

OnLine Resources	DISCUSSIONS AND CASE STUDIES
The National Center for Case Studies in Science	Go to http://ublib.buffalo.edu/libraries/projects/cases/case.html.
ERIC OnLine ED450434	*Facilitating Classroom Discussion: Lessons from Student-Led Discussions*, by Muller, Heidi L., 2000, presents several excerpts from student-led discussions as examples of how students are able to facilitate a class-long discussion on a controversial topic.
ERIC OnLine ED466265	*The Role of Class Discussion in the Learning-Centered Classroom*, by Cross, K. Patricia, 2002.
ERIC OnLine ED455221	*The Case Study Method: Critical Thinking Enhanced by Effective Teacher Questioning Skills*, by Wood, Alexander T., and Anderson, Carol H., 2001.

Check this textbook's website at http://education.college.hmco.com/students for additional links.

Self-Directed Instruction

The need to customize learning experiences has taken on greater importance as a result of the diversification of American classrooms (Allan & Tomlinson, 2000). Teachers accommodate individual student differences (see Topic 8) through their choice of content, methods, process, and products (Tomlinson, 2001), and often through the use of approaches such as **one-on-one sessions** (as when a mathematics teacher during a problem-solving task provides direct "over the shoulder" assistance to an individual student) and **small heterogeneous groupings** (as when an English teacher groups students by reading ability and joins a more challenged group during the reading of a poem like "The Raven"). However, the purpose of this Topic is to focus on **Self-Directed Instruction,** a more independent form of study than teacher-centered approaches like lecture and discussions or the differentiated instructional approaches described above.

Approaches to Self-Directed Instruction

Self-Directed Instruction shifts the responsibility for learning to the student: The student must rely on his or her own initiative to bring his or her learning to a successful outcome (Gibbons, 2003). Typically, the teacher defines the parameters of the tasks by defining the process, content, and products. In some cases, all students might have the same content but can choose their products (the principle of gravity might be the topic, but students are free to write an essay or draw a diagram). In other cases students select the content and the product is defined (students choose one of the wars America fought in, but all the students must draw a timeline). Such self-directed instruction differs from the typical tasks given students during practice and group activities because (1) it takes a longer time to complete (self-directed tasks are usually multiday or week projects); and (2) the focus is on the responsibility of the individual students for their work and products (with as little intervention by the teacher as possible). Self-directed instruction is sometimes misunderstood to mean that students work only by themselves. In fact, although each student must do his or her own work, many tasks are completed while students work together or consult with the teacher.

Teacher's Tip

Particularly at the beginning of the year, teachers need to give students more structure and checkpoints for self-directed instruction.

Keys to Self-Directed Instruction

Self-Directed Instruction, whether organized as an assignment, contract, or a packet (as will be discussed in the following sections), has a number of crucial attributes.

1. **The teacher must clearly define the scope of the instruction.** One or more multiple lessons must be about the assigned task and the timeline for completion, which must be clearly articulated verbally and in writing by the teacher. It is a best practice to present an example of a finished product or a rubric and then place students in groups to discuss the project and ask questions.

2. **The teacher must clearly delineate the limits of acceptable collaboration with peers.** In addition, the teacher should discuss the nature of plagiarism in the context of ethical behavior.

3. **Students take charge of their own learning.** Not only are students expected to make judgments about the content, but they must also **pace themselves** within limits set by the teacher's milestones. In some cases the teacher organizes resources into packets or in a library or learning resource center to facilitate access to the content. Depending on the nature of the tasks, the teacher may leave the content to be more open-ended. In both cases, students need to monitor their own progress and independently collect information to complete the prescribed task.

4. **Direct teacher supervision is minimized.** After an overview or modeling of the task, the teacher responds to students' questions. The teacher should then minimize supervision so that students take charge of their own learning. It is prudent to establish timelines and review drafts of their products, but the students should be expected to proceed as directed and the teacher should limit his or her further input to content matters.

5. **Learning has specific and measurable objectives or outcomes.** These can be communicated by a list of objectives and/or an assessment rubric (see Unit 7).

6. **The teacher sets a minimum standard.** Such a standard is set for page length, components of the product, and the knowledge it represents, but students are encouraged to go beyond the minimum set by the grading scheme.

7. **Optional objectives allow for additional effort by students.** The teacher may provide the options, or students can propose creative alternatives for the teacher's approval.

8. **Students set their own pace within the milestones or deadlines.** When it is an in-class assignment, other activities are available to those who choose to finish faster. Often, the teacher provides time in which students can choose to work on their projects in class, do other homework in school, or work on other assignments for other classes.

9. In addition to acquiring knowledge in the domain, **the teacher's goal is for the learners to practice and exhibit life skills** such as:
   a. Self-direction.
   b. Responsibility.
   c. Decision making.
   d. Resourcefulness.
   e. Accountability.
   f. Time management.
   g. Creativity.
   These kinds of dispositions are as much the focus of self-directed instruction as is traditional content. Talking with students individually and as a group about these attitudes is crucial to their development.

Learning Packets

Learning packets are used to organize learning tasks for the classroom or for homework. Learning packet tasks might be based solely on one topic for all students and the only resource might be the textbook. Or the packet might include different content for each student and have multiple materials (supplemental readings, charts, pictures, practice items) in each packet. The kinds of resources, products, and skills listed in Table 33.1 can be used to define the learning packet's tasks and evaluation scheme.

Students can work in groups or individually. There should be a minimum set of tasks and some optional tasks. Time is scheduled for students to work on their packets in class, at home, and/or in the learning resource center, and packets are turned in for evaluation upon completion.

Library and Learning Resource Centers

Most schools have expanded the traditional concept of a library. Formerly just a place to house books, libraries now include an array of resources such as computers, Internet access, CDs or films of experiments or documentaries, and so forth. These **Learning Resource Centers (LRCs)** are ideal for facilitating self-directed, self-paced learning. However, self-directed learning requires a high degree of planning and numerous resources. Such planning pays off with highly active and motivated students.

The following ideas for planning a task in which all the students cover the same content over a four-day period should be helpful.

Step 1. Select a topic for an upcoming lesson that you had planned to offer by using a more traditional lecture, discussion, or group activity.

Step 2. Identify resources in the LRC and create additional resources for the students to use to learn the content independently; alert the LRC about your plans.

Step 3. Create a learning packet with directions, timeline, rubric, and list of objectives and organizers. The objectives should be written along the following lines:

    a. "View the Encarta CD and record the following information: . . ."

    b. "Go to the following Internet site . . . and write a summary of your perceptions."

    c. "Use the *Encyclopedia Britannica* to identify five major . . ."

    d. "Create a graphic image with at least five elements on . . ."

Step 4. Model for students a completed packet based on the objectives.

Step 5. Explain that all students will spend the next four days in the LRC (with you). As students finish, they should bring the packet to you. You will review the packets, give them an oral exam on what they have learned, and assign them a grade or tell them to redo some objectives or reread their materials for another oral exam. As soon as students complete the task, they can use the time for other schoolwork.

Step 6. Go to the LRC and let the students begin working while you circulate and make yourself available for clarifications, discussions, and oral exams. You should plan to monitor and engage students who you know have less self-discipline and/or who are not putting their time to good use.

Step 7. Debrief the students in a whole-class discussion about their knowledge with an eye to emphasizing Big Ideas and Procedural Knowledge.

If you gave four days in the LRC for completion of the project, the first time you use this approach you may find that the time is too short. If so, announce an additional couple of days. When this is used effectively, the more self-disciplined students complete their projects early and you have more time to work with the less motivated students, drawing on your interpersonal skills to motivate them. In some cases a few students might come to you three or four times before their packet and oral exam are satisfactory to you, but this is one of the best ways to get to know your students and to position yourself to help them become more successful in their schoolwork.

Teacher's Tip

Your Library Media Specialist can be one of your greatest assets in gathering the materials your students can use for individualized projects. Enlist his or her support early in the development stage of your lesson.

Teacher's Tip

If the task involves using the Internet at school, teachers may want to identify the links beforehand, but in all cases, teachers must monitor the students.

Teacher's Tip

"WebQuests" are usually teacher- or student-created websites that are excellent resources for the creation of learning centers. WebQuests have taken on a standard form that allows for self-paced and independent student work. You can create or use **WebQuests** from the Internet with your students, but you must first carefully scrutinized them.

Learning Contracts

The **learning contract** method has the following attributes:

1. It is a prearranged, written agreement between the teacher and the student (and sometimes the parent).
2. The student commits to doing specific learning tasks within a given time frame to earn a specified grade.
3. The learning is self-directed once the contract is signed.
4. The contract is unique to each student.

Learning contracts can be powerful tools for building self-control and a sense of self-satisfaction. Many contracts are structured around independent projects that students are assigned. Others are created for students who are interested in an idea or topic and would like you to incorporate the extra work into your evaluation and grading. This is not the same as not doing their work and asking for "extra credit work" to make up for prior failures.

Learning contracts can be very effective with students who are highly self-motivated and who need enrichment. In addition, they can be effectively used with students who fall behind in their schoolwork. Students who have fallen behind should not be excused from the original work requirement, but a contract might be negotiated for a timeline to make up the work while keeping up with the ongoing class requirements.

 What is your philosophy on "extra credit work"? Should it be used? If so, when?

A learning contract should include the following:

1. Student's name
2. Date
3. Reason for the contract
4. Objectives, which should be written in unambiguous language, such as "The student will . . . :
   a. . . . neatly outline Chapter 12 in no less than two pages, free of misspellings and grammatical errors." (or refer the student to a rubric such as the **Six-Trait Analytical Writing Rubric** described in Topic 14)
   b. . . . make a five-minute presentation to the class on . . ."
5. Due date
6. Outcome: "If completed on time and as specified, the student will receive an A and the assignment will be worth 20 points."
7. Signature of teacher, student, and parents

Table 33.1 gives a list of options for developing individualized instruction goals, objectives, directions, tasks, and rubrics. It describes the many skills, products, and resources that can be applied to Self-Directed Instruction.

Teacher's Tip

You might consider using a **Learning Contract** by requiring all students in the second half of the year to have at least one independent study learning contract. Each student would be expected to select a topic that he or she is interested in and to propose what he or she would like to do. The contract formalizes the expectations.

Table 33.1 **SELF-DIRECTED INSTRUCTION OPTIONS**

Skills: *What students practice or demonstrate*		
Classifying	Communicating	Comparing/contrasting
Computing	Creating	Critiquing
Demonstrating	Drawing conclusions	Evaluating
Investigating	Listening	Measuring
Preparing	Problem solving	Reading
Record keeping	Researching	Summarizing
Thinking	Vocabulary development	Writing

Products: *What students create*		
Advertisements	Collages	Diagrams
Diary entries	Dioramas	Displays
Editorials	Essays	Experiments
Games	Graphic images	Graphs
Interviews	Journal entries	Letters
Models	News stories	Pictures
Poems	Puzzles	Reports
Scrapbooks	Timelines	Etc.

Resources: *What students use to gather information*		
Art supplies	Audiotapes	CDs
Computers	Filmstrips	Flash cards
Games	Globes	Graphic images
Internet hookups	Laser discs	Library books
Magazines	Maps	Newspapers
Pamphlets	Pictures	Posters
Puzzles	Tapes	Textbooks
Timelines	Videotapes	Scientific apparatus
		Etc.

Source: Adapted from Schurr et al. (1995).

Assignment 33.1 | **DEVELOP A SELF-DIRECTED INSTRUCTION LESSON**

INTASC STANDARDS 1–8

Based on your assigned lesson plan topic from Topic 13, create a **Learning Packet** for a self-directed approach in a Learning Resource Center and explain how you would implement your lesson and debrief the students in a whole-class format. Be prepared to turn the assignment in to your professor and to discuss it in class.

OnLine Resources	SELF-DIRECTED INSTRUCTION
University of South Florida	For directions on how to create WebQuests and WebQuests from different domains, go to http://www.coedu.usf.edu/webquest/.
ERIC OnLine EJ636462	*Contract Grading: Encouraging Commitment to the Learning Process Through Voice in the Evaluation Process,* by Hiller, Tammy Bunn, and Hietapelto, Amy B., 2001, explains how to negotiate and renegotiate contracts, outlines limitations and challenges, and highlights ways in which contract grading assists in learning management concepts.
ERIC OnLine ED475517	*Activities for Differentiated Instruction Addressing All Levels of Bloom's Taxonomy and Eight Multiple Intelligences,* edited by Rule, Audrey C., and Lord, Linda Hurley, 2003, contains thirteen curriculum units integrating Benjamin S. Bloom's levels of cognitive understanding with Howard Gardner's eight domains of intelligence to provide a framework for individualized instruction.

Check this textbook's website at http://education.college.hmco.com/students for additional links.

Practice and Homework

For the Reflective Practitioner

Practice is the best of all instructors. PUBLILIUS SYRUS

ractice should be incorporated into the Instructional Sequence (refer to Topic 20) as either an **in-class assignment** or an **out-of-class assignment** (homework). **Homework,** as explained in Topic 13 on reading, may be used to practice or to create a baseline of information prior to instruction. We will discuss both approaches to learning in this Topic. However, before doing so, I need to elaborate on two important concepts, Automaticity and Overlearning.

Automaticity and Overlearning

In Topic 12, the term *Automaticity* was introduced as it pertained to the importance of vocabulary in reading. In this Topic, it refers to the importance of students mastering Procedural Knowledge processes so that the procedure occurs rapidly "within their heads" and with little conscious effort, like adding 2 plus 2 for adults. This way, you don't have to commit substantial memory to the process and thus free up memory for reconstructing and making meaning of knowledge that is more complex (Willingham, 2003a, 2003b). As an example, in mathematics, if the process of solving equations as a result of instruction in algebra does not become automatic for the student, the more complex operations of calculus become more difficult to process.

Overlearning is how thinking processes become automatic. It is learning something to a point of mastery so that it can be replicated repeatedly, automatically, and over extended years. As an example, repetition with mathematical problem solving is intended for this purpose, and most of us, even though we do not use the multiplication basic skill frequently, are able to simultaneously remember the value of numbers, recall and utilize the basic skill of multiplying numbers like 24×300, and produce an answer—all within our mind's eye. This automaticity is due to overlearning, which requires practice—not just explanation or exposure to the concepts by the teacher. Practice in the Basic Skills and Procedural Knowledge skills of the domain is the gateway to becoming apprentices in domains, and it opens the door for students to become experts (Ericsson, 1996). Sustained practice over the time period of a course, a semester, a year, or several years is the overlearning strategy that allows students to develop automaticity.

Practice

Teachers create assignments or tasks so that students can overlearn Procedural Knowledge and Basic Skills. In this learning process, students are taught something (through lecture, group activity, modeling, etc.), then practice the knowledge by applying it to new content under the supervision of the teacher, and then practice again, but on their own (see Topic 20). Ideally, both practices would take place prior to the formal assessment. The teacher weighs time constraints, degree of difficulty, and the expectation that students must take responsibility for their own learning to determine how much practice he or she will require or allow to be optional and whether the assignment will be an in-class or out-of-class assignment.

Most teachers associate practice with skills like reading, writing, and arithmetic. Demonstrating a procedure in the domain and following this with student practice is a common approach used in teaching mathematics, science, foreign language, and theater. However, social studies and literature can also be practiced. For example, when a lower-level Procedural Knowledge skill such as finding longitude and latitude is taught in geography, students could be given longitudes and latitudes and required to find cities or landmarks. They could also be given cities and expected to calculate their longitudes and latitudes. In English class, the teacher could model the process of analyzing plot and conflict in a short story (Procedural Knowledge) in a dialogue with students in class, and the students would be asked to practice applying the same process to a new short story.

Teacher instruction and/or modeling of a procedure should be followed by both Guided Practice and Independent Practice. Students should be expected to apply a method they have just learned or, after a short review by the teacher, a method they learned previously.

Guided Practice

Guided Practice ALWAYS takes place at school in a classroom, library, studio, laboratory, computer room, or athletic field where the teacher can observe and give feedback. In this method, the teacher actively interacts with students, providing **"over-the-shoulder instruction"** to an individual or group. Students can be expected to apply the knowledge as individuals, or they can be allowed to complete their individual assignments in groups. They are permitted to consult with other students while working, but not to copy results. Each student is responsible for his or her assigned project or task; however, when working in groups each student must produce his or her own product so that you know he or she has practiced. The best way to motivate students to take these kinds of assignments seriously is to create engaging, meaningful, and challenging tasks. Such tasks are usually graded, but they are typically given a lower value than a test since they are the students' "practice." In Guided Practice organized in groups, the teacher can give both group and individual grades, but never just group grades.

Independent Practice

Independent Practice can take place in school or as homework. The student is expected to complete the task without (or with very little) assistance from the teacher, other students, or anyone else. It is best to have an Independent Practice follow a Guided Practice as an in-class activity or a homework assignment, but it can be used as a substitute for Guided Practice with provision for teacher feedback, given time constraints. However, the teacher should never lose sight of the fact that it is the practice that leads to mastery.

Independent Practice is also graded to ensure that students take the assignment seriously. It is typically given a lower value than a test and a higher value than Guided Practice.

Teacher Supervision of Practice

Practicing in the classroom is an excellent way to "break up" the routine of teacher-centered instruction. As a general rule, once the teacher has taught the knowledge and explained the directions, he or she should minimize responses to questions from students, at least directly. Instead, the teacher could use the Socratic method to draw the analysis and conclusion (answer) out of the students who pose questions. Questions should be redirected to another student in the group or to a student in another group.

If a student persists in asking questions of the teacher after weeks of using the practice approach, the teacher might ask the student if he or she understands the content before the group activity begins. The teacher could counsel the student privately. This encourages listening skills, metacognition, and responsibility and demonstrates that the student knew or should have known the answer. A teacher who does not handle questions this way will have taught students that they do not have to pay attention, and will have begun an unending process of answering questions.

DEVELOP A GUIDED PRACTICE LESSON

Assignment 34.1

INTASC STANDARDS 1–8
Based on your assigned lesson plan topic from Topic 13, create a content presentation and Guided Practice in the Class Notes format. Be prepared to turn the assignment in to your professor and to discuss it in class.

Homework

Homework is a form of independent practice. Teachers have traditionally depended on it to further students' education, using the home as a place for practice. Parents often see homework as an indicator of a productive classroom and their teenager's development.

The Value of Homework

There are advocates and opponents of homework. Disagreements about the value of homework stem in large measure from what individuals identify as its purpose as well as from the complexity of measuring its academic effects (Cooper, 2001). Advocates believe homework improves not only academic performance but also study habits, develops autonomy and self-discipline, promotes efficiency by effectively using both the classroom and the home for learning, and facilitates parental involvement in children's education. Such results lead them to conclude that homework is too valuable not to be used as a method. And research demonstrates that homework has a positive long-term, if not short-term, effect on students' academic success (Cooper, 1989, 2001; Lamare, 1997). Objections to homework seem to stem from poorly thought-out homework assignments and policies and cultural factors that have resulted in parents not making homework a priority.

When homework is well conceived and required in moderation, it can be an effective Strategy for developing students' potential. O'Rourke-Ferra's (1998) article "Did You Complete All Your Homework Tonight Dear?" is an excellent summary of research and opinions on and about homework. Go to this book's website for a link to this ERIC online article, ED425862.

Teacher's Tip

It is appropriate to expect students to read passages from the basal text and complete an assignment started in class, apply a skill taught in class, or apply a concept that was modeled in class. Assignments that require resources from the community library, material from a store (poster paper), or parent supervisions must be planned and announced well in advance of the due date. Ask yourself this question: "If I were a parent, would I think this assignment was beneficial and worth the time and effort?"

For the Reflective Practitioner

Half of all high school students who do more than 10 hours of homework a week will go on to earn a bachelor's degree.
Only 16 percent of high school students doing less than 3 hours of homework a week will graduate from college.　　ROSENBAUM (2001)

Because homework is an out-of-class task and requires integration into family life, certain challenges must be minimized so that students (and their parents) can more easily meet the teacher's expectations. The permeable family makes it a challenge for some parents to commit the time needed to supervise or even check homework, and sometimes the student must work after school for the family's financial stability. Some parents feel that homework is less important than social or athletic events and that it intrudes on their lifestyle. Teachers, therefore, have the additional challenge of persuading parents that homework is crucial to their teenager's future and that the parent, teacher, and student make up a team that needs to use homework to maximize learning. On their part, teachers should weed out unnecessary and mundane assignments and make sure the goals of homework are legitimate.

The Goals of Homework

In homework that is assigned appropriately, the student has four goals:

- To practice skills learned in class.
- To learn a baseline of information in advance of a lesson, usually as a reading homework assignment.
- To apply concepts learned in the classroom by completing assignments.
- To learn self-discipline.

Homework is valuable because it can:

- Promote important study habits.
- Improve students' attitudes.
- Make efficient use of home and class time.
- Promote productive relationships between parents and their teens.
- Improve academic performance.

Parents' Duties

Whereas teachers provide a consistent learning environment in their classrooms, each home is unique, and parents (or caregivers as the case may be) should not be viewed as a substitute for the teacher, because not all parents have the appropriate training. Therefore, when designing homework, make sure the student's success will be based on his or her own level of participation in the classroom learning process that led up to the assignment. Parents can be called upon and should be expected to monitor their teenagers so that they complete their homework as prescribed and on time (Cooper & Gerston, 2002).

While teachers express frustration with students who do not do homework, parents express frustration when their teenagers are given too many seemingly trivial assignments, when assignments are not clearly explained, or when the necessary content instruction did not precede the homework task.

Teachers should send a letter to parents at the beginning of the school year encouraging them to adopt the following practices:

1. Provide a specific and consistent time each day for homework so that it becomes a valuable part of the daily routine at home (such as following an after-school activity, or immediately before or after dinner).

Teacher's Tip

Teachers should also consider holding a homework seminar for parents during the first week of class and/or explaining homework at the open house and at parent-teacher meetings.

2. If students are allowed to do their homework in their bedrooms but performance starts to wane, designate a specific place where homework is to be done that is in your presence (such as at the kitchen table).

3. Limit distractions by eliminating TV and music during homework.

4. Check the student's understanding of the assignment before he or she starts.

5. If there is a problem in understanding the assignment, the student should contact a study club member or homework buddy. However, students should not give answers to or receive answers from other students.

6. Students should not do homework with their friends; homework is independent practice, unless it is a group project.

7. If the student encounters a problem, ask questions to help the student arrive at a conclusion.

8. Never do a teenager's homework by telling him or her the answers.

9. Expect the work to be neat and orderly.

10. Check the work for accuracy if you have the expertise.

Teachers' Duties

Teachers must also give greater attention to the value and importance of homework. Consistency, frequency, and reasonableness are crucial standards. Teachers should consider adopting the following policies and practices:

1. Only homework that students should know how to do if they were paying attention in class will be assigned.

2. Reading assignments will follow a prereading activity and/or be followed by bell work or a postreading activity. Students will be held accountable for reasonable factual information.

3. Homework assignments will always be doable and will not need any particular expertise to complete, if the teenager was paying attention in school.

4. The assignment will be clear and definite, and the student will be able to do it at home, even if he or she does not have computers or other specialized materials.

5. Students will be held accountable: They will not be allowed to shift the blame for not doing homework to parents or anyone else ("the dog ate my paper"). It is the student's responsibility to get his or her homework done.

6. Students will be assigned to a study club or homework colleague to get assignments when they are absent and to clarify assignments if they are confused upon reading the assignment at home.

7. The amount of time students will be expected to spend on homework will be limited. (I suggest an average of one-half hour a day, Monday through Thursday.)

8. Meaningful homework will be assigned on a consistent basis, perhaps every Monday through Thursday. The schoolwide policy will be checked before this schedule is established.

9. Homework will be collected, read, and graded, and feedback will be provided within two days of receipt. Marking will include positive comments as well as notes about mistakes. Homework that reflects improvement will be noted as such.

10. Students will be required to use a homework planner.

Teacher's Tip

Second Chances. *Even though your standard should be that all homework must be turned in on time, there are times when a student has a legitimate reason for not turning in homework on time. Giving a second chance requires your professional judgment, but it should be accompanied by a clear message about the Standards and future expectations. See Benson (2000) for additional suggestions on homework.*

Teacher's Tip

During the first day of class, create **Homework Colleagues.** *In pairs of two or three, students exchange phone numbers, and they are then expected to call their colleague if they miss class or need a clarification on how to complete the assignment.*

11. Students—not the teacher—will be responsible for the daily check-in and checkout of homework. Students will be responsible for delivering homework to the teacher.
12. There will be some mandatory and some optional homework.
13. There will be options: For example, students will be able to choose between creating an essay or creating an image to express their ideas.
14. Assignments will be written on the chalkboard at the beginning of class, not at the end as an afterthought.
15. As students leave, they will be reminded about the homework due the next day.

 How much should homework be worth in your grading system (versus tests, exams, quizzes, and in-class practice)?

Assignment 34.2

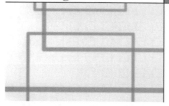

INTEGRATE HOMEWORK INTO YOUR LESSON PLAN

INTASC STANDARDS 1–8, 10

Based on your assigned lesson plan topic from Topic 13, prepare a handout for your students to be given out the day before the lesson starts on Monday that designates the homework that will be due on Monday, Tuesday, Wednesday, and Thursday of your topic lesson plan. Be prepared to turn in your assignment to the professor and to discuss your ideas in class.

OnLine Resources	PRACTICE AND HOMEWORK
The Homework Spot	http://www.homeworkspot.com/.
ERIC OnLine ED477945	*Homework Tips for Parents* (Consejos para los padres sobre la tarea escola), District of Columbia, 2003.
ERIC OnLine ED444702	*Improving Academic Achievement Through Creative Alternatives to Traditional Homework Strategies*, by Diersen, Kimberly, 2000, describes strategies targeted to eighth-graders in all subject areas who failed to complete homework assignments.
ERIC OnLine ED435956	*Strategies to Improve Student Motivation to Complete Homework Assignments*, by Watland, M., Sigourney, D., Mallek, C., and Fraser, E., 1999, describes a program designed to increase student motivation to complete homework assignments.

Check this textbook's website at http://education.college.hmco.com/students for additional links.

Field Trips and Guest Speakers

Field trips and **guest speakers** provide a different context, stimulus, and voice than the teacher-led classroom. The time commitment to field trips and guest speakers can be considerable, so their use should be based on the students' needs and weighed against lost opportunities to teach more efficiently with other methods. So that they do not drift into "fun-only" activities, field trips and guest speakers should be integrated into a comprehensive lesson plan; that is, they should not be stand-alone events and should serve as a motivating device to stimulate the acquisition of important concepts.

> **Teacher's Tip**
>
> As a prelude to a trip or guest speaker, have students write about what they hope to learn from the experience.

Field Trips

The field trip can be used as a motivating device prior to classroom instruction about the field trip's topic, a content presentation in the middle of a lesson, or a culminating activity at the end of the Instructional Sequence. Regardless of when the trip takes place, a briefing and debriefing should be part of the Instructional Sequence.

Many teachers use field trips as rewards that students must earn. While this is a common practice, it implies that the field trip is not an essential part of an important planned learning experience. When a trip is used as a reward for students who are achieving or who do not have behavior problems, the students who might be motivated to improve their behavior or performance by the active learning experience are deprived of the opportunity to do so.

Field Trip Venues

The following are some local venues for field trips that have educational value:

Archeological dig	Military base
Art museum	Newspaper or TV station
Factory	Performing arts venue
Farm	Reenactment site (such as
History museum	historic site Williamsburg)
Laboratory	Science museum
Nature and ecology park	State park
Municipal building	

Virtual field trips can be taken over the Internet (Mandel, 2002). For example, you can search the database of the Smithsonian Institution at **http://educate.si.edu/** for virtual field trips students can take in the classroom. Virtual field trip sites often offer streaming video and slide shows as an alternative to being at the site. The Curry School of Education at the University of Virginia provides a guide and more than twenty-five examples of lesson plans for field trips at **http://curry.edschool.virginia.edu/curry/class/Museums/Teacher_Guide/**.

Best Practices for Field Trips

You will need to commit a great deal of your time to planning the trip if you want to avoid certain hazards. The following are useful guidelines:

1. Make a pretrip visit before deciding to take the students.
2. Take the time to meet with your administration and explain your educational goals.
3. Decide if you will run the tour or if a guide from the venue will do so.
4. Verify and confirm all arrangements in writing (transportation, meals, departure and return information, additional supervision).
5. Make arrangements for students with special needs.
6. Create clear rules about conduct for the students.
7. Review appropriate conduct and attire with the students.
8. Invite parents to serve as additional supervisors.
9. Create an attachment to the school's standard permission slip that includes a statement of the educational goals.
10. Take roll before, during, and after the trip to keep track of students.
11. Preview the trip with students.
12. Provide each student with a "guide sheet" or questions to answer while on the trip.
13. Provide instruction before and after the trip.
14. Give students specific tasks to be completed as a result of the trip.
15. Debrief the students about the field trip.

Teacher's Tip

One alternative to an actual field trip is visiting the field trip site and recording your visit on videotape. Schools often have camcorders and digital cameras for this purpose.

Guest Speakers

Guest speakers invited into your classroom can provide powerful learning experiences (Poling, 2000). They can also be disasters. Many potential speakers are experts in very particularized areas and are unable to adapt their knowledge and presentation to the middle or high school classroom. Many other people who want to come to your classroom have biased agendas and will attempt to indoctrinate your students. And some guest speakers are performers with no substantive background in the content they propose to represent. You need to decide if a guest speaker is the best source of information for the students.

Best Practices for Guest Speakers

To ensure an excellent outcome, you should set expectations for your classroom visitors. In addition, you should do the following:

1. If at all possible, preview the speaker before extending the invitation. If that is not possible, meet with the speaker or call a reference from a recent presentation. Deciding to invite the speaker solely on the basis of a brief phone conversation is extremely risky.
2. Obtain your principal's approval.
3. Communicate all the arrangements (arrival time, length of presentation, number of students) verbally, and verify and confirm them in writing. Send the speaker a map; alert the front desk; and have someone meet the person at the entrance to the school.
4. Clearly state the focus of the presentation and your expectations. If you cannot reach an agreement, do not run the risk; it would be better to decline the opportunity. Remember, your credibility is on the line.
5. Limit the time to no more than two-thirds of your class time.
6. Encourage an active presentation based on active learning strategies.

7. Encourage guest speakers to use Realia, music, artwork, primary documents, pictures, apparatusus, handouts, and visual aids, if appropriate.
8. Suggest the value of storytelling and anecdotal stories, and warn the speaker to avoid preaching.
9. Prepare students by reviewing etiquette and questioning skills.
10. Provide instruction about the topic as part of a comprehensive lesson before and after the presentation.
11. Require students to prepare questions for the visitor.
12. Give students specific assignments to be completed as a result of the presentation.
13. Send a thank-you note from the class.

Can you share a good example of a guest speaker or field trip in your local area? Can you recall a good experience from your middle or high school years to share with the class?

OnLine Resources	FIELD TRIPS AND GUEST SPEAKERS
Tramline's Virtual Field Trips	http://www.field-guides.com/vft/
Utah Education Network	http://www.uen.org/utahlink/tours/
ERIC OnLine ED398030	*Field Trips: Maximizing the Experience*, by Millan, Deborah A., 1995.
ERIC OnLine ED455107	*Community Connections for Science Education, Volume I: Building Successful Partnerships*, by Robertson, William C., 2001.
ERIC OnLine ED446901	*Virtual Field Trips in the Earth Science Classroom*, by Woerner, Janet J., 1999.

Check this textbook's website at http://education.college.hmco.com/students **for additional links.**

Media- and Computer-Based Resources

Media (video and sound recordings, whether on tape or disc or digital or analog) and computer resources (handhelds, PCs, specific and general content CD's, the Internet, digital projectors, etc.) are so familiar to students that it is essential that teachers incorporate these assets into the instructional pattern as easily and frequently as they use the overhead projector, textbook, and chalkboard.

When using these resources in lectures, teachers should seamlessly integrate them into the teacher talk. When used as part of task assignments in Guided or Independent Practice and in group or individual activities, the kind of protocol described in Topic 13 on reading should be adapted to the resource. That is, you should preview, as an example, the video's content as well as explain the tasks, provide time for the students to complete the tasks, and then debrief the expected new knowledge.

Media- and computer-based resources have become so varied that they defy clear distinctions, but generally speaking they fall into two groups:

1. **Proprietary resources,** which include:
   a. *Integrated assets,* which are the materials that come with a textbook, and
   b. *Freestanding assets* that can be purchased to support your instruction in your discipline but are independent of your textbook.

2. **Public domain or quasi–public domain resources** are freestanding assets and are typically available at no cost. Anything like a ".gov" website, a video recording you made of a *NOVA* program, or a rented video of a feature film can be used in a classroom.

Media

The use of video and sound resources in a classroom should not be the passive activity experienced by consumers in movie theaters or on the living room couch. In a classroom, video and sound should be an integral part of a choreographed lesson.

Video and audio appeal to multiple senses and the affective domain with sound and images that provide cognitive information. Sound recordings are not used as frequently as they once were because of the widespread availability of video. However, video is, arguably, the most misused technology in the classroom. A growing number of teachers show entire videos of historical feature films or television science shows as examples, as rewards, over multiple days, or as entertainment while they perform other duties. Some school districts have facilitated the misuse of videos by providing an approved list of videos that teachers can show so that they do not have to preview a video for the administration's approval. Classrooms are not effective settings for video presentations, but they are ideally suited for discussions and for students to test their thinking.

Teachers should use classroom time to maximize the kind of learning that can only take place in classrooms and schools. Showing videos as a substitute for teaching is bad practice.

The Key Clips Approach

Whether it is a video designed specifically for an educational purpose, such as a *NOVA* or History Channel production or a feature film that can be used for the same purpose, such as *Romeo and Juliet* or *Glory*, showing the entire video is often unnecessary and an unproductive use of classroom time. When previewing the video, identify the key clips you need so that the video doesn't become a substitute for the kind of interactive, thinking activities that are the essential part of classroom learning.

This **Key Clips approach** is the best practice for using freestanding video or audio productions because it is effective, efficient, and appropriate to a classroom setting and ensures that the video is grounded in a lesson. In this approach, the teacher shows only a 10- to 20-minute clip of the video to make a very specific point related to the lesson.

Best Practices Using Media

The following practices should be used when making sound and video part of your instruction.

1. Sound recordings and videos may be integrated into a comprehensive lesson plan in the following ways:
   a. As an attention-getter to stimulate students' interest and followed by an explanation and examination of the recording.
   b. As an integral part of a content presentation.
   c. As a closing or summary following a content presentation followed by a debriefing.
2. Only use a clip, no more than about 10 to 20 minutes, to achieve your objective. Most media segments developed as integrated assets are designed for 15- to 30-minute attention spans.
3. Hold students accountable for the content.
4. The procedure should include an introduction, directions on what to look or listen for (if not a handout of objectives), and a debriefing.

Computer Resources

The **personal computer** and the **Internet** continue to change the way we live, work, and learn. Nevertheless, despite the continuous decline in the cost of an entry-level computer and the ease of Internet access, teachers cannot plan tasks on the assumption that every household has a computer and access to the Internet. Assigning homework that requires a computer or the Internet is inappropriate unless the teacher is sure that all students have access to these technologies.

Hardware Considerations and Configurations

The teacher who has a computer at school and one at home (or a laptop) that connect to the Internet and to printers can spend less time on everyday planning and administrative tasks and more time on creative endeavors essential to quality instruction. With this kind of asset, this teacher can create more engaging lectures and structure more meaningful active learning experiences.

Teacher's Tip

Students come to school familiar with various forms of popular music, like country and rock 'n' roll. Schools should introduce students to what they do not know. Playing **classical music** as students enter your class, at transitions, and when leaving class is often soothing, a signal of a change in activity, and engaging.

Teacher's Tip

Be sure to check your state, district, and school policies regarding use of videos and access to the Internet by students under your supervision.

For the Reflective Practitioner

The Digital Divide. In 2001, over 70 percent of whites and Asians regularly used computers and over 59 percent used the Internet; in contrast, as few as 55 percent of Latinos and blacks used computers and 39 percent used the Internet.

NATIONAL TELECOMMUNICATIONS AND INFORMATION ADMINISTRATION (NTIA) (2002)

Topic 36: **Media- and Computer-Based Resources**

Teacher's Tip

In a calculus course, hand-held devices like a graphing calculator are commonplace. However, it is likely that handhelds will become more prominent in the future. Go to http://education.ti.com/us/solution/social.html for information on the use of handhelds in most teaching fields at the middle and high school level.

At the time of this publication, the ideal configuration for a school might include the following scenario. Assuming a class size of twenty-five students, the school would provide a computer with an Internet connection, a scanner, a digital camera, and a printer for each teacher, a large monitor or a projector for whole-class instruction, and five computer stations with Internet connections for group work. If there is also a computer laboratory with twenty-five stations or twenty-five stations in the Learning Resource Center (LRC) that can be reserved, all twenty-five students could use a station at the same time during an assigned task. If the school is networked with a website that supports list serves and individual classroom or teachers' websites, the school can be said to provide a comprehensive platform of options for using technology to teach.

The reality is very different. Believers in the use of digital technology are alarmed by reports of computers stacked in corners and never used. Teachers point to antiquated equipment and the lack of a comprehensive platform as inhibiting their use of the technology (NCES, 2000). Administrators complain of budget constraints and the difficulty of even keeping working light bulbs in overhead projectors. All of this is true.

However, the promise of digital technology is too great for us not to overcome such problems. And progress is being made. In a 2000 study, most public school teachers (84 percent) reported having at least one computer in their classrooms. Approximately half of the public school teachers who had computers or the Internet available in their schools used them for classroom instruction. Sixty-one percent of teachers assigned students to use these technologies for word processing or creating spreadsheets, and about 50 percent assigned tasks requiring Internet research, drills, and solving problems and analyzing data (NCES, 2000).

Teacher Uses of Computers

Teachers can become more effective by using computers to learn and gather content information, create teaching materials, accompany instructional activities, and assist with administrative tasks.

Content

No matter how many courses you took in your teaching field, you will never know all the content. And just when you feel you are getting a really good command of your courses, you may have your assignment changed. Teachers have always found obtaining **background content** a challenge once they have left the university. Proprietary, freestanding **content-specific software** can be a valuable resource for background information, and the content can often be used with students as well. However, the Internet (see following section) provides much of the same and more extensive offerings at no cost. For a relatively small investment, freestanding **general content software** such as *Compton's Interactive Encyclopedia, The Grolier Encyclopedia,* and *Encarta* provide a wealth of background information at a relatively small cost.

Instruction

Teachers can use **application software** such as *Corel Word Perfect, Microsoft Office,* and *PowerPoint* to create high-quality handouts and images as transparencies or for projection.

The content-specific software that is integrated with the textbook is selected as part of the textbook adoption process and thus gives teachers the opportunity to ensure its quality. When selecting textbooks, you should evaluate the quality of the software along with the book. For freestanding software there are

Teacher's Tip

Contact the IRS or your accountant, but in most cases the cost of a home Internet connection and PC is tax-deductible.

a number of websites that offer descriptions and evaluations. The California Instructional Technology Clearing House for the California public schools provides teachers' evaluations of software at **http://clearinghouse.k12.ca.us/** and is a good starting point for identifying and selecting popular software packages. Your learning resources coordinator may ask you for suggestions, or the PTA might have funds for teachers who want software for their classrooms.

Administrative Tasks

Administrative tasks are a necessary part of a teacher's life. Application software can make maintaining grades; communicating with parents, administrators, classroom visitors, and colleagues; and documenting interactions with students and parents less burdensome and time-consuming.

Microsoft Works and *AppleWorks* are low-cost application software packages that combine a word processor, database, and spreadsheet into an integrated program. Besides letting you write letters, they allow you to create a grade book that adds and calculates averages and totals automatically. An address book created in the database can insert names or any other data elements into letters, so that you can send parents personalized communications and status reports on their children. Tent cards for open houses can also be created with a database, as well as mailing labels and envelopes. A calendar for planning is one of many templates. One of the main advantages of such software is that it preserves a document to be used again, so that the teacher does not have to recreate it. A second advantage is that the appearance of documents makes a positive statement about your professionalism.

Student Uses of Computers

Sixty-five percent of middle and high school students report having the use of a computer at home, and almost all students have been exposed to computers (Horatio Alger Association, 2003). Many students are far more knowledgeable about the capabilities of computers and the nuances of software than their teachers. Where secondary-level teachers should have greater expertise is in the integration of these technologies with their domain knowledge to produce meaningful learning experiences.

Content

Freestanding digital encyclopedias for adults are also typically well suited for use with middle and high school students. An increasing number of publishers are accompanying their textbooks with software for computers and Internet sites for students.

Teacher and Student Uses of the Internet

Most of the best practices described for teacher and student use of computers also apply to using the Internet. However, websites are dynamic and largely unregulated, and therefore require special screening before they are used.

Standards for Selecting Websites

A primary consideration is the validity of a website's content. Some websites are inaccurate, biased, and purposefully misleading. This makes websites different from a textbook or software package, which has typically undergone considerable review and editing to ensure accuracy and a balanced presentation.

You can minimize the risks of invalid or inaccurate information by focusing on websites sponsored by recognized and reputable institutions, such as museums, school districts, universities, libraries, and national organizations.

Teacher's Tip

Transparency acetates can be purchased at any office supply store. There are two types of transparencies, depending on the kind of printer you have access to, a color printer or laser printer. You can create transparencies by placing them in the paper bin of the printer. Generally make sure the type font is not less than size 20 for readability. Because the transparencies can be expensive, it is wise to print out your image or document on standard paper, as a draft.

Teacher's Tip

Be careful! Even what appear to be reputable sources carry potentially unregulated advertisements to support their websites, and some give advertising space with little or no editorial standards.

The extension ".com" (dot-com) is used for commercial enterprises, and the content of such sites is unregulated. The websites of educational institutions (.edu), nonprofit organizations (.org), and government institutions (.gov) are generally more reliable. It is most important to look at these extensions. As an example, http://www.whitehouse.gov is the official site of the U.S. president's residence, but www.whitehouse.com is a pornography site.

Content and Instruction

The content area topics in Unit 8 for your discipline identify a number of websites, and additional websites are located at this book's website. However, given the dynamic nature of the Internet, a search in any search engine can produce specific websites for lesson plans and for content to be used in a lesson that you create. As an example, the Frog at http://froggy.lbl.gov/#study offers an award-winning interactive frog dissection kit, and the *Index of Resources to American History* at http://vlib.iue.it/history/USA/, originally developed by the University of Kansas History Department, is a gateway to topics on American history. In English, a search for Shakespeare produces over 6 million sites.

Whatever the content and Strategy you select to teach with, there is almost certainly something on the Internet that will make the lesson better:

- Pictures, images, and documents can enhance lessons or can be used by students who are gathering information for projects and reports. Yahoo maintains a gallery of images at http://gallery.yahoo.com/. At this site you can search for names, places, things, and events. "Thumbnail" images are displayed of items like Shakespeare, atoms, Newton, various kinds of cells, Gettysburg, and so on, and these can be turned into images for use in the classroom.

- Publishers' websites, such as the ClassZone developed by Houghton Mifflin at http://www.classzone.com/, offer resources geared to their textbooks, but often they can be used even if your school has not adopted the text.

- There are also online textbooks. The University of Colorado has a website gateway to online science books at http://spot.colorado.edu/~dubin/bookmarks/b/1240.html.

- Virtual activities are available from websites. Interactive manipulations, full-motion video tours or sequenced still pictures, or dynamic simulations can be found in websites such as the National Library of Virtual Manipulatives at http://matti.usu.edu/nlvm/nav/grade_g_4.html. Learn French online from the BBC can be found at http://www.bbc.co.uk/languages/french/index.shtml, and the Anne Frank house in Holland has a virtual tour of Anne Frank's home and hiding place at http://www.annefrank.com/.

- **WebQuests** are usually teacher-created or student-created websites. When you type "WebQuest" AND your topic in a search engine, you will find WebQuests for your discipline that use what is increasingly becoming a standard form: introduction, task, process, resources, evaluation, conclusion, and teacher background. Go to the University of South Florida for examples of geography WebQuests at http://www.coedu.usf.edu/webquest/.

- Real-time activities include the *National Geographic Index* for expeditions; your class can travel with experts in specific regions or by types of journey at http://www.nationalgeographic.com/congotrek/.

Safety

Safety is a significant consideration for teachers who have their students use the Internet in school. It is always better to err on the side of caution. Teachers should preview and prescribe sites to be used in lessons. Students should not be allowed to roam the Internet unsupervised. The Center for Innovation in Engineering and Science at http://www.k12science.org/ offers a basic set of best practices that you should follow when incorporating student use of the Internet.

Suppose a student informs you that, for religious reasons, his or her parents do not allow him or her to watch videos or use the Internet. How would you handle this?

Administrative Tasks

Teachers can gain considerable relief from paperwork by effectively using the Internet.

- E-mail can be an effective tool for communicating with parents about classroom activities, with students, and with other teachers. The same considerations that go into deciding whether to give parents your phone number apply to e-mail. Not all parents or students have home computers, so e-mail cannot be the only form of communication. Free e-mail service is available from http://www.yahoo.com and http://www.juno.com/.

- School-based websites are now being supported by school districts. A one-day seminar is sufficient for most teachers to learn the basic techniques of creating and maintaining a simple website. Listing homework, changes in planned curriculum, special events, lesson plan summaries, links for activities that parents can do with their children, and classroom rules on your website can further the aims of the classroom experience.

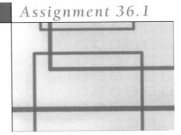

WEBSITE EVALUATIONS

Assignment 36.1

INTASC STANDARDS 1–8

Search the Internet to find five websites that you can use for your lesson plan topic from Topic 13, and explain how they would be integrated into your Instructional Sequences. Be prepared to turn in to your professor (1) a page from each Internet site that is representative of the resource and (2) a paper explaining how these resources would be used. Be prepared to discuss this assignment in class.

OnLine Resources

Check this textbook's website at http://education.college.hmco.com/students for online links that are periodically updated to reflect new resources as they become available.

Assessing Student Learning

George Abbott.

Assessment

The purpose of **assessment** is twofold: (a) to provide teachers and students with information and insight into students' success (or failure) in the learning process; and (b) to provide teachers with feedback on their teaching effectiveness (or ineffectiveness) (Daws & Singh, 1999). Your approach to assessment should, and likely will, grow out of your philosophical approach to instruction. Teachers who believe that evaluation should take place after they finish telling the students what they need to know usually prefer objective paper-and-pencil tests given at one point in time. However, if your philosophy is that students learn in increments, learn by doing and by being required to think, and can demonstrate their learning in a multiplicity of ways, then you will want to use a variety of evaluation approaches at different times throughout the year. This is not to say that paper-and-pencil tests are inappropriate, but they should be part of a larger repertoire of assessment tools used to measure different kinds of learning.

Evaluation using **teacher-made assessments** (discussed in more detail in Topics 39 and 40), such as questions, quizzes, reports, and presentations, occurs on a daily basis in classrooms. **High-stakes testing**, the typically state-mandated standardized tests at various grade levels, is a relatively new phenomenon. Its purpose is to provide comparative data by student, school, district, and state and to implement the Standards-based approach to education established nationally in 2002 when President Bush signed into law the **No Child Left Behind Act.**

In both teacher-made assessment and high-stakes testing, it is relatively easy to measure Information Knowledge. Measuring Procedural Knowledge is more of a challenge in both kinds of testing.

The use of traditional paper-and-pencil teacher-made and standardized tests has drawn both criticism and support. Proponents of standardized high-stakes tests feel that such tests lead to a clear focus on Standards, provide data that can help identify and disseminate effective practices, and provide scores that can be compared by the student, school, district, and state. One major disadvantage is that teachers feel compelled to "teach to the test" rather than to create engaging lessons and allow the test to measure students' knowledge. Another is that we do not know how much the problem of student failure is due to schools and teachers as opposed to communities, poverty, and parents—yet it is only students, schools, and teachers that are being measured by the tests. In addition, these tests only measure what students can demonstrate on just one day. Standardized tests have also been criticized for cultural bias. Conversely, alternative assessments are very powerful (see Topic 38) but are time-consuming for students to complete and for teachers to evaluate, and teacher bias can skew results (Snowman & Biehler, 2003).

For the Reflective Practitioner

Ordinary talent is measurable, uncommon talent is difficult to measure and genius not at all.

BROTHERS GRIMM, QUOTED BY KARL JASPERS

Teacher's Tip

Good teaching begins with figuring out what you plan to evaluate (Information Knowledge, Procedural Knowledge, Basic Skills, Academic Disposition, and/or a Big Idea) and how you plan to assess the new knowledge.

Just as excellent teachers accommodate diverse learners by using a variety of teaching Strategies, so they need to provide a variety of vehicles for students to demonstrate their knowledge. A product assessment (see Topic 38) offers a different way in which students can express their understanding than a traditional paper-and-pencil test, and thus offers a different avenue to success (Snowman & Biehler, 2003). Howard Gardner's Multiple Intelligences (review Topic 7) promotes multiple forms of assessment so that students can use both their well-developed and less-developed intelligences.

Purposes of Assessment

There are a number of purposes for assessment that teachers should keep in the forefront of their thinking as they develop lesson plans. Assessments are used:

1. To determine the knowledge needs of students.
2. To provide learners with information on their progress.
3. To improve teaching, learning, and remediation.
4. To provide a basis for assigning grades and for making decisions about promoting students to the next grade level (see Stiggins, 2004).

High-Stakes Testing

The state's movement to assess students' progress every few years, usually in a pattern such as all third-, sixth-, and tenth-grade students, is known as **High-Stakes Testing.** Like the SAT and AP tests, these tests are almost exclusively paper-and-pencil tests and evaluations of knowledge that can be demonstrated in that form. The normative data gathered from statewide testing are being used not only as assessment information about students' progress, but also as a way to "grade" schools, draw inferences about teachers, and provide incentives to school districts to reform. For these reasons, and because of the typical one-time approach of these tests, the term *high stakes* has taken on a particularly onerous meaning (Amrein & Berliner, 2003; Lattimore, 2001).

> **For the Reflective Practitioner**
>
> 66
> *If there is anything that education does not lack today, it is critics.*

Not all of these high-stakes tests cover all subjects. They tend to focus on reading, writing, and calculating skills. High-stakes testing is an ideological and political issue as well as an educational issue, and each teacher should respond to it based on his or her personal ethics. By becoming a teacher, you have not given up the right—and perhaps you have even taken on a greater duty—to advocate your view of the role of high-stakes testing in your own school, district, and state. Regardless of your personal position, high-stakes testing is a reality that teachers must address. However, it will not be the focus of this Unit because this book focuses on options that are directly under your control.

Classroom Assessment

It is easy to lose sight of the purpose of assessment, which is for the teacher to get feedback on how well the student is learning. The term *classroom assessment* refers to the different options for evaluating students that are available to teachers to assess what they have taught. Formal, objective teacher-made tests and quizzes composed of multiple choice, matching, etc. have been traditional and arguably overdone. We often overlook the ongoing, although informal, feedback that occurs in every class (a casual look of approval, etc.) and in the hallways of middle and high schools (casually mentioning to a student that you recognize the increased effort while at a school function). Alternative Assessments and more creative, objective measures like the crossword puzzle assignment in the **Preface** are intended to diversify the evaluation strategies for classroom assessment.

Although there are concerns about the subjectivity of even the more objective forms of testing and about the amount of time dedicated to evaluation rather than teaching, the emphasis on objective tests is based on legitimate questions about the subjectivity of a teacher's observations and even more formal subjective assessments. Parents' and school districts' demands for "proof" beyond teachers' observations and commonsense findings have led to greater emphasis on formal, documented assessment. Thus a challenge for teachers is to make sure that assessment is as objective as possible, even when using alternative, more subjective assessments. True-false, multiple-choice, and matching tests and rubrics tend to insulate a teacher from accusations of favoritism or prejudice against a student. Accommodating individual differences is one thing, but partiality and discrimination are another. Teachers have to guard against the more subtle problem of the **"halo effect,"** which is when teachers—often unknowingly—tend to grade some students' work product more favorably than is warranted. Such bias can also work against students who have traditionally done poorly or who are behavior problems. These issues, along with increases in class size, have led to "defensive" testing, in which teachers test to document students' failures, rather than to remedy them.

The term *alternative assessment* is often used to refer to the full range of evaluation options, other than the **traditional assessment** of a paper-and-pencil test. Almost all of the assignments in this text are alternative assignments. Many of them are also **authentic assessments.** They are "authentic" because they replicate activities from the real world of teaching (Smith, Smith, & De Lisi, 2001). For example, finding information on the Internet and preparing lesson plans are authentic activities because teachers do them in the course of their jobs. A great advantage of alternative assessment is that it has students take responsibility for constructing and expressing their knowledge. Alternative assessment usually requires students to construct their understanding of new information and combines, in an almost seamless way, instruction and student performance. Authentic and performance assessment are further discussed in the next topic.

The Importance of Feedback

Feedback is the centerpiece of assessment because it leads to intervention and reduces learning deficiencies. Just telling students their performance level—that is, giving them points or grades—does not necessarily lead to change and improvement. For this reason, teachers should carefully distinguish between assessment and grading (see Topic 40). How you approach assessment will have an impact, for better or worse, on the climate of your classroom. The following sections describe types of feedback that should be helpful in communicating about performance to students and their parents.

For the Reflective Practitioner

Honest criticism is hard to take, particularly from a relative, a friend, an acquaintance, or a stranger.   FRANKLIN P. JONES

Rubrics

Rubrics identify the teacher's expectation of what students will learn from the experience that is about to take place (see Boston, 2002). They restructure the traditional disjointed learning-evaluation process from one in which students learn and are then evaluated to one in which learning and evaluation are seamless (see the next topic for a more detailed explanation of rubrics).

Topic 37: **Assessment**

Checklists

Checklists might best be thought of as simplified rubrics, and a new word that has appeared in the literature is *"checkbric,"* which denotes the combined elements of a rubric and a checklist. In both cases, they are intended to define what is needed before the task begins so that students' prospects for success are higher.

Pretests or Preassessment

Pretests can be used to teach test-taking skills and assess current knowledge. They give students a "heads-up" about important material. Like rubrics, they occur prior to the instructional process. Pretests tell teachers about students' prior knowledge and needs so that feedback of a remedial nature is less likely to be required.

Practice Tests

Practice tests can be given as practice in advance of the "real" test. They also give students a "heads-up" about what to expect and can serve as a review when combined with the Socratic method.

Assessment Progress Reports

Assessment progress reports (which are internal reports, not the required report cards) allow students to receive feedback as they progress through a project. Students should also be expected to monitor and report their own progress. Using a rubric and progress reports, the teacher can give feedback and guide students to take responsibility for the quality and pace of their work. Typically, students are given a form that requires them to report the time spent on a project each day, the problems encountered, and the important benchmarks or activities completed ("read the passage, created an outline, drafted the report").

Informal Feedback

Informal feedback is part of the daily routine. It can be as simple as a thumbs-up, low-key admonition, quiet questioning of an individual student about his or her performance, or a word of praise. If a student is not doing well, depending on the frequency of his or her poor performance, the teacher will need more formal documentation of the reasons for the failure because additional intervention involving school personnel or parents might be needed.

Written Assessments

Written assessments by teachers are the norm. They need to be carefully crafted to direct the student to reflection and intervention. This is different from subtracting or tallying points or marking right and wrong answers. Students who have done well receive statements of encouragement, while students who have not done well receive suggestions about how to improve. The student can be required to perform tasks to remediate knowledge (look up the wrong answers, further explain the answers), or the teacher can provide a prompt about behaviors ("If you pay more attention in class, I am sure your understanding will improve.").

Interviews

Interviews with students help teachers understand students' approaches to alternative evaluations and traditional tests and help students discuss their acquired knowledge or behaviors. As a general rule, it is best to ask open-ended questions that focus on the learning experience and that allow students to freely articulate their strengths and shortcomings.

1. For alternative assessment, interviews can be the assessment. They can include questions such as these:
   a. What did you like about the project?
   b. What part did you find the most difficult?
   c. What would you do differently?
2. For traditional assessment, questions while reviewing a test might include the following:
   a. What was it about finding the solution that gave you a problem, do you think?
   b. Do you think you could find the solution now with a new problem?
   c. Why did this question give you a problem?

These kinds of questions put the student at ease and provide the teacher with diagnostic information to help the student improve. Interviews are very efficient, as long as other students are occupied with other work, and they provide an opportunity for promoting remedies in a less stressful way.

Peer Assessment

Peer assessment can be used in either alternative or traditional testing. Students should not be asked to score other students' work, nor should they record grades. The primary purpose is to give feedback—grades are the teacher's responsibility. Peer assessment is most effective when it is integrated into the learning experience as part of the drafting and rewriting process, rather than tacked on to the end of a project. It should include verbal and written feedback, usually by pairs of students. It is authentic because it is what takes place in the real world when adults help other adults succeed. The teacher needs to create an environment of trust so that peer reviews are a positive socialization process for students.

Have you ever participated in peer assessment? How did you feel about other students correcting your work?

Self-Assessment

Self-assessment can be very effective for student presentations, particularly if they are videotaped. Rating scales for voice projection, mannerisms, eye contact, and other relevant factors can encourage objectivity and self-reflection and can provide a structured form for constructive feedback. In writing assignments, self-assessment is as difficult for teens as for adults; we tend not to see our own grammatical and spelling errors and logical inconsistencies. If assessment rubrics are given out at the beginning of the task, students can be expected to check off required components as a self-assessment and to turn them in when that task is completed.

Class Review

Class review should be conducted after an assessment by reteaching the items that all students did poorly on. Involving the whole class in a teacher-led review is one strategy, and putting students into groups to review mistakes is another approach.

Why do some students fail? This is one of the most difficult questions to answer in education, yet it often goes unasked. Some teachers say, "I taught the same material to twenty-five students and five failed, so it has to be the five students' failure." Is it really that simple?

Topic 37: **Assessment**

Assignment 37.1 **SCHOLARSHIP ON ASSESSMENT IN YOUR SUBJECT AREA**

INTASC STANDARDS 1–3, 7, 8

Find an article on the Internet on assessment in your teaching field, and list five key ideas from the article that are important to assessment issues in your content area and that would be helpful to your colleagues. Be prepared to turn in both a page from the Internet article and your five key ideas to your professor and to share your ideas in class.

OnLine Resources

Check this textbook's website at http://education.college.hmco.com/students for online links that are periodically updated to reflect new resources as they become available.

Alternative Assessment

lternative assessment includes *authentic, product,* and *performance assessments,* and the terms are frequently used interchangeably. **Authentic assessment** usually requires students to demonstrate knowledge and skills the way they might be used in the real world outside the classroom, such as by writing a letter to an elected official on a community issue in social studies. In **product assessment** students create products rather than take paper-and-pencil tests; for example, they may make a flow chart of an experiment in chemistry. **Performance assessment,** for the purpose of this textbook, involves the evaluation of the skills demonstrated during a process, such as a presentation, laboratory task, or performance, rather than the production of an end product. Performance and product assessments may or may not be authentic, but authentic assessments are almost always either performance or product assessments. An important part of the alternative assessment approach is the use of rubrics.

The Importance of Rubrics

The use of **rubrics** is one of the best ways to help students succeed at tasks and master content. Rubrics can be powerful because they transfer responsibility for learning to students by creating a process that focuses on students' motivation and self-evaluation. A rubric clearly identifies what a student needs to do by defining the required components of a task, the performance standards they should meet, and the point values that will be used to evaluate their performance (Boston, 2002; Kist, 2001).

Analytic rubrics articulate a level of performance for each criterion, while **holistic rubrics** articulate a total level of performance. The level of performance is defined by **descriptors** that determine the assessment and grade. As an example, if an assignment required sources, the rubric's descriptors would say that for "Poor," there would be 4–5 sources; for "Good," 5–9 sources; and for "Excellent," 10–15 sources. Rubrics should always be given to students before they begin the task assignment so that there is little room for disagreement about expectations.

There are different kinds of rubrics; Table 38.1 is a Grid Rubric. You can find numerous kinds of rubrics and articles on the proper use of rubrics on the Internet; go to MiddleWeb at **http://www.middleweb.com/rubricsHG.html** and the Chicago Public Schools at **http://intranet.cps.k12.il.us/Assessments/Ideas_and_Rubrics/Rubric_Bank/rubric_bank.html** for examples. RubiStar at **http://rubistar.4teachers.org/index.php** is a free online rubric generator. Table 38.1 was created using this free service for an assignment requiring students to create a graph.

Table 38.1 | **RUBRIC EXAMPLE**

Category	Assessment/Point Value			
	Excellent 4	**Good** 3	**Fair** 2	**Poor** 1
Type of Graph Chosen	Graph fits the data well and makes it easy to interpret.	Graph is adequate and does not distort the data, but interpretation of the data is somewhat difficult.	Graph distorts the data somewhat and interpretation of the data is somewhat difficult.	Graph seriously distorts the data, making interpretation almost impossible.
Neatness and Attractiveness	Exceptionally well designed, neat, and attractive. Colors that go well together are used to make the graph more readable. A ruler and graph paper (or graphing computer program) are used.	Neat and relatively attractive. A ruler and graph paper (or graphing computer program) are used to make the graph more readable.	Lines are neatly drawn but the graph appears quite plain.	Appears messy and "thrown together" in a hurry. Lines are visibly crooked.
Accuracy of Plot	All points are plotted correctly and are easy to see. A ruler is used to neatly connect the points or make the bars, if not using a computerized graphing program.	All points are plotted correctly and are easy to see.	All points are plotted correctly.	Points are not plotted correctly OR extra points were included.
Data Table	Data in the table is well organized, accurate, and easy to read.	Data in the table is organized, accurate, and easy to read.	Data in the table is accurate and easy to read.	Data in the table is not accurate and/or cannot be read.
Title	Title is creative and clearly relates to the problem being graphed (includes dependent and independent variable). It is printed at the top of the graph.	Title clearly relates to the problem being graphed (includes dependent and independent variable) and is printed at the top of the graph.	A title is present at the top of the graph.	A title is not present.
Labeling of X axis	The X axis has a clear, neat label that describes the units used for the independent variable (e.g., days, months, participants' names).	The X axis has a clear label that describes the units used for the independent variable.	The X axis has a label.	The X axis is not labeled.

Table 38.1 | **continued**

Category	Assessment/Point Value			
	Excellent **4**	**Good** **3**	**Fair** **2**	**Poor** **1**
Labeling of Y axis	The Y axis has a clear, neat label that describes the units and the dependent variable (e.g., % of dog food eaten; degree of satisfaction).	The Y axis has a clear label that describes the units and the dependent variable (e.g., % of dog food eaten; degree of satisfaction).	The Y axis has a label.	The Y axis is not labeled.

Permission Granted by ALTec. Development of this resource was supported, in part, by the US Department of Education awards to ALTec (Advanced Learning Technologies) at the University of Kansas Center for Research on Learning. These include Regional Technology in Education Consortium 1995–2002, awards #R302A50008 and #R302A000015. This resource does not necessarily reflect the policies of the US Department of Education. Copyright 1995–2004 ALTEC, the University of Kansas.

A **checklist** is often less detailed than a rubric and thus requires more imagination and self-initiative on the part of the student. Checklists may be given to students before an assignment to foster self-evaluation, or they may just be used by the teacher to score a product or performance with a greater degree of consistency. **Models** or **examples** can be used as an alternative to a rubric. The disadvantage of models is that students tend to duplicate what they see, which reduces individual creativity and initiative.

With writing assignments, presentations, portfolios, and projects, students should be given an assessment rubric before they start the task. Using rubrics clearly delegates responsibility to the learner and should eliminate most confusion about how well the student performed. Providing students with rubrics, checklists, and examples of end products also helps teachers structure their own thinking about the process and their expectations. As a result, the degree of subjectivity that is part of all nonobjective testing should be minimized. Teachers need to be able to demonstrate to parents and administrators what standard the students were expected to attain.

Authentic Assessments

Authentic assessment relies on **products** created by students as an integral part of the learning experience. Products are unlikely to be authentic unless they are created in a real-world context. The following characteristics are associated with authentic assessment:

1. The product simulates a real-world activity, such as giving a verbal presentation, creating a written proposal, interviewing, or flowcharting a set of events.
2. The assessment is preceded by relevant instruction on content and form.
3. The assessment is both an evaluation and a learning experience. Students developing a presentation are learning during the preparation stage and during the presentation itself.
4. The performance or product allows for individual creativity, interests, and strengths.

Topic 38: **Alternative Assessment**

5. Students are expected to develop the information necessary for the assessment activity with a minimum of teacher supervision.
6. Students progress at different rates to produce high-quality results.
7. Scoring of the product or performance is consistent, but it allows for individual differences and creativity.
8. Feedback addresses strengths and weaknesses.

Product Assessment

The middle and high school classroom should include all forms of assessment. Whereas traditional, standardized paper-and-pencil tests create anxiety, focus on a single point-in-time performance, and provide for only one format and results, product assessment is integrated into the learning process, usually has multiple and sequential opportunities for feedback, and may have multiple acceptable responses. Well-designed product assessments can ensure mastery of Information Knowledge similar to a paper-and-pencil test, but a paper-and-pencil test can rarely be designed to achieve the outcomes of product assessments. The capacity of product assessments to accommodate individual differences and intelligences facilitates the development of the whole person and allows the teacher to model the kind of acknowledgment of individual differences important to a society.

In lieu of a paper-and-pencil test, students could create the following kinds of products.

1. **Portfolios:** These are collections of a student's work that provide a cumulative record of their development (Lockledge & Hayn, 2000). A portfolio is not the same thing as a folder in the classroom into which students place their completed assignments. The best practice is to set an expectation that students will create and maintain a portfolio from materials that reflect their successes and that it will include both materials from the classroom folder and original work they choose to add. Students can be expected to rank the items in importance and write comments about each item and how it could have been improved. Teachers might encourage more reflective reporting by asking why the student selected the item and where he or she got the idea. Students should be given responsibility for their portfolios to demonstrate what they know and what they can do.
2. **Posterboards and collages:** These are usually based on a topic that students are assigned or that they select from the content of the course. Students are asked to depict the topic (such as the solar system) using these media.
3. **Fact-findings:** The students first decide what facts to gather and then gather them and present them in paper-and-pencil form or in posterboards.
4. **Response journals:** These require students to write their thoughts and feelings.
5. **Letters:** A student can write a letter by taking on the persona of a person who must explain a topic to someone else. In social studies, an example would be the view of a soldier from Baghdad on the Iraq war.
6. **Word webs:** Students take one word from a lesson and create a web of ideas.
7. **Idea lists:** After a lesson, students list the main ideas and their reasons for selecting them.
8. **Headlines:** Much as in idea lists, students create catchy headlines using knowledge from the topic.
9. **Newspaper articles:** Students create newspaper articles about a topic.
10. **Chalkboard journals:** Students contribute ideas from their personal journals to be recorded on the chalkboard.
11. **Proposals:** In government class, students investigate a problem in the community and develop a proposal for how to solve it.

12. **Ideas of the week:** At the end of each week students volunteer a Big Idea and explain its importance. Usually, the teacher selects three volunteers and puts their ideas on the board. This is an assessment because it gives the teacher an idea of what the students found to be important in the week's lessons. Students who never volunteer should be told at the beginning of the week that they will need to provide a Big Idea by the end of the week.

Performance Assessment

The two most common methods used for performance assessment are questioning and observation. Teacher questioning should be an ongoing, systematic activity; it should include feedback; and the teacher should award and record points for participation and the accuracy of student responses (see Topic 28).

Observation is used extensively to determine a student's progress. Behaviors as well as demonstrations of knowledge are observed and recorded as part of the daily routine, during group discussions, during prescribed activities, and as students work on assignments. It is unrealistic to think that a teacher can evaluate every student every day using product or traditional assessments, but the teacher can rotate the students to be observed. Five students may be the focus of the teacher's particular attention one day, and five other students the next day.

CREATE A PRODUCT ASSIGNMENT AND ASSESSMENT RUBRIC *Assignment 38.1*

INTASC STANDARDS 1, 2, 3, 7, 8

Go to the Idea Corporation's site at http://www.idecorp.com/assessrubric.pdf for a rubric for creating rubrics. Create a product assignment and an analytic rubric based on your assigned lesson plan topic from Topic 13. You can use RubiStar at http://rubistar.4teachers.org/index.php to create your rubric or create your own. Be prepared to share your ideas with your classmates and to turn the assignment in to the professor.

OnLine Resources	ASSESSMENT AND RUBRICS
Chicago Public Schools	Find *Scoring Rubrics* on their website at http://intranet.cps.k12.il.us/Assessments/Ideas_and_Rubrics/Intro_Scoring/intro_scoring.html.
ERIC OnLine ED432938	*The Art and Science of Classroom Assessment: The Missing Part of Pedagogy*, by Brookhart, Susan M., 1999.
ERIC OnLine ED443880	*The Role of Classroom Assessment in Teaching and Learning*, CSE Technical Report, by Shepard, Lorrie A., 2000.
ERIC OnLine ED452974	*Using Portfolios Across the Curriculum*, edited by Lockledge, Ann, and Hayn, Judith, 2000.

Check this textbook's website at http://education.college.hmco.com/students **for additional links.**

Traditional Assessment

Teacher's Tip

Remember, ideally you want all students to succeed. Providing them with the topics for a test or a comprehensive list of possible test questions or vocabulary can help them do that.

Teacher's Tip

Included with your middle or high school textbook ancillary materials are typically sample tests or a test bank. While the temptation to use the test (as is) is great, it is wise to use those materials to create your own test.

Traditional assessment refers to quizzes and tests that are often objective—that is, in which each question has one discrete answer ("solve $2x + 6 \times 25 + 15x$" or answer "When did Columbus discover America?"). Essay tests or short answer tests are less objective, but teachers typically expect students to include objective information in the answers.

Objective and essay questions appear to be the most common forms in use today, both in **teacher-made tests** and in the **standardized tests** used in **high-stakes testing.** Most traditional assessments use paper and pencils, although computer-based tests are becoming more common.

The popularity of traditional tests has a great deal to do with the ease with which they can be scored and the ease of comparing the quantitative, relatively objective scores across a class. It can be argued that alternative assessment provides an opportunity to demonstrate all forms of knowledge and skills far better than traditional assessment. Teachers usually find it necessary to use both forms of assessment and, arguably, are wise to do so.

Traditional Tests

Traditional teacher-made tests can evaluate the kinds of thinking that we associate with Bloom's *Taxonomy of Educational Objectives* (1956). Teachers can use Bloom's taxonomy when creating traditional tests by structuring questions that draw from all six levels of the taxonomy. When using traditional tests, teachers should emphasize items that focus on the higher objectives of performing evaluation, synthesis, analysis, and application as well as the lower objectives of gaining knowledge and comprehension. Teachers often give fewer points for knowledge and comprehension questions and more points for evaluation, synthesis, analysis, and application questions. The emphasis on evaluating higher-level thinking is crucial in helping students acquire Procedural Knowledge.

Most of the following types of tests will be familiar to you as a student. As a teacher, you will need to consider the implications and nuances of each one's structure.

Essay and Short Answer Exams

Essay and short answer exams can be used in both middle and high school, although the expectations are different for both sets of students.

Advantages: They are usually easy to construct; eliminate guessing; require recall of knowledge; and support a teacher's language arts goals by letting students organize Information Knowledge and express it in a unique form.

Disadvantages: They take more time to score; are more subjective; and usually take more time to administer than true-false tests.

Advice:

1. Create a rubric and a list of expected correct answers or components of answers to reduce subjectivity.
2. Score one question at a time for all the students, rather than all questions for one student.
3. Take off points for errors in spelling, handwriting, and grammar; give positive points for correct content.
4. Have some questions that are required of all students and some from which students can select, but do not have optional bonus questions.

Lead Phrase Approach

One way to approach higher-order traditional testing is to provide a "lead phrase" for students to complete. A teacher may provide leads for the students to expand upon that are based on Bloom's taxonomy. Evaluation leads would be phrases such as "The best event was . . ." Synthesis leads would be phrases such as "What if . . . ?" and "I wonder whether . . . ?" Analysis leads would be phrases such as "It's like . . . ," "Compared to . . . ," and "Why would . . . ?" Application leads would be phrases such as "Based on . . . ," "If . . . , then . . . ," and "Another example of *x* is . . . ."

Mixed Vocabulary Approach

In this approach the teacher provides perhaps ten vocabulary words in alphabetical order, and students are expected to weave a story out of them. In this manner, students would create an essay.

Fill-in-the-Blank and Completion Test Items

Fill-in-the-blank and **completion items** typically require simple recall.

Advantages: They are usually easy to construct; eliminate guessing; require recall of knowledge; support spelling skills; and are relatively easy to grade.

Disadvantages: They take more time to administer and to score than true-false tests.

Advice:

1. Create an answer sheet of correct answers.
2. When testing for definitions, put the term in the question, and require students to supply the definition.
3. There should be no more than two blanks per question.
4. Take points off for spelling and handwriting errors, and give positive points for correct content.
5. Do not take sentences directly from the textbook.

True-False Tests

True-false tests may be the most widely used tests because they are so easy to construct and grade.

Advantages: They can cover a lot of material in a short period of time; are easy to score; provide quantitative comparative scores for students; and are relatively uncontestable.

Disadvantages: They encourage guessing; can be poorly phrased and confusing; tend to focus on facts, although care can be taken to create higher-level true-false questions; and because key terms must be used in the item, there is little recall.

Advice:

1. Have no more than one concept in a question.
2. For some questions, require additional written elaboration (this is a modified true-false item).

Topic 39: **Traditional Assessment**

3. Since most students guess "true," make more than half of the questions false.
4. Avoid clues such as "all," "never," and "only."
5. Avoid double negatives.
6. Avoid complex and compound sentences.
7. Avoid giving clues in the choice of grammar.
8. Avoid the trivial.
9. Do not take wording directly from the text.
10. Make the test an application by providing a reading, problem, diagram, graph, or image and having students answer true or false based on their Procedural Knowledge.

Multiple-Choice Tests

Multiple-choice tests have a distinct advantage over true-false tests in that they require students to choose among multiple answers.

Advantages: Same as true-false; work well for concepts with closely related potentially correct answers; reduce guessing possibilities; and can be constructed to require the choice of the "best" answer as well as the only correct answer.

Disadvantages: Require little recall because key terms are included as options; time and skill are needed to construct plausible wrong answers; and they tend to focus on facts, although higher-order test items can be created.

Advice:

1. Stems (the phrases before the possible answers) should be either questions or incomplete statements.
2. Make sure there is only one correct answer.
3. All options should be plausible.
4. Do not use "all of the above" or "none of the above."
5. An approximately equal number of correct answers should appear in each position (a test of twenty stems with four answers each should have five correct answers in the first position, and so on).
6. Four possible answers per question is a good amount. They should be all nouns, all verb phrases, and so on.
7. Make the test an application by providing a reading, graph, diagram, or image, and have students make choices based on their Procedural Knowledge.

Matching Tests

Matching tests have a problem column and a response column. They can consist of terms and definitions, causes and effects, dates or people and events, and problems and solutions.

Advantages: Same as true-false; focus students on key ideas; reduce guessing possibilities; can be constructed to require choice of "best" answer as well as the only correct answer; and require less paper.

Disadvantages: Require no recall; and developing homogeneous columns (columns with all like items, such as names on the left and what the people did on the right) takes time and skill.

Advice:

1. Place like items in one column and their matching definitions or events in the other column.
2. Number the left column and use letters for the right column.
3. Make sure there is only one correct answer.
4. Provide more items in the response column than in the problem column.

5. Keep the test to one page, with fifteen or fewer items.
6. Disperse responses throughout the list.
7. Arrange responses in alphabetical or some other logical order.
8. Keep responses short.
9. Make the test an application by providing a reading, graph, problem, diagram, or image, and have students answer based on their Procedural Knowledge.

Alternatives to Traditional Tests

The following approaches are neither alternative assessments nor traditional paper-and-pencil tests. These alternative forms of testing add variety to a teacher's testing palette and can be used to accommodate student differences.

Oral Exams

Oral exams, in which the teacher calls on students one at a time and asks questions—perhaps at the teacher's desk—quickly determine students' knowledge. Oral exams are effective because they individualize the test to the student by varying the pace and phrasing, and the student has a chance to explain his or her thinking.

Teachers can allow students to choose a verbal quiz while others complete a paper-and-pencil assessment, but they also should require all students to select the oral exam option a couple of times a semester. Oral exams should be documented with a checklist, or the teacher can use a paper-and-pencil test to guide the questions asked. Engaging students one-on-one is a powerful experience, the student gets a chance to interact with the teacher in a more personl way, and the teacher learns more about each student's thinking processes and personality.

Classroom Jeopardy

Classroom Jeopardy simulates the popular television program. When all students have the opportunity to be contestants, it can serve as a test rather than as a review. Students often enjoy this kind of assessment so much so that they do not think of it as a test.

Pupil-Produced Tests

In **pupil-produced tests,** students construct test items that make up the pool of questions from which the teacher constructs the actual test. This approach gives students a sense of control over the test because they helped create it.

Take-Home Tests

Take-home tests often set a higher standard than in-class tests because the amount of time is relatively unlimited. An honor system must accompany such tests, and parents as well as other students must be excluded from helping. The advantage of this kind of test is that it doesn't compete with important instructional time.

Crossword Puzzles

Crossword puzzles usually are effective in testing facts, definitions, and vocabulary, but they can also be created to test relationships between concepts and facts if the teacher creates the clues to require higher-order thinking. Puzzlemaker at **http://puzzlemaker.com/** is an excellent tool for creating crossword puzzles and word scrambles.

Word Scrambles

In **word scrambles** letters of the word are scrambled, and students must study the definition and reorder the letters to figure out the word. Like Jeopardy and crossword puzzles, word scrambles are less stressful because of their gamelike qualities.

Assignment 39.1 **CREATE A TRADITIONAL TEST**

INTASC STANDARDS 1–3, 7, 8

Based on your lesson plan topic from Topic 13, create a grade-appropriate traditional test with no fewer than fifteen items and identify which questions meet which of Bloom's categories. Be prepared to share your test with the class and to turn in the assignment to your professor.

OnLine Resources

Check this textbook's website at http://education.college.hmco.com/students for online links that are periodically updated to reflect new resources as they become available.

Grading

This Topic offers practical strategies by which you can manage the assessment process that involves organizing and evaluating the typical paper-based products submitted by students in your courses.

Assessment Management

The assessment process involves creating the assessment (see previous Topics in this Unit), **Assessment Administration** (giving a test), **Initial Assessment, Marking** (commenting and scoring), and **Grade Recording.** Table 40.1 focuses on what a teacher does once he or she has the product in hand. The terms *grading, scoring,* and *marking* are often used interchangeably, but, as explained in Table 40.1 and Topics 14 and 37, *marking* is the phase when we give the all-important written **feedback** by **commenting** on the work and assigning the point values needed for record keeping.

Teacher's Tip

Before your first assignment or test, you should have a candid talk about ethics, cheating, and plagiarism. You should also review the repercussions of cheating, which should have been sent to students' homes in written form at the beginning of the year.

Table 40.1 | **THE GRADING PROCESS**

Phase 1: Initial Evaluation	Phase 2: Marking (Commenting and Scoring)	Phase 3: Grading and Recording
Start with the papers in random order to avoid bias, and don't look at the names.	The papers are in five stacks: A's, B's, C's, D's, and F's.	Record overall comments next to the score on the back of the final page.
Make an initial "eyeball" assessment without markings or in pencil.	Use a *Rubric, Answer Key, Point Scale,* etc., and indicate either points lost or received for individual items. In marking, comments should include *questions, directions, suggestions,* and *referrals* to pages in the text or Class Notes tagged to specific items (see Topic 14).	Assign *Final Grade* if different from total score or indicate both (e.g., "95% or–A") and put the papers in alphabetical order.
End with the papers in five stacks: A's, B's, C's, D's, and F's.	Move papers from one stack to the other based on *within-grade consistency* and *between-grade consistency.*	Record numeric grade in grade book (numeric grades can be calculated in a spreadsheet, whereas "C+" and such cannot.)
If necessary, modify your expectations based on patterns in the results.	If necessary, modify your expectations based on patterns in the results, and reassign scores to individual items. Total and record scores on the back of the final page.	Return papers to students, give statistics on the grades ("90% of the class got A's"), and review key concepts missed and/or open class to questions about the assignment and the assessment.

There is substantial evidence that (a) students focus on points and grades to the detriment of learning from their mistakes; (b) parents and students view the points and grades through a competitive lens; and (c) because teachers fear conflict with students and parents over their assessments, there is point and grade inflation (William & Black, 1996).

Establishing and communicating your grading system to students and parents should be a top priority. Your expectations and expertise will tell students what they should know and be able to do by the end of the school year. But feedback in oral and written form on a daily and weekly basis is the goal of assessment. It should be straightforward and as simple as possible and then used to reshape your teaching practices. Some of the following strategies will vary based on whether the assessment product is a test with mathematical problems, true/false and multiple-choice questions in history, a term paper, a project, or some other form.

Best Practices for Grading

Your credibility as a teacher is on the line with each assessment you administer. Plagiarism and cheating must be prevented to ensure fairness. The following tips on testing should be helpful.

1. Define plagiarism and cheating and give concrete examples during your discussion of your grading practice and ethics.
2. Never sit down during a test, but circulate around the room.
3. Give two versions of a test.
4. Arrange desks so that students are lined in rows, not grouped.
5. Have students clear all materials from around their area during a test.
6. If you observe a student cheating with materials, collect the materials during the test, but deal with the student after class.
7. If you observe a student cheating by looking at another student's paper ("wandering eyes"), record the time and event, but deal with the student after class.
8. On assignments, make it clear whether students can collaborate or whether it is to be an **exclusive work product.**
9. When talking with a student about your suspicions, explain your observations without using the word *cheating,* listen carefully to the student's response, keep the student's welfare in mind, be prepared for excuses, explain your conclusion after hearing the explanation, and inform the student of the action you will take.
10. Establish a grading scale, such as A = 90–100 . . . F = 60–69. Typically this will likely be prescribed by your school or school district.
11. Establish categories and their weights during a grading period: for example, 100 points for participation; 100 points for correct answers from questioning; 200 points for four tests; 200 points for the authentic assessment project.
12. Announce the scale, categories, and weights of the assessments in writing to parents and students at the beginning of the marking period.
13. Drop the lowest grade or two as an alternative to requiring makeup tests for absences. This way you do not have to create a another version of the test and you do not have to do additional scoring.
14. Vary the value of questions based on Bloom's taxonomy, with the greatest weight to higher-level abilities.
15. Grade all papers within two days of receipt, and return them on the third day.

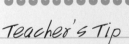

16. Shuffle the papers before scoring to avoid bias, rather than always grading students in a certain order.
17. Record the grades on the back of the paper in ink so students do not know what other students' grades are, unless they deliberately share them.
18. Record the numeric grades in a software package or grade book.
19. When possible, post correct answers on the board for students to review and record on their papers.
20. After returning papers, go over items on which all students generally did less well than expected, and answer students' questions about other items.
21. As a self-assessment, have students write reasons why questions were not answered correctly on their papers.
22. Require parents to sign all assessments below a C grade.
23. Encourage comments from parents.
24. Have students maintain a file folder with all their assessments.
25. If you make a mistake in scoring, admit it and change the grade. Otherwise, do not change grades.
26. Talk with a student who has done poorly in two consecutive assessments.
27. If the student does poorly on the next test, call the parent: Do not wait until a conference.
28. Consider carefully whether to give extra work as an option to help students improve poor grades (this is not the same thing as giving all students the opportunity to redo or resubmit an assignment). Extra credit is contrary to the basic principle that you know what they need to know, you teach what they need to know, and you assess them on what they need to know.
29. Use a numeric grading scheme so that you can record grades in a spreadsheet or database that automatically compiles totals, percentages, and averages.

Teacher's Tip

Frequent testing and multiple forms of assessment are a best practice that gives students multiple opportunities and formats in which to demonstrate what they know.

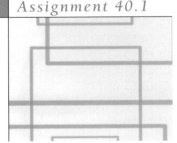

Teacher's Tip

When grading subjective tests and assignments, don't look at the students' names until after you have evaluated the assignment, so that you can avoid bias.

> **As students complete a test, should they bring them up, should you collect them, or should they do other work? What are the pros and cons of these strategies?** ❓

> **Suppose a student became confrontational over a grade you assigned and accused you of bias. How would you respond?** ❓

GRADING SCHEME

Assignment 40.1

INTASC STANDARDS 1–3, 7, 8

Tensions over grades can be particularly disruptive to teacher-student and teacher-parent relationships. A well-thought-out grading scheme and clear communication about grading are essential. Contact a practicing teacher. Interview the teacher and obtain copies of his or her grading scheme and communications with parents. Develop a letter to parents explaining your approach to grading. Be prepared to turn in the assignment to your professor and share your ideas with the class.

GRADES

Assignment 40.2

INTASC STANDARDS 1–3, 7, 8

Indicate what you think are the current statistics based on a 2002–2003 survey of middle and high school students shown in the following chart, and be prepared to discuss your ideas in class.

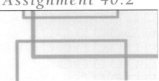

Question	Your Subject Field (Indicate your estimate as a %.)		Average for All Subject Fields (Indicate your estimate as a %.)	
High school students' report of grades	Mostly A's	%	Mostly A's	%
	Mostly A's/B's	%	Mostly A's/B's	%
	Mostly B's	%	Mostly B's	%
	Mostly B's/C's	%	Mostly B's/C's	%
	Mostly C's/below	%	Mostly C's/below	%
High school students' report of hours per week of homework	No data available		1–5	%
			6–1	%
			11–15	%
			16–20	%
			20 plus	%

Note to Professor: The answers based on a national survey appear in the PowerPoint slides that accompany this text.

OnLine Resources	GRADING AND REPORTING
Preventing Academic Dishonesty	Go to http://teaching.berkeley.edu/bgd/prevent.html for an excellent explanation of plagiarism.
ERIC OnLine ED470592	*Score Normalization as a Fair Grading Practice,* by Winters, R. Scott, 2002.
ERIC OnLine ED423309	*Teacher Comments on Report Cards,* by Brualdi, Amy, 1998.

Check this textbook's website at http://education.college.hmco.com/students for additional links.

Content Area Trends, Standards, and Teaching Methods

Dan Rosandich (www.danscartoons.com)

Current Trends in Content Areas

This Unit introduces you to your chosen craft as a teacher of *English, Mathematics, Science, Social Studies, World Language, The Arts* (visual arts, music, and performing arts like dance and theater), or *Physical Education and Health*. These teaching fields are collectively referred to as **Academic Domains** (or Domains), **Content Areas,** or **Subject Fields.** The Topics in this unit will present:

For the Reflective Practitioner

Remember, it is the teacher AND student against the content, not the teacher and content against the student.
J. B. MAYO

1. An introduction to each of these academic domains.
2. Listings of the related major professional associations (also referred to as learned societies) in your field.
3. A compilation of the major journals in your teaching field.
4. Internet resources that can be accessed most easily through this book's website.
5. Authentic assignments that will enable you to develop your instructional planning skills to meet Standards-based education expectations.
6. Best practices for teaching in your field.

We begin by analyzing the differences between the domains and showing how these differences affect teaching and learning.

Curriculum, Academic Domains, and Literacy

The curriculum leading to high school graduation is, in effect, society's attempt to define domain and discipline literacy—the minimum understanding society believes the population should have in a range of subject fields. In theory, by progressing through a series of courses in each academic domain while in middle and high school, students will develop sufficient knowledge to succeed in the workforce or to advance in additional academic pursuits both specific Basic Skills and higher forms of knowledge.

Common Ground of the Academic Domains

The professional literature of the individual domains leads us to conclude that all the domains share five themes:

1. **The Need for Greater Knowledge.** Each professional organization representing a domain calls for greater student understanding in ITS disciplines. Each of the learned societies defines what it perceives to be the minimum literacy based on criteria IT has developed. The case for greater literacy is typically based on arguments supporting the development of "human capital," concerns about American competitiveness, the expansion of a democratic ideology, and the need to advance the intellectual frontiers of its domain. And most cite advances in technology and communication as the catalysts that are

Teacher's Tip

Most learned societies have national and state councils or chapters. Joining them is one of the ways that you can influence policy in your teaching field.

precipitating their call for greater knowledge. No professional society has a literacy standard that calls for simply maintaining current levels of knowledge.

For teachers, this raises one of the most difficult dilemmas they may face during planning: how to achieve a balance between what is referred to as "Depth and Breadth." How much depth should they go into in any topic, and should they teach the topic at all? Student enthusiasm and the acquisition of Procedural Knowledge often benefit from more in-depth and time-consuming investigations into a topic, but such investigations limit students' exposure to the breadth of knowledge in the domain. Almost all the domains call for a balance, but they define only the breadth of knowledge to be achieved.

 How do you think this problem of depth and breadth will affect your lesson planning and instruction?

 Can you make a case for requiring more course work in your discipline? If so, what courses in your field or in another discipline would you eliminate?

2. **Competing Conceptions of Standards.** Standards-based educational reform with high-stakes testing is the current movement that is being used to define general and domain literacy. The No Child Left Behind (NCLB) legislation is the formalization of the strategy to increase overall literacy by defining higher standards and closing the knowledge gap between individual students and between segments of the U.S. population. As a new teacher you are entering the profession at the beginning of a new era in American education.

NCLB is relying on learned societies to articulate domain standards and organizations of school administrators like the American Association of School Administrators (AASA) and other professional organizations to suggest how to reconcile the competing demands between disciplines. In the end, it is local or state school boards or legislatures that mandate the curriculum and requirements based on regulations emanating from NCLB.

Most professional organizations include secondary teachers and university faculty from the disciplines (for example, chemistry professors) and education (such as science education professors), and in some cases from the general public or other interested parties. The focus of these learned societies is typically on both pedagogy and content. The Standards the societies articulate take on different forms. They can be as brief as those given by the *National Council of Teachers of English* (NCTE) (**http://www.ncte.org/**) or as detailed and extensive as those given by the *National Science Teachers Association* and the National Academy of Sciences' *National Science Education Standards* (NSES) (**http://www.nap.edu/readingroom/books/nses/html/**). What the domains have in common is internal disagreements that stem in part from differing views of what it is to be literate. In addition, there are multiple societies and agencies recommending THEIR standards; for example, the National Geography Standards are much more detailed than the standards recommended by the umbrella organization for social studies, the National Council for the Social Studies.

Shamos (1995), in writing about scientific literacy, identified three levels of literacy that epitomize thinking in all the domains: (a) **cultural literacy:** the person knows numerous terms and definitions; (b) **functional literacy:** the person can coherently converse, read, and write using these terms and definitions; and (c) **true literacy:** the person knows something of the "enterprise and conceptual schemes" of the domain. In all domains, the highest standard appears to be that all students should be able to **"do"** a subject, such as social studies, science, or theater (true literacy), as opposed to just **"knowing about"** social studies, science, or theater (cultural and functional literacy). But they also seem to have conceded that the American culture and time constraints make such a goal impossible. Within this context, each of the disciplines has articulated and developed standards that it believes should be used by the states to shape their K–12 curriculum, and these standards are likely to be the driving force in whatever goals you will set for your subject matter (see **http://edstandards.org/Standards.html#Subject**).

How do you think your practices would differ based on which of these three literacies you felt was most important?

---

3. **The Need for Interdisciplinary and Cross-Disciplinary Knowledge.** At one time, individuals such as Nicolaus Copernicus, Leonardo da Vinci, or William Shakespeare could transform the world, single-handedly it seemed, by conceptualizing things differently or perfecting a new art form. But most scientific advancements today are made by teams. Even new art forms like film require the cooperation of individuals who understand different media and new technologies. All domains thrive through collaboration. The recognition of this phenomenon is reflected in standards that often include interdisciplinary and cross-disciplinary knowledge and teacher practices that call for more cooperative, collaboration, and group learning strategies.

4. **Concern over Class Size.** Classes that are too large are a concern for many of the learned societies. Research shows that larger class size adversely impacts student achievement (Bracey, 1995; Wenglinsky, 1997). It affects the dialogue and participation level of the INDIVIDUAL student, the instructional strategies, and the personal attention given by the teacher (an expert) to each student that allows the student to reconstruct knowledge (Egelson, Patrick, & Charles, 1996; Krieger, 2002). There is a general recognition that with smaller classes teachers COULD restructure their pedagogy to have more in-depth dialogues with students and COULD require more tasks leading to the more detailed evaluations, feedback, and remediation that are essential to "do" the discipline as opposed to just "knowing about" it. It is less clear that all teachers WOULD IN FACT change to suit the new opportunities of smaller classes (Scudder, 2001).

Teachers have great autonomy in deciding how much time outside of school they will spend in planning lessons and evaluating students' work products. A one-hour planning period during school is certainly insufficient to achieve excellence. Smaller classes might also give teachers an incentive to increase the time they spend on course preparation using strategies better suited to smaller classes and to employ assessments that require more time-consuming evaluations (Deutsch, 2003).

How differently do you think you would teach if you had classes of ten students, rather than thirty-five?

Topic 41: **Current Trends in Content Areas**

5. **Awareness of the Information Age.** Most of the learned societies articulate an understanding of the changes and opportunities presented by the Internet and related technologies. Adjusting to the expanding information available through such vehicles as the Internet and its delivery systems requires teachers to reconsider the traditional emphasis on teaching what they know as opposed to focusing on techniques to find, access, interpret, and use information.

 Can you identify specific examples of how the Internet has impacted your domain?

Discipline and Domain Differences

The academic disciplines and domains are, simply put, different; and the individuals who participate in the community of practice of each discipline share a way of thinking and effectively create unique academic cultures among their members (Becher, 1989; Shulman, 1974; Shulman & Quinlan, 1996; Snow, 1974; Stodolsky, 1988). As an example, individuals in scientific communities are much more collaborative than in other areas and tend to see their disciplines as having a more fixed body of knowledge. Individuals in social studies and English tend to see their domains as places to challenge values and stimulate individuals intellectually (Biglan, 1973; Feldmen, 1976; Pohlman, 1976).

The various teaching approaches have many common elements (to which this book is largely dedicated), but their applications vary by domain and discipline as well as by level within a discipline (first-year French as opposed to third-year French, as an example). This variety is most demonstrable in the elementary school setting, where excellent teachers take on new personas and reconfigure their instruction based on the domain they are teaching, an art that does not have to be practiced at the secondary level, where teachers specialize in a domain. The following are some ways in which the academic domains differ that make teaching and learning unique experiences for the teacher and student.

Problem Solving

If viewed as the most common ground of all learning, problem solving can be thought of as the place where Procedural and Information Knowledge are joined and where the student's Academic Disposition affords him or her a repertoire of learned and rehearsed strategies to apply to a problem. However, it is a very different problem-solving task to author and edit an essay, solve a multipart mathematics problem, analyze the multiple perspectives of an historical event, or phrase a sentence in a second language (Doyle, 1992; Kieran, 1992). The kind of thinking used during problem solving in these domains differs based on the executive processes of the discipline.

Pace

Each discipline has a unique pace that is evident during teacher talk. When visiting classrooms in the preparation of this text, I observed that the pace of teacher talk appeared faster in foreign language and mathematics and slower in social studies and literature. This is not surprising given the goals of the disciplines. In a conversational third-year Spanish class, the teacher relies on students instantaneously processing the new vocabulary and grammar used in the teacher talk and then responding using self-shaped vocabulary and grammar. Being bilingual requires thinking in the other language, and the speed of response indicates whether the student is translating the language or thinking in it.

In mathematics, students are expected to respond to discrete, relatively short problem sets by proposing to the teacher the next step to solve the problem. This requires having in mind the correct, although perhaps arcane, vocabulary, procedure, numeric examples, and solution. If a problem has eight steps, the student must retain all eight steps in his or her mind's eye to arrive at a correct solution. In mathematics, speed is important in order to retain all the steps and to internalize the Procedural Knowledge. Thus in mathematics, one observes an instructional pace that seems to rely on and encourage nondivergent processing as an important component of success.

In social studies and literature, the pace appears slower, in part because speed is not essential to internalizing Procedural Knowledge and, indeed, not prized when considering values; the domain's content is less sequential and more divergent; there is often not "ONE" answer or interpretation; the teacher talk uses more familiar, accessible vocabulary that is less easily lost because it is given at a slower pace; and students can draw upon general and previously used vocabulary to articulate answers.

Because teachers have been immersed in their content field as "majors" or "minors," they have become accustomed to a certain dispositional pace, and because they are experts relative to their students, they process information more rapidly than their students. This superior ability often leaves nonapprentice students without the essential skills to progress in the domain and discourages some students from becoming apprentices.

Structure

In Algebra 1 and German 2, teachers must cover a specific, sequential body of knowledge to prepare students for Algebra 2 and German 3. Each course is a step leading toward more complex knowledge; for example, one must know addition before one can do algebra. Social studies and English do not have the same constraints. The social studies and literature domains might be said to have layers of knowledge (see Figure 41.1), so that the American Revolution is covered generally in first grade and then more thoroughly explored in middle and high school grades. Figure 41.1 depicts this difference between disciplines.

Figure 41.1 | **VERTICAL AND HORIZONTAL LEARNING**

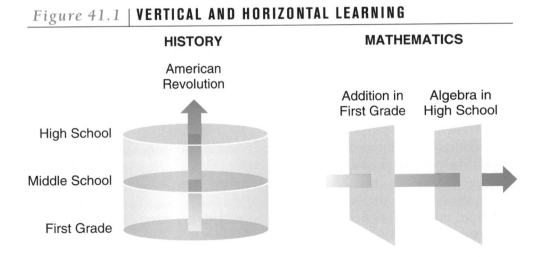

Consistency

Precisely for the reasons explained in the last section, science, mathematics, and foreign language, it can be argued, can only be learned if studied incrementally, sequentially, and almost every night in preparation for the next day's lesson, and this may account for why foreign language learning shares some of the same anxiety features as science and mathematics (Horwitz, 2001; Taylor & Fraser, 2003). They are **"cumulative" disciplines** in that each bit of knowledge directly builds on the previous day's knowledge in a way that is not always required in social studies, health education, and literature. As an example, in social studies one can learn about the northern, middle, and southern colonies separately from the slave trade even though knowing about both would be helpful in understanding the development of the thirteen colonies. But to progress to the next learning task in a second language, it is essential to know the vocabulary and sentence structure from the day before.

The consistency of attentiveness needed in mathematics, science, and language learning is made more difficult to achieve by school schedule disruptions, absences, and the permeable family. Because self-discipline is needed to achieve the consistent regimen for success in some disciplines more than others and the challenges facing teenagers make such a commitment difficult for some, students exit and enter some domains on the basis of the amount of required daily commitment. The ability tracking that starts in middle school most often means moving students to exploratory courses or subjects like social studies and English because they are viewed as having a lower degree of difficulty than science and mathematics based on this one criterion, not students' ability or inclination.

Degree of Difficulty

Plato and Aristotle, over 2,000 years ago, believed that mathematical thinking was of the highest order because it demanded a high level of abstraction. And such ability appears to be even more prized today: Technological advancement depends on it, and it seems to be the one in the shortest supply. Few would argue that mathematics is not immediately more abstract than history. But few historians would agree that abstraction is not necessary in the discipline of history, either. Educators focus on students' cultural and psychological traits and ineffective teaching methods as the greatest impediments to success in a domain, rather than the degree of abstraction, because to do otherwise would mean that attaining literacy in all domains might be an impossible goal.

Jerome Bruner (1960) maintained, "Any subject can be taught effectively in some intellectually honest form to any child at any stage of development" (p. 13). That we stubbornly hold on to the belief that under the right circumstances we can teach and students can learn just about anything, at least as the knowledge is defined at the secondary level, is a reflection of the egalitarian philosophy that is a hallmark of democratic societies.

 Do you agree with this idea? Given the right circumstances, do you think everyone in your class could learn calculus?

CONVERSING WITH STUDENTS FROM OTHER DISCIPLINES

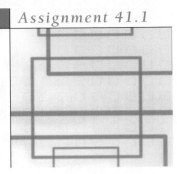

INTASC STANDARDS 1–8

Although you have made a decision to teach a specific subject area and want to learn as much about it as possible, understanding your teaching field in the context of the standards and issues in other fields can give you insights into your teaching practices that would not otherwise be possible. After reading the Topic for your domain/discipline in this Unit, select one other subject field and be prepared to engage in a discussion of the topic with fellow students who have selected it as their teaching area.

OnLine Resources

Check this textbook's website at http://education.college.hmco.com/students for online links that are periodically updated to reflect new resources as they become available.

English Education

The following professional organizations, journals, and standards play an essential role in English education and the development of your teaching practices.

THE NATIONAL COUNCIL OF TEACHERS OF ENGLISH — NCTE

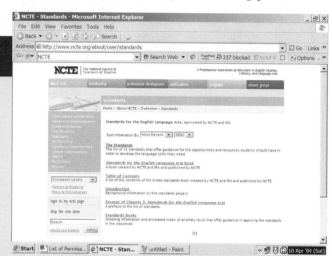

Professional Organizations for Teachers of English

National Council of Teachers of English http://www.ncte.org/

International Reading Association http://www.reading.org/

National Communication Association http://www.natcom.org/

Related Organizations

American Communication Association
http://www.americancomm.org/index.html

Academy of American Poets http://www.poets.org/

American Comparative Literature Association
http://www.acla.org/

American Folklore Society http://www.afsnet.org/

American Literature Association
http://www.calstatela.edu/academic/english/ala2/index.html

Association of Literary Scholars and Critics
http://www.bu.edu/literary/

Modern Language Association http://www.mla.org

Association for Education in Journalism and Mass Communication
http://www.aejmc.org/

American Forensics Association
http://www.americanforensics.org/

Speech, Debate and Theater Association
http://www.nfhs.org/

Association of Teachers of Technical Writing
http://www.attw.org/

Selected Journals

English Journal

Written Communication

Voices from the Middle

Classroom Notes

English Education

The Reading Teacher

Journal of Adolescent and Adult Literacy

Reading Research Quarterly

Argumentation Advocacy

The Forensic Educator

Communication Teacher

Quarterly Journal of Speech

Communication Monographs

Communications Education

Composition Studies

Academic Writing

Enculturation

JAC: A Journal of Composition Theory (formerly *Journal of Advanced Composition*)

Journal of Teaching Writing

The Writing Instructor

National and State Standards

National Standards for English Education (developed by NCTE and IRA)
http://www.ncte.org/about/over/standards/110846.htm

National Standards and Competencies for Speaking, Listening, and Media Literacy
http://www.natcom.org/Instruction/K-12/K12stdspr.htm

INTASC Standards for English Teacher Education (in development) http://www.ccsso.org/

Your state standards http://edstandards.org/Standards.html#State or
http://www.aligntoachieve.org/AchievePhaseII/basic-search.cfm

ENGLISH STANDARDS

Assignment 42.1

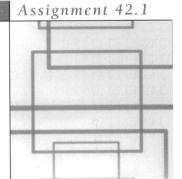

INTASC STANDARDS 1, 7, 9

Visit each of the above standards websites so that you can become familiar with your state and national standards. Reflect on the standards, and be prepared to discuss the relationship of your state standards to the national standards and what additional preparation you think you would need to have your students reach these standards. In a one-page report, list five to ten national and state standards that you believe could be achieved in a lesson plan based on your assigned topic from Topic 13, Assignment 13.1. Be prepared to turn in the assignment to your professor and to discuss your ideas in class.

DOWNLOAD BONUS COURSE MATERIALS AND ASSIGNMENTS

Assignment 42.2

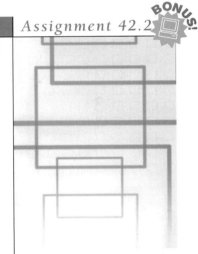

INTASC STANDARDS 1, 7, 9

At http://education.college.hmco.com/students you will find downloadable documents that will assist you in applying the knowledge you have learned from your professor and this book to develop the kind of practical lesson plans you will need as a new teacher for your domain or discipline. The materials that you should download are:

1. Copies from Internet-based resources.
2. Authentic lesson-planning assignments for this Topic (found only at the textbook website) that might be assigned by your professor, such as creating a topic lesson statement of goals, creating Class Notes for the first daily lesson, creating a complete thematic lesson, and more.
3. Examples and templates of a Unit Plan's Statement of Goals (see Topic 19, Assignment 19.1) and a teacher's Class Notes (see Topic 20, Assignment 20.1) for your use.

Introduction to English Education

anguage Arts, English, and *English Education* are all terms used to refer to instruction in literature, composition, speech communication, and/or reading. The term *Language Arts* is most often used to refer to elementary education instruction in English. *English Education* is the most common term used to refer to English education in middle and high schools. The trend to have reading specialists in secondary schools has resulted in English teachers having their students apply reading skills to literature in the same way that history teachers rely on reading in history classes.

For the Reflective Practitioner

In science one tries to tell people, in such a way as to be understood by everyone, something that no one ever knew before. But in poetry, it's the exact opposite.   PAUL DIRAC

Topic 42: **English Education**

Mandel (1980) identified the three primary approaches to instruction in current-day English education:

- **The Process-Approach Model** emphasizes use of literature, writing, and speaking for individual growth.
- **The Mastery Model** emphasizes diagnosis of students' needs, clear objectives, and evaluation of skills and knowledge.
- **The Heritage Model** calls for a core of knowledge based on the "great works" (also known as the **"Canon"**) as essential to cultural transmission. A contemporary version of the Canon has been developed in Massachusetts in cooperation with the American Diploma Project (ADP) (refer to Topic 11), and many of the Canon's works are available at Project Gutenberg at **http://www.promo.net/pg/**. This ADP version of the Canon is based on a need to have students learn to read different kinds of texts or "genres" with different degrees of rigor and selections that are culturally rich (Gallagher, Knapp, & Noble, 1993). To view the Massachusetts list, go to **http:// www.achieve.org/dstore.nsf/Lookup/MA_Reading/$file/MA_Reading.pdf**.

Teacher's Tip

Many English teachers serve as advisors to school newspapers and yearbook editions. Students acting as journalists can have difficulty learning the limits of editorializing and can misrepresent the facts. For this reason, it is advisable to have a member of the administration approve final copy. The outcome of the Hazelwood Case (at **ED321253** the Supreme Court on "Hazelwood": A Reversal on Regulation of Student Expression. ERIC Digest No. 8. Eveslage, Thomas, 1988) gives the school the right to censure, but this can place the moderator in an awkward and difficult position as an arbitrator between the students, parents, and administration.

The topics taught by English teachers typically include writing, reading, oral communication, literature, and sometimes theater and drama (see Topic 47). The first three (writing, reading, and oral communication) are often classified as Basic Skills; although these would be every teacher's responsibility, they are most closely associated with English teachers. ADP has identified a Procedural Knowledge approach to English with its Benchmarks (go to **http://www. achieve.org/dstore.nsf/Lookup/ADP_english/$file/ADP_english.pdf**) organized into Language, Communication, Writing, Research, Logic, Informational Texts, Media, and Literature. The study of literature is consistently the focus of English education and is intended to provoke reflection on the cosmos, society, and the human experience (see Standards 1 and 2 at NCTE: **http://www.ncte. org/about/over/standards/110846.htm**). As a result, English teachers, like social studies teachers, often find themselves engaged in discussions of personal virtues and societal values.

By the late nineteenth century, the patchwork curriculum of American secondary schools was viewed as inadequate for the rapidly changing society. Instruction in composition, speech, literature, and reading was an integral part of the landscape, but the content of these areas was inconsistent, as were the required years of study.

In 1892, the Committee of Ten (National Education Association, 1892), led by Harvard President Charles Eliot, identified the *Canon* of literary works, which consisted mainly of British classics. This standard for what a college-bound student should know in "English" was adopted as a prerequisite for admission to most colleges and was the driving force in shaping high school English curriculums and textbook content. The Canon is still referred to today, albeit in a changed form, and which of the great works should be in or out of the Canon is still debated in the current academic literature (Gere & Shaheen, 2001).

Founded in 1911, **The National Council of Teachers of English (NCTE)** has influenced the direction of both the education of English teachers and the K–12 English curriculum. It gave a voice to English education from the perspective of teachers of English and the secondary school, which advocated from its inception a wider selection of literature than had been advocated by the original colleges' Canon. The focus on literature by both the Committee of Ten and NCTE during this period led to the assimilation of what were mostly separate composition courses into English literature courses where composition was also taught. While formal instruction in grammatical rules and other composition subjects continued in the early part of the twentieth century, Squire and Applebee (1968) reported that English teachers in 1968 spent only 15.7 percent of their class time emphasizing composition.

In 1917 the National Joint Committee on English issued a report entitled *Reorganization of English in Secondary Schools,* which was influenced by John Dewey's progressive ideas. The implementation of this progressive philosophy shifted the emphasis of secondary English education from one primarily defined by colleges to one focused on a curriculum that prepared students for life with practical writing, verbal communication, and reading skills and literature.

In 1935, NCTE's landmark report, *An Experience Curriculum in English* (NCTE, 1935), reinforced the core of reading, writing, literature, and verbal communication as the focus of secondary English education and also argued for authentic experiences rather than the more traditional Canon and prescriptive practices for writing. The "**Tripod**" made up of *composition* (including rhetoric), *literature* (an expanded Canon with works more relevant to students), and *language* (a new term that included grammar and linguistics) became the hallmark English education curriculum by the 1950s. It called for teachers of English to explicitly teach the formal properties of the novel, short story, poem, and stage play and the rules of composition and grammar.

Approaches to Writing

By 1967, an alternative model to the formal "rules and properties" approach to teaching composition was proposed based on what is referred to as the "Dartmouth Seminar" (Dixon, 1967). This **process approach** would encourage English to be used by students to explore and express themselves. Writing (also see Topics 12 and 14) became viewed as a process in which students express ideas with increasing degrees of sophistication rather than one in which students simply learn to **apply** grammar rules by being exposed to time-honored examples of "good" texts (Chomsky, 1957; Emig, 1971; Nystrand, Greene, & Wiemelt, 1993).

Interest in writing instruction took on new meaning with *Newsweek*'s article "Why Johnny Can't Write" (December, 8, 1975), which decried the state of writing skills among the more diverse baby boom population of college students. Applebee (1981, 1984), who investigated the problem for the National Institute of Education (NIE), found that (a) most writing assignments in secondary schools were informative, rather than expressive or persuasive; (b) the audience was the teacher, rather than an "authentic audience"; (c) writing was often taking notes or filling in blanks; and (d) most writing assignments were two or three sentences or, at most, the infamous five-paragraph essay. There was a growing recognition that (a) teaching writing was not the sole responsibility of English teachers; (b) writing was not a mechanical process, but a cognitive-social process; and (c) the Procedural Knowledge of the disciplines required students to learn the conventions of the various domains. This awareness led to the writing-across-the curriculum movement (Faigley, 1986) and to the adoption of best practices such as greater use of journals (Fulwiler, 1987); greater writer-reader interaction (Gere & Stevens, 1985; Nystrand, 1986); authentic writing assignments (Cohen & Riel, 1989); and the use of portfolios (Nystrand, 1990; Sunstein, & Lovell, 2000). Two contemporary movements evolved out of this growing body of research and theory. The writing workshop approach (go to the Anneburg/CPB online workshop number 4 by Lucy Calkins at http://www. learner.org/channel/workshops/hswriting/) is a

Teacher's Tip

Many districts have "approved" or "banned" books and movies. A clear rationale for your use of any books, movies, or even Internet sites is essential for anything not preapproved and should be cleared with the school administration.

formal teaching mechanism that emphasizes process. The genre approach (Cope & Kalatzis, 1993) emphasizes the Procedural Knowledge of writing and may offer the best balance of product and process, while accommodating the social context of students. It focuses on students learning to use narration, argument, description, explanation, and instruction genres to convey their ideas, regardless of the discipline or domain (Devitt, 2004; Gallagher et al., 1993).

Approaches to Literature

There are several competing theories of how to interpret literature that in turn affect the teaching of literary works. These approaches deal with Procedural Knowledge, that is, knowing how to use and think about the knowledge in a discipline. Four of the most widely accepted theories are as follows:

- **New Criticism** maintains that literature instruction should focus on a "close reading" of the literary piece that deciphers the meaning by analyzing its author's choices of language, techniques, and form (Blake & Blake, 2002; Gallagher, 1997).
- **The Transaction Approach** focuses on the reader, arguing that interpretation of literature should be based on the reader creating, in effect, a new text as a result of the integration of the author's ideas and the reader's ideas (Rosenblatt 1938/1968).
- **Reader's Response** also focuses on the reader, but is more personal and introspective. It purports that literature produces a highly personal interpretation and responses, and that these reflect the reader's psychological state (Bleich 1978; Holland, 1975; Karolides, 2000).
- **Interpretive Communities** focuses on the sociological and cultural contexts that shape readers' negotiation of the meaning of literature (Dillon, 1982; Fish, 1980).

Students' ability to read literature and move from literal to interpretive approaches, to see different perspectives, to understand temporal contexts, and to understand different genres is a Procedural Knowledge that is crucial to making use of literature as intended by the NCTE standards (particularly 1 and 2). Teachers play a crucial role in the development of this Academic Disposition (Morrow, 1992; Purves, 1993), but it is also dependent on students' maturation (Applebee, 1977; Many, 1991), exposure to reading (Hartman, 1995; Lehr, 1988), and social experiences (Hynds, 1989).

The most common Instructional Sequence in literature education is as follows: The students complete the task of reading a passage; then the teacher asks questions with students offering short answers; and finally the teacher debriefs the short answers to elaborate, clarify, or correct them in **whole-class discussions** (Agee, 2000). The teacher typically uses the debriefing to provide a scaffold for the students and to model an expert's **"close reading"** that reveals the author's intent and strategies and the compelling ideas of the story line (Applebee, 1993; Marshall, Smagorinski, & Smith, 1995). Marshall found that in this **whole-class, teacher-centered model,** students have relatively little opportunity to develop their own conception of the text because the teacher dominates the discussion. This may account for why students, at least according to one study, prefer small-group discussions (Alvermann et al., 1996). However, **small-group discussions,** as an alternative to whole-class discussions, have been demonstrated to not be as effective for debriefing literary works, but this may be due to variables such as lack of teacher attentiveness, not the small-group format (Nystrand & Gamoran, 1991). Both theatrical enactments and writing assignments that are part of the

Instructional Sequence have positive effects on literature instruction (Marshall, 1987; Wilhelm, 1997).

Best Practices for Teaching Literature

While there are many strategies that are effective in teaching literature (Strickland & Strickland, 2002), the following basic approaches are essential.

- Teacher talk should be "gentle inquisitions" characterized by substantial and sustained discussions that use open-ended questions and follow-up questions based on students' responses (Eeds & Wells, 1989; Nystrand & Gamoran, 1991).
- When using small groups, a whole-class discussion should be planned as a precursor to small-group work to provide the scaffold base. The tasks (focus questions, graphic organizer, writing assignment, and so on) for the groups need to be well structured to build on that base, and the groups must be attended to by periodic teacher visits. Teachers who are inattentive to group interactions may not achieve the desired benefits because of status issues among peers in small groups or domination of a group by one student (Lewis, 1997).
- Reenactments, visuals, storyboards, or transparencies of the vocabulary and main characters, places, or other components should be used as an **"Attention-Getter"** or **Prereading** activity in the instructional pattern (see Topic 20).
- A variety of writing tasks (see Topic 14) as part of a postreading activity have been demonstrated to have enduring positive effects and should consistently be used (Marshall, 1987).

Speech Communication

While speech communication could also have been included as a literacy or basic skills topic (in 1978, Title II of the Elementary and Secondary Education Act of 1965 was amended to include "effective oral communication" as a Basic Skill), information on speech education has particular relevance to English teachers who are called upon to teach communication or public speaking skills courses.

Because of the relationship of speech, literature, and theater, English teachers find themselves with multiple courses and extracurricular responsibilities such as debate club and theater. Most recent data indicate that at least thirty states require oral communication as part of an integrated language-arts curriculum, and for most of the others it is an elective typically offered in a half-year course (Hall, Morreale, & Gaudino, 1999).

One of the most notable changes in speech education came in 1976 and was evidenced in the change of the journal title *The Speech Teacher* to *Communication Education*. This new conceptualization broadened the discipline from just speech education to include such topics as mass communication, listening, oral interpretation, and drama. For the secondary teacher of a speech communication class, the focus is on the art of public speaking.

Anxiety about public speaking is one of the primary focal points of research in teaching speech communication because it is perceived as an underlying impediment for many individuals. We know that students who are academically successful generally have lower anxiety levels about public speaking (Rosenfeld et al., 1995) and that students who are guided through a systematic preparation for public speaking assignments can significantly improve their performances.

For the Reflective Practitioner

Good communication is as stimulating as black coffee and just as hard to sleep after.

ANNE MORROW LINDBERGH

Topic 42: **English Education**

Teacher's Tip

You should require students to seek your approval for all topics for a speech so that you avoid controversies brought on by props, pictures, and presentations that might be offensive or possibly too sexually explicit.

Success is linked to a teacher structuring assignments so that students are required to spend time preparing for a speaking assignment by developing visual aids, rehearsing silently, rehearsing out loud, and preparing speaking notes (Menzel & Carrell, 1994). The impact of such training on students' critical thinking capacities can be transferred to other disciplines as well, leading to greater overall academic success (Allen et al., 1999; Berkowitz, Hunt, & Louden, 1999).

Best Practices for Teaching Oral Communication

- Provide opportunities for multiple forms of presentation, such as leading discussion groups, lecturing, giving dramatic readings, telling stories, conducting read-alouds, and conducting interviews.
- As part of your lesson on public speaking, encourage positive "self-talk" as a way to minimize negative thoughts about potential shortcomings of the upcoming performance. **Self-talk** is the quiet conversations that you have with yourself prior to, during, and after a presentation. Self-statements like "way to go" and "you can do this" are the kinds of positive statements that can improve performance.
- Create a step-by-step process for speech preparation with periodic input from the teacher. The process should include students' research, development of the topic, creation of speaking notes and aids, and rehearsal.
- Model the process of developing and delivering a speech.
- Videotape student presentations and ask for student reflections to enhance your individual feedback.

OnLine Resources	ENGLISH EDUCATION
National Communication Association	Go to NCA's Communication Teacher Resources Online at http://www.natcom.org/resources_links.htm.
Project Gutenberg	Find an extensive collection of literature classics at http://gutenberg.net/catalog.
ERIC OnLine ED461108	*Position on the Teaching of English: Assumptions and Practices*, by NCTE, 1997.
ERIC OnLine ED462701	*Learning to Write: From Choosing the Topic to Final Draft*, by Asser, Hiie, and Poom-Valickis, Katrin, 2002.
ERIC OnLine ED440426	*Basic Communication Course Annual*, Vol. 12, edited by Hugenberg, Lawrence W., 2000, provides tips in seven essays relating to instruction in the basic communication course.

Check this textbook's website at http://education.college.hmco.com/students **for additional links.**

Mathematics Education

The following professional organizations, journals, and standards play an essential role in Mathematics education and the development of your teaching practices.

THE NATIONAL COUNCIL OF TEACHERS OF MATHEMATICS — NCTM

Learned Societies for Teachers of Mathematics

National Council of Teachers of Mathematics
http://www.nctm.org

Mathematical Sciences Education Board
http://www7.nationalacademies.org/mseb/

Mathematics Association of America http://www.maa.org/

Council for Technology in Mathematics Education
http://mathforum.org/library/

American Association for the Advancement of Science
http://www.aaas.org/

National Science Foundation http://www.nsf.gov/

National Academies of Science http://www.nas.edu/

Related Organizations

Association for Women in Mathematics
http://www.awm-math.org/

European Mathematical Association
http://www.emis.ams.org/ems-general.html

Society for Industrial and Applied Mathematics
http://www.siam.org/index.htm

Selected Journals

Mathematics Teaching in the Middle School

Mathematics Teacher

School Science and Mathematics

Teaching Children Mathematics

Online Journal for School Mathematics

Journal for Research in Mathematics Education

SIAM Journal on Discrete Mathematics and for other SIAM journals at http://epubs.siam.org/

American Mathematical Monthly

Mathematics Magazine

Mathematics Horizons

Teaching Mathematics and Its Applications: An International Journal of the IMA

National and State Standards

NCTM provides:

- An introduction to mathematics standards, Principles and Standards for School Mathematics (PSSM)
  http://www.nctm.org/standards/introducing.htm
- An interactive link http://standards.nctm.org/

The Anneberg/CPB, a comprehensive guide to the mathematics and science education reform movement http://www.learner.org/theguide/

Your state standards http://edstandards.org/Standards.html#State or http://www.aligntoachieve.org/AchievePhaseII/basic-search.cfm

---

Assignment 43.1   **MATHEMATICS STANDARDS**

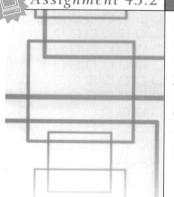

INTASC STANDARDS 1, 7, 9

Visit each of the above standards websites so that you can become familiar with your state and national standards. Reflect on the standards and be prepared to discuss the relationship of your state standards to the national standards and what additional preparation you think you would need to have your students reach these standards. In a one-page report, list five to ten national and state standards that you believe could be achieved in a lesson plan based on your assigned topic from Topic 13, Assignment 13.1. Be prepared to turn in the assignment to your professor and to discuss your ideas in class.

BONUS!

Assignment 43.2   **DOWNLOAD BONUS COURSE MATERIALS AND ASSIGNMENTS**

INTASC STANDARDS 7 AND 9

At http://education.college.hmco.com/students you will find downloadable documents that will assist you in applying the knowledge you have learned from your professor and this book to develop the kind of practical lesson plans you will need as a new teacher for your domain or discipline. The materials that you should download are:

1. Copies from Internet-based resources.
2. Authentic lesson-planning assignments for this Topic (found only at the textbook website) that might be assigned by your professor, such as creating a topic lesson statement of goals, creating Class Notes for the first daily lesson, creating a complete thematic lesson, and more.
3. Examples and templates of a Unit Plan's Statement of Goals (see Topic 19, Assignment 19.1) and a teacher's Class Notes (see Topic 20, Assignment 20.1) for your use.

Introduction to Mathematics Education

In 1980, the National Council of Teachers of Mathematics (NCTM) issued a statement, *An Agenda for Action: Recommendations for School Mathematics for the 1980s,* arguing that mathematics instruction should be focused more on problem solving than on drill and practice. A number of reports called for reform of mathematics education, several of which are considered key NCTM reports and standards. These are listed below along with related documents of the Mathematical Sciences Education Board (MSEB) of the National Academy of Sciences.

- *Curriculum and Evaluation Standards for School Mathematics*, NCTM (1989), also known as "**The Standards**," can be found at http://standards.nctm.org/.
- *Everybody Counts: A Report to the Nation on the Future of Mathematics Education* (1989) delineated a need for reform; go to http://www7.nationalacademies.org/mseb/MSEB_Publications_List.html.
- *Reshaping School Mathematics: A Philosophy and Framework for Curriculum* (1990, pp. 37–39) stated six principles that should shape mathematics curriculum and instruction; go to http://www7.nationalacademies.org/mseb/MSEB_Publications_List.html.

   Principle 1. Mathematics education must focus on the development of **mathematics power** (the ability to compute, calculate, use rules, and apply formulas quickly and confidently).

   Principle 2. Calculators and computers should be used throughout the mathematics community.

   Principle 3. Relevant application should be an integral part of the curriculum.

   Principle 4. Each part of the curriculum should be justified on its own merits.

   Principle 5. Curriculum choices should be consistent with contemporary standards for school mathematics.

   Principle 6. Mathematics instruction at all levels should foster active student involvement.

- *Professional Standards for Teaching Mathematics* (NCTM, 1991).
- *Assessment Standards for School Mathematics* (NCTM, 1995).

In 2000, NCTM updated the national mathematics standards with the publication of *Principles and Standards for School Mathematics* (NCTM, 2000). This document established six broad principles that should guide mathematics education: Equity, Curriculum, Teaching, Learning, Assessment, and Technology. Subsequently a number of websites (listed later in this topic and at this book's website) have been developed to provide models of excellent instruction.

For the Reflective Practitioner

Do not worry about your difficulties in Mathematics. I can assure you—mine are still greater.

ALBERT EINSTEIN

The Practice of Mathematics Education

Fewer than 20 percent of school districts require more than three years of mathematics, according to NAEP (National Assessment of Educational Progress) data for the year 2000, and 30 percent require two years or less (see http://nces.ed.gov/nationsreportcard/). The NCTM reports at the close of the twentieth century recommended that students take more mathematics classes at the secondary level to achieve the literacy needed for the twenty-first century. This kind of mathematics literacy was defined as "**Mathematics Power**" (NCTM, 1989) and consisted of both procedural fluency and conceptual understanding in subjects such as algebra, geometry, trigonometry, functions, statistics, probability, and discrete mathematics. While one would not think that these two goals of **procedural fluency** and **conceptual understanding** would compete for the teacher's time and focus, delivering the right mix as part of a lesson plan is a significant and crucial challenge for mathematics teachers.

Research indicates that a balance of instruction in concepts and student practice must be created for students to learn mathematics (Kilpatrick, Swafford, & Findella, 2001; Knapp et al., 1995; Rittle-Johnson, Siegler, & Alibali, 2001). Teachers should strive to ensure procedural fluency by giving homework assignments and saving classroom time for the teacher to focus on conceptual understanding. But that assumes that American students routinely complete homework assignments to develop their procedural fluency and do not need much class time to acquire it (Travers & Westbury, 1989). Because of cultural differences that lead to Japanese students doing homework, only 40 percent of a Japanese teacher's time is spent developing students' procedural fluency, whereas a U.S. teacher spends as much as 90 percent of his or her time developing students' procedural fluency (Stigler & Hiebert, 1999). The mathematics topics in American schools are also more watered down than they are in some other countries where students are doing better (Travers & Westbury, 1989). In the United States, where family and cultural factors also might make practice during school time more of a necessity, a greater number of students perceive themselves as nonapprentices. This can lead teachers to resort to excessive drill and practice in class to meet the standards of a high-stakes testing regime, which leads to rote learning without mastery of concepts.

A second tenet of mathematics education is that you must start with what the student knows. However, there is widespread agreement that the diversity of the classroom makes finding a common starting point difficult. Uncovering what students know is a difficult task because students' presentations of ideas are not always fully formed, they have apprehensions about potential negative peer perceptions, the classroom climate may inhibit feedback, and students may have math anxiety (Ball, 1997; Ma, 2003; Taylor & Fraser, 2003).

The third principle of mathematics education stresses the importance of discoursing with students so that they reveal their mathematical thinking, reflect on it, refine it, and make adjustments (Knuth & Peressini, 2001). The discourse between the teacher and student, and between student and student, allows for multiple perspectives and what Hiebert et al. (1997) called "cognitive conflict" as a way to force reconstruction of ideas.

Finally, technology has proved to be an important tool in mathematics instruction (Gilliland, 2002). The use of hand-held calculators has been demonstrated to consistently produce positive results (Crouws & Cebulla, 1999; Gilliland, 2002; Hembree & Dessart, 1992). And more recently, computers appear to be most effective with higher-order applications and less effective with drill exercises (The Education Trust, 1998).

One criticism, in spite of reforms in mathematics education, is that the instructional pattern has been consistent and predictable for nearly a century (Hoetker & Ahlbrand, 1969; Stigler & Hiebert, 1997). Davis and Hersh (1981) describe the "ordinary mathematics class" as follows:

> We have problems to solve, or a method of calculation to explain, or a theorem to prove. The main work will be done in writing, usually on the blackboard [now on an overhead projector]. If the problems are solved, the theorems proved, or the calculations completed, then the teacher and the class know they have completed the daily task. (p. 3)

Davis and Hersh (1981) go on to report that when there is student confusion, the teacher's typical response is to repeat the same steps only more slowly, more loudly, and in greater detail. Although there has been dissatisfaction with the level of mathematics literacy among Americans and there have been many reform movements over the decades, there is little evidence that the process of mathematics instruction at the secondary level has substantially changed. The criticism continues to be focused on the following (Conference Board of the Mathematical Sciences, 1975; Stigler & Hiebert, 1997; Silver, 1998; Spillane & Zeuli, 1999):

1. Classes fail to help students develop concepts or connect those concepts to procedures.
2. There is too much emphasis on teaching procedures.
3. Teacher talk tends to be statements choreographed with demonstration of the procedure, but the concepts are not explained or developed.
4. Seatwork is primarily an unchallenging practice of a procedure that has just been demonstrated rather than a new application or group activity where students attempt to reconstruct new knowledge.
5. The curriculum is undemanding and repetitive.

Best Practices for Teaching Mathematics

The current standards and research suggest a number of best practices for mathematics instruction.

- Structure learning of concepts and skills into problem-solving activities: Present problems as intellectual challenges and exhibit enthusiasm in exploring possible solutions.
- Use hands-on activities, visuals, and didactic materials.
- When teaching concepts via tasks, preview the concepts and debrief how the tasks reflect the concepts.
- Model mathematical thinking by verbally sharing your own metacognitive process as you progress through a problem-solution set.
- Require students to provide explanations and justifications: Ask them to explain why they selected the solution and why it works.
- Focus on the analysis of multiple solution methods.
- Focus on conceptual development: Emphasize the correctness of the mathematical reasoning, rather than the correct answers.
- Hold students accountable for completion of tasks.
- If students have been taught the Procedural Knowledge to perform the task, resist the urge to intervene and provide the solution: Make them figure it out.
- Don't overpractice procedures before students understand them; they have more difficulty making sense of them later.
- Treat mistakes as new learning opportunities.

For more on these topics, see Kilpatrick et al. (2001), Spillane and Zeuli (1999), Grouws and Smith (2000), Fennema, Sowder, and Carpenter (1999), Stein et al. (2000), and Boyer (2002).

For the Reflective Practitioner

For information and benchmarks on mathematics as a basic skill, go to the American Diploma Project at http://www.achieve.org/achieve.nsf/AmericanDiplomaProject?OpenForm.

OnLine Resources	MATHEMATICS EDUCATION
Eisenhower National Clearinghouse for Mathematics and Science Education	Go to http://www.enc.org/ for comprehensive lesson plans and standards.
NCTM Illuminations Website	Go to http://illuminations.nctm.org/ for extensive concrete examples and vignettes on how to teach to the standards.
Modeling Middle School Mathematics	Go to http://www.enc.org/resources/records/contents/0,1240,025622,00.shtm for online videos modeling best practices in mathematics at the middle school level.
ERIC OnLine ED465514	*ED Thoughts: What We Know About Mathematics Teaching and Learning*, edited by Sutton, John, and Krueger, Alice, 2002, is a concise summary of research on teaching mathematics.

Check this textbook's website at http://education.college.hmco.com/students for additional links.

Science Education

The following professional organizations, journals, and standards play an essential role in science education and the development of your teaching practices.

THE NATIONAL SCIENCE TEACHERS ASSOCIATION — NSTA

Reprinted with the permission of National Science Teachers Association.

Professional Organizations for Teachers of Science

National Science Teachers Association http://www.nsta.org/

National Academy of Sciences http://www.nas.edu/

American Association for the Advancement of Science http://www.aaas.org/

Eisenhower National Clearinghouse http://www.enc.org/

National Science Foundation http://www.nsf.gov/

National Association for Research in Science Teaching http://www2.educ.sfu.ca/narstsite/

National Middle Level Science Teachers Association http://www.nmlsta.org/

Related Organizations

American Association of Physics Teachers http://www.aapt.org/

National Association of Biology Teachers http://www.nabt.org/

American Chemistry Society http://www.chemistry.org/portal/a/c/s/1/home.html

Chemical Heritage Foundation http://www.chemheritage.org/

American Association of Physics Teachers http://www.aapt.org

American Institute of Physics http://www.aip.org/

Physics Teaching Resource Agents http://www.aapt.org/PTRA/index.cfm

Selected Journals

Science Education

Journal of Science Teacher Education

The Science Educator

School Science Review

School Science and Mathematics

The Science Teacher

Studies in Science Education

Journal of Research in Science Teaching

Research in Science Teaching (Australia)

The Chemical Educator

The International Journal of Science Education (Europe)

Related Organizations

American Society of Plant Biologists http://www.aspb.org/

National Association of Geoscience Teachers
http://www.nagt.org/

National Earth Science Teachers Association
http://www.nesta.org/

Geological Society of America
http://www.geosociety.org/educate

National Association of Geology Teachers http://www.nagt.org/

History of Science Society http://www.hssonline.org/

National and State Standards

Project 2061 Benchmarks http://www.project2061.org/tools/benchol/bolintro.htm

The National Science Education Standards http://stills.nap.edu/html/nses/

INTASC Standards for Science Teacher Education
http://www.ccsso.org/content/pdfs/ScienceStandards.pdf

Your state standards http://edstandards.org/Standards.html#State or
http://www.aligntoachieve.org/AchievePhaseII/basic-search.cfm

Assignment 44.1   ## SCIENCE STANDARDS

INTASC STANDARDS 1, 7, 9

Visit each of the above standards websites so that you can become familiar with your state and national standards. Reflect on the standards and be prepared to discuss the relationship of your state standards to the national standards and what additional preparation you think you would need to have your students reach these standards. In a one-page report, list five to ten national and state standards that you believe could be achieved in a lesson plan based on your assigned topic from Topic 13, Assignment 13.1. Be prepared to turn in the assignment to your professor and to discuss your ideas in class.

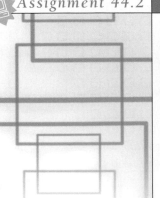

Assignment 44.2   ## DOWNLOAD BONUS COURSE MATERIALS AND ASSIGNMENTS

INTASC STANDARDS 7 AND 9

AT http://education.college.hmco.com/students you will find downloadable documents that will assist you in applying the knowledge you have learned from your professor and this book to develop the kind of practical lesson plans you will need as a new teacher for your domain or discipline. The materials that you should download are:

1. Copies from Internet-based resources.
2. Authentic lesson-planning assignments for this Topic (found only at the textbook website) that might be assigned by your professor, such as creating a topic lesson statement of goals, creating Class Notes for the first daily lesson, creating a complete thematic lesson, and more.
3. Examples and templates of a Unit Plan's Statement of Goals (see Topic 19, Assignment 19.1) and a teacher's Class Notes (see Topic 20, Assignment 20.1) for your use.

Introduction to Science Education

The dynamic and explosive developments in science and technology during the last fifty years have been a major factor in shaping the unique demands on science educators. Unlike domain knowledge in history and literature, for example, where changes tend to be new interpretations, science teachers' domain knowledge, if not current at even the middle and high school levels, is inaccurate. Unlike textbooks at the secondary level in social studies and literature, which may not have the latest information but are still useable without being inaccurate, science text materials are easily outdated. Arguably, more than in any other domain, science teachers are in need of **"in-service" training** and timely teaching materials so that they can stay current with their Information and Procedural Knowledge.

The state of science instruction as the nation moved into World War II reflected the science and technology of the times and a pedagogy consisting primarily of explanations about topics such as aviation, photography, and radio. Students would read the narrative text of out-of-date topics introduced by the teacher. Scientific method, experiments, hypothesizing, and analysis of data were reserved primarily for the university experience. With the development of the atomic bomb at the end of World War II and the launching of *Sputnik*, the first satellite, in 1957 by the USSR, a period of reform in science education began in American schools.

In the late fifties and early sixties, the National Science Foundation (NSF) played a lead role in advancing science education by establishing over 400 institutes at colleges and universities. These centers offered up-to-date and advanced training to teachers and eventually were providing some training to over half of all secondary math and science teachers in the nation (Raizen, 1991). NSF created what was known as the "alphabet curricula" because it used acronyms like "STS" for science, technology, and society. These materials were developed by teams of scientists for use in the classrooms to fill the void left by out-of-date textbooks and pedagogy. The materials were theoretical in nature, encouraged discovery pedagogy (i.e., science should be taught as a process of discovering the unknown), were oriented toward college-bound students, and used quantitative techniques with few of the practical explanations of the early fifties (Mathews, 1994).

In 1970, the National Science Teachers Association (NSTA) identified "scientific literacy" as its most important goal (NSTA, 1971) and emphasized the need to teach students about science so that they could understand their world and acquire the tools for acquiring new scientific knowledge. Following the *Nation at Risk* report (National Commission on Excellence in Education, 1983), which cited science and math acumen as particularly lacking in American high school graduates, in 1985 the American Association for the Advancement of Science (AAAS) organized what became known as Project 2061 (2061 is the year Halley's comet can again be observed from earth), which was set as the goal for a "scientific literate society"). Project 2061's "Benchmarks" emphasized the societal problem of achieving scientific literacy, which consisted of **Cultural Literacy** (knowing numerous terms and definitions from science) and **Functional Literacy** (being able to coherently converse, read, and write using scientific terms and definitions) (Shamos, 1995). Whether science

For the Reflective Practitioner

Aristotle maintained that women have fewer teeth than men; although he was twice married, it never occurred to him to verify this statement by examining his wives' mouths.
BERTRAND RUSSELL

For the Reflective Practitioner

The most exciting phrase to hear in science, the one that heralds new discoveries, is not "Eureka!" (I found it!) but "That's funny . . ."
ISAAC ASIMOV

For the Reflective Practitioner

The important thing in science is not so much to obtain new facts as to discover new ways of thinking about them.
SIR WILLIAM BRAGG

should emphasize cultural literacy or functional literacy is still debated today (Rutherford & Ahlgren, 1990; Shamos, 1995). The publication *Benchmarks for Science Literacy* (AAAS, 1993) focused on and promoted functional literacy and identified the Basic Skills, Information and Procedural Knowledge, and habits of mind that every high school student should possess in science, mathematics, and technology by high school graduation.

The National Science Teachers Association (NSTA) and the National Academy of Sciences (NAS) through the National Research Council published the *National Science Education Standards* (NRC, 1996) with specific standards for grades 5 through 8 and 9 through 12 (go to http://www.nap.edu/readingroom/books/nses/html/). The "Standards," which share most of the same goals and philosophy as Project 2061 and the *Benchmarks for Science Literacy,* anticipate that individuals should be able to also "do" science (Kemp, 2000). All these reports have shaped the current focus of science education and will guide your practice in the classroom.

Best Practices for Teaching Science

The following are a number of practices that are important to high-quality science instruction.

- Continuously emphasize the reliance on and development of empirical evidence as the centerpiece of the scientific method by using **Inquiry-Based Teaching Strategies.** Such approaches rely on teachers to create situations in which students take on the role of scientist. Students take the initiative to observe and question phenomena; pose explanations about what they see; devise and conduct tests to support or contradict their theories; analyze data; draw conclusions from experimental data; and design and build models.
- Model and then guide students in conducting investigations by setting up problems and resources, rather than lecturing on topics.
- Include a variety of investigation formats, such as laboratory work, fieldwork, and work in Microcomputer-Based Labs (MBLs).
- Create and use graphical representations or physical models during your teacher talk, such as anatomical figures and graphic organizers depicting processes.
- Design tasks that require comparing and classifying the results of experiments and data.
- Require students to formulate logical and cohesive verbal and written explanations based on investigations.
- Develop authentic observation and writing skills by creating opportunities for students to take notes and render their conclusions in observation notes.
- Plan and incorporate multiple analogies and examples into your teacher talk to create a bridge from what students know to what they don't know.
- Guide students into converting "Why" questions into "How" questions, because the latter can be validated.
- Plan detailed and sequential questions as part of your teacher talk: Begin lessons with a question that deals with a Big Idea (see Topics 11 and 20).
- Treat mistakes as learning experiences.
- Have students read and interpret primary scientific documents so they develop their literacy in the domain-specific content.
- Use multiple assessments and various types of assessments (see Topic 37).

OnLine Resources	SCIENCE EDUCATION
The Source Book for Teaching Science	For this gateway to resources for teaching science, go to http://www.csun.edu/~vceed002/.
The Clickable Periodic Table	Go to http://www.ch.cam.ac.uk/magnus/PeriodicTable.html.
The Virtual Body	Go to http://www.medtropolis.com/VBody.asp.
ERIC OnLine ED433242	*Inquiry and Problem Solving*, edited by Thorson, Annette, 1999, provides examples of inquiry and problem-solving instructional approaches.
ERIC OnLine ED391504	*Scientific Thinking Is in the Mind's Eye*, by Ganguly, Indrani, 1995, demonstrates the effectiveness of analogies.

Check this textbook's website at http://education.college.hmco.com/students for additional links.

Social Studies Education

The following professional organizations, journals, and standards play an essential role in social studies education and the development of your teaching practices.

THE NATIONAL COUNCIL FOR THE SOCIAL STUDIES — NCSS

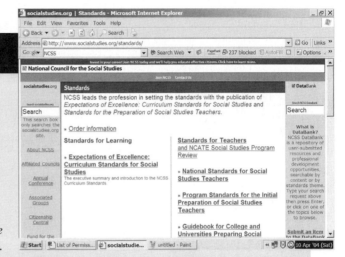

Copyright by the National Council for the Social Studies. Reprinted with permission.

Professional Organizations for Teachers of Social Studies

National Council for the Social Studies (NCSS)
http://www.ncss.org/

Related Organizations

National Center for History in the Schools
http://www.sscnet.ucla.edu/nchs/

Organization of American Historians http://www.oah.org/

American Historical Association http://www.theaha.org/

National Council for History Education
http://www.history.org/nche

American Studies Association
http://www.georgetown.edu/crossroads/asainfo.html

National Council on Economic Education
http://www.ncee.org

National Association of Economic Educators
http://ecedweb.unomaha.edu/naee/naeepamp.htm

National Council for Geographic Education
http://www.ncge.org

Association of American Geographers
http://www.aag.org/intro.html

American Geographical Society
http://www.amergeog.org/Index.html

Selected Journals

Journal of Social Studies Research

Social Education

International Journal of Social Education

Social Studies

Social Studies Professional

Theory and Research in Social Education

National Geographic

American Anthropologist

Cultural Anthropology

The American Political Science Review

PS: Political Science and Politics

Journal of Geography

Geographical Review

FOCUS on Geography Magazine

Journal of American Studies

Journal of Economics Education

American Economic Review

American Economist

Related Organizations	Selected Journals
Center for Civic Education http://www.civiced.org/index.html	*History Teacher*
	History and Theory
American Political Science Association http://www.apsanet.org/	*Journal of American History*
	The American Historical Review
American Anthropological Association http://www.aaanet.org	*The Historical Journal of American History*
American Psychological Association http://www.apa.org	*Psychological Review*
	Political Science and Politics
American Sociological Association http://www.asanet.org	*American Sociological Review*
	Sociological Theory

National and State Standards

Expectations of Excellence: Curriculum Standards for Social Studies
http://www.socialstudies.org/standards/

National History Standards http://www.sscnet.ucla.edu/nchs/standards/thinkingk-4.html

National Economic Standards http://www.economicsamerica.org/standards/contents.html

National Geography Standards http://www.ncge.org/publications/tutorial/standards/

National Standards for Civics and Government http://www.civiced.org/curriculum.html

INTASC Standards for Social Studies Teacher Education (in development) http://www.ccsso.org/

Your state standards http://edstandards.org/Standards.html#State or
http://www.aligntoachieve.org/AchievePhaseII/basic-search.cfm

---

SOCIAL STUDIES STANDARDS
Assignment 45.1

INTASC STANDARDS 1, 7, 9

Visit each of the above standards websites so that you can become familiar with your state and national standards. Reflect on the standards and be prepared to discuss the relationship of your state standards to the national standards and what additional preparation you think you would need to have your students reach these standards. In a one-page report, list five to ten national and state standards that you believe could be achieved in a lesson plan based on your assigned topic from Topic 13, Assignment 13.1. Be prepared to turn in the assignment to your professor and to discuss your ideas in class.

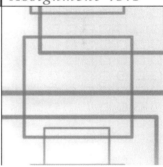

DOWNLOAD BONUS COURSE MATERIALS AND ASSIGNMENTS
Assignment 45.2

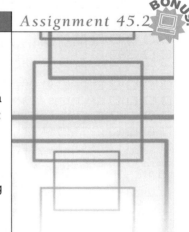

INTASC STANDARDS 7 AND 9

At http://education.college.hmco.com/students you will find downloadable documents that will assist you in applying the knowledge you have learned from your professor and this book to develop the kind of practical lesson plans you will need as a new teacher for your domain or discipline. The materials that you should download are:

1. Copies from Internet-based resources.
2. Authentic lesson-planning assignments for this Topic (found only at the textbook website) that might be assigned by your professor, such as creating a topic lesson statement of goals, creating Class Notes for the first daily lesson, creating a complete thematic lesson, and more.
3. Examples and templates of a Unit Plan's Statement of Goals (see Topic 19, Assignment 19.1) and a teacher's Class Notes (see Topic 20, Assignment 20.1) for your use.

Introduction to Social Studies Education

The terms *Social Studies* and *Social Sciences* are often used interchangeably and are at times a source of confusion. *Social Studies* is the preferred term, in part because it is more inclusive. *Social Sciences* typically refers only to the academic disciplines of sociology, psychology, and sometimes economics and anthropology. The term *Social Studies* includes the aforementioned social sciences as well as history, geography, political science, and philosophy. However, in the professional literature, these terms are often used interchangeably.

Background

History, geography, and civics (instruction in government, patriotism, and democratic values) were the autonomous subjects that were the mainstay of a secondary education in the nineteenth century. However, there were indications that change was coming when the 1893 *Report of the Committee of Ten on Secondary School Studies* advocated an interdisciplinary approach in the social studies. By 1916, the National Education Association's (NEA) Committee on the Social Studies was urging the creation of a curriculum focused on "man as a member of social groups" that included the perspectives of the relatively newly formed and influential social sciences. This NEA report established *social studies* as the name of the content area.

The National Council for the Social Studies (NCSS) was formed in 1921. Since that time, the NCSS has launched a number of curricula initiatives and adopted a number of influential position statements that affect the separate disciplines taught under the umbrella of social studies. Position statements from academic freedom to multiculturalism can be found at the NCSS website at http://www.socialstudies.org/positions/.

In 1989, the NCSS published *Essential Skills of a Social Studies Education*, which established a broad set of Basics Skills and executive processes that should be included in K–12 social studies programs. In 1990, the NCSS published *Social Studies for Citizens for a Strong and Free Nation* (see Table 45.2), which articulated a set of beliefs and values that should be part of the scope and sequence of all state social studies programs. These beliefs and values serve as the theoretical framework for promoting a democratic ideology.

Finally, in 1994, NCSS published *Expectations of Excellence: Curriculum Standards for Social Studies*. Citing the need to promote civic ideals and principles for life in the twenty-first century, the standards consist of ten interdisciplinary **themes** (see Table 45.1) and **strands** that serve as a guide for developing social studies curricula and establishing course standards in all of the social studies fields.

These themes were a significant departure from the past, when the curriculum standards were defined in terms of teaching certain content, such as the Civil War in American history, the two-party system in civics, or South America in geography. In Assignment 45.1, you should have noted that these standards are heavily weighted toward Procedural Knowledge as opposed to Information Knowledge. As an example, consider the **Theme** *"Culture"* and the related **Strand**: "*Compare ways in which people from different cultures think about and deal with their physical environment and social conditions.*" It does not mention any one culture, that is, Information Knowledge. In the past, teaching would have prescribed what historical or contemporary culture

For the Reflective Practitioner

My own in-house youth consultant, my son, is almost thirteen and knows with astonishing details the genealogy of Frodo Baggins from Lord of the Rings *or the battles of Luke Skywalker's rebellion against the Empire in* Star Wars. *Yet, he did not know until recently that Abraham Lincoln was born in a log cabin. He knows because I told him. "They don't teach us much history in school, Dad," he said.*

CLARENCE PAGE

Table 45.1 | **THE TEN NCSS THEMES**

NCSS Theme	Primary Social Studies Discipline(s)
CULTURE	Anthropology and Geography
TIME, CONTINUITY, AND CHANGE	History
PEOPLE, PLACES, AND ENVIRONMENTS	Geography and Anthropology
INDIVIDUAL DEVELOPMENT AND IDENTITY	Sociology and Psychology
INDIVIDUALS, GROUPS, AND INSTITUTIONS	Political Science, Sociology, and Anthropology
POWER, AUTHORITY, AND GOVERNANCE	Political Science
PRODUCTION, DISTRIBUTION, AND CONSUMPTION	Economics
SCIENCE, TECHNOLOGY, AND SOCIETY	History, Anthropology, and Political Science
GLOBAL CONNECTIONS	Geography, Anthropology, and Political Science
CIVIC IDEALS AND PRACTICES	Political Science and History

should be studied. Under this new framework, Procedural Knowledge could be used to understand various topics: prehistoric humans, ethnic neighborhoods in America, early civilizations, regionalization of the American colonies, and contemporary comparisons of people in northern and southern climates. At the NCSS website (www.socialstudies.org) you can find lesson plans and a more detailed explanation of each of the themes.

Gaining agreement on a set of content standards in the social studies disciplines is more controversial than securing a consensus on approaches to instruction (Bain, 1995; Cornbleth & Waugh, 1995; Nash, Crabtree, & Dunn, 1997). By focusing on Procedural Knowledge, the NCSS was able to avoid the ideological differences that become most apparent when defining Information Knowledge.

Divergent Interests and Challenges in Social Studies

Social studies teachers are not only expected to transmit Procedural Knowledge and Information Knowledge like teachers of science and mathematics, but they are also expected to promote democratic values and prepare students for citizenship. In social studies, ambiguity and differences of opinion can arise from almost identical facts; this characteristic draws many individuals to the field, but it is both a blessing and a curse. It is a blessing in that it can make a classroom dynamic, although some people may feel that this dynamism takes on new meaning with popular commentators such the "liberal" Al Frankin and the "conservative"

Rush Limbaugh. It is a curse because social studies standards are subject to ideological influences. As an example, the economics and geography standards moved to a finalization with relatively little controversy. But the National Center for History in the Schools report, **National Standards for History** (1996) at http://www.sscnet.ucla.edu/nchs/standards/thinkingk-4. html, still remains controversial today (Symcox, 2002). In history, any decision to include or exclude a person, place, or event is subject to criticism on ideological grounds.

> **?** *Assume you are a consultant to a textbook company and they have told you that they are out of text space and have only enough room for a paragraph on Ben Franklin OR Sojourner Truth. Who would you include, and what would be your justification?*

Multicultural Education and Cultural Literacy

In what are known as the "**Culture Wars**," some educators have charged that history standards have elevated the importance of relatively minor historical figures and events for the sake of diversity and have created a loss of "proportionality" for the sake of "political correctness" (Hertzberg, 1982; Hughes, 1994; Ravitch, 1985, 2003a, 2003b). Others have claimed that certain groups, individuals, and events have been omitted altogether or not given adequate weight because of bias or American Eurocentrism, if not Ethnocentrism (Gitlin, 1995). E. D. Hirsch (1987) has proposed in **Cultural Literacy: What Every American Needs to Know** a core of Information Knowledge based on the argument that it is the "glue" that binds a culture and society together. Even if all of us were to agree that a more structured core of Information Knowledge is needed, the problem remains as to what should it be?

For the Reflective Practitioner

I think it would be a good idea.

MAHATMA GANDHI, WHEN ASKED WHAT HE THOUGHT OF WESTERN CIVILIZATION

When taken to extremes, **Multicultural Education** and **Cultural Literacy** are depicted in the education literature as the opposing forces in this fight for the minds and hearts of American youth and the future of civilization. Advocates of Cultural Literacy are depicted as promoting the superiority of Western civilization and U.S. culture in much the same way Hitler promoted German superiority. And Multiculturalists are portrayed as moral relativists who fail to appreciate the unique advancements brought about by the traditions of Western civilization that are reflected in American culture today. However, both Multicultural Education and Cultural Literacy are vital to the success of social studies teachers because both provide insights into our shared human experience and allow people to bond in the common task of providing for the common welfare of the inhabitants of the planet. For essays on this topic, go to the Core Knowledge website at http://www.coreknowledge.org/CKproto2/about/articles/centrst.htm.

For the Reflective Practitioner

Any man who is under thirty and is not a liberal has no heart; any man who is over thirty and is not a conservative has no brains.

WINSTON CHURCHILL

Subjectivity and Interpretation

Continuing with the history discipline as our example, the general public often misperceives "history" as a fixed series of facts (Nasch, Crabtree, & Dunn, 1997; Whelan, 1992). But those working at the expert level know that history is manufactured and always reflects the author's or teacher's perspective, sometimes with prejudice or deceit, sometimes perhaps unknowingly with bias because of "ideological blinders," and often not presented with appropriate distinctions between facts and interpretations (Ravitch, 2003a, 2003b). Biased interpretations (either liberal or conservative) find their way into middle and high school textbooks and classrooms in spite of the best of intentions of publishers and textbook consultants (see Cornbleth & Waugh, 1995; Evans, 1990; Gitlin, 1995; Ravitch, 2003a, 2003b). In history, therefore, it is essential to focus on the Procedural Knowledge that will empower students to become their own interpreters. This begins with an understanding that history is an account, not an event (Bain, 1997; Werner, 2000).

Indoctrination and Enculturation

The transmission of democratic principles has been an expectation for American schools, and social studies teachers in particular, since the nation's founding. The NCSS in *Social Studies for Citizens for a Strong and Free Nation* (NCSS, 1990) defined a set of democratic beliefs that should be promoted in social studies classrooms (and arguably in every classroom). These are presented in Table 45.2.

Table 45.2 | **NCSS DEMOCRATIC BELIEFS**

Rights of the Individual	Freedoms of the Individual
Right to life	Freedom to participate in the political process
Right to liberty	Freedom of worship
Right to dignity	Freedom of thought
Right to security	Freedom of conscience
Right to equality of opportunity	Freedom of assembly
Right to justice	Freedom of inquiry
Right to privacy	Freedom of expression
Right to private ownership of property	

Responsibilities of the Individual	Beliefs Concerning Societal Conditions and Governmental Responsibilities
To respect human life	Societies need laws that are accepted by the majority of the people.
To respect the rights of others	Dissenting minorities are protected.
To be tolerant	Government is elected by the people.
To be honest	Government respects and protects individual rights.
To be compassionate	Government respects and protects individual freedoms.
To demonstrate self-control	Government guarantees civil liberties.
To participate in the democratic process	Government works for the common good.
To respect the property of others	

"Promoting" beliefs such as these in a democratic state can be controversial, however, because of differences over how the principles should be applied in specific cases, such as abortion, war, or poverty. How much they should assert their own opinion is one of the great challenges for social studies teachers (see Topic 32 on leading discussions and Kelley's approaches to this challenge).

 What is the difference between indoctrination and enculturation? Can you define each of these terms? Have you ever been indoctrinated?

Textbook-Based Instruction

Social studies teaching has been characterized as heavily reliant on textbooks (Goodlad, 1984; Ogawa, 2001), usually lecture oriented with an occasional film and weekly quizzes (Cuban, 1991; Ravitch & Finn, 1987), and excessively focused on facts (Onsko, 1990; Spoehr & Spoehr, 1994). National survey results of students in 1987 indicated that 97 percent of the students participated in lecture at least some of the time, 89 percent of students used the textbook weekly, 83 percent memorized information, and 68 percent reported not having written long reports (Applebee, Langer, & Mullis, 1987). In another study, only about 5 percent of lessons called on students to acquire Procedural Knowledge (Leinhardt, 1993). Is it any wonder that Goodland (1984) found that students ranked social studies less important than most other subjects? The following section outlines some best practices that can be used to engage students.

Best Practices for Teaching Social Studies

The following best practices are recommended social studies strategies. They are based on the works of Newmann (1990), Onsko (1990), Leinhardt (1997), Kelley (1986), Kaplan (2002), Beardsley (2003), and others, as well as NCSS position statements.

- Frame lessons in terms of a Big Idea and encourage students to examine the idea.
- Serve more as an interlocutor than a lecturer.
- Draw analogies to current events that force students to draw "close" comparisons.
- Relish and let your students see you enjoy the complexity and ambiguity of social studies.
- Model the characteristics of a thoughtful person by showing interest in students' ideas and their suggestions for solving problems, by modeling problem-solving processes rather than just giving answers, and by acknowledging the difficulties involved in gaining a clear understanding of problematic topics.
- Rely less on the textbook materials and use multiple sources, including primary documents.
- Ensure that classroom interactions focus on sustained examination of a few topics rather than on superficial coverage of many by focusing on Procedural Knowledge applications to the content.
- Pose questions rather than promote answers.
- Suggest ideas that may be beyond students' experiences.
- Press students to clarify or justify their assertions rather than merely accepting and reinforcing them indiscriminately.
- Give students sufficient time to think before being required to answer questions.

- Encourage students to generate original, unpopular, and unconventional ideas in the course of the interaction.
- Treat the textbook as a companion for the Big Ideas you will develop.
- Use simulations and reenactments to create active learning lessons.

OnLine Resources	SOCIAL STUDIES EDUCATION
National Geographic	See the *National Standards Related Lessons and Activities* at http://www.nationalgeographic.com/xpeditions/standards/.
Gateway to World History	Go to http://vlib.iue.it/history/index.html. Go to http://www.academicinfo.net/hist.html#meta.
Gateway to American History	Go to http://vlib.iue.it/history/USA/.
NCSS	at position papers at http://www.socialstudies.org/positions/ *Social Studies in the Middle* and *A Vision of Powerful Teaching and Learning in the Social Studies: Building Social Understanding and Civic Efficacy.*
ERIC OnLine ED410141	*Handbook on Teaching Social Issues* (NCSS Bulletin 93), edited by Evans, Ronald W., and Saxe, David Warren, 1996, is an extensive anthology of teaching strategies for social studies.

Check this textbook's website at http://education.college.hmco.com/students for additional links.

topic 46

World/Foreign Language Education

The following professional organizations, journals, and standards play an essential role in World/Foreign Language education and the development of your teaching practices.

THE AMERICAN COUNCIL FOR TEACHERS OF FOREIGN LANGUAGE—ACTFL

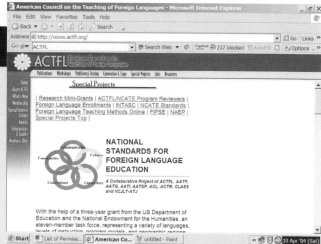

Reprinted with permission of the American Council for Teachers of Foreign Language.

Professional Organizations for Foreign Language Teachers

American Council on the Teaching of Foreign Languages
http://www.actfl.org/

Modern Language Association http://www.mla.org

American Association of Applied Linguistics http://www.aaal.org/

Related Organizations

American Federation of Teachers of French
http://www.frenchteachers.org/

American Association of Teachers of German http://www.aatg.org

American Association of Teachers of Italian
http://www.italianstudies.org/aati/

American Association of Teachers of Spanish and Portuguese
http://www.aatsp.org/ScriptContent/Index.cfm

American Classical League http://www.aclclassics.org/

American Councils for International Education
http://www.americancouncils.org/home.asp?PageID=1

Akzidenz Grotesk BE http://www.all-languages.org.uk/

Teachers of English to Speakers of Other Languages, Inc.
http://www.tesol.org

American Association of Teachers of Slavic and Eastern European
Languages http://aatseel.org/

American Association of Teachers of Arabic http://www.wm.edu/aata/

Selected Journals

Applied Linguistics

Foreign Language Annals

Language Learning

Language Learning and Technology

The Modern Language Journal

Studies in Second Language Acquisition

TESOL Quarterly

(*TESOL Journal* and *TESOL Matters* ceased publication with their Fall 2003 issues and are replaced by *Essential Teacher*)

The French Review

Hispania

Dutch Unterrichtspraxis

Related Organizations

Association of Teachers of Japanese
http://www.colorado.edu/ealld/atj/

Chinese Language Teachers Association
http://clta.deall.ohio-state.edu/

National and State Standards

Standards for Foreign Language Learning: Preparing for the 21st Century (published in 1996 and 1999)
http://www.actfl.org/index.cfm?weburl=/public/articles/details.cfm?id=33 and go to Publications

Your state standards http://edstandards.org/Standards.html#State or
http://www.aligntoachieve.org/AchievePhaseII/basic-search.cfm

---

WORLD LANGUAGE STANDARDS

Assignment 46.1

INTASC STANDARDS 1, 7, 9

Visit each of the above standards websites so that you can become familiar with your state and national standards. Be prepared to reflect on the standards and to discuss the relationship of your state standards to the national standards and what additional preparation you think you would need to have your students reach these standards. In a one-page report, list five to ten national and state standards that you believe could be achieved in a lesson plan based on your assigned topic from Topic 13, Assignment 13.1. Be prepared to turn in the assignment to your professor and to discuss your ideas in class.

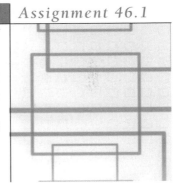

DOWNLOAD BONUS COURSE MATERIALS AND ASSIGNMENTS

Assignment 46.2 **BONUS!**

INTASC STANDARDS 7 AND 9

At http://education.college.hmco.com/students you will find downloadable documents that will assist you in applying the knowledge you have learned from your professor and this book to develop the kind of practical lesson plans you will need as a new teacher for your domain or discipline. The materials that you should download are:

1. Copies from Internet-based resources.
2. Authentic lesson-planning assignments for this Topic (found only at the textbook website) that might be assigned by your professor, such as creating a topic lesson statement of goals, creating Class Notes for the first daily lesson, creating a complete thematic lesson, and more.
3. Examples and templates of a Unit Plan's Statement of Goals (see Topic 19, Assignment 19.1) and a teacher's Class Notes (see Topic 20, Assignment 20.1) for your use.

Introduction to Foreign Language Education

The terms *world, second,* and *foreign* in **Second Language Acquisition Education** are used to refer to learning a language that is other than one's native language. So for students in Japan learning English, or students in St. Louis learning French, the language to be learned is referred to as the **"Target Language"** or **"L2"** (L1 is the student's native language). The world languages domain includes the burgeoning field of teaching English as a second language (common acronyms are **ESL** and **ESOL**: *English as a Second Language;* **TESOL:** *Teaching*

Topic 46: **World/Foreign Language Education**

English to Speakers of Other Languages; and **ELL:** *English Language Learners*). This specialty has been brought to the forefront in large measure by a growing multicultural student population with limited English proficiency. The focus of this chapter is on teaching a language other than English (L2) to students in American middle and high school settings.

While the advantages of being bilingual are apparent in the twenty-first century, the strong monolingual tradition of the United States means that L2 instruction is delivered predominately at the middle and high school level, rather than in communities as a natural, everyday process or at the elementary school level with other important subjects, as in Europe. This impediment contributes to the anxiety of students who are expected to learn a new language as they enter secondary education (Horwitz, 2001; Kim, 2001).

Mediation is the term used to describe the human process of using language to interact with the world and one another. And it is through mediation—interactions with other human beings using language to reflect ideas—that we acquire our existing language and learn to produce language (Ellis, 1997). The mediation path includes both (1) internal processes (what Vygotsky, 1986, called **"private speech"**) by which we clarify our thoughts and express them through language, and (2) external processes like direct instruction, textbooks, conversations, and visuals used in classrooms. While these external processes may motivate and lower anxiety levels for L2 learning, it is students' private speech that moves them beyond their existing linguistic competence (Vygotsky, 1986).

Language Acquisition (LA) involves proficiency in four forms: speaking, reading, listening, and writing. Research on how children acquire their first language has been a driving force in creating the current standards and methods in second language acquisition. This research indicates that humans have an innate ability—a **"language acquisition device" (LAD)**—that allows them to process and create language. The structure of language is universal because the essential elements in all languages (verbs, phrases, cadence, emphasis, and so on) are substantially the same; for classic presentations of theory regarding "Universal Grammar," refer to Chomsky (1965) and White (1989).

A key variable in successful language acquisition is the quality and quantity of **"input"** (the language you hear), and there is a consensus that **"output"** (the language you speak) is necessary, particularly for a high level of competence (Ellis, 1997; Krashen, 1982; Lightbrown, 1985; Long, 1983; Swain, 1995). **"Intake"** is the student's reconstruction of the input and is essential to the ultimate goal of output, the ability to think and converse in a second language (VanPatten & Cadierno, 1993). This intake is integrated into what Selinker (1974) called **"interlanguage,"** the language of the learner, which can be developed with effective instruction. From this line of research, a number of fundamental principles have evolved:

1. Foreign language is best learned in context, just as children learn their first language in the context of family and friends and in daily interactions with the environment.
2. Students exposed only to exercises that focus on structure learn more slowly than those who are immersed in conversation (Lightbrown, 1985).
3. Learners need conversation in the language because, as they interact with other students and the teacher, they develop greater comprehension of the

form of the language and move more from conscious to unconscious rules (Ellis, 1994).

4. Although children may have an advantage in achieving nativelike fluency in the long run, new language may actually be easier to learn and more rapid for the adult than for the child.

5. Teenagers (everyone, for that matter) learn best by integrating new concepts and material into already existing cognitive structures, not by rote memory (Krashen, Long, & Scarcella, 1979).

6. Teenagers' inhibitions about making errors in front of peers are a mitigating factor in language learning (Rubin, 1975).

7. "Good L2 learners" are enthusiastic and accurate guessers; are motivated to communicate in the new language; take advantage of practice opportunities; are attentive to the speech of others; and pay attention to meaning and structure (Oxford, 2001).

8. The input must be "comprehensible." New input must be within students' grasp and based on their prior knowledge, the context, and cues like gestures (Krashen, 1982).

This line of research has affected traditional methods that concentrated on the grammar (the how) and the vocabulary (the what) of a second language. The shift in focus to communication, which includes the why, whom, and when of a second language, is reflected in the current standards.

In 1986 the American Council on the Teaching of Foreign Languages established oral proficiency guidelines with a scale ranging from 0 for "no functional proficiency" to 5 for "educated native speaker." These are known as the **ACTFL Oral Proficiency Guidelines** and can be found at http://www.sil.org/lingualinks/ LANGUAGELEARNING/OtherResources/ACTFLProficiencyGuidelines/TheACTFL Guidelines.htm. This proficiency model grew out of the U.S. government language training schools and therefore was not developed for the purposes of instruction or curricula at the middle or high school levels (Bachman & Savignon, 1986; Lange, 1990). These ACTFL's **Standards for Foreign Language Learning (SFLL)** inspired the development in 1999 of the **ACTFL Performance Guidelines for K–12 Learners** (go to http://www.actfl.org/i4a/pages/index.cfm?pageid=1 and select Publications) which put forth a contemporary vision of language education that is reflected in the "Five C's"—the five goals of foreign language study:

- **Communication:** to speak in languages other than English
- **Cultures:** to gain knowledge and understanding of other cultures
- **Connections:** to use foreign language to understand other disciplines and to acquire information in other language communities
- **Comparisons:** to develop insights through comparative language and culture
- **Communities:** to participate in multilingual communities

The performance standards established three benchmark levels of expertise and six categories of language use:

1. **Benchmarks**
   a. Novice Learner (K–4, 5–8, 9–10)
   b. Intermediate Learner (K–8, 7–12)
   c. Pre-Advanced Learner (K–12)
2. **Domains** (categories of language use)
   a. Comprehensibility (How well is the student understood?)
   b. Comprehension (How well does the student understand?)
   c. Language Control (How accurate is the student's language?)

d. Vocabulary Usage (How extensive and applicable is the student's language?)

e. Communication Strategies (How do students maintain communication?)

f. Cultural Awareness (How is students' cultural understanding reflected in their communication?)

Best Practices in Foreign Language Education

Based on the fundamental principles stated above, the performance and proficiency standards suggest a number of best practices.

1. Create a low-anxiety classroom characterized by a thoughtful teacher who collaborates with students during dialogues to help them see errors and who integrates information about the culture with the instruction.

2. Permit "safe" responses and encourage risk taking.

3. Use scaffolding (in which the expert teacher takes control of portions of the dialogue outside the students' range) to improve success.

4. Incorporate simulations, reenactments, plays, choral recitations, and so forth to facilitate context.

5. Use diaries or journals for students to express their frustrations.

6. Use mixed-ability pairs and groups to create more opportunities for students to converse with more expert speakers.

7. Allow wait time so students can develop their best available response.

8. Be explicit, overt, and relevant in instruction, and provide plenty of practice with varied L2 tasks involving authentic materials.

9. Do not tie strategy training solely to the class at hand; provide strategies that are transferable to future language tasks beyond a given class.

10. Employ authentic creative activities that require students to create travel brochures, food menus, stories, and other original items.

11. Use authentic materials (magazines, videos, brochures, music, food, cultural artifacts, monuments, history) from native language communities.

12. Use the prewriting, drafting, and revising methodology (see Topic 14).

13. Use the prereading, reading, and postreading methodology (see Topic 13).

14. Connect vocabulary to text structure, student interest, or background knowledge.

15. Focus on engagement with the language, then accuracy.

16. Use English as appropriate to provide overviews, make comparisons, clarify, and explain patterns and structures.

OnLine Resources	FOREIGN LANGUAGE EDUCATION
Speakeasy	To find multiple listings of resources for multiple languages, go to http://www.speakeasy.org/~dbrick/Hot/foreign.html.
ERIC OnLine ED474368	*Decreasing Anxiety and Frustration in the Spanish Language Classroom*, by Haskin, J., Smith, M., de Lourdes, H., and Racine, M., 2003.
ERIC OnLine ED448594	*Slow Down! The Importance of Repetition, Planning, and Recycling in Language Teaching*, by Brown, Steven, 2000.
ERIC OnLine ED472671	*The Use of the Computer in Developing L2 Reading Comprehension: Literature Review and Its Implications*, by Kim, Myonghee, 2002, examines the effect of the computer on developing L2 reading comprehension.

Check this textbook's website at http://education.college.hmco.com/students **for additional links.**

Fine and Performing Arts Education

The following professional organizations, journals, and standards play an essential role in Dance, Music, Theater, and Visual Arts education and the development of your teaching practices.

ARTSEDGE WEBSITE

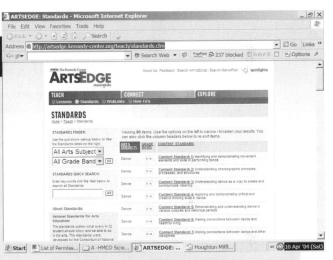

Reprinted with permission of ArtsEdge/The John F. Kennedy Center for the Performing Arts

Professional Organizations of Teachers of Fine and Performing Arts

National Art Education Association (http://www.naea-reston.org/)

National Association of Music Education (http://www.menc.org/)

Educational Theater Association (http://www.edta.org/)

National Dance Education Association (http://www.ndeo.org/)

Related Organizations

American Alliance for Theater and Education http://www.aate.com/

American Music Conference http://www.amc-music.com/about_us.htm

Americans for the Arts http://www.artsusa.org

Arts Education Partnership http://aep-arts.org/

Kennedy Center's ArtsEdge http://artsedge.kennedy-center.org/

National Assembly of State Arts Agencies http://www.nasaa-arts.org/

National Endowment for the Arts http://arts.endow.gov/

American Choral Directors Association http://acdaonline.org/

American Council for the Arts http://www.artsusa.org/issues/artsed/index.asp

Selected Journals

Music Educators Journal

Teaching Music

Journal of Research in Music Education

General Music Today

Art Education

Art Journal

Arts and Activities

International Journal of Education and the Arts

Arts Education Policy Review

Art Education

Studies in Art Education

Journal of Aesthetic Education

Visual Arts Research

International Journal of Education and the Arts

Stage of Art

Youth Theater Journal

Related Organizations

National School Orchestra Association and American String Teachers http://www.astaweb.com/

National Dance Association http://www.aahperd.org/nda/template.cfm?template=main.html

American Alliance of Health, Physical Education, Recreation and Dance http://www.aahperd.org/index.html

Selected Journals

Journal of Physical Education, Recreation and Dance

Journal of Dance Education

Dramatics

Teaching Theater

National and State Standards

The National Standards for Arts Education (Dance, Music, Visual Arts, and Theater) http://artsedge.kennedy-center.org/teach/standards.cfm

The National Standards for Music Education http://www.menc.org/publication/books/standards.htm

INTASC Standards for Arts Teacher Education http://www.ccsso.org/content/pdfs/ArtsStandards.pdf

Your state standards http://edstandards.org/Standards.html#State or http://www.aligntoachieve.org/AchievePhaseII/basic-search.cfm

---

Assignment 47.1

FINE AND PERFORMING ARTS STANDARDS

INTASC STANDARDS 1, 7, 9

Visit each of the above standards websites so that you can become familiar with your state and national standards. Reflect on the standards and be prepared to discuss the relationship of your state standards to the national standards and what additional preparation you think you would need to have your students reach these standards. In a one-page report, list five to ten national and state standards that you believe could be achieved in a lesson plan based on your assigned topic from Topic 13, Assignment 13.1. Be prepared to turn in the assignment to your professor and to discuss your ideas in class.

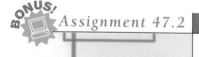

Assignment 47.2

DOWNLOAD BONUS COURSE MATERIALS AND ASSIGNMENTS

INTASC STANDARD 9

At http://education.college.hmco.com/students you will find downloadable documents that will assist you in applying the knowledge you have learned from your professor and this book to develop the kind of practical lesson plans you will need as a new teacher for your domain or discipline. The materials that you should download are:

1. Copies from Internet-based resources.
2. Authentic lesson-planning assignments for this Topic (found only at the textbook website) that might be assigned by your professor, such as creating a topic lesson statement of goals, creating Class Notes for the first daily lesson, creating a complete thematic lesson, and more.
3. Examples and templates of a Unit Plan's Statement of Goals (see Topic 19, Assignment 19.1) and a teacher's Class Notes (see Topic 20, Assignment 20.1) for your use.

Introduction to Arts Education

"Arts Education" is a diverse domain including music, theater, dance, and visual arts, or "the Arts." Like other domains, the Arts share some common themes from a pedagogical, historical, and school organization perspective. For example, few would expect, at the middle or high school level, that a teacher trained in visual arts would be able to teach music any more than a French teacher would be expected to teach German. On the other hand, a biology teacher is often expected to also teach chemistry, and a music teacher might be able to teach theater.

Teacher training in the Arts is often offered by the music, visual art, dance, or theater departments rather than the college of education. It can also be argued that the divide between apprentices and nonapprentices in the Arts is substantially different than in other domains because of the amount of independent practice required to become proficient or even be a novice in the field. As a result, the line between apprentices and nonapprentices is more clearly marked and is not a question of providing a more or less rigorous version of a topic, as in physics. Rather, performance courses and appreciation courses in the Arts are more distinct, with the latter including appreciation courses for nonapprentices and infusion into other disciplines.

Advocacy for the Arts

Because few university admission policies require education in the Arts and also because the Arts lack a utilitarian orientation like the other domains, Arts education has been viewed as a luxury. The 35th Annual Phi Delta Kappa/Gallup Poll of the Public's Attitudes Toward the Public Schools, taken in 2003 (see **http://www.pdkintl.org/kappan/kpollpdf.htm**), indicated that 80 percent of the public felt that the No Child Left Behind focus on back to basics will mean even less emphasis on the arts. Unlike other domains, the Arts have often been learned outside the school setting through private instruction, after-school programs, museum programs, instruction in proprietary dance studios, and so forth. And historically the Arts were viewed as elitist and more appropriate for females, which added to the challenges of adopting them into the general curriculum (Broudy, 1990).

Perception and self-discipline play a key role in the Arts, in terms of both understanding the concepts and improving one's individual performance. Moreover, though music, dance, theater, and visual arts instruction takes place in classrooms, it also involves after-school activities like performances, recitals, and art exhibitions, which can produce the kind of time burden that teachers in other disciplines do not experience unless they volunteer for an extracurricular duty like coaching a sport. Dance is often part of the Physical Education curriculum. Art and theater teachers can find themselves embroiled in freedom of expression and community standards issues in much the same way English teachers are required to deal with literature that might be viewed as inappropriate for middle or high school students.

All of these Arts disciplines can have both "studio" experiences for **"Arts making,"** where knowledge is gained through practice and performance, and **"Arts appreciation,"** which can be learned in a classroom setting through demonstration, films, audio, and so forth or outside the classroom through audience participation in

For the Reflective Practitioner

Music has charms to soothe the savage beast, to soften rocks, or bend a knotted oak.

WILLIAM CONGREVE, *THE MOURNING BRIDE,* ACT 1, SCENE 1

For the Reflective Practitioner

Every child is an artist. The problem is how to remain an artist once he grows up. PABLO PICASSO

venues like museums or symphony concerts. Arts appreciation, which provides a practical way to introduce arts education into the curriculum as a requirement for all students, is a relatively recent phenomenon (Broudy, 1990). Music and visual arts instruction is offered in most of the nation's public secondary schools (90 percent and 93 percent, respectively), while dance and drama/theater (14 percent and 48 percent, respectively) are offered less frequently (Carey et al., 2002).

Data from the ten-year National Education Longitudinal Survey (NELS) of 25,000 students was used to characterize students as *"high Arts students"* and *"low Arts students"* based on their exposure to the Arts and to develop correlations with students' success in school. In the study, high Arts students earned better grades and scores on standardized tests than the general population in the study and, when specifically compared to low Arts students, were less likely to drop out of school, watched fewer hours of television, had a more positive self-concept, and were more involved in community service (Catterall, 1998). High Arts students in band and orchestra also performed better in math, reinforcing the often-claimed relationship between music and mathematics (Catterall, Chapleau, & Iwanaga, 1999; Vaughn, 2000). In spite of these favorable statistics, the public persists in feeling (excepting those who themselves have come to appreciate high art) that art education is desirable but not necessary (Broudy, 1990; Hanks, 1975).

Historical Perspective on Arts Education

Music and theater have been part of American schools since the 1600s, even if they involved nothing more than singing songs and reenacting historical events in highly religious settings (Leonhard & House, 1972). But by the 1800s visual arts had found their way into the public schools, and drawing was seen as an important vocational skill (Efland, 1985; Eisner & Ecker, 1971). By the early 1900s vocal music instruction was beginning to be required in public schools and elective instrumental music instruction was added to the curriculum with a primary goal of performing through school bands and orchestras.

The most significant changes in Arts education were precipitated by technology advancements. The phonograph and films and videos made it possible for schools to expose students to the Arts as they were performed or created at the expert level. Such recordings and images provided exemplars for studio classes, but their availability also made it possible to broaden the concept of Arts education to include appreciation of the arts by nonapprentices who had little interest in performance. Although the first music appreciation course was offered in the 1890s, the focus of Arts education remained on performance and studio classes through the 1940s (Broudy, 1990; Lanier, 1974). It was only in the 1980s that the Getty Center for Education in the Arts proposed Disciplined-Based Arts Education (DBAE) as a strategy to expand Arts appreciation (Goodwin, 2000).

Disciplined-Based Arts Education

DBAE is a conceptual framework that originated in the visual arts. It ensures that all students, not just artistically talented students, are involved in the study of the arts as a part of their general education. It also promotes integrating the Arts into the curriculum (including art and period music into social studies and English classes, for example) to permit students to understand and participate in an art form within the structure of a typical school day (Goodwin, 2000).

DBAE gave a unifying approach to the Arts, meaning that students should study musical, theatrical, dance, and visual art from the following four discipline perspectives, depending on their interest:

1. **Production:** creating or performing
2. **History:** studying the historical and cultural background of works of art
3. **Aesthetics:** discovering the nature and philosophy of the Arts
4. **Criticism:** making informed judgments about the Arts

DBAE was not without controversy, however, because it assumed that:

1. Arts teachers should serve as resources for classroom teachers in other disciplines.
2. Teachers do not have to be artists to teach students about visual art.
3. Teachers do not have to sing or play an instrument to teach students about music.
4. Teachers can incorporate dance and movement, simulations, historical reenactments, and productions of literary works into an active classroom.

These assumptions conflicted with those of many practicing artists, for whom it is a heartfelt and deeply imbedded belief that one must "do art" to some degree to fully appreciate it.

Arts and Multiple Intelligences

Howard Gardner's (1983) landmark book *Frames of Mind: The Theory of Multiple Intelligences* proposed a new model of thinking about intelligence (discussed previously in Topic 7). Gardner initially formulated seven different types of intelligence: linguistic, logical/mathematical, musical, spatial, bodily kinesthetic, interpersonal, and intrapersonal. The first two are the ones that have been most valued in schools; the next three are usually associated with the arts; and the final two are called "personal intelligences." From the Art community's perspective, this formulation underscored the importance of the arts in teaching and learning. By their very nature, schools focus primarily on linguistic and logical/mathematical intelligence and, as social settings, engage and shape interpersonal and intrapersonal intelligence. The Arts focus on musical, kinetic, and spatial intelligence and build upon and integrate them into the other forms of intelligence.

Standards

In the 1980s, President George Bush Sr.'s attempt at national educational goals was not successfully negotiated through the Congress and did not include a mandate for Arts education (Jennings, 1995). However, through President Clinton's "Goals 2000" bill, Arts education was included and resulted in the publication of the *National Standards for Arts Education: What Every Young American Should Know and Be Able to Do in the Arts* (Consortium of National Art Education Associations, 1994; go to **http://artsedge.kennedy-center.org/ teach/standards.cfm**). The standards for the four disciplines of music, visual art, dance, and theater are divided by grades K–4, 5–8, and 9–12. At the 9–12 level, the standards establish "proficient" and "advanced" achievement standards in each discipline and call for a curriculum for Arts education that will ensure literacy for all students, not just apprentices. Table 47.1 lists the standards for the Proficient level in dance, music, theater, and visual arts.

Table 47.1 | HIGH SCHOOL ARTS STANDARDS: PROFICIENT LEVEL

Dance (9–12)

1: Identifying and demonstrating movement elements and skills in performing dance
2: Understanding choreographic principles, processes, and structures
3: Understanding dance as a way to create and communicate meaning
4: Applying and demonstrating critical and creative thinking skills in dance
5: Demonstrating and understanding dance in various cultures and historical periods
6: Making connections between dance and healthful living
7: Making connections between dance and other disciplines

Music (9–12)

1: Singing, alone and with others, a varied repertoire of music
2: Performing on instruments, alone and with others, a varied repertoire of music
3: Improvising melodies, variations, and accompaniments
4: Composing and arranging music within specified guidelines
5: Reading and notating music
6: Listening to, analyzing, and describing music
7: Evaluating music and music performances
8: Understanding relationships between music, the other arts, and disciplines outside the arts
9: Understanding music in relation to history and culture

Theater (9–12)

1: Script writing through improvising, writing, and refining scripts based on personal experience and heritage, imagination, literature, and history
2: Acting by developing, communicating, and sustaining characters in improvisations and informal or formal productions
3: Designing and producing by conceptualizing and realizing artistic interpretations for informal or formal productions
4: Directing by interpreting dramatic texts and organizing and conducting rehearsals for informal or formal productions
5: Researching by evaluating and synthesizing cultural and historical information to support artistic choices
6: Comparing and integrating art forms by analyzing traditional theater, dance, music, visual arts, and new art forms
7: Analyzing, critiquing, and constructing meanings from informal and formal, theater film, television, and electronic media productions
8: Understanding context by analyzing the role of theater, film, television, and electronic media in the past and the present

Visual Arts (9–12)

1: Understanding and applying media, techniques, and processes
2: Using knowledge of structures and functions
3: Choosing and evaluating a range of subject matter, symbols, and ideas
4: Understanding the visual arts in relation to history and cultures
5: Reflecting upon and assessing the characteristics and merits of their work and the work of others
6: Making connections between visual arts and other disciplines

Best Practices for Arts Education

The following best practices for teaching the Arts to middle and high school students are drawn from the works cited previously.

- Ground your teaching in the principles of DBAE.
- Pursue instruction as a process of inquiry into a specific art form, an artist, a time period, a unique contribution, and so forth.
- Use culturally rich and diverse art forms as well as traditional works of art.
- Facilitate student inquiry, interpretation, discussion, writing, and the creation of student works.
- Have students model their own art experiences by sharing and explaining their works with the class.
- Have students critique their own products.
- Collaborate with other teachers to integrate the arts into the other domains.
- Identify and facilitate the use of art resources in the community with guest speakers, field trips to performances, ethnic festivals, and so forth.
- Use technology to communicate about the arts, access information about the arts, and facilitate students' art making. Many museums have extensive websites.
- Use videotape for self-critiques of performances in theater, music, and dance.
- Promote student-led rehearsals.

OnLine Resources	THE ARTS
OnLine Classics	Go to http://www.onlineclassics.com/DCTV/html/index.html for streaming video of theater, dance, and symphonic performances.
ERIC OnLine ED455550	*Readers Theater: An Introduction to Classroom Performance*, by Ratliff, Gerald Lee, 2000, advocates the use of Readers Theater to "dramatize" literature in classroom performance.
ERIC OnLine EJ636173	*Bach and Rock in the Music Classroom*, by Ponick, F. S., 2000, focuses on approaches to using popular music in music education.

Check this textbook's website at http://education.college.hmco.com/students **for additional links.**

Physical and Health Education

The following professional organizations, journals, and standards play an essential role in Physical and Health education and the development of your teaching practices.

THE AMERICAN ALLIANCE FOR HEALTH, PHYSICAL EDUCATION, RECREATION AND DANCE

Reprinted from http://www.aahperd.org/naspe/ template.cfm?template=about-welcome.html (2004) with permission of The National Association for Sport and Physical Education (NASPE), 1900 Association Drove, Reston, VA 20191-1599.

Professional Organizations for Teachers of Health and Physical Education

National Association for Sport and Physical Education http://www.aahperd.org/naspe/template.cfm?template=main.html

American Association for Health Education http://www.aahperd.org/aahe/

American Alliance for Health, Physical Education, Recreation and Dance http://www.aahperd.org/

Related Organizations

American Association for Active Lifestyles and Fitness http://www.aahperd.org/aaalf/template.cfm?template=main.html

American Association for Leisure and Recreation http://www.aahperd.org/aalr/template.cfm?template=main.html

National Association for Girls and Women in Sport http://www.aahperd.org/nagws/template.cfm?template=main.html

National Dance Association http://www.aahperd.org/nda/template.cfm?template=main.html

Research Consortium http://www.aahperd.org/research/template.cfm?template=main.html

Selected Journals

Journal of Teaching in Physical Education

Physical Education Digest

The Physical Educator

Journal of Physical Education, Recreation and Dance

Journal of Teaching in Physical Education

Physical and Health Education Journal

International Journal of Sport Psychology

Isokinetics and Exercise Science

Journal of Sport and Social Issues

Measurement in Physical Education and Exercise Science

Adapted Physical Activity Quarterly

Journal of School Health

Strategies: A Journal for Physical and Sport Educators

National and State Standards	Selected Journals
Physical Education Standards http://www.aahperd.org/NASPE/template.cfm?template= publications-nationalstandards.html Health Education Standards http://www.aahperd.org/aahe/pdf_files/standards.pdf Your state standards http://edstandards.org/Standards.html#State	*Research Quarterly for Exercise and Sport* *Applied Research in Coaching and Athletics Annual* *Exercise and Sport Sciences Reviews* *Human Movement Science* *Advances in Health Education* *American Journal of Health Education* *Health Education and Behavior* *Journal of Nutrition Education and Behavior* *Quest*

PHYSICAL AND HEALTH EDUCATION STANDARDS

Assignment 48.1

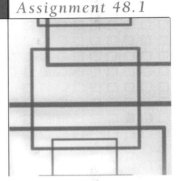

INTASC STANDARDS 1, 7, 9

Visit each of the above standards websites so that you can become familiar with your state and national standards. Reflect on the standards and be prepared to discuss the relationship of your state standards to the national standards and what additional preparation you think you would need to have your students reach these standards. In a one-page report, list five to ten national and state standards that you believe could be achieved in a lesson plan based on your assigned topic from Topic 13, Assignment 13.1. Be prepared to turn in the assignment to your professor and to discuss your ideas in class.

DOWNLOAD BONUS COURSE MATERIALS AND ASSIGNMENTS

Assignment 48.2

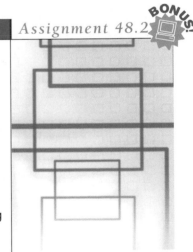

INTASC STANDARDS 7 AND 9

At http://education.college.hmco.com/students you will find downloadable documents that will assist you in applying the knowledge you have learned from your professor and this book to develop the kind of practical lesson plans you will need as a new teacher for your domain or discipline. The materials that you should download are:

1. Copies from Internet-based resources.
2. Authentic lesson-planning assignments for this Topic (found only at the textbook website) that might be assigned by your professor, such as creating a topic lesson statement of goals, creating Class Notes for the first daily lesson, creating a complete thematic lesson, and more.
3. Examples and templates of a Unit Plan's Statement of Goals (see Topic 19, Assignment 19.1) and a teacher's Class Notes (see Topic 20, Assignment 20.1) for your use.

Introduction to Physical Education

Physical education (PE) is required in every school in the United States, but the amount of time and days of the week devoted to it vary greatly (Pate et al., 1995). The U.S. Department of Health and Human Services national health objectives, **Healthy People 2010,** at http://www.healthypeople.gov/document/html/volume2/22Physical.htm#_Toc490380803 include two key objectives that affect middle and high schools:

1. **Objective 22-9:** Increase the proportion of adolescents who participate in daily school physical education by 50 percent. In 1999, 29 percent of students in grades 9 through 12 participated in daily school physical education.
2. **Objective 22-10:** Increase the proportion of adolescents who spend at least 50 percent of school physical education class time being physically active. In 1999, 38 percent of students in grades 9 through 12 were physically active in physical education classes more than 20 minutes, three to five days per week.

In *Moving into the Future: National Standards for Physical Education* (NASPE, 2004), the National Association for Sport and Physical Education (NASPE) stated that a physically educated person:

1. Has learned skills necessary to perform a variety of physical activities.
2. Is physically fit.
3. Participates regularly in physical activity.
4. Knows the implications of and the benefits from involvement in physical activities.
5. Values physical activity and its contribution to a healthful lifestyle.

On the basis of these attributes, the standards for students are categorized for grades K, 2, 4, 6, 8, 10, and 12 with sample performance benchmarks and a variety of assessment techniques for assessing student achievement. The school-based standards indicate that a physically educated student:

1. Demonstrates competency in many movement forms and proficiency in a few movement forms.
2. Applies involvement concepts and principles to the learning and development of motor skills.
3. Exhibits a physically active lifestyle.
4. Achieves and maintains a health-enhancing level of physical fitness.
5. Demonstrates responsible personal and social behavior in physical activity settings.
6. Demonstrates understanding and respect for differences among people in physical activity settings.
7. Understands that physical activity provides opportunities for enjoyment, challenge, self-expression, and social interaction.

For the Reflective Practitioner

Sports serve society by providing vivid examples of excellence.

GEORGE F. WILL

Goals of Physical Education

Since the 1850s, when physical education was formally introduced into schools, the emphasis on exercise has expanded to include the behavioral competencies and motor skills needed for lifelong engagement in healthy and satisfying physical activity. This change in the goals of physical education is due primarily to societal forces and demographic changes. The diversity of students enrolled in secondary education and the longevity of the American population because of the increased quality of health care and advancements in nutrition and medicine have increased the need for education about the benefits of physical fitness and a lifetime of physical activity. In spite of this significant societal issue, physical education subject matter is still perceived by its teachers as being socially and philosophically marginalized compared to the "academic" subjects (Lock, Telljohann, & Price, 1995; Sparkes & Templin, 1992).

Of the current adult American population, 24 percent are considered totally sedentary, 54 percent are not active enough, nearly two-thirds of U.S. adults are overweight, and one-third are obese (Van Camp, 1993) (go to National Institutes of Health at **http://win.niddk.nih.gov/statistics/index.htm**), and this more sedentary lifestyle begins with adolescence (Kelder, Perry, & Klepp, 1993). Although the physical exertion in PE classes, along with exposure in such classes to activities that might be adopted as part of a healthy lifestyle, is beneficial, the traditional approach to PE classes is questionable as a motivating device to help students become physically active on a continuing basis (Aarts et al., 1997; Sallis et al., 1992).

> ### For the Reflective Practitioner
>
> *The only way to keep your health is to eat what you don't want, drink what you don't like, and do what you'd rather not.* MARK TWAIN

Sport performance of an activity is the traditional notion of a physical education class, where there is instruction about a "sport" (dance, baseball, swimming, games) and then the opportunity to play or perform the sport. This method gives students the opportunity to develop motor skills, an aesthetic appreciation of the activity, success in a new challenge, exposure to an activity that sometimes leads to becoming an apprentice, and habits that may remain with them after their secondary education experience. Team and individual activities requiring competition and cooperation also allow students to test and develop the character traits and interpersonal skills needed for careers and citizenship. Team sports (after-school programs where students compete in teams against other schools) and intramurals (activities during or after school in which students compete in teams within schools) are also school-sponsored avenues for apprentices and nonapprentices that serve as positive, structured socialization settings in the middle and high school milieu.

The knowledge of physical education evolves out of performance. That is, one becomes knowledgeable about baseball by playing baseball, even if at the nonapprentice level. In this sense, physical education is like the Arts, which are best learned by "doing Art." Also, like the Arts, there are multiple non-school-based venues in which to participate in supervised athletic activities, such as little leagues. A model for how students relate to sports suggests that students may have one of two orientations:(1) **Mastery orientation,** whereby students gain personal satisfaction from activities by learning and mastering tasks; or (2) **Ego orientation,** whereby students find personal satisfaction from competing and excelling (Duda, 1992; Treasure & Roberts, 1995).

Programs of physical education classes, team sports, and intramurals aim at motivating teenagers to adopt both a mastery orientation and a healthy lifestyle. It is unlikely that one can change students from an ego to a mastery orientation (or vice versa), but students can be influenced to consider their orientations and alter or moderate their behaviors (Treasure & Roberts, 1995). Given the current state of obesity in children and teens and other measures of fitness, one would have to ask if the traditional sports-specific motor skills approach to the physical education class is the best approach to a healthy lifestyle (Pate et al., 1995; Taggart, 1985). However, the current emphasis in the public media toward weight control, nutrition, and moderate forms of exercise is influencing curricula in schools, particularly Health Education (see next section).

Challenges of Physical Education Instruction

Given the above challenges, there are a number of variables that uniquely affect physical education's quest to achieve goals and that need to be considered by the successful instructor (Griffin, 1985). Physical appearance and control of their "look" are paramount concerns for many middle and high school students, and these are impacted by physical education activities. The process of changing into gym clothing raises additional issues related to students' comfort level with degrees of modesty (Luke & Sinclair, 1991). Students complain that the traditional class periods are too brief for meaningful enjoyment given the time it takes to get to the gym, change clothing, and change back again (Rice, 1988). In addition, individuals' failures and shortcomings during activities in gym classes are obvious to peers, unlike receiving an F on a confidential report card, and, for some students, the activities are "too" competitive (Tannehill et al., 1994; Treasure & Roberts, 1995).

Another issue is that social expectations based on gender differences affect student participation (Griffin, 1992; Streitmatter, 1994). Because physical activity is traditionally associated with masculine tendencies, females are routinely socialized not to participate and excel, and boys are expected to do extremely well. Thus coeducational classes can be humiliating for males of limited athletic skill (Griffin, 1985), and girls can also feel intimated (Hutchinson, 1995).

As someone considering a profession in physical education and therefore interested in PE, do you think your experience in middle and high school PE classes differed from that of students who were less interested in physical education? If so, how?

On the other hand, 85 percent of high school students report that they like physical education (although 40 percent like it less than most other subjects) (Rice, 1988; Tannehill et al., 1994). Students report they like physical education because of the variety of activities, the atmosphere of fun, and the immediate, obvious, positive feedback they receive when they succeed in an activity (Luke & Sinclair, 1991; Tannehill & Zakrajsek, 1993; Tannehill et al., 1994). Seventy percent of students express a clear preference for learning team sport skills in physical education classes. The advantage of team sports in physical education classes is that individuals can experience competition and cooperation simultaneously. In such activities, teachers who create a task-oriented environment by emphasizing improvement, hard work, and self-satisfaction bring out the best in all students, even those who are ego oriented and tend toward goal achievement and "winning at all cost" (Duda, 1996). To maximize the opportunities to learn in physical education, a range of factors must be available. These include time for physical education in the schedule, reasonable class size, adequate facilities and equipment, good planning, and a variety of course offerings that accommodate different skill levels (NASPE, 1992, 1995, 1996, 2004).

Adapted Physical Education

Federal law mandates that physical education be provided to students with disabilities. It defines adapted physical education as the development of:

1. Physical and motor skills.
2. Fundamental motor skills and patterns (such as throwing, catching, walking, and running).

3. Skills in aquatics, dance, and individual and group games and sports (including intramural and lifetime sports).

Meeting the physical education needs of students with disabilities offers excellent opportunities for the teacher to model the civic values that can emerge out of a quality, inclusive, physical education program (Block & Zeman, 1996). An excellent website for information on adapted physical education is Physical Education Central at **http://www.pecentral.org/adapted/adaptedmenu.html**.

Best Practices for Physical Education

The following best practices for teachers of physical education stem from the works cited previously in this Topic and Landin (1994), Silverman, Kulinna, and Crull (1995), Kwak (1993), and Graham et al. (1993).

- Communicate the purpose and usefulness of the activity.
- Use multiple and precise verbal cues during explanation and demonstration, and encourage students to use the same cues during "self-talk" and metacognitive rehearsals of the task.
- Fully and explicitly demonstrate the tasks, graduating from simplistic to more complex versions in step-by-step presentations.
- Provide multiple opportunities for students to perform tasks after each step, along with supportive feedback.
- Manage activities through vigilant supervision and frequent praise.
- Encourage students to think about their techniques during tasks, and ask them to report their thinking.
- Teach fewer activities to allow for more instruction, demonstration, and practice.
- Use videos of experts as models, teacher modeling, and student-to-student modeling.
- Attribute success to effort and ability; do not make praise contingent on accomplishment.

Health Education

Health education is typically delivered in a traditional class setting and is unique in that it combines elements of social studies instruction and science instruction (a person majoring in health education should review both of those topics). One of the particular problems facing health educators is dealing with controversial issues: The marriage of science and social studies places health education teachers on thin ice. The inclusion of topics like teen suicides, sexually transmitted diseases (STDs), child abuse, teen pregnancy, and addiction can give rise to conflicts about grade-appropriate material, local community standards, religious values, and parental rights. For this reason, teachers of health science should rely heavily on policies that define the curriculum, on teaching materials that have been adopted by the school board, and on well-scripted lesson plans that document goals, content, and methods. You should be open to allowing parents and community members to preview lessons and attend classes, if not help teach them with you.

In 1991 the Joint Committee on Health Education Terminology defined health literacy as "the capacity of an individual to obtain, interpret, and understand basic health information and services and the competence to use such

For the Reflective Practitioner

Be careful about reading health books. You may die of a misprint.
MARK TWAIN

information and services in ways which are health-enhancing." Then in 1995 the Joint Committee on National Health Education Standards published *National Health Education Standards: Achieving Health Literacy.* This publication outlined seven health education standards:

1. Students will comprehend concepts related to health promotion and disease prevention.
2. Students will demonstrate the ability to access valid health information and health promotion products and services.
3. Students will demonstrate the ability to practice health-enhancing behaviors and reduce health risks.
4. Students will analyze the influence of culture media, technology, and other factors on health.
5. Students will demonstrate the ability to use interpersonal communication skills to enhance health.
6. Students will demonstrate the ability to use goal-setting and decision-making skills to enhance health.
7. Students will demonstrate the ability to advocate for personal, family, and community health.

These standards should be the focus of health education lessons so that students can be taught how to make informed decisions.

OnLine Resources	PHYSICAL AND HEALTH EDUCATION
PECentarl	For this gateway website for information and lesson plans for physical education teachers, go to http://www.pecentral.org/.
PBS Teachers Resources	To find lesson plans on health education by topic, go to http://www.pbs.org/teachersource/health.htm.
ERIC OnLine ED470726	*Physical Activity and Sport for the Secondary School Student* (5th ed.), edited by Dougherty, Neil J., 2002, includes texts by twenty-six authors on contemporary physical activities and sports forms. It provides students with an overview of the various physical activities, the skill techniques required, safety, scoring, rules and etiquette, strategies, equipment, and related terminology.
ERIC OnLine ED470729	*Liability and Safety in Physical Education and Sport: A Practitioner's Guide to the Legal Aspects of Teaching and Coaching in Elementary and Secondary Schools,* by Hart, James E., and Ritson, Robert J., 2002.

Check this textbook's website at http://education.college.hmco.com/students for additional links.

Conclusion: Advice for Beginning Teachers

The transition from college to your profession is the start of a new journey. With this thought in mind, you need a plan for your first few years. The following suggestions are adapted from a class presentation to students in their final internship (Cruz, 2004).

1. Plan to be a better professional.
   a. Continue your education; go to graduate school.
   b. Join a professional organization.
   c. Read professional journals.
   d. Attend professional development conferences and workshops.
   e. Make a presentation at a regional conference of your professional organization.
   f. Volunteer for one out-of-class assignment at school.
   g. When you are ready, mentor a new teacher.
2. Plan to be a better teacher.
   a. Take risks, experiment, and adopt new teaching strategies.
   b. Use your summers to recharge your batteries; try to avoid teaching during the summer.
   c. Focus on doing a few things really well by setting a few reasonable goals for improvement each year.
   d. Ask your students for feedback on what you can do better.
   e. Ask a colleague to look over some of your lessons and to provide advice.
   f. Always be on the lookout for ideas to improve your lessons.
   g. When you make a mistake, admit it, correct it, and move on.
   h. Model lifelong learning for your students.
3. Plan to be a better person.
   a. Keep a perspective on both your successes and failures; rewards are intrinsic and not immediate.
   b. Avoid negative colleagues and friends; choose to be upbeat and positive.
   c. Care about your students, but remember that you are their teacher, not their friend.
   d. Develop a life that is separate from school with friends and loved ones and with exercise, hobbies, and reading.
   e. Learn to laugh at yourself and enjoy the moment.
   f. You can't accomplish everything in a day; learn to pace yourself.

On behalf of Houghton Mifflin and myself, we hope this book is helpful to your becoming the excellent teacher that is within us all.

Enjoy Your Students!

Topic/Number	Page	Assignments	Subject Matter Expertise	Learning & Development	Diverse Learners	Multiple Instructional Strategies	Motivation & Classroom Management	Communication Skills	Instructional Planning	Assessment	Professional Commitment & Responsibility	Partnerships
		INTASC STANDARD #	**1**	**2**	**3**	**4**	**5**	**6**	**7**	**8**	**9**	**10**
P.1	i	Crossword Puzzles		2	3	4	5		7	8		
S.1	xi	Teacher Standards: A Contrary View									9	10
S.2	xiv	GEM Search	1	2		4			7			
1.1	12	Code of Ethics									9	10
2.1	24	Interview with a Practicing Teacher	1	2	3	4	5	6	7	8	9	10
2.2		New Teacher Expectations	1	2	3	4	5	6	7	8	9	10
2.3		What Are Middle and High School Students Thinking?		2	3		5	6				10
4.1		Preparations for an Interview with a Middle School Student		2	3		5		7		9	10
4.2		Interview a Middle School Student	1	2	3	4	5	6	7	8	9	10
4.3		State Middle School and High School Curricula							7	8	9	
4.4		Thematic Teaching	1	2	3	4			7	8	9	
4.5		Exploratory Courses	1	2	3	4			7		9	
4.6		Expert Opinions on Middle School	1	2	3	4	5	6	7	8	9	10
5.1		Interview a High School Student		2	3			6			9	10
5.2		Current Scholarship on Schoolwide Topics	1	2	3	4	5	6	7	8	9	10
6.1		Behavioral Objectives	1						7	8		
7.1		Myers-Briggs Personality Type		2	3	4	5	6	7		9	
7.2		Learning Styles		2	3	4	5	6	7		9	
7.3		Multiple Intelligences		2	3	4	5	6	7	8		
8.1		Conversing with Students from Other Disciplines	1	2	3	4	5	6	7	8		
8.2		Reflection on Diversity	1		3		5	6		8		
8.3		Stereotypes and Bias	1		3			6		8		
8.4		Current Scholarship on Student Diversity	1	2	3	4	5	6	7	8	9	10
9.1		Student Nonverbal Behaviors		2	3		5	6				

		INTASC STANDARD #	1	2	3	4	5	6	7	8	9	10
9.2		Classroom Observation		2		4		6	7			
10.1		What Is the State of Affairs?		2	3	4	5	6	7	8		
11.1		National and State Standards	1						7	8		
11.2		Application of Concepts							7	8		
11.3		Web of Knowledge	1			4						
12.1		Read-Aloud in Your Discipline	1	2	3	4	5	6	7	8		
13.1		Subject Area Reading Materials and Topic Lesson Plan Content	1	2	3	4	5	6	7	8		
13.2		Subject Area Reading Plan	1	2	3	4	5	6	7	8		
13.3		Internet-Based Image Integration	1	2	3	4	5	6	7	8		
13.4		Expert Opinions on Reading	1	2	3	4	5	6	7	8	9	10
14.1		Create a Writing Assignment	1	2	3	4	5	6	7	8		
15.1		Scholarship on Student Discipline		2	3		5	6	7			10
16.1		Classroom Tour	1	2		4						
16.2		Classroom Expectations		2	3		5	6	7		9	10
17.1		Letter to Parents			3		5		7		9	10
17.2		Open House Presentation			3		5		7		9	10
18.1		Create a Syllabus	1	2	3	4	5	6	7	8		
19.1		Lesson Plan Statement of Goals: Example and Template	1	2	3	4	5	6	7	8		
20.1		Class Notes: Example and Template	1	2	3	4	5	6	7	8		
21.1		Internet Search for Ideas on Active Learning	1	2	3	4	5	6	7	8		
22.1		Develop a Lesson on Concept Formation	1	2	3	4	5	6	7			
24.1		Develop an Lesson on Inductive and Deductive Reasoning	1	2	3	4	5	6	7			
24.2		Restructuring Lessons for Critical Thinking	1	2	3	4	5	6	7			
25.1		Why Is Juneau Warmer? A Collaborate Assignment	1	2	3	4	5	6	7			
25.2		Develop a Lesson Using Hypothesis Formation	1	2	3	4	5	6	7			
25.3		Develop a Lesson Using Decision Making	1	2	3	4	5	6	7			
25.4		Develop a Lesson Using Advance Organizers	1	2	3	4	5	6	7			
25.5		Develop a List, Group, and Label Lesson	1	2	3	4	5	6	7			
27.1		Create Lectures Based on Types	1	2	3	4	5	6	7			

INTASC STANDARD #		1	2	3	4	5	6	7	8	9	10
27.2	Create Lectures Using Different Organizations	1	2	3	4	5	6	7			
28.1	Questioning for a Content Presentation	1	2	3	4	5	6	7			
28.2	Questions Based on Bloom's Taxonomy	1	2	3	4	5	6	7	8		
30.1	Develop a Teacher-Centered Graphic Organizers Lesson	1	2	3	4	5	6	7			
30.2	Develop a Student-Centered Graphic Organizers Lesson	1	2	3	4	5	6	7	8		
31.1	Cooperative Learning Lesson	1	2	3	4	5	6	7	8		
32.1	Develop a Discussion Guidelines Lesson	1	2	3	4	5	6	7			
32.2	Develop a Discussion Lesson	1	2	3	4	5	6	7			
32.3	Develop a Case Study Lesson	1	2	3	4	5	6	7			
33.1	Develop a Self-Directed Instruction Lesson	1	2	3	4	5	6	7	8		
34.1	Develop a Guided Practice Lesson	1	2	3	4	5	6	7	8		
34.2	Integrate Homework into Your Lesson Plan	1	2	3	4	5	6	7	8		10
36.1	Website Evaluations	1	2	3	4	5	6	7	8		
37.1	Scholarship on Assessment in Your Subject Area	1	2	3				7	8		
38.1	Create a Product Assignment and Assessment Rubric	1	2	3				7	8		
39.1	Create a Traditional Test	1	2	3				7	8		
40.1	Grading Scheme	1	2	3				7	8		
40.2	Grades	1	2	3				7	8		
Students Should go to *Bonus Course Materials* at this Book's Website to print these Assignments											
42.1	English Standards	1						7		9	
42.2	Download Bonus Course Materials and Assignments							7		9	
42.3	Create a Lesson Plan Statement of Goals: Writing Skills	1	2	3	4	5	6	7	8		
42.4	Create a Topic Lesson Statement of Goals: Literature	1	2	3	4	5	6	7	8		
42.5	Create Class Notes for the First Daily Lesson: Literature	1	2	3	4	5	6	7	8		
42.6	Create a Complete Topic Lesson: Literature	1	2	3	4	5	6	7	8		

	INTASC STANDARD #	1	2	3	4	5	6	7	8	9	10
42.7	Lesson Planning Statement of Goals: Speech/Communication	1	2	3	4	5	6	7	8		
43.1	Mathematics Standards	1						7		9	
43.2	Download Bonus Course Materials and Assignments							7		9	
43.3	Create a Topic Lesson Statement of Goals: Mathematics	1	2	3	4	5	6	7	8		
43.4	Create Class Notes for the First Daily Lesson: Mathematics	1	2	3	4	5	6	7	8		
43.5	Create a Complete Thematic Lesson: Mathematics	1	2	3	4	5	6	7	8		
43.6	Lesson Plan Statement of Goals: Graphic Calculator	1	2	3	4	5	6	7	8		
43.7	Lesson Plan Statement of Goals: Algebra	1	2	3	4	5	6	7	8		
44.1	Science Standards	1						7		9	
44.2	Download Bonus Course Materials and Assignments							7		9	
44.3	Create a Topic Lesson Statement of Goals: Science	1	2	3	4	5	6	7	8		
44.4	Create Class Notes for the First Daily Lesson: Science	1	2	3	4	5	6	7	8		
44.5	Create a Complete Topic Lesson: Science	1	2	3	4	5	6	7	8		
44.6	Lesson Plan Statement of Goals: Physics	1	2	3	4	5	6	7	8		
44.7	Lesson Plan Statement of Goals: Biology	1	2	3	4	5	6	7	8		
45.1	Social Studies Standards	1						7		9	
45.2	Download Bonus Course Materials and Assignments							7		9	
45.3	Create a Topic Lesson Statement of Goals: Social Studies	1	2	3	4	5	6	7	8		
45.4	Create Class Notes for the First Daily Lesson: Social Studies	1	2	3	4	5	6	7	8		
45.5	Create a Complete Thematic Lesson: Social Studies	1	2	3	4	5	6	7	8		
45.6	Social Studies Lesson Planning Statement of Goals: Current Events	1	2	3	4	5	6	7	8		
46.1	World Language Standards	1						7		9	
46.2	Download Bonus Course Materials and Assignments							7		9	

	INTASC STANDARD #	1	2	3	4	5	6	7	8	9	10
46.3	Create a Topic Lesson Statement of Goals: World Language	1	2	3	4	5	6	7	8		
46.4	Create Class Notes for the First Daily Lesson: World Language	1	2	3	4	5	6	7	8		
46.5	Create a Complete Thematic Lesson: World Language	1	2	3	4	5	6	7	8		
46.6	Language Lesson Planning Statement of Goals	1	2	3	4	5	6	7	8		
47.1	Arts Standards	1						7		9	
47.2	Download Bonus Course Materials and Assignments							7		9	
47.3	Create a Topic Lesson Statement of Goals: Arts	1	2	3	4	5	6	7	8		
47.4	Create Class Notes for the First Daily Lesson: Arts	1	2	3	4	5	6	7	8		
47.5	Create a Complete Thematic Lesson: Arts	1	2	3	4	5	6	7	8		
47.6	Infused Arts Lesson Planning Statement of Goals: Arts	1	2	3	4	5	6	7	8		
48.1	Physical and Health Education Standards	1						7		9	
48.2	Download Bonus Course Materials and Assignments							7		9	
48.3	Lesson Planning Statement of Goals: Physical Education	1	2	3	4	5	6	7	8		
48.4	Create Class Notes for the First Daily Lesson: Physical Education	1	2	3	4	5	6	7	8		
48.5	Create Class Notes for 4 More Activities: Physical Education	1	2	3	4	5	6	7	8		
48.6	Lesson Planning Statement of Goals: Health Education	1	2	3	4	5	6	7	8		
48.7	Create Class Notes for the First Daily Lesson: Health Education	1	2	3	4	5	6	7	8		
48.8	Create a Complete Thematic Lesson: Health Education	1	2	3	4	5	6	7	8		

References

Aarts, H., Paulussen, T., Willemse, G., Schaalma, H., Bolman, C., & De Nooyer, J. (1997). *Prevention of cardiovascular diseases: A review of international studies on the promotion of physical activity among youth.* The Hague/Woerden/ Maastricht: Dutch Heart Foundation, NIGZ, Maastricht University.

Abrams, Scott. (2001). *Using journals with reluctant writers: Building portfolios for middle and high school students.* (ERIC Document Reproduction Service No. ED442109)

Abu-Hilal, M. M. (2000). A structural model of attitudes towards school subjects, academic aspiration and achievement. *Educational Psychology: An International Journal of Experimental Educational Psychology* 20 (1): 75–84.

Adams, G., & Engelmann, S. (1996). *Research on direct instruction: 20 years beyond DISTAR.* Seattle, WA: Educational Achievement Systems.

Adams, R. S., & Biddle, B. J. (1970). *Realities of teaching: Explorations with video tape.* New York: Holt, Rinehart & Winston.

Adler, P. (1992). Socialization to gender roles: Popularity among elementary schools for boys and girls. *Sociology of Education* 65: 169–187.

Agee, J. (2000). *What is effective literature instruction? A study of experienced high school English teachers in differing grade- and ability-level classes.* (ERIC Document Reproduction Service No. EJ650287)

Alcock, M. A., & Ryan, P. M. (2000). Type, teaching and learning. *Journal of Psychological Type* 52: 5–10.

Alderman, M. (1999). *Motivation for achievement: Possibilities for teaching and learning.* Hillsdale, NJ: Lawrence Erlbaum.

Allan, S. D., & Tomlinson, C. A. (2000). *Leadership for differentiating schools and classrooms.* (ERIC Document Reproduction Service No. ED469218)

Allen, M., Berkowitz, S., Hunt, S., & Louden, A. (1999). A meta-analysis of the impact of forensics and communication education on critical thinking. *Communication Education* 48 (1): 18–30.

Allington, R. L., & Johnston, P. H. (2000). *What do we know about effective fourth grade teachers and their classrooms?* Albany, NY: National Research Center for English Learning and Achievement. Retrieved July 9, 2001, from http://cela.albany.edu/4thgrade/index.html

Alvermann, D. E., Young, J. P., Weaver, D., Hinchman, K. A., Moore, D. W., Phelps, S. F., Thrasch, E. D., & Zalewski, P. (1996). Middle and high school students' perceptions of how they experience text-based discussions. A multicase study. *Reading Research Quarterly* 31: 244–267.

American Association for the Advancement of Science. (1993). *Benchmarks for science literacy.* New York: Oxford University Press.

American Council on the Teaching of Foreign Languages. (1986). *ACTFL proficiency guidelines.* Retrieved November 3, 2003, from http://www.sil.org/lingualinks/LANGUAGELEARNING/OtherResources/ACTFLProficiencyGuidelines/TheACTFLGuidelines.htm

American Council on the Teaching of Foreign Languages. (1999a). *Performance guidelines for K–12 learners.* Retrieved November 3, 2003, from http://www.actfl.org/public/articles/index.cfm?cat=29

American Council on the Teaching of Foreign Languages. (1999b). *Standards for foreign language earning* (SFLL). Retrieved November 3, 2003, from http://www.actfl.org/public/articles/details.cfm?id=33

American Diploma Project. (2004). *Ready or not: Creating a high school diploma that counts.* Washington, DC: Archive, Inc., the Education Trust, and the Thomas B. Fordham Foundation.

Amrein, A. L., & Berliner, D. C. (2003). The testing divide: New research on the intended and unintended impact of high-stakes testing. *Peer Review* 5 (2): 31–32.

Anderson, J. F., Anderson, P. A., Murphy, M. A., & Wendt, Wasco N. (1985). Teacher's reports of students' nonverbal communication in the classroom: A developmental study in grades K–12. *Communication Education* 34 (4): 292–307.

Anderson, L. (1981). Instruction and time-on-task: A review. *Journal of Curriculum Studies* 13: 289–303.

Anderson, T. (2000). *New teacher-mentor project: Moving teachers into the second millennium* (Schoolwide Northwest, 4–5). Portland, OR: Northwest Regional Educational Laboratory. Retrieved December 17, 2003, from http://www.nwrac.org/pub/schoolwide/spring00/indexl.html

Applebee, A. N. (1981) *Writing in the secondary school* (Research Report No 21). Urbana, IL: National Council of Teachers of English.

Applebee, A. N. (1984) *Contexts for learning to write: Studies of secondary school instruction.* Norwood, NJ: Ablex.

Applebee, A., Langer, J., & Mullis, I. (1987). *The nation's report card: Literature and U.S. history.* Princeton, NJ: Education Testing Service.

Applebee, A. N. (1977). ERIC/RCS report: The elements of a response to a literary work: What we have learned. *Research in the Teaching of English* 11: 255–271.

Applebee, A. N. (1991). Informal reasoning and writing instruction. In J. Voss, D. Perkins, & J. Segal (Eds.), *Informal reasoning and education* (pp. 401–414). Hillsdale, NJ: Lawrence Erlbaum.

Applebee, A. N. (1993). *Literature in the secondary school: Studies of curriculum and instruction in the United*

States (NCTE Research Report No. 25). Urbana IL: National Council of Teachers of English.

Aria, C. (2002). *The use of humor in vocabulary Instruction.* (ERIC Document Reproduction Service No. ED463537)

Aristotle. (W. R. Roberts, Trans.). (1954). *Rhetoric.* New York: The Modern Library.

Aronson, R. (2001). *At-risk students defy the odds: Overcoming barriers to educational success.* (ERIC Document Reproduction Service No. ED454598)

Ashton, P. (1984). Teacher efficacy: A motivational paradigm for effective teacher education. *Journal of Teacher Education* 35 (5): 28–32.

Atkinson, J. (1974). *Motivation and achievement.* Washington, DC: V. H. Winston.

Atkinson, J., & Feather, N. (1966). *A theory of achievement motivation.* New York: Wiley & Sons.

Ausubel, David P. (1963). *The psychology of meaningful verbal learning: An introduction to school learning.* New York: Grune & Stratton.

Ausubel, David P. (1967). *Learning theory and classroom practice.* Ontario: Ontario Institute for Studies in Education.

Ausubel, David P. (1968). *Educational psychology: A cognitive view.* New York: Holt, Rinehart & Winston.

Avery, P., & Graves, M. (1997, March/April). Young learners: Reading of social studies text. *Social Studies for the Young Learner,* pp. 10–14.

Bachman, L., & Savignon, S. J. (1986). The evaluation of communicative language proficiency: A critique of oral interview. *Modern Language Journal* 70: 380–390.

Bain, R. B. (1995, February 22). The world-history standards: A teacher's perspective. *Education Week,* pp. 34, 36.

Bain, R. B. (1997). *Teaching history as an epistemic act: Notes from a practioner.* Paper presented at the annual meeting of the American Historical Association, New York.

Baker, J. H. (1913). *Report of the committee of the National Council of Education on economy of time in education* (Bulletin No. 38). Washington, DC: U.S. Government Printing Office.

Baldwin, R. S., et al. (1982). The impact of subschemata on metaphorical processing. *Reading Research Quarterly* 4: 528–543.

Ball, D. L. (1997). From the general to the particular: Knowing our own students as learners of mathematics. *The Mathematics Teacher* 90 (9): 732–737.

Ball, S. J., & Goodson, I. (1985). Understanding teachers: Concepts and contexts. In S. J. Ball & I. F. Goodson (Eds.), *Teachers' lives and careers* (pp. 1–26). London: Falmer Press.

Bandura, A. (1986). *Social foundations of thought and action.* Englewood Cliffs, NJ: Prentice-Hall.

Bandura, A. (1997). *Self-efficacy: The exercise of control.* New York: W. H. Freeman.

Barr, L., Dittmar, M., Roberts, E., & Sheraden, M. (2000). *Enhancing student achievement through the improvement of listening skills.* (ERIC Document Reproduction Service No. ED465999)

Barton, J. (1995). Conducting effective classroom discussions. *Journal of Reading* 38 (5): 346–350.

Baumann, J. F., Jones, L. A., & Siefert-Kessell, N. (1993). Using think-a-louds to enhance children's comprehension monitoring abilities. *The Reading Teacher* 47: 184–193.

Bean, J. T., Singer, H., Sorter, J., & Frazee, C. (1986). The effect of metacognitive instruction in outline and graphic organizer construction on student comprehension in a tenth-grade world history class. *Journal of Reading Behavior* 18: 153–169.

Bean, John C., Drenk, D., & Lee, F. D. (1982). Microtheme strategies for developing cognitive skills. In C. W. Griffin (Ed.), *Teaching writing in all disciplines* (New Directions for Teaching and Learning, No. 12)(pp. 27–38). San Francisco: Jossey-Bass.

Beane, J. (1997). *Curriculum integration: Designing the core of democratic education.* New York: Teachers College Press.

Beardsley, D. A. (2003). *Secondary social studies starters and extensions.* (ERIC Document Reproduction Service No. ED474167)

Bearman, A., Feagin, C., Bottoms, G., & Tanner, B. (2003). *Instructional strategies: How teachers teach matters.* (ERIC Document Reproduction Service No. ED479271)

Becher, T. (1989). *Academic tribes and territories: Intellectual enquiry and the cultures of disciplines.* Bristol, PA: Open University Press.

Beck, I. L., McKeown, M. G., Hamilton, R. L., & Kucan, L. (1998). Getting at the meaning: How to help students *unpack* difficult text. *American Educator* 22 (1–2): 66–71.

Beck, I. L., McKeown, M. G., & Omanson, R. C. (1987). The effects and uses of diverse vocabulary instructional techniques. In M. C. McKeown & M. E. Curtis (Eds.), *The nature of vocabulary acquisition.* Hillsdale, NJ: Lawrence Erlbaum.

Beck, I. L., McKeown, M. G., Sandora, C., Kucan, L., & Worthy, J. (1996). Questioning the author: A yearlong classroom implementation to engage students with text. *Elementary School Journal* 96: 385–414.

Beeth, M. E. (1998). Teaching for conceptual change: Using status as a metacognitive tool. *Science Education* 82: 343–356.

Beeth, M. E., Ozdemir, O., & Yuruk, N. (2003). *The role of metacognition in facilitating conceptual change.* (ERIC Document Reproduction Service No. ED477315)

Bellack, A. A., Kliebord, H. M., Hyman, R. T., & Smith, F. (1966). *The language of the classroom.* New York: Teachers College Press.

Benson, B. P. (2003). *How to meet standards, motivate students, and still enjoy teaching! Four practices that improve student learning.* (ERIC Document Reproduction Service No. ED473258)

Benson, S. H. (2000). Make mine an A. *Education Leadership* 57 (5): 30–32.

Bereiter, C., & Scardamalia, M. (1986). Level of inquiry into the nature of expertise in writing. In E. Z. Rothkopf (Ed.), *Review of research in education* (Vol. 13, pp. 259–282). Washington, DC: American Education Research Association.

Berk, R. A. (2003). *Professors are from Mars, students are from snickers: How to write and deliver humor in the classroom and in professional presentations.* (ERIC Document Reproduction Service No. ED479152)

Berkowitz, A. M., Hunt, S., & Louden, A. (1999). A meta-analysis of the impact of forensics and communication education on critical thinking. *Communication Education* 48 (1): 18–30.

Berkowitz, S. J. (1986). Effects of instruction in text organization on sixth-grade students' memory for expository reading. *Reading Research Quarterly* 21: 161–178.

Berliner, D. (1994). Expertise: The wonder of exemplary performances. In J. N. Mangiere & C. C. Block (Eds.), *Creating powerful thinking in teachers and students: Diverse perspectives* (pp. 161–186). Fort Worth, TX: Harcourt Brace College.

Berliner, D. C. (1988). *The development of expertise in pedagogy.* Washington, DC: American Association of Colleges for Teacher Education.

Bernard, B. (1991). *Fostering resiliency in kids: Protective factors in the family, school and community.* Portland, OR: Northwest Regional Educational Laboratory.

Bernoff, R. (1992). *Teaching thinking skills.* Presentation at the University of South Florida.

Beyer, B. K. (1988). *Developing a thinking skills program.* Boston: Allyn & Bacon.

Biglan, A. (1973). The characteristics of subject matter in different academic areas. *Journal of Applied Psychology* 57: 195–203.

Black, Susan. (2000, August). The praise problem. *American School Board Journal* 187 (8): 38–40.

Blake, B. E., & Blake, R. W. (2002). *Literacy and learning: A reference handbook.* (ERIC Document Reproduction Service No. ED472809)

Blatt, M., & Kohlberg, L. (1975). The effects of classroom moral discussion upon children's level of moral judgment. *Journal of Moral Education* 4: 129–161.

Bleich, D. (1978). *Subjective criticism.* Baltimore, MD: Johns Hopkins University Press.

Block, C. (2001). *Think analogies: Learning to connect words and relationships.* (ERIC Document Reproduction Service No. ED471006)

Block, M., & Zeman, R. (1996). Including students with disabilities in regular physical education: Effects on nondisabled children. *Adapted Physical Activity Quarterly* 13: 38–49.

Bloom, B. (1956). *Taxonomy of educational objectives: Handbook 1: Cognitive domain.* New York: David McKay.

Blumefeld, P. C., Soloway, E., & Marx, R. W. (1991). Motivating project-based learning: Sustaining the doing, supporting the learning. *Educational Psychologist* 26: 369–398.

Bonus, M., & Riordan, L. (1998). *Increasing student on-task behavior through the use of specific seating arrangements.* (ERIC Document Reproduction Service No. ED422129)

Bonwell, C. C., & Eison, J. A. (1991). *Active learning: Creating excitement in the classroom* (ASHE-ERIC Higher Education Report No. 1). Washington, DC: George Washington University School of Education and Human Development.

Borg, W. R., Kelley, M. L., Langer, P., & Gall, M. (1970). *The minicourse: A microteaching approach to teacher education.* London: Collier-MacMillan.

Borisoff, D., & Arliss, L. (Eds.). (2001). *Women and men communicating: Challenges and changes* (2nd ed.). Prospect Heights, IL: Waveland Press.

Boston, C. (Ed). (2002). *Understanding scoring rubrics: A guide for teachers.* (ERIC Document Reproduction Service No. ED471518)

Bourdieu, P. (1986). The forms of capital. In J. Richardson (Ed.), *Handbook of theory and research for the sociology of education* (pp. 241–258). Westport, CT: Greenwood.

Bowker, A., Bukowski, W. M., Hymel, S., & Sippola, L. K. (2000). Coping with daily hassles in the peer group during early adolescence: Variations as a function of peer experience. *Journal of Research on Adolescence* 10 (2): 211–243.

Boyer, K. R. (2002). Using active learning strategies to motivate students. *Teaching in the Middle School* 8 (1): 48–51.

Bracey, G. (1995). Research oozes into practice: The case of class size. *Phi Delta Kappan* 77 (1): 89–91.

Brady, M., Clinton, D., Sweeney, J., Peterson, M., & Poynor, H. (1977). *Instructional dimensions study.* Washington, DC: Kirschner Associates.

Brandt, R., & Perkins, D. N. (2000). The evolving science of learning. In R. S. Brandt (Ed.), *Education in a new era* (Chapter 7, pp. 159–184). Alexandria, VA: ASCD Yearbook, Association for Supervision and Curriculum Development.

Brent, R., & Anderson, P. (1993). Developing children's listening strategies. *The Reading Teacher* 47 (2): 122–126.

Brett, A., Rothlein, R., & Hurley, M. (1996). Vocabulary acquisition from listening to stories and explanations of target words. *Elementary School Journal* 96 (4): 415–418.

Brewster, C., & Railsback, J. (2001). *Supporting beginning teachers: How administrators, teachers, and policymakers can help new teachers succeed.* Portland, OR: Northwest Regional Educational Laboratory. (ERIC Document Reproduction Service No. ED455619)

Bridges, D. (1979). *Education, democracy and discussion.* Windsor, England: NFER.

Briggs, T. H. (1920). *The junior high school.* Boston: Houghton Mifflin.

Brogan, B. R., & Brogan, W. A. (1995). The Socratic questioner: Teaching and learning in the dialogical classroom. *Educational Forum* 59 (3): 288–296.

Bromley, K. (1993). *Journaling: Engagements in reading, writing, and thinking*. New York: Scholastic. (ERIC Document Reproduction Service No. ED371387)

Brophy, J. (1986). *On motivating students*. East Lansing, MI: Institute for Research on Teaching, Michigan State University. (ERIC Document Reproduction Service No. ED276724)

Brophy, J. E., & Good, T. L. (1986). Teacher behavior and student achievement. In M. C. Wittrock (Ed.), *Handbook of research on teaching* (3rd ed., pp. 328–377). New York: Macmillan.

Broudy, S. (1990). The role of music in general education. *Bulletin of the Council for Research in Music Education* 105: 23–43.

Brown, G. (1975). *Microteaching: A programme of teaching skills*. New York: Harper & Row.

Brown, J. (2004, July 25). Teachers, here's yet another challenge. *Tampa Tribune*, p. 6.

Brown, J. S., Collins, A., & Duguid, P. (1989). Situated cognition and the culture of learning. *Educational Researcher* 18 (1): 32–42.

Brown, R., & Evans, W. P. (2002). Extracurricular activity and ethnicity: Creating greater school connection among diverse student populations. *Urban Education* 37 (1): 41–58.

Bruner, J. (1960). *The process of education*. New York: Random House/Vintage Books.

Bruner, J. (1990). *Acts of meaning*. Cambridge: Harvard University Press.

Bruner J. (1996). *The culture of education*. Cambridge, Mass: Harvard University Press.

Brylinsky, J. A., & Moore, J. (1984). The identification of body build stereotypes in your children. *Journal of Research in Personality* 28: 170–181.

Burgoon, J. K., Stern, L. A., & Dillman, L. (1995). *Interpersonal adaptation: Dyadic interaction patterns*. New York: Cambridge University Press.

Caldwell, J., Huitt, W., & Graeber, A. (1982). Time spent in learning: Implications from research.

Elementary School Journal 82 (5): 471–480.

Campbell, C. P., & Simpson, C. R. (1992). *The self-fulfilling prophecy: Implication for the training and learning process*. (ERIC Document Reproduction Service No. ED353377)

Canady, R. L., & Rettig, M. D. (1995). *Block scheduling: A catalyst for change in high schools*. Princeton, NJ: Eye on Education.

Canfield, A. (2002). *Body, identity and interaction: Interpreting nonverbal communication*. (ERIC Document Reproduction Service No. ED473237)

Canfield, J., & Siccone, F. (1993). *101 ways to develop student self-esteem and responsibility. Volume 1: The teacher as a coach*. Needham Heights, MA: Simon & Schuster.

Canter, L., & Canter, M. (2001). *Lee Canter's assertive discipline*. Los Angeles: Canter & Associates.

Carey, J. C., Fleming, S. D., & Roberts, D. Y. (1989). The Myers-Briggs Types Indicator as a measure of aspects of cognitive style. *Measurement and Evaluation in Counseling and Development* 22 (2): 94–99.

Carey, N., Kleiner, B., Porch, R., & Farris, E. (2002). *Arts education in public elementary and secondary schools: 1999–2000* (Statistical Analysis Report). (ERIC Document Reproduction Service No. ED467892)

Carnegie Council on Adolescent Development. (1989). *Turning points: Preparing America for the 21st century*. New York: Carnegie Corporation.

Carnegie Foundation for the Advancement of Teaching. (1906). *First annual report*. New York: Carnegie Corporation.

Carnine, D. W. (1993). Effective teaching for higher cognitive functioning. *Educational Technology* 33 (10): 29–33.

Carroll, J. (1963). A model for school learning. *Teachers College Record* 64: 723–733.

Carroll, J. (1994). The Copernican Plan evaluated: The evolution of

a revolution. *Phi Delta Kappan* 76 (2): 112–113.

Case, R. (1988). *Intellectual development: Birth to adulthood*. New York: Academic Press.

Caskey, M. (2002). A lingering question for middle school: What is the fate of integrated curriculum? (Issues in Education). *Childhood Education* 78 (2): 97–99.

Catterall, J. S. (1998). *Involvement in the arts and success in secondary school*. Washington, DC: Americans for the Arts, Monograph 1 (9).

Catterall, J. S., Chapleau, R., & Iwanaga, J. (1999). *Involvement in the arts and human development: Extending an analysis of general associations and introducing the special cases of intensive involvement in music and theatre arts*. Unpublished manuscript. The Imagination Project, Graduate School of Education and Information Studies, University of California at Los Angeles.

Cawetli, G. (Ed.). (1995). *Handbook of research on improving student achievement*. Arlington, VA: Education Research Service.

Cazden, C. B. (1993). Vygotsky, Hymes and Bakhtin. In E. A. Forman, N. Minick, & C. A. Stone (Eds.), *Context for learning: Sociocultural dynamics in children's development* (pp. 197–212). New York: Oxford University Press.

Center for Educational Reform. (1998). *A nation still at risk: An educational manifesto*. Washington, DC: Author.

Chall, J. S., Jacobs, V. A., & Baldwin, L. E. (1990). *The reading crisis: Why poor children fall behind*. Cambridge: Harvard University Press.

Chall, J., Jacobs, V., & Baldwin, L. (1996). The reading, writing and language connection. In J. Shimron (Ed.), *Literacy and education: Essays in memory of Dina Feitelson* (pp. 33–48). Cresskil, NJ: Hampton Press.

Chance, P. (1986). *Thinking in the classroom: A survey of programs*. New York: Teachers College Press.

Checkley, K. (2000). Serving gifted students in the regular classroom. *ASCD's Curriculum Update*, p. 5.

Chethik, N. (1994, August 19). Boys, too, shortchanged in classroom. *Cleveland Plain Dealer*, p. 5.

Chomsky, N. (1957). *Syntactic structures*. The Hague: Mouton.

Chomsky, N. (1965). *Aspects of theory of syntax*. Cambridge: MIT Press.

Christie, F. (1998). Science and apprenticeship: The pedagogic discourse. In J. R. Martin & R. Vell (Eds.), *Reading science: Critical and functional perspectives on discourses of science* (pp. 152–177). London: Routledge.

Ciaccio, J. (2000). A teacher's chance for immortality. *Education Digest* 65 (6): 44–48.

Close, E., & Ramsey, K. (Eds.). (2000). Planning for the job interview. *English Journal* 89 (5): 143–146.

Codding, J. B., & Rothman, R. (1999). Just passing through: The life of an American high school. In D. D. Marsh & J. D. Codding (Eds.), *The new American high school* (pp. 3–17). Thousand Oaks, CA: Corwin Press.

Cohen, E. (1986). *Designing group work: Strategies for the heterogeneous classroom*. New York: Teachers College Press.

Cohen, M., & Riel, M. (1989). The effect of distant audiences on stdents' writing. *American Educational Research Journal* 26 (2): 143–159.

Colby, K. M. (1961). On the greater amplifying power of causal-correlative over interrogative input on free association in an experimental psychoanalytic situation. *Journal of Nervous and Mental Disease* 133: 233–239.

Coleman, D. (2000). *Working with emotional intelligence*. New York: Bantam Doubleday Dell.

Coleman, J. S., Campbell, E. Q., Hobson, C. J., McPartland, J., Mood, A. M., Weinfield, F. D., & York, L. R. (1966). *Equality of educational opportunity*. Washington, DC: U.S. Government Printing Office.

Collins, R. (1988). The vividness effect: Elusive or illusory? *Journal of Experimental Social Psychology* 24 (1): 1–18.

Coloroso, B. (2002). *Kids are worth it! Giving your child the gift of inner discipline*. New York: Avon Books/Harper Collins.

Comer, J. (1997). *Waiting for a miracle: Why schools can't solve our problems—and how we can*. New York: Dutton.

Commission on Teaching and the American Future. (1996). *What matters most: Teaching for America's future*. New York: NCTAE.

Conant, J. B. (1959). *The American high school today. A first report to interested citizens*. New York: McGraw-Hill.

Conference Board of the Mathematical Sciences. (1975). *Overview and analysis of school mathematics, grades K–12*. Washington, DC: Author.

Connell, J. P. (1991). Context, self and action: A motivational analysis of self-system process across the life-span. In D. Cicchetti (Ed.), *The self in transition: Infancy to childhood*. Chicago: University of Chicago Press.

Consortium of National Arts Education Associations. (1994). *National standards for arts education: What every young American should know and be able to do in the arts*. Retrieved August 2004 from **http://artsedge. kennedy-center.org/teach/ standards.cfm**

Cooper, H. (1989). Synthesis on research on homework. *Educational Leadership* 47 (3): 85–91.

Cooper, H. (2001). Homework for all—in moderation. *Educational Leadership* (7): 34–38.

Cooper, M., & Gersten, R. M. (2002). *A teacher's guide to homework tips for parents: Talking points for presenters to use with transparencies*. (ERIC Document Reproduction Service No. ED468048)

Cope, B., & Kalatzis, M. (1993). Introduction: How a genre approach to literacy can transform the way writing is taught. In B. Cope & M. Kalatzis (Eds.), *The power of literacy: A genre approach to teaching writing* (pp. 1–21). Pittsburgh: University of Pittsburgh Press.

Copeland, T., Davis, K., Foley, B., Morely, B., & Nyman, K. (2001). *Improving middle school students' academic success through motivational strategies*. (ERIC Document Reproduction Service No. EDR455463)

Cornbleth, C., & Waugh, D. (1995). *The great speckled bird: Multicultural politics and education policymaking*. New York: St. Martin's Press.

Cortes, E. C. (2000). *The children are watching: How the media teach about diversity*. New York: Teachers College Press.

Costa, A. L. (1991). The school as a home for the mind. In A. L. Costa (Ed.), *Developing minds: A resource for teaching thinking* (rev. ed., Vol. 1). Alexandria, VA: Association for Supervision and Curriculum Development.

Costa, A. L., & Loveall, R. A. (2002). The legacy of Hilda Taba. *Journal of Curriculum and Supervision* 18 (1): 56–62.

Cothran, D. J., & Ennis, C. D. (2000). Building bridges to student engagement: Communicating respect and care for students in urban high schools. *Journal of Research and Development in Education* 33 (2): 106–117.

Cotton, K. (1990). School-wide and classroom discipline. Northwest Regional Educational Laboratory, Portland, OR. Retrieved November 3, 2003, from **http://www. nwrel.org/scpd/sirs/5/cu9.html**

Cotton, K. (2001). *New small learning communities: Findings from recent literature*. Northwest Regional Educational Laboratory, Portland, OR. Retrieved February 15, 2003, from **http://www.nwrel.org/ scpd/sirs/nslc.pdf**

Cotton, K. (2003). *Educational time factors*. Close-up #8. Northwest Regional Educational Laboratory, Portland, OR. Retrieved November 3, 2003, from **http://www.nwrel.org/ scpd/sirs/4/cu8.html**

Couch, R. (1993). Synectics and imagery: Developing creative thinking through images. In *Art, science and visual literacy: Selected readings from the annual conference of the*

International Visual Literacy Association (24th), Pittsburgh, PA, September 30–October 4, 1992. (ERIC Document Reproduction Service No. ED 363330)

Covello, V., & McCallum, D. B. (1997). The determinants of trust and credibility in environmental risk communication: An empirical study. *Risk Analysis* 17: 43–54.

Cross, K. P. (1977). *Accent on learning.* Washington, DC: Jossey-Bass.

Crouws, D. A., & Cebulla, K. J. (1999). Mathematics. In G. Carwelti (Ed.), *Handbook of research on improving student achievement* (pp. 117–134). Arlington, VA: Education Research Service.

Cruickshank, D. (1986). Profile of an effective teacher. *Educational Horizons* 64 (2): 80–86.

Cruz, B. (2004). *Lecture to graduating social studies education majors.* University of South Florida.

Cuban, Larry. (1984). *How teachers taught: Constancy and change in American classrooms, 1890–1980.* New York: Longman.

Cuban, L. (1991). History of teaching social studies. In J. P. Shaver (Ed.), *Handbook of research on social studies teaching and learning* (pp. 197–209). New York: Macmillan.

Cuff W. A. (1966). Reported in Alexander, W. M. (1984), The middle school emerges and flourishes, in *Perspectives: Middle School Education, 1964–1984,* edited by J. Lounsbury. Columbus, OH: National Middle School Association.

Cummins, J. (1999). *BICS and CALP: Clarifying the distinction.* (ERIC Document Reproduction Service No. ED438551)

Curwin, R., & Mendler, A. (1988). *Discipline with dignity.* Alexandria, VA: Association for Supervision and Curriculum Development.

Cusik, J. (Ed.). (2002). *Innovative techniques for large-group instruction* (An NSTA Press Journals Collection). Arlington, VA: NSTA Press.

Daly, J. A., & Suite, A. (1981). Classroom seating choice: Teacher perceptions of students. *Journal of Experimental Education* 50 (2): 64–69.

Danielson, C. (1996). *Enhancing professional practice: A framework for teaching.* Alexandria, VA: Association for Supervision and Curriculum Development.

Daresh, J. C. (2003). *Teachers mentoring teachers: A practical approach to helping new and experienced staff.* (ERIC Document Reproduction Service No. ED473040)

Darling, A. L., & Civikly, J. M. (1987). The effect of teacher humor on student perceptions of classroom communication climate. *Journal of Classroom Interaction* 22 (1): 24–30.

Davis, P., & Hersh, R. (1981). *The mathematical experience.* Boston: Houghton Mifflin.

Davison, A., & Green, G. M. (Eds.). (1988). *Linguistic complexity and text comprehension: Readability issues reconsidered.* Hillsdale, NJ: Lawrence Erlbaum.

Daws, N., & Singh, B. (1999). Formative assessment strategies in secondary science. *School Science Review* 80 (293): 71–78.

Deci, E. L., Koestner, R., & Ryan, R. M. (2001). Extrinsic rewards and intrinsic motivation in education: Reconsidered once again. *Review of Educational Research* 71 (1): 1–27.

Deci, E. L., & Ryan, R. M. (1985). *Intrinsic motivation and self-determination in human behavior.* New York: Plenum.

Dekeyrel, A., Dernovish, J., Epperly, A., & McKay, V. (2000). *Using motivation strategies to improve academic achievement of middle school students.* (ERIC Document Reproduction Service No. ED443550)

Delefes, P., & Jackson, B. (1972). Teacher-pupil interaction as a function of location in the classroom. *Psychology in the Schools* 9: 119–123.

DePaul, A. (2000). *Survival guide for new teachers: How new teachers can work effectively with veteran teachers, parents, principals, and teacher educators.* Washington, DC: U.S. Department of Education. Retrieved March 26, 2001, from **http://www.ed.gov/pubs/survivalguide/**

Deutsch, F. M. (2003). How small classes benefit high school students. *NASSP Bulletin* 87 (635): 35–44.

Devitt, A. J. (2004). *Writing genres.* Carbondale: Southern Illinois University Press.

Dewey, J. (1916). *Democracy and education.* New York: Macmillan.

Dewey J. (1980). *School and society.* Carbondale: Southern Illinois University Press. (Original work published in 1899)

Dickinson, T. S., & Erb, T. O. (Eds.). (1997). *We gain more then we give: Teaming in middle schools.* Columbus, OH: National Middle School Association.

Dillon, G. L. (1982). Styles of reading. *Poetics Today* 3 (2): 77–88.

Dillon, J. T. (1981a). Duration of response to teacher question and statement. *Contemporary Educational Psychology* 6: 1–11.

Dillon, J. T. (1981b). To question or not to question during discussion: 1. Questioning and discussion. *Journal of Teacher Education* 32 (5): 51–55.

Dillon, J. T. (1981c). To question or not to question during discussion: II. Non-questioning techniques. *Journal of Teacher Education* 32 (6): 15–20.

diSessa, A. (1993). Toward an epistemology of physics. *Cognition and Instruction* 10: 105–225.

Dixon, J. (1967). *Growth through English: A report based on the Dartmouth Seminar, 1966.* Reading, England: National Association for the Teaching of English.

Dole, J. A., Valencia, S. W., Greer, E. A., & Wardrop, J. L. (1991). Effects of two types of prereading instruction on the comprehension of narrative and expository text. *Reading Research Quarterly* 26: 142–159.

Dornbusch, S. M., & Ritter, P. L. (1988). Parents of high school students: A neglected resource. *Educational Horizons* 66: 75–77.

Douglas, A. M. (1970). An experiment in seminar methods. *International Journal of Electrical Engineering Education* 4: 19–22.

Doyle, W. (1986). Classroom organization and management. In M. C. Wittrock (Ed.), *Handbook of research on teaching* (3rd ed.). New York: Macmillan.

Doyle, W. (1992). Curriculum and pedagogy. In P. W. Jackson (Ed.), *Handbook of research on curriculum* (pp. 486–516). New York: Macmillan.

Dragseth, K., Weymouth, C., & Du, Y. (2003). *Gender differences and student learning.* (ERIC Document Reproduction Service No. ED477525)

Draper, T. M., Barskdale-Ladd, M. A. & Radencich, M. C. (2000). Reading and writing habits of preservice teachers. *Reading Horizons* 40 (3): 185–203.

Dreikurs, R. (1998). *Maintaining sanity in the classroom: Classroom management techniques.* Washington, DC: Accelerated Development.

Dreikurs, Rudolf, Grunwald, B. B., & Pepper, F. C. (1982). *Maintaining sanity in the classroom: Classroom management techniques* (2nd ed.). New York: Harper Collins.

Duda, J. L. (1992). Motivation in sport settings: A goal perspective approach. In G. Roberts (Ed.), *Motivation in sport and exercise* (pp. 57–91). Champaign, IL: Human Kinetics.

Duda, J. L. (1996). Maximizing motivation in sport and physical education among children and adolescents: The case for great task involvement. *Quest* 48: 290–302.

Duhon, G. M. (2002). *Racism in the classroom: Case studies.* (ERIC Document Reproduction Service No. ED464052)

Duit, R. (1999). Conceptual change approaches in science education. In W. Schnotz, S. Vosniadou, & M. Carretero (Eds.), *New perspective on conceptual change* (pp. 263–282). Oxford: Elsevier.

Duke, N., Bennett-Armistead, V., & Roberts, E. (2003). Filling the great void: Why we should bring nonfiction into the early-grade classroom. *American Educator* 27 (1): 30–35, 46–48.

Dunn, R., & Dunn, K. (1987). Dispelling outmoded beliefs about student learning. *Educational Leadership* 44 (6): 55–62.

Dunston, P. J. (1992). A critique of graphic organizer research. *Reading Research and Instruction* 31 (2): 57–65.

Duplass, J. A. (1996a). Charts, tables, graphs and diagrams: An approach for the social studies teacher. *The Social Studies* 87 (1): 32–39.

Duplass, J. A. (1996b). Proposition 187: A metaphors strategy for reflective inquiry. *Social Studies Review* 35 (2): 8–13.

Duplass, J. A. (2004). *Teaching elementary social studies: What every elementary school teacher should know.* Boston: Houghton Mifflin.

Dykman, B. M., & Reis, H. T. (1979). Personality correlates of classroom seating position. *Journal of Educational Psychology* 71 (3): 346–354.

Education Department of South Australia. (1988). *Developing the classroom group: A manual for the inservice trainer* (Report No. 4). Adelaide, South Australia: Govern Printer of South Australia.

The Education Trust. (1998). *Education watch: The 1998 education trust state and national data book,* 11. Washington, DC: The Education Trust.

The Education Trust. (2003). *The ABCs of "AYP": Raising achievement for all students.* (ERIC Reproduction Document Service No. ED478280)

Edwards-Groves, C. J. (2001). *Lessons from the classroom: What we learn about effective pedagogy from teacher-student interactions.* (ERIC Document Reproduction Service No. ED456441)

Eeds, M., & Wells, D. (1989). Grand conversations: An exploration of meaning construction in literature study groups. *Research in Teaching of English* 23: 4–29.

Efland, A. (1985). Introduction of music and drawing in the Boston schools: Two studies of education reform. In *The history of art education; Proceedings from the Penn State conference.* The Pennsylvania State University College of Arts and Architecture School of Visual Art, State College, PA.

Egelson, P., Patrick H., & Charles, M. A. (1996). *Does class size make a difference? Recent findings from state and district initiatives.* (ERIC Document Reproduction Service No. ED398644)

Eggen, P., & Kauchak, D. (2001). *Educational psychology: Windows on classrooms* (5th ed.). Upper Saddle River, NJ: Prentice Hall.

Eichhorn, D. H. (1966). *The middle school.* New York: Center for Applied Research in Education.

Eisenhart, M., Finkel, E., & Marion, S. F. (1996). Creating the conditions for scientific literacy: A reexamination. *American Educational Research Journal* 33 (2): 261–295.

Eisner, E., & Ecker, D. (1971). Some historical development in art education. In *Concepts in art and art education: An anthology of current issues.* New York: MacMillan.

Ekman, P., & Friesen, W. V. (1969). The repertoire of nonverbal behavior: Categories, origins, usage and coding. *Semiotica* 1: 49–98.

Elbow, P. (1998). *Writing without teachers* (2nd ed.). Oxford: Oxford University Press.

El-Hindi, A. E. (1996). Enhancing metacognition awareness of college learners. *Reading Horizons* 36 (3): 215–230.

Elhoweris, H. (2001). *Cooperative learning: Effective approach to a multicultural society.* (ERIC Document Reproduction Service No. ED457225)

Elias, J. A., & Stewart, B. R. (1991). The effects of similarity and dissimilarity of student and teacher personality type on student grades. *The Marketing Educator* 17: 42–51.

Elias, M. J. (2001). Easing transitions with social-emotional learning. *Principal Leadership* 1 (7): 20–25.

Elias, M. J., Arnold, H., & Hussey, C. (Eds.). (2003). *EQ + IQ = best leadership practices for caring and successful schools.* Thousand Oaks, CA: Corwin Press.

Elkind, D. (1984). *Ties that stress.* Cambridge MA: Harvard University Press.

Elliot, D. L., & Woodward, A. (Eds.). (1990). *Textbooks and schooling in the United States* (89th Yearbook,

Part I). Berkeley, CA: National Society for the Study of Education.

Ellis, R. (1994). *The study of second language acquisition*. Oxford: Oxford University Press.

Ellis, R. (1997). *SLA research and language teaching*. Oxford: Oxford University Press.

Ellsworth, J. A. (2003). *The ABC's of group work: Building community in schools. A workbook for high school and college*. (ERIC Document Reproduction Service No. ED474075)

Emig, J. (1971). *The composing process of twelfth graders*. Urbana, IL: National Council of Teachers of English.

Emmer, E., Evertson, C., & Worsham, M. (2003). *Classroom management for secondary teachers* (6th ed.). Boston: Pearson Allyn & Bacon.

Ennis, C. D. (1994). Knowledge and beliefs underlying curricular expertise. *Quest* 46: 164–175.

Ennis, R. H. (1987). A taxonomy of critical thinking dispositions and abilities. In J. B. Barron & R. J. Sternberg (Eds.), *Teaching thinking skills: Theory and practice* (pp. 1–26). New York: W. H. Freeman.

Epstein, J. (1984). School policy and parent involvement: Research results. *Educational Horizons* 62: 70–72.

Epstein, J., & Dauber, S. (1991). School programs and teacher practices of parent involvement in inner-city elementary and middle schools. *Elementary School Journal* 91: 289–306.

Ericsson, K. A. (1996). The acquisitions of expert performance: An introduction to some of the issues. In K. A. Ericsson (Ed.), *The road to excellence* (pp. 1–50). Hillsdale, NJ: Lawrence Erlbaum.

Erskine, C. A., & Tomkin, A. (1964). Evaluation of the effect of the group discussion method in a complex teaching programme. *Journal of Medical Education* 38: 1036–1942.

Eskeles-Gottfried, A., Fleming, J., & Gottfried, A. (1998). Role of cognitively stimulating home environment in children's academic intrinsic motivation: A longitudinal study. *Child Development* 69: 1448–1460.

Evans, R. W. (1990). History, sociology and social responsibility. *Social Science Record* 27 (2): 11–17.

Evers, W. M. (2001). Standards and accountability. In T. Moe (Ed.), *A primer on America's schools*. Stanford, CA: Hoover Institutional Press.

Everson, H. T. (1997, March 24–28). *Do metacognition skills and learning strategies transfer across domains?* Paper presented at the annual meeting of the American Educational Research Association, Chicago, IL. (ERIC Document Reproduction Service No. ED410262)

Everston, C. (1980). *Differences in instructional activities in high- and low-achieving junior high classes*. Paper presented at the annual meeting of the American Educational Research Association, Boston. (ERIC Document Reproduction Service No. ED195546)

Faigley, L. (1986). Competing theories of process. *College English* 48 (6): 527–542.

Farner, C. D. (1996). Mending the broken circle. *Learning* August: 27–29.

Feldmen, K. A. (1976). The superior college teacher from the student's view. *Research in Higher Education* 5: 243–288.

Fennema, E., Sowder, J., & Carpenter, T. P. (1999). Creating classrooms that promote understanding. In E. Fennema & T. A. Romberg (Eds.), *Mathematics classrooms that promote understanding* (pp. 185–199). Mahwah, NJ: Lawrence Erlbaum.

Fenstermacher, G. D. (1994). The know and the known: The nature of knowledge in research on teaching. In L. Darling-Hammond (Ed.), *Review of research in education* (Vol. 20, pp. 1–54). Washington, DC: American Education Research Association.

Ferreira, M. (2000). *Caring teachers: Adolescents' perspectives*. (ERIC Document Reproduction Service No. ED441682)

Fersh, S. (1993). *Integrating the transnational/cultural dimension*. (Fastback 361). Bloomington, IN: Phi Delta Kappa Educational Foundation. (ERIC Document Reproduction Service No. ED362233)

Fish, S. (1980). *Is there a text in this class? The authority of interpretive communities*. Cambridge, MA: Harvard University Press.

Fitzgerald, F. (1979). *America revisited: History schoolbooks in the 20th century*. Boston: Little, Brown.

Fitzgerald, J., & Stamm, C. (1990). Effects of group conferences on first graders' revisions in writing. *Written Communication* 7 (1): 96–135.

Flavell, J. J. (1976). Metacognitive aspects of problem solving. In L. Resnick (Ed.), *The nature of intelligence* (pp. 231–235). Hillsdale, NJ: Lawrence Erlbaum.

Flood, J., & Lapp, D (1986). Types of text: The match between what students read in basal and what they encounter in tests. *Reading Research Quarterly* 121: 284–297.

Flower, L. (1990). Negotiating academic discourse. In L. Flower, V. Stein, J. Ackerman, M. J. Kantz, K. McCormick, & W. C. Peck (Eds.), *Reading-to-write: Exploring a cognitive social process* (pp. 221–252). Oxford: Oxford University Press.

Flower, L. S. (1994). *The construction of negotiated meaning: A social cognitive theory of writing*. Carbondale: Southern Illinois University Press.

Flower, L. S., & Hayes, J. R. (1981). A cognitive process theory of writing. *College Composition and Communication* 32 (4): 365–387.

Flower, L. S., & Hayes, J. R. (1984). Images, plans and prose: The representation of meaning in writing. *Written Communication* 1 (1): 120–160.

Flower, L. S., Stein, V., Ackerman, J. M., Kantz, P., McCormick, K., & Peck, W. (1990). *Reading to write: Exploring a cognitive and social process*. New York: Oxford University Press.

Forte, I., & Schurr, S. (1993). *The definitive middle school guide*. Nashville: Incentive Publications, pp. 19–20, 31.

Foster, R. M., & Horner, J. T. (1988). National profile of agricultural teacher educators and state supervisors of vocational agriculture by MBTI preference type. *Journal of the American Association of*

Teacher Educators in Agriculture 29 (3): 20–27.

Fowler, W. (1995). School size and student outcomes. *Advances in Educational Productivity* 5: 3–26.

Frederick, W. (1977). The use of classroom time in high schools above and below the median reading score. *Urban Education* 11: 459–464.

Freedman, S. W. (1992). Outside-in and inside-out: Peer response groups in two ninth-grade classes. *Research in the Teaching of English* 26 (1): 71–107.

Freytag, C. E. (2001). *Teacher-parent communication: Starting the year off right.* (ERIC Document Reproduction Service No. ED460087)

Friedman, P. (1986). *Listening processes: Attention, understanding, evaluation* (2nd ed.). Washington, DC: National Education Association.

Friedrich, G., & Cooper, P. (1999). First day. In J. Daly, G. Friedrich, & A. Vangelisti (Eds.), *Teaching communication: Theory, research and methods* (pp. 287–296). Hillsdale, NJ: Lawrence Erlbaum.

Frymier, A., & Thompson, C. (1992). Perceived teacher affinity-seeking in relation to perceived teacher credibility. *Communication Education* 41: 388–399.

Fulwiler, T. (Ed.). (1987). *The journal book.* Portsmouth, NH: Boynton-Cook.

Gage, N. L., & Berliner, D. C. (1998). *Educational psychology* (6th ed.). Boston: Houghton Mifflin.

Gagne, R. M. (1965). *The conditions of learning.* New York: Holt, Rinehart and Winston.

Gagne, R. M., Briggs, L. J., & Wagner, W. W. (1992). *Principles of instruction design* (4th ed.). Orlando, FL: Harcourt Brace Jovanovich.

Gagnon, G. W., & Collay, M. (2001). *Designing for learning: Six elements in constructivist classrooms.* (ERIC Document Reproduction Service No. ED451136)

Gallagher, C. (1997). The history of literary criticism. *Daedalus* 126 (1): 133–153.

Gallagher, M., Knapp, P., & Noble, G. (1993). Genre in practice. In B. Cope & M. Kalatzis (Eds.), *The power of literacy: A genre approach to teaching writing* (pp. 179–202). Pittsburgh: University of Pittsburgh Press.

Garcia, E. G. (1991). *The education of linguistically and culturally diverse students: Effective instructional practices* (National Center for Research on Cultural Diversity and Second Language Learning Education Practice Report: 1). Washington, DC: U.S. Department of Education.

Garcia, E. G. (2001). *Hispanic education in the United States: Raices y Alas. Critical issues of contemporary American education.* Lanham, MD: Rowman & Littlefield.

Gardner, H. (1983). *Frames of mind: The theory of multiple intelligences.* New York: Basic Books.

Garger, S., & Guild, P. (1984). Learning styles: The crucial differences. *Curriculum Review* 23 (1): 9–12.

Geismar, T. J., & Pullease, B. G. (1996). The trimester: A competency based model of block scheduling: Research brief. *NASSP Bulletin* 80 (581): 95–105.

George, P. (2000/2001). The evolution of middle schools. *Educational Leadership* 58 (4): 40–44.

George, P., & Shewey, K. (1994). *New evidence for the middle school.* Columbus, OH: National Middle School Association.

Georgiady, N. P., & Romano, L. G. (2002). *Positive parent-teacher conferences* (Fastback 491). (ERIC Document Reproduction Service No. ED478537)

Gere, A., & Stevens, R. (1985). The language of writing groups: How oral response shapes revision. In S. Freedman (Ed.), *The acquisition of written language: Revisions and responses* (pp. 85–105). Norwood, NJ: Ablex.

Gere, A. R., & Shaheen, P. (Eds). (2001). *Making American literatures in high school and college* (Classroom Practices in Teaching English, 31). Urbana, IL: National Council of Teachers of English.

Giancola, S. P. (2000). *Adolescent behavior problems: Peer pressure "is"*

all it's cracked up to be. (ERIC Document Reproduction Service No. ED448384)

Gibbons, M. (2003). *The self-directed learning handbook: Challenging adolescent students to excel* (Jossey-Bass Education Series). San Francisco, CA: Jossey-Bass.

Gilbert, M. C. (1996). Attitudinal patterns and perceptions of math and science among fifth-grade through seventh-grade girls and boys. *Sex Roles* 35 (7/8): 489–506.

Gilliland, K. (2002). Calculators in the classroom. *Mathematics Teaching in the Middle School* 8 (3): 150–151.

Gilstrap, R. L., Bierman, C., & McKnight, T. R. (1992). *Improving instruction in middle schools* (Fastback 331). Bloomington, IN: Phi Delta Kappa Educational Foundation.

Gitlin, T. (1995). *The twilight of common dreams: Why America is wracked by culture wars.* New York: Henry Holt.

Glasser, W. (1997). *Choice theory: A new psychology of personal freedom.* New York: Harper Collins.

Goldberg, M. F. (2000). *Profiles of leadership in education.* (ERIC Document Reproduction Service No. ED459508)

Goldman, C., & Wong, E. (1997). Stress and the college student. *Education* 117: 604.

Goldsmith, L. T., & Shifter, D. (1994). *Characteristics of a model for the development of mathematical teaching* (Center for the Development of Teaching Paper Series). Newton, MA: Center for the Development of Teaching, Education Development Center.

Gollnick, D., & Chinn, P. (2002). *Multi-cultural education in a pluralistic society* (6th ed.). New York: Merrill/Macmillan.

Good, T. L. (1982). How teachers' expectations affect results. *American Education* 18 (10): 25–32.

Good, T. L., & Brophy, J. E. (1986). School effects. In M. C. Wittrock (Ed.), *Handbook of research on teaching* (3rd ed.). New York: Macmillan.

Good, T. L., Brophy, J. E. (2000). *Looking in classrooms* (8th ed.). New York: Addison-Wesley/Longman.

Goodlad, J. (1984). *A place called school: Prospects for the future.* New York: McGraw-Hill.

Goodlad, John I., Soder, Roger, & Sirotnik, Kenneth, A. (Eds.). (1990). *The moral dimensions of teaching.* San Francisco: Jossey-Bass.

Goodman, K. S., Shannon, P., Freeman, Y. S., & Murphy, S. (1988). *Report card on basal readers.* Katonah, NY: Richard Cowen.

Goodwin, M. (2000). Achievements or disasters. *Arts Education Policy Review* 101 (3): 7–8.

Gordon, E. W. (1999). *Education and justice: A view from the back of the bus.* New York: Teachers College Press.

Gordon, L. (1993). *People, types and tiger stripes* (3rd ed.). Gainesville, FL: Center for Applications of Psychological Type.

Gorham, J., & Christophel, D. M. (1990). The relationship of teachers' use of humor in the classroom to immediacy and student learning. *Communication Education* 39: 46–52.

Goza, B. (1993). Graffiti needs assessment: Involving students in the first class session. *Journal of Management Education* 17: 99–106.

Graham, K. C., Hussey, K., Taylor, K., & Werner, P. (1993). A study of verbal presentations of three effective teachers. *Research Quarterly of Exercise and Sport* 64: 87a (Abstract).

Green, T. F. (1971). *The activities of teaching.* New York: McGraw-Hill Book Company.

Sternberg, R. J. (1992). CATL A program of Comprehensive Abilities Testing. In B. R. Giffor & M. C. O'Connor (Eds.) *Changing assessments: Alternative views of aptitude, achievement and instruction* (pp 213–274). Boston: Kluwer Academic.

Greenleaf, C., Schoenbach, R., Cziko, C., & Mueller, F. (2001).

Apprenticing adolescent readers to academic literacy. *Harvard Educational Review* 71 (1): 79–129.

Gregorc, A. F. (1979). Learning/teaching styles: Potent forces behind them. *Educational Leadership* 36 (4): 234–236.

Gregorc, A. F., & Ward, H. B. (1977). A new definition for individual. *NASSP Bulletin* 61 (406): 20–26.

Griffin, P. (1985). Equity in the gym: What are the hurdles? *Canadian Association of Health, Physical Education, Recreation Journal* 55 (2): 23–26.

Griffin, P. (1992). Changing the game: Homophobia, sexism and lesbians in sport. *Quest* 44: 251–265.

Grigorenko, E. L., & Sternberg, R. J. (2000). *Teaching for successful intelligence to increase student learning and achievement.* Arlington Heights, IL: SkyLight Professional Development.

Grolnick, W. S., & Ryan, R. M. (1989). Parent styles associated with children's self-regulation and competence in school. *Journal of Educational Psychology* 81 (2): 143–154.

Grossman, P. L. (1989). A study in contrast: Sources of pedagogical content knowledge for secondary English. *Journal of Teacher Education* 40 (5): 24–32.

Grouws, D. A., & Smith, M. S. (2000). NAEP findings on the preparation and practices of mathematics teachers. In E. A. Silver & P. A. Kennedy (Eds.), *Results from the seventh mathematics assessment of the National Assessment of Educational Progress* (pp. 107–140). Reston, VA: National Council of Teachers of Mathematics.

Gurtler, L. (2002). *Humor in educational contexts.* (ERIC Document Reproduction Service No. ED470407)

Haberman, M. (1991). The pedagogy of poverty versus good teaching. *Phi Delta Kappan* 73 (4): 290–294.

Haberman, M. (1995). *Star teachers of children in poverty.* West Lafayette, IN: Kappa Delta Pi.

Hackman, D. G. (1997). *Student-led conference at the middle level.* (ERIC Document Reproduction Service No. ED407171)

Hall, B. I., Morreale, S. P., & Gaudino, J. L. (1999). A survey of the status of oral communication in the K–12 public education system in the United States. *Communication Education* 48 (2): 139–148.

Hall, R., & Sandler, B. (1982). *The classroom climate: A chilly one for women?* Washington, DC: Association of American Colleges Project on the Status and Education of Women.

Hallinan, M. T. (2000). *Ability group effects on high school learning.* (ERIC Document Reproduction Service No. 467684)

Hallinan, M. T., & Kubitschek, W. N. (1999). Curriculum differentiation and high school achievement. *Social Psychology of Education* 2: 1–22

Hampel, R. L. (2002). Historical perspectives on small schools. *Phi Delta Kappan* 83 (5): 357–363.

Hanks, N. (1975). The arts in the school: A 200 year struggle. *American Education* 11 (6): 16–23.

Harari, H., & McDavid, J. (1973). Name stereotypes and teachers' expectations. *Journal of Educational Psychology* 65 (2): 222–225.

Hart, B., & Risley, T. R. (2003). The early catastrophe: The 30 million word gap. *American Educator* 27 (1) 4–9.

Hartman, D. K. (1995). Eight readers reading: The intertextual links of proficient readers reading multiple passages. *Reading Research Quarterly* 30: 520–561.

Hayes, J. R., & Flower, L. S. (1980). Identifying the organization of writing process. In L. W. Gregg & E. R. Steinberg (Eds.), *Cognitive processes in writing* (pp. 3–30). Hillsdale, NJ: Lawrence Erlbaum.

Hayward, P. A. (2001). *Students' initial impressions of teaching effectiveness: An analysis of structured response items.* (ERIC Document Reproduction Service No. ED465979)

Hembree, R. & Dessart, D. J. (1992). Research on calculators in mathematics education. In J. T. Fey (Ed.). *Calculators in mathematics education*. 1992 yearbook of the National Council of Teachers of Mathematics (pp. 22–31). Reston, VA: National Council of Teachers of Mathematics. National Education Association of the United States (1918). *Cardinal principles of secondary education*. Washington, DC: Government Printing Office.

Hennessey, M. G. (1999). *Probing the dimensions of metacognition: Implications for conceptual change teaching-learning*. Paper presented at the annual meeting of the National Association for Research in Science Teaching, Boston.

Hertzberg, H. W. (1982). The teaching of history. In M. Kammen (Ed.), *The past before us: Contemporary historical writing in the United States* (pp. 474–504). Ithaca, NY: Cornell University Press.

Hester, V. (2001). *Responding to student writing: Locating our theory/practice among communities*. (ERIC Document Reproduction Service No. ED451539)

Hewlett, S. (1991). *When the bow breaks: The cost of neglecting our children*. New York: Harper Collins.

Hidi, S., & Harackiewicx, J. M. (2000). Motivating the academically unmotivated: A critical issue for the 21st century. *Review of Educational Research* 70: 151–179.

Hiebert, J., Carpenter, T. P., Fennema, E., Fuson, K. C., Wearne, D., Murracy, H., Olivier, A., & Human, P. (1997). *Making sense: Teaching and learning mathematics with understanding*. Portsmouth, NH: Heinemann.

Hill, D. J. (1988). *Humor in the classroom: A handbook for teachers (and other entertainers!)*. Springfield, IL: Charles C. Thomas.

Hirsch, E. D. (1987). *Cultural literacy: What every American needs to know*. New York: Houghton Mifflin.

Hirsch, E. D., Jr. (1996). *The schools we need and why we don't have them*. New York: Doubleday.

Hirsch, E. D. (2001). Seeking breadth and depth in the curriculum. *Education Leadership* 59 (2): 22–25.

Hixson, J., & Tinzmann, M. (1991). Who are the at-risk students of the 1990's? North Central Regional Education Laboratory Website. Retrieved from **http://www/ncrel.org/sdrs/areas/rpl_essay/equity**

Hoetker, J., & Ahlbrand, W. (1969). The persistence of the recitation. *American Educational Research Journal* 6: 145–167.

Hogan, K., & Pressley, M. (1997). Scaffolding scientific competencies within classroom communities of inquiry. In K. Hogan & M. Pressley (Eds.), *Scaffolding student learning: Instructional approaches and issues* (pp. 74–107). Cambridge, MA: Brookline Books.

Holland, N. (1975). *Five readers reading*. New Haven, CT: Yale University Press.

Holloway, J. H. (2002). Extracurricular activities and student motivation. *Educational Leadership* 60 (1): 80–81.

Hootstein, E. (1995). Motivational strategies of middle school social studies teachers. *Social Education* 59 (1): 23–26.

Horatio Alger Association. (2003). *The state of the nation's youth*. Alexandria, VA: Horatio Alger Association of Distinguished Citizens.

Horwitz, E. K. (2001). Language anxiety and achievement. *Annual Review of Applied Linguistics* 21: 112–126.

Housner, L. D., & Griffey, D. C. (1985). Teacher cognition: Differences in planning and interactive decision making between experienced and inexperienced teachers. *Research Quarterly for Exercise and Sport* 56: 45–53.

Howe, Michael, Davidson, J. W., & Sloboda, J. A. (1998). Innate talents: Reality or myth? *Behavioral and Brain Sciences* (21): 399–442.

Howley, C. (1996). The Matthew principle: A West Virginia publication? *Education Policy Analysis Archives* 3(1). Retrieved December 17, 2003,

from **http://epaa.asu.edu/epaa/v3n18.html**

Hoyt, L. (2002). *Make it real: Strategies for success with informational texts*. Portsmouth, NH: Heinemann.

Hudley, C., Daoud, A., Hershberg, R., Wright-Castro, R., & Polanco, T. (2002). *Factors supporting school engagement and achievement among adolescents*. (ERIC Document Reproduction Service No. ED465774)

Hudson, L. (2002). *The first day of class: Establishing rapport as well as ground rules*. (ERIC Document Reproduction Service No. ED467618)

Hughes, R. (1994). *Culture of complaint: A passionate look into the ailing heart of America*. New York: Warner.

Huitt, W. (1995). *A systems model of the teaching/learning process*. Valdosta, GA: College of Education, Valdosta State University.

Hunsberger, B., & Cavanagh, B. (1988). Physical attractiveness and children's expectations of potential teachers. *Psychology in the Schools* 25 (1): 40–74.

Hunter, M. (1982). *Mastery teaching*. California: Corwin Press.

Hurt, T., Scot, M., & McCroskey, J. (1981). *Communication in the classroom*. Menlo Park, CA: Addison-Wesley.

Hutchinson, G. E. (1995). Gender-fair teaching in physical education. *Journal of Physical Education, Recreation and Dance* 66 (91): 42–47.

Hynds, S. (1989). Bringing life to literature and literature to life. Social constructs and context of four adolescent readers. *Research in the Teaching of English* 23: 30–61.

Imel, S. (2001). *Learning communities/communities of practice* (Trends and Issues Alert No. 26). (ERIC Document Reproduction Service No. ED452434)

Ingram, M. A. (2000). *Extrinsic motivators and incentives: Challenge and controversy*. (ERIC Document Reproduction Service No. ED448127)

Jacobs, G. M., Power, M. A., & Inn, L. (2002). *The teacher's sourcebook for cooperative learning: Practical techniques, basic principles, and frequently asked questions.* Thousand Oaks, CA: Corwin Press.

Jacques, D. (1992). *Learning in groups* (2nd ed.). Houston, TX: Gulf.

Jalongo, M. R. (1995). Promoting active listening in the classroom. *Childhood Education* 72 (1): 13–18.

Jenks, C. J. (2003). *Process writing checklist.* (ERIC Document Reproduction Service No. ED479389)

Jennings, J. F. (Ed.). (1995). *National issues in education; Goals 2000 and school-to-work.* Bloomington, IN: Phi Delta Kappa Educational Foundation.

Johannessen, L. R. (1984). Making small groups work: Controversy is the key. *English Journal* 73 (2): 63–65.

Johannessen, L. R. (2002). *Let's get started: Strategies for initiating authentic discussion.* (ERIC Document Reproduction Service No. ED471394)

Johnson, A. B., Charner, I., & White, R. (2003). *Curriculum integration in context: An exploration of how structures and circumstances affect design and implementation.* (ERIC Document Reproduction Service No. ED473644)

Johnson, A. P. (2002). *Using thinking skills to enhance learning.* (ERIC Document Reproduction Service No. ED471387)

Johnson, D. W., Johnson, H., & Maruyama, G. (1983). Interdependence and interpersonal attraction among heterogeneous and homogeneous individuals: A theoretical formulation and a meta-analysis of the research. *Review of Educational Research* 53: 5–54.

Johnson, D. W., Johnson, H., Stanne, M., & Garibaldi, A. (1990). Impact of group processing on achievement in cooperative groups. *Journal of Social Psychology* 130: 507–516.

Johnson, D. W., & Johnson, R. (1989). *Cooperation and competition: Theory and research.* Edina, MN: Interaction.

Johnson, D. W., Maruyama, C., Johnson, R., Nelson, D., & Skon, L. (1981). Effects of cooperative, competitive, and individualistic goal structures on achievement: A meta-analysis. *Psychological Bulletin* 89: 47–62.

Johnston, H. J. (1984). *A synthesis of research findings on middle level education.* In John H. Lounsbury (Ed.), *Perspectives: Middle school education, 1964–1984.* Columbus, OH: National Middle School Association.

Johnston, J. H. (2004). Departmental papers. Secondary Education Department, University of South Florida.

Joint Committee on Health Education Terminology. (1991). *Report of the 1990 Joint Committee on Health Education Terminology.* Reston, VA: Association for the Advancement of Health Education.

Joint Committee on National Health Education Standards. (1995). *National health education standards: Achieving health literacy.* Atlanta, GA: American Cancer Society.

Jonassen, D. H. (1996). *Computers in the classroom: Mindtools for critical thinking.* Eaglewoods, NJ: Merrill/Prentice Hall.

Jones, A., & Brown, M. (2003, August 9). Federal gauges leave most students behind. *Tampa Tribune,* pp. 1, 10.

Jones, V and Jones L. (2001). *Comprehensive classroom management: Motivating and managing students* (3rd ed.). Boston: Allyn & Bacon.

Jordon, W. J., & Nettles, S. M. (1999). *How students invest their time out of school: Effects on school engagement, perceptions of life chances, and achievement* (Report No. 29). (ERIC Document Reproduction Service No. ED428174)

Kagan, S. (1989). The structural approach to cooperative learning. *Education Leadership* 47 (4): 12–15.

Kagan, S. (1993). The structural approach to cooperative learning. In D. D. Holt (Ed.), *Cooperative learning: A response to linguistic and cultural diversity.* (ERIC Document Reproduction Service No. ED355813)

Kagan, S. (1994). *Cooperative learning.* San Clemente, CA: Kagan Cooperative Learning.

Kalsounis, T. (1987). *Teaching social studies in the elementary school: The basics for citizenship* (2nd ed.). Englewood Cliffs, NJ: Prentice-Hall.

Kaplan, S. N. (2002). Awakening and elaborating: Differentiation in social studies content and instruction. *Gifted Child Today Magazine* 25 (3): 18–23.

Kariuki, P., & Davis, R. (2000). *The effects of positive discipline techniques as they relate to transition times in the middle school classroom.* (ERIC Document Reproduction Service No. ED450119)

Karlin, R. (2000, April 5). More students in special-ed taking regents. *Albany Times Union,* p. B2.

Karolides, N. J. (Ed.). (2000). *Reader response in secondary and college classrooms* (2nd ed.). Mahwah, NJ: Lawrence Erlbaum.Karp, D. A., & Yoels, E. W. C. (1976). The college classroom: Some observations on the meaning of student participation. *Sociology and Social Research* 60: 421–439.

Kelder, S. H., Perry, C. L., & Klepp, K.-I. (1993). Communitywide youth exercise promotion: Long term outcomes of the Minnesota Hearth Health Program and the Class of 1989 study. *Journal of School Health* 63: 218–223.

Kelley, T. E. (1986). Discussing controversial issues: Four perspectives on the teacher's role. *Theory and Research in Social Education* 14 (2): 112–138.

Kemp, A. C. (2000). *Science educators' view of the goals of scientific literacy for all: An interpretive review of the literature.* Paper presented at the annual meeting of the National Association for Research in Science Teaching, New Orleans, LA. (ERIC Document Reproduction Service No. ED454099)

Kent, H., & Fisher, D. (1997, March 24–28). *Association between teacher personality and classroom environment.* AERA, Chicago. (ERIC Document Reproduction Service No. ED407395)

Kieran, C. (1992). The learning and teaching of school algebra. In D. A. Grouws (Ed.), *Handbook of research on mathematics teaching and learning* (pp. 390–419). New York: Macmillan.

Kilpatrick, J., Swafford, J., & Findella, B. (Eds.). (2001). *Adding it up: Helping children learn mathematics.* Washington, DC: National Academy Press.

Kim, Y. (2001). *Foreign language anxiety as an individual difference variable in performance: From an interactionist's perspective.* (ERIC Document Reproduction Service No. ED457695)

Kirk, S., Gallagher, J. J., & Anastasiow, N. J. (2003). *Educating exceptional children.* Boston: Houghton Mifflin.

Kist, B. (2001). *Using rubrics: Teacher to teacher.* (ERIC Document Reproduction Service No. ED458392)

Kliebard, H. M. (1995). *The struggle for the American curriculum: 1983–1958* (2nd ed.). New York: Routledge.

Knapp, M. S., Adleman, N. E., Marder, C., McCollum, H., Needels, M. C., & Padilla, C. (1995). *Teaching for meaning in high-poverty classrooms.* New York: Teachers College Press.

Knight, C., Halpen, G., & Halpen, G. (1992). *The effects of learning environment accommodation on the achievement of second graders.* Paper presented at the annual meeting of the American Educational Research Association, San Francisco.

Knuth, E., & Peressini, D. (2001). Unpacking the nature of discourse in mathematics classrooms. *Mathematics Teaching in the Middle School* 6 (5): 320–325.

Kohlberg, L. (1981). Essays on moral development, I. In *The psychology of moral development: Moral stages and the idea of justice.* San Francisco: Harper & Row.

Kohlberg, L. (1984). Essays on moral development, II. In *The psychology of moral development: Moral stages and the idea of justice.* San Francisco: Harper & Row.

Kohlberg, L. (1987). *Child psychology and childhood education: A cognitive-developmental view.* New York: Longman.

Kohn, Alfie. (1993). *Punished by rewards: The trouble with gold stars, incentive plans, A's, praise and other bribes.* New York: Houghton Mifflin.

Kolb, D. A. (1981). Learning styles and disciplinary differences. In Chickering, A. (Ed.), *The modern American college.* San Francisco: Jossey-Bass.

Kolbe, K. (1990). *The conative connection.* Reading, MA: Addison-Wesley Publishing Company, Inc.

Konopak, B. C., Martin, S. H., & Martin, M. A. (1990). Using writing strategy to enhance sixth-grade students' comprehension of content material. *Journal of Reading Behavior* 22: 19–37.

Koos, L. V. (1920). *The junior high school.* New York: Harcourt, Brace, and Howe.

Kounin, J. S. (1970). *Discipline and group management in classrooms.* New York: Holt, Rinehart and Winston.

Krashen, S. (1982). *Principles and practice in second language acquisition.* Oxford, England: Pergamon Press.

Krashen, S. D., Long, M. A., & Scarcella, R. C. (1979). Age, rate and eventual attainment in second language acquisition. *TESOL Quarterly* 13: 573–582.

Krieger, J. D. (2002). *Teacher/student interactions in public elementary schools when class size is a factor.* (ERIC Document Reproduction Service No. ED479874)

Kuhn, D., & Dean, D. (2003). *Metacognition and critical thinking.* (ERIC Document Reproduction Service No. ED477930)

Kulik, J. A., & McKeachie, W. J. (1975). The evaluation of teachers in higher education. In F. N. Kerlinger (Ed.), *Review of research in education.* Itasca, IL: Peacock.

Kwak, C. (1993). *The initial effects of various task presentation conditions on students' performance of the lacrosse throw.* Unpublished doctoral dissertation, University of South Carolina, Columbia.

Labaree, David F. (1999). Too easy a target: The trouble with ed schools and the implications for the university. *Academe* 85 (1): 34–39.

Labaree, David F. (2000). On the nature of teaching and teacher education: Difficult practices that look easy. *Journal of Teacher Education* 51 (3): 228–233.

Ladson-Billings, G. (1994). *The dreamweavers: Successful teachers of African American children.* San Francisco: Jossey-Bass.

Lake, K. (1994). Integrated curriculum: *Close-Up #16.* School Improvement Research Series. Northwest Regional Education Laboratory. Retrieved February 3, 2004, from **http://www.nwrel.org/**

Lamare, J. (1997). Sacramento start: An evaluation report (No. BBB34917). Sacramento, CA: Sacrament Neighborhoods Planning and Development Services Department.

Lamber, N., & McCombs. B. (1998). Introduction: Learner-centered school and classrooms as a direction for school reform. In N. Lanber & B. McCombs (Eds.) *How students learn: Reforming school through learner-centered education* (pp. 1–22). Washington, DC: American Psychological Association.

Landau, B. M., & Gathercoal, F. (2000). Creating peaceful classrooms: Judicious discipline and class meetings. *Phi Delta Kappan* 81 (6): 450–452, 454.

Landin, D. (1994). The role of verbal cues in skill learning. *Quest* 46: 299–313.

Landsverk, R. A. (2000). *The new teacher welcome packet, Fall 2000.* (ERIC Document Reproduction Service No. ED453164)

Lang, D. E. (2002). *Teacher interactions within the physical environment: How teachers alter their space and/or routines because of classroom character.* (ERIC Document Reproduction Service No. ED472265)

Lange, D. L. (1990). Sketching the crisis and exploring different perspectives in foreign language curriculum. In D. W. Birckbichler (Ed.), *New perspective and new direction in foreign language education* (pp. 77–109) (American Council on the Teaching of Foreign Languages Series). Lincolnwood, IL: National Textbook.

Langer, J. A., & Applebee, A. N. (1986). Reading and writing instruction: Toward a theory of teaching and learning. In E. Z. Rothkoph (Ed.), *Review of research in education* (Vol. 13, pp. 171–194). Washington, DC: American Educational Research Association.

Lanier, V. (1974). A plague on all your houses: The tragedy of art education. *Art Education* 27 (3): 12–15.

Larkin, M. (2002). *Using scaffolded instruction to optimize learning.* (ERIC Document Reproduction Service No. ED474301)

Lattimore, R. (2001). The wrath of high-stakes tests. *Urban Review* 33 (1): 57–67.

Lawton, E. (1994). Integrating curriculum: A slow but positive process. *Schools in the Middle* 4 (2): 27–30.

Leavitt, H. J. (1951). Some effects of certain communication patterns on group performance. *Journal of Abnormal and Social Psychology* 46: 38–50.

Lehr, S. (1988). The child's developing sense of theme as a response to literature. *Reading Research Quarterly* 23: 337–357.

Leinhardt, G. (1993). Weaving instructional explanation in history. *British Journal of Educational Psychology* 63: 46–74.

Leinhardt, G. (1997). Instructional explanations in history. *International Journal of Educational Research* 27: 221–232.

Leonhard, C., & House, R. H. (1972). *Foundations and principles of music education.* New York: McGraw-Hill.

Leonard, L. J. (2001). *Erosion of instructional time: Teacher concerns.* (ERIC Document Reproduction Service No. ED460119)

Leslie, Connie. (1999). Separate and unequal? *Newsweek.* Retrieved February 3, 1999, from http://web3.inforac-custom.com

Leu, D., & Kinzer, C. K. (1999). *Effective literacy instruction, K–8* (4th ed.). Upper Saddle River, NJ: Prentice-Hall.

Levin, J., & Nolan, J. (2000). *Philosophical approaches to classroom management.* Boston: Allyn & Bacon.

Lewis, C. (1997). The social drama of literature discussion in a fifth/sixth grade classroom. *Research in the Teaching of English* 31: 163–204.

Lightbrown, P. (1985). Great expectations: Second-language acquisition research and classroom teaching. *Applied Linguistics* 6: 173–189.

Linn, R. L. (2002). *Accountability systems: Implications of requirements of the No Child Left Behind Act of 2001 (CSE Technical Report).* (ERIC Document Reproduction Service No. ED467440)

Livingston, J. A. (2003). *Metacognition: An overview.* (ERIC Document Reproduction Service No. ED474273)

Lock, R. S., Telljohann, S. K., & Price, J. H. (1995). Characteristics of elementary school principals and their support for the physical education program. *Perceptual and Motor Skills* 81: 307–315.

Lockledge, A., & Hayn, J. (Eds.). (2000). *Using portfolios across the curriculum.* (ERIC Document Reproduction Service No. ED452974)

Logan, J. (2003). *Classroom management: Techniques, policies, procedures, and programs to insure discipline "rules" in your classroom.* (ERIC Document Reproduction Service No. ED479639)

Long, M. H. (1983). Native speaker/non-native speaker conversation in the second language classroom. In M. A. Clarke & J. Handscomb (Eds.), *On TESOL '82: Pacific perspective on language learning and teaching* (pp. 207–225). Washington, DC: TESOL.

Lortie, D. C. (1975, 2002). *Schoolteacher: A sociological study.* Chicago: University of Chicago Press.

Lounsbury, J. H., & Clark, D. (1990). *Inside grade six: From apathy to excitement.* Reston, VA: National Association of Secondary School Principals.

Lounsbury, J. H., & Johnston, J. H. (1988). *Life in the three 6th grades.*

Reston, VA: National Association of Secondary School Principals.

Loveless, T. (2003). *The tracking and ability grouping debate.* Thomas B. Fordham Foundation. Retrieved July 2003 from http://www.edexcellence.net/library/track.html

Lucas, B. G., & Lusthaus, C. S. (1978). The decisional participation of parents in elementary and secondary Schools. *High School Journal* 61 (5): 211–220.

Luke, M. D., & Sinclair, G. D. (1991). Gender differences in adolescents' attitude toward school physical education. *Journal of Teaching in Physical Education* 11: 31–46.

Ma, X. (2003). Effects of early acceleration of students in mathematics on attitudes toward mathematics and mathematics anxiety. *Teachers College Record* 105 (3): 438–464.

MacDonald, C. (1991). *Children's awareness of their popularity and social acceptability.* Paper presented at the biennial meeting of the Society of Research in Child Development, Seattle, WA. (ERIC Document Reproduction Service No. ED332816)

MacIntyre A. (1981). *After Virtue.* Notre Dame, Ind.: University of Notre Dame Press.

Mandel, B. J. (Ed.). (1980). *Three language-arts curriculum models: Pre-kindergarten through college.* Urbana, IL: National Council of Teachers of English.

Mandel, S. (2002). *Cybertrips in social studies: Online field trips for all ages.* (ERIC Document Reproduction Service No. ED473024)

Manger, T., Eikeland, O., & Asbjornsen, A. (2002). Effects of social-cognitive training on students' locus of control. *School Psychology International* 23 (3): 342–354.

Manhood, W. (1987). Metaphors in social studies instruction. *Theory and Research in Social Education* 15: 285–297.

Many, J. E. (1991). The effects of stance and age level on children's literary response. *Journal of Reading Behavior* 23: 61–85.

Marshall, J. D. (1987). The effects of writing on students' understanding of literary texts. *Research in the Teaching of English* 21: 30–63.

Marshall, J. D., Smagorinski, P., & Smith, M. W. (1995). *The language of interpretation: Patterns of discourse in discussions of literature.* Urbana, IL: National Council of Teachers of English.

Martinez, M., & Brady, J. (2002). *All over the map: State policies to improve high schools.* (ERIC Document Reproduction Service No. ED467576)

Martorella, P. H. (1988). Students' understanding of metaphorical concepts in international relations. *Social Science Record* 25: 46–49.

Marzano, R. J., Gaddy, B. B., & Dean, C. (2000). *What works in classroom instruction.* (ERIC Document Reproduction Service No. ED468434)

Maslow, A. H. (1968). *Toward a psychology of being* (2nd ed.). Princeton, NJ: Van Nostrand.

Maslow, A. H. (1970). *Motivation and personality* (2nd ed.). New York: Harper & Row.

Maslow, A. H., & Mintz, N. L. (1956). Effect of esthetic surroundings: Initial effects of three esthetic conditions upon perceiving "energy" and "well-being" in faces. *Journal of Psychology* 41: 254–357.

Massachusetts Advocacy Center. (1990). *Locked in/locked out: Tracking and placement practices in public schools.* Boston: Eusey Press.

Mathematical Sciences Education Board. (1989). *Everybody counts: A report to the nation on the future of mathematics education.* Washington, DC: National Academy Press.

Mathematical Sciences Education Board. (1990). *Reshaping school mathematics: A philosophy and framework for curriculum.* Washington, DC: National Academy Press.

Mathews, M. R. (1994). *Science teaching: The role of history and philosophy of science.* New York: Routledge.

Maulding, W. S. (2002). *Emotional intelligence and successful leadership.* (ERIC Document Reproduction Service No. ED470793)

McCarthy, K. J. (2000). *The effects of student activity participation, gender, ethnicity, and socio-economic level on high school student grade point averages and attendance.* (ERIC Document Reproduction Service No. ED457173)

McCombs, B. L. (2000, August). *Addressing the personal domain: The need for a learner-centered framework.* Paper presented at the annual meeting of the American Psychological Association, Washington, DC.

McCombs, B. L., & Whisler, J. S. (1997). *The learner-centered classroom and school: Strategies for increasing student motivation and achievement.* San Francisco: Jossey-Bass.

McCormick, T. E., & Noriega, T. (1986). Low versus high expectations: A review of teacher expectancy effects on minority students. *Journal of Educational Equality and Leadership* 3: 224–234.

McCroskey, J. C., & McVetta, R. W. (1978). Classroom seating arrangement: Instructional communication theory versus student preferences. *Communication Education* 27: 101–102.

McDonald, J. P., & Naso, P. (1986, May). *Teacher as learner: The impact of technology.* Unpublished paper, Educational Technology Center, Harvard Graduate School of Education.

McEwing, C. K., Dickinson, T. S., & Jenkins, D. M. (1996). *American's middle schools: Practices and progress, a 25 year perspective.* Columbus, OH: National Middle School Association.

McGinnis, J. C. (1995). Enhancing classroom management through proactive rules and procedures. *Psychology in the Schools* 32 (3): 220–224.

McGuinness, C. (1999). *From thinking skills to thinking classrooms: A review and evaluation of approaches for developing pupils' thinking.* Nottingham: DFEE Publications.

McTighe, J. & Wiggins, G. (2004). *Understanding by design professional development workbook.* Alexandria, VA: Association for Supervision & Career Development.

Mead, N., & Rubin, D. (1985). *Assessing listening and speaking skills.* (ERIC Document Reproduction Service No. ED263626)

Melton, G. (Ed.). (1984). The junior high school: Success and failures. In John H. Lounsbury (Ed.), *Perspectives: Middle school education.* Columbus, OH: National Middle School Association.

Meltzer, J. (2001). *Supporting adolescent literacy across the content areas: Perspectives on policy and practice.* (ERIC Document Reproduction Service No. ED459442)

Mendler, A. N. (1992). *What do I do when . . . ? How to achieve discipline with dignity in the classroom.* Bloomington, IN: National Educational Service.

Menzel, K. E., & Carrell, L. J. (1994). The relationship between preparation and performance in public speaking. *Communication Education* 43(1): 17–26. (ERIC Document Reproduction Service No. EJ486194)

Merrill, M. D. (2002). First principles of instruction. *Educational Technology Research and Development* 50 (3): 43–59.

Meyer, D. K. (1993). What is scaffolded instruction? Definitions, distinguishing features and misnomers. In D. J. Lev & C. K. Kinzer (Eds.), *Examining central issues in literacy research, theory and practice* (pp. 41–53). Chicago: National Reading Conference.

Michael, J. A. (1991). Art education: Nature or nurture? *Art Education* 44 (4): 16–23.

Michaelsen, L. K., Fink, L. D., & Knight, A. (1997). Designing effective group activities: Lesson for classroom teaching and faculty development. *To Improve the Academy* 16: 373–398.

Miller, G. A. (1956). The magical number seven, plus or minus two: Some limits on our capacity for processing information. *Psychological Review* 63: 81–97.

Miller, J. (1997). Using educational technologies to promote vocabulary development among heterogeneously-grouped fifth grades. *28 Takes on 21st Century Literacy Instruction.*

Mishler, E. G. (1978). Studies in dialogue and discourse: III. Utterance structure and utterance function in interrogative sequences. *Journal of Psycholinguistic Research* 7: 279–305.

Moir, E. (2003). *Launching the next generation of teachers through quality induction.* (ERIC Document Reproduction Service No. ED479764)

Moje, E., Young, J. P., Readence, J., & Moore, D. (2000). Reinventing adolescent literacy for new times: Perennial and millennial issues. *Journal of Adolescent and Adult Literacy* 43 (5): 400–410.

Moles, O. C. (Ed.). (2000). *Reaching all families: Creating family-friendly schools. Beginning of the school year activities.* (ERIC Document Reproduction Service No. ED447961)

Moore, A. (2002). Small-size schools: A historical review and synthesis of research on variables affecting students. Doctoral dissertation, University of South Dakota. *Dissertation Abstracts International* 63: 1652.

Moore, D. S. (1995). The craft of teaching. *Focus* 15 (2): 5–8.

Moore, D. W., & Readence, J. E. (1984). A quantitative and qualitative review of graphic organizer research. *Journal of Educational Research* 78 (1): 11–17.

Moran, C. (1996). Short-term mood change. Perceived funniness and the effect of humor stimuli. *Behavioral Medicine* 22: 1–32.

Morrow, L. M. (1992). The impact of a literature-based program on literacy achievement, use of literature and attitudes of children from minority backgrounds. *Reading Research Quarterly* 27: 250–276.

Mottet, T. P. (2002). *Student communication behaviors and their influence on teachers and teaching in the American classroom: A review of the recent communication research.* Pyatigorsk, Russia. (ERIC Document Reproduction Service No. ED466546)

Mottet, T. P., Beebe, S. A., Paulsel, M. L., & Raffeld, P. (2002). Teachers' preferential treatments of students: The effects of student classroom communication behaviors on teachers' evaluation of student essays, cited in Mottet, T. P. (2000).

Muller, H. L. (2000). *Facilitating classroom discussion: Lessons from student-led discussions.* (ERIC Document Reproduction Service No. ED450434)

Murdock, T. B., Anderman, L. H., & Hodge, S. A. (2000). Middle-grade predictors of students' motivation and behavior in high school. *Journal of Adolescent Research* 15 (3): 327–351.

Murnane, R. J., & Levy, F. (1996). *Taking the new basic skills: Principles for educating children to thrive in changing economy.* New York: The Free Press.

Murphy, S. (1996). *The achievement zone.* New York: G. P. Putnam's Sons.

Nagy, W., & Scott, J. (2000). Vocabulary processes. In M. Kamil, P. Mosenthal, P. Pearson, & R. Barr (Eds.), *Handbook of reading research* (pp. 269–284). Mahwah, NJ: Lawrence Erlbaum.

Nash, G. B., Crabtree, C., & Dunn, R. E. (1997). *History on trial: Culture wars and the teaching of the past.* New York: Alfred A. Knopf.

NASPE. (1992). *Program guidelines and appraisal checklist for physical education, secondary.* Reston, VA: Author.

NASPE. (1995). *Developmentally appropriate physical education, middle school.* Reston, VA: Author.

NASPE. (1996). *Developmentally appropriate physical education, secondary.* Reston, VA: Author.

NASPE. (2004). *Moving into the future: National standards for physical education, A guide to content and assessment* (2nd ed.). Reston, VA: Author. (Originally published 1995)

National Center for Educational Statistics (NCES). (2000). *Teachers' tools of the twenty-first century: A report on teachers' use of technology.* Washington, DC: U.S. Department of Education.

National Center for History in the Schools. (1994). *National standards for world history: Exploring paths to the present.* Los Angeles, CA: Author.

National Center for History in the Schools. (1996). *National standards for history.* Los Angeles, CA: Author.

National Commission on Excellence in Education. (1983). *A nation at risk.* Washington, DC: U.S. Government Printing Office.

National Commission on Teaching and the American Future (NCTAF). (1996). *What matters most: Teaching for America's future.* Retrieved April 20, 2004, from **http://www. nctaf.org/publications/ whatmattersmost.html**

National Commission on Writing in America's Schools and Colleges. (2003, April). *The neglected "R": The need for a writing revolution.* Princeton, NJ: College Entrance Examination Board.

National Council for Teachers of Mathematics. (1980). *An agenda for action: Recommendations for school mathematics in the 1980s.* Reston, VA: Author.

National Council for Teachers of Mathematics. (1989). *Curriculum and evaluation standards for school mathematics.* Reston, VA: Author.

National Education Association. (1892). *Report of the Committee of Ten.* Washington, DC: U.S. Government Printing Office.

National Education Association. (1893). *Report of the Committee of Ten on secondary school studies.* Washington, DC: U.S. Government Printing Office.

National Education Association. (1894). *Report of the Committee of Ten on secondary school studies with reports of the conferences arranged by the committee.* New York: American Book Co.

National Education Association. (1895). *Report of the Committee of Fifteen on elementary education, with reports of the sub-committees: On the training of teacher; On the correlation of studies in elementary education; On the organization of city school systems.* New York: American Book Co.

National Education Association of the United States. (1918). *Cardinal principles of secondary education.* Washington, DC: U.S. Government Printing Office.

National Middle School Association. (1982). *This we believe.* Columbus, OH: Author.

National Middle School Association. (2003). *This we believe: Successful schools for young adolescents.* Columbus, OH: Author.

National Research Center on Education in the Inner Cities. (2000). How small classes help teachers do their best: Recommendations from a national invitational conference. *CEIC Review* 9 (2). (ERIC Document Reproduction Service No. ED440198)

National Research Council. (1996). *National science education standards.* Washington, DC: Antinal Academy Press.

National Science Teachers Association. (1971). NTSA position statement on school science education for the 70's. *The Science Teacher* 38: 46–51.

National Telecommunications and Information Administration (NTIA). U.S. Department of Commerce. (2000). *Falling through the net: Toward digital inclusion.* Washington, DC: Author.

Nauta, M. M., & Kokaly, M. (2001). Assessing role model influences on students' academic and vocational decisions. *Journal of Career Assessment* 9 (1): 81–99.

Naylor, D., & Diem, R. (1987). *Elementary and middle school social studies.* New York: Random House.

NCSS. (1989). The essentials of social studies: In search of scope and sequence for social studies. *Social Education* 53 (6): 376–385.

NCSS. (1990). *Social studies for citizens for a strong and free nation.* Social Studies Curriculum Planning Resources. Washington, DC: Author.

NCSS. (1994). *Expectations of excellence: Curriculum standards for social studies.* Washington, DC: Author.

NCTE. (1917). *Reorganization of English in secondary schools.*

Urbana, IL: National Council of Teachers of English.

NCTE. (1935). *An experience curriculum in English.* Urbana, IL: National Council of Teachers of English.

NCTE. (1997). *NCTE's position on the teaching of English: Assumptions and practices.* (ERIC Document Reproduction Service No. ED461108)

NCTM. (1991). *Professional standards for teaching mathematics.* Reston, VA: Author.

NCTM. (1995). *Assessment standards for school mathematics.* Reston, VA: Author.

NCTM. (2000). *Principles and standards for school mathematics.* Reston, VA: Author.

Nelson, S. M., Gallagher, J. J., & Coleman, M. R. (1993). Cooperative learning from two different perspectives. *Roeper Review* 16 (2): 117–121. (ERIC Document Reproduction Service No. EJ479457)

Nettles, S. M. (1989). The role of community involvement in fostering investment behavior in low-income black adolescents: A theoretical approach. *Journal of Adolescent Research* 4: 190–210.

Newman, F. M., & Associates. (1996). *Authentic achievement: Restructuring schools for intellectual quality.* San Francisco: Jossey-Bass.

Newmann, F. (Ed.). (1988). *Higher order thinking in high school social studies: An analysis of classrooms, teachers, students, and leadership.* Madison: University of Wisconsin, National Center on Effective Secondary Schools.

Newmann, F. M. (1990). Higher order thinking in teaching social studies. *Journal of Curriculum Studies* 22: 41–56.

Nielsen, D. L. (1986). The nature of ground in farfetched metaphors. *Metaphors and Symbolic Activity* 1 (14): 127–138.

Nodding, N. (1992). *The challenge to care in schools.* New York: Teachers College Press.

North Central Regional Educational Lab. (2002). *Understanding the No Child Left Behind Act of 2001: A*

quick key to reading. Naperville, IL: North Central Regional Educational Lab. (ERIC Document Reproduction Service No. ED467523)

Norton, R. W. (1983). *Communication style: Theory, applications and measures.* Beverly Hills, CA: Sage.

Novak, J. D. (1993). How do we learn our lesson? Taking students through the process. *The Science Teacher* 60 (3): 50–55.

Novak, J. D., Gowin, D. B., & Johansen, G. T. (1983). The use of concept mapping and knowledge mapping with junior high school science students. *Science Education* 67: 625–645.

Numeracy Task Force. (2004). *Numeracy matters: Final report, implementation of the national numeracy strategy.* Retrieved January 4, 2004, from http://www.dfes.gov.uk/numeracy/contents.shtml

Nussbaum, J. F. (1992). Effective teaching behaviors. *Communication Education* 41: 167–180.

Nystrand, M. (1986). *The structure of written communication: Studies in reciprocity between writers and readers.* Orlando, FL: Orlando Academic Press.

Nystrand, M. (1990). Sharing words: The effects of readers on developing writers. *Written Communication* 7 (1): 3–24.

Nystrand, M., & Gamoran, A. (1991). Instructional discourse, student engagement, and literature achievement. *Research in the Teaching of English* 25: 261–290.

Nystrand, M., Greene, S., & Wiemelt, J. (1993). Where did composition come from? An intellectual history. *Written Communication* 10 (3): 267–333.

O'Brien, T. P. (1999). Relationships among selected characteristics of college students and cognitive style preferences. *College Student Journal* 25 (1): 492–500.

Ogawa, M. (2001). *Building multiple historical perspectives: An investigation of how middle school students are influenced by different perspectives.* (ERIC Document Reproduction Service No. ED453108)

Onsko, J. J. (1990). Comparing teachers' instruction to promote students' thinking. *Journal of Curriculum Studies* 22: 443–461.

Ortony, A. (1979). *Metaphor and thought*. New York: Cambridge University Press.

Oxford, R. (2001). Language learning styles and strategies. In M. Celce-Murcia (Ed.), *Teaching English as a second or foreign language* (3rd ed.). Boston: Heinle & Heinle.

Owca, S., Pawlak, E., & Pronobis, M. (2003). *Improving student academic success through the promotion of listening skills*. (ERIC Document Reproduction Service No. ED478233)

Packer, J., & Brain, J. D. (1978). Cognitive style and teacher-student compatibility. *Journal of Educational Psychology* 70 (5): 864–871.

Padron, Y. N., Waxman, H. C., & Rivera, H. H. (2002). *Educating Hispanic students: Obstacles and avenues to improved academic achievement* (Educational Practice Report 8). (ERIC Document Reproduction Service No. ED470554)

Pagares, M. F. (1992). *Teachers' beliefs and educational research*. Review of Educational Research, 62(3), 307–332.

Parker, D. A. (2003). *Confident communication: Speaking tips for educators*. Thousand Oaks, CA: Corwin Press.

Parker, W. C. (2001). Classroom discussion: Models for leading seminars and deliberations. *Social Education* 65 (2): 111–115.

Parkes, J., & Harris, M. (2002). The purposes of a syllabus. *College Teaching* 50 (2): 55–61.

Pastoll, G. (2002). *Motivating people to learn*. (ERIC Document Reproduction Service No. ED475354)

Pate, R. R., Small, M. L., Ross, J. L., Young, J. C., Flint, K. H., & Warren, C. W. (1995). School physical education. *Journal of School Health* 65: 312–318.

Patrick, C., Hisley, J., & Kempler, T. (2000). "What's everybody so excited about?" The effects of teacher enthusiasm on student intrinsic motivation and vitality. *Journal of Experimental Education* 68 (3): 217–236.

Payne, R. K. (2001). *Framework for understanding poverty*. Highlands, TX: Aha Process, Inc.

Peck, M. S. (1997). *The road less traveled*. New York: Simon & Schuster.

Perkins, D., Jay, E., & Tishman, S. (1992). Beyond abilities: A dispositional theory of thinking. *Merrill-Palmer Quarterly* 39 (1): 1–21.

Perkins, D. N. (1992). *Smart schools: From training memories to educating minds*. New York: The Free Press.

Perkins, D., Jay, E., & Tishman, S. (in press). Beyond abilities: A dispositional theory of thinking. *The Merrill-Palmer Quarterly* 39 (1): 1–21.

Peterson, D. W. (2001). *On the road: In search of excellence in middle level education*. (ERIC Document Reproduction Service No. ED451930)

Peterson, P. L., & Clark, C. M. (1978). Teachers' reports of their cognitive processes during teaching. *American Educational Research Journal* 15 (4): 555–565.

Petrei, H. (1979). Metaphor and learning. In A. Ortony (Ed.), *Metaphor and thought* (pp. 438–461). New York: Cambridge University Press.

Phi Delta Kappa. (1998, March). The Charter School Movement. *Phi Delta Kappan* 79 (7): 448–498.

Philips, D. C. (1995). The good, bad and the ugly: The many faces of constructivism. *Educational Researcher* 24: 5–12.

Piaget, J. (1972). *The psychology of the child*. New York: Basic Books.

Pines, H. A., & Larkin, J. E. (2003). *When teachers call on students: Avoidance behavior in the classroom*. (ERIC Document Reproduction Service No. ED479918)

Pisapia, J., & Westfall, A. L. (1997). *Alternative high school scheduling: A view from the teacher's desk* (Research Report). (ERIC Document Reproduction Service No. ED411335)

Pohlman, J. T. (1976). A description of effective college teaching in five disciplines as measured by student rating. *Research in Higher Education* 4: 335–346.

Poling, L. G. (2000). The real world: Community speakers in the classroom. *Social Education* 64 (4): 8–10.

Pollak, J., & Freda, P. (1997). Humor, learning, and socialization in middle level classrooms. *Clearing House* 70 (4): 176–178.

Popper, S. H. (1967). *The American middle school: An organizational analysis*. Waltham, MA: Blais-Dell Publishing Company.

Porter, A. C. (1989). External standards and good teaching: The pros and cons of telling teachers what to do. *Educational Evaluation and Policy Analysis* 11 (4): 343–356.

Posner, G. J., Strike, K. A., Hewson, P. W., & Gertzog, W. A. (1982). Accommodation of a scientific conception: Toward a theory of conceptual change. *Science Education* 66: 221–227.

Powell, A. G., Farrar, E., & Cohen, D. K. (1985). *The shopping mall high school: Winners and losers in the educational marketplace*. Boston: Houghton Mifflin.

Powell, R. R., Skoog, G., Troutman, P., & Jones, C. (1996). *Standing on the edge of middle-level curriculum reform: Factors influencing the sustainability of a non-linear integrative learning environment*. Paper presented at the annual meeting of the American Educational Research Association, New York.

Prewitt, V. R. (2003). The constructs of wisdom in human development and consciousness. (ERIC Document Reproduction Service No. ED475466)

Prior, P. (1998). Contextualizing instructors' responses to writing in the college classroom. In N. Nelson & R. Calfee (Eds.), *The reading-writing connection: Yearbook of the National Society for the Study of Education* (pp. 153–177). Chicago: University of Chicago Press.

Proctor, C. (1984). Teacher expectations: A model for school improvement. *Elementary School Journal* 84 (4): 469–481.

Public Agenda. (1997). *Getting by: What American teenagers really think about their schools.* New York: Author.

Puntambekar, S., & duBoulay, B. (1997). Design and development of MIST: A system to help students develop metacognition. *Journal of Education Computing Research* 16 (109): 1–35.

Purves, A. C. (1993). Toward a reevaluation of reader response and school literature. *Language Arts* 70: 348–361.

Queen, J. A., et al. (1997). *Responsible classroom management for teacher and students.* Upper Saddle River, NJ: Merrill/Prentice-Hall.

Raizen, S. A. (1991). The reform of science education in the U.S.A. Déjà vu or de novo? *Studies in Science Education* 19: 1–14.

Ravitch, D. (1985). *The schools we deserve: Reflections on the educational crises of our time.* New York: Basic Books.

Ravitch, D. (2003a). *The language police: How pressure groups restrict what students learn.* New York: Knopf.

Ravitch, D. (2003b). Thin gruel: How the language police drain the life and content from our texts. *American Educator* 27 (3): 6–19.

Ravitch, D., & Finn, C. E. (1987). *What do our 17-year-olds know? A report on the First National Assessment of History and Literature.* New York: Harper & Row.

Readence, J. E., Baldwin, R. S., & Rickelmanm, R. J. (1983). Work knowledge and metaphorical interpretation. *Research in Teaching English* 17: 349–358.

Readence, J. E., et al. (1986). Direct instruction in processing metaphors. *Journal of Reading Behavior* 18: 325–340.

Renniger, K. A., & Snyder, S. S. (1983). Effect of cognitive style on perceived satisfaction and performance among students and teacher. *Journal of Education Psychology* 75 (5): 668–676.

Resnick, L. B. (1987). *Education and learning to think.* Washington, DC: National Academy Press.

Resnick, L. B. (1999). Foreword. In D. D. March & J. B. Codding et al. (Eds.), *In the new American high school.* Thousand Oaks, CA: Corwin Press.

Resnick, L. B., & Klopfer, L. E. (1989). Toward the thinking curriculum: An overview. In L. B. Resnick & L. E. Klopfer (Eds.), *Toward the thinking curriculum: Current cognitive research* (pp. 1–18). Alexandria, VA: Association of Supervision and Curriculum Development.

Rice, P. L. (1988). Attitudes of high school students toward physical education activities, teachers and personal health. *Physical Educator* 45 (2): 94–99.

Richards, J. C. (2001). *What do teachers and their students think and know about reading? An exploratory study.* (ERIC Document Reproduction Service No. ED464043)

Richardson, V. (1996). The role of attitudes and beliefs in learning to teach. In J. Sikula (Ed.), *Handbook of research on teacher education* (2nd ed., pp. 102–119). New York: Macmillan.

Richey, R. C. (Ed.). (2000). *The legacy of Robert M. Gagne.* (ERIC Document Reproduction Service No. ED445674)

Richmond, V. P., Gorham, J. S., & McCroskey, J. C. (1986). The relationship between selected immediacy behaviors and cognitive learning. In M. C. McLaughlin (Ed.), *Communication Yearbook 10.* Beverly Hills, CA: Sage.

Richmond, V. P., & McCroskey, J. C. (1995). *Communication apprehension, avoidance, and effectiveness.* Scottsdale, AZ: Gorsuch Scarisbrick.

Richmond, V. P., & McCroskey, J. C. (1999). *Nonverbal behavior in interpersonal relations* (4th ed.). Boston: Allyn & Bacon.

Richmond, V. P., McCroskey, J. C., & Payne, S. (1987). *Nonverbal behavior in interpersonal relations.* Englewood Cliffs, NJ: Prentice-Hall.

Ridling, Z. (1994). *The effects of three seating arrangements on teachers' use of selective interactive verbal behaviors.* (ERIC Document

Reproduction Service No. ED369757)

Riecken, T. J., & Miller, M. R. (1990). Introducing children to problem solving and decision making by using children's literature. *The Social Studies* 81 (2): 59–64.

Rinehart, S. D., Barksdale-Ladd, M. A., & Paterson, J. J. (1994). Story recall through prereading instruction. Use of advance organizers combined with teacher-guided discussion. In E. G. Sturtevant & W. M. Linek (Eds.), *Pathways for literacy: Learners teach and teachers learn* (pp. 237–247). Pittsburg, KS: College Reading Association.

Risinger, C. F. (1987). *Improving writing skills through social studies.* (ERIC Document Reproduction Service No. ED285829)

Risko, V. J., Vukelich, C., & Roskos, K. (2002). Preparing teachers for reflective practice: Intentions, contradictions, and possibilities. *Language Arts* 80 (2): 134–144.

Rittle-Johnson, B., Siegler, R., & Alibali, M. (2001). Developing conceptual understanding and procedural skill in mathematics: An interactive process. *Journal of Education Psychology* 93 (2): 346–362.

Roby, T. W. (1981). *Bull sessions, quiz shows and discussions.* Paper presented at the annual meeting of the American Education Research Association, Los Angeles.

Rolle, J. R. (2002). *The role of communication in effective leadership.* (ERIC Document Reproduction Service No. ED467282)

Rosenbaum, J. E. (2001). *Beyond college for all.* New York: Russell Sage.

Rosenblatt, L. M. (1968). *Literature as exploration.* New York: Modern Language Association. (Original work published in 1938)

Rosenfeld, L. B. (1995). Communication Apprehension and Self-Perceived Communication Competence of Academically Gifted Students. *Communication Education* 44 (1): 79–86. (ERIC Document Reproduction Service No. EJ497375)

Rosenthal, R. (1987). Pygmalion effects. Existence, magnitude, and social importance. *Educational Research* 9: 37–41.

Rosenthal, R., & Jacobson, L. (1968). *Pygmalion in the classroom.* New York: Holt.

Ross, B., & Munby, H. (1991). Concept mapping and misconceptions: A study of high school students' understanding of acids and bases. *International Journal of Science Education* 13 (1): 11–24.

Rowe, M. B. (1972). *Wait time and rewards as instructional variables, their influence in language, logic and fate control.* Paper presented at the National Association for Research in Science Teaching, Chicago, IL. (ERIC Document Reproduction Service No. ED061103)

Rowe, M. B. (1974). Pausing phenomena: Influence on quality of instruction. *Journal of Psycholinguistic Research* 3: 203–233.

Rowe, M. B. (1987). Wait time: Slowing down may be a way of speeding up. *American Educator* 11 (1): 38–43, 47.

Rowe, W. G., & O'Brien, J. (2002). The role of Golem, Pygmalion, and Galatea effects on opportunistic behavior in the classroom. *Journal of Management Education* 26 (6): 612–628.

Roy, P. S. (1998). *Teacher behaviors that affect discipline referrals and off-task behaviors.* Paper presented at the annual Research Colloquium at the State University of West Georgia. (ERIC Document Reproduction Service No. ED 422306)

Rubin, J. (1975). What the "good language learner" can teach us. *TESOL Quarterly* 9: 41–51.

Ruddell, M. R. (1997). *Teaching content reading and writing* (2nd ed.). (ERIC Document Reproduction Service No. ED401526)

Ruhl, K. L., Hughes, C. A., & Schloss, P. J. (1987, Winter). Using the pause procedure to enhance lecture recall. *Teacher Education and Special Education* 10: 14–18.

Ruiz-Primo, M. A., & Shavelson, R. J. (1996). Problems and issues in the use of concept maps in science as-

sessment. *Journal of Research in Science Teaching* 33 (6): 569–600.

Rumelhar, D. E. (1982). Schemata: The building blocks of cognition. In J. Guthrie (Ed.), *Comprehension and teaching: Research reviews* (pp. 3–26). Newark, DE: International Reading Association.

Russell, J. F. (1997). Relationships between the implementation of middle-level program concepts and student achievement. *Journal of Curriculum and Supervision* 12: 169–185.

Rutherford, F. J., & Ahlgren, A. (1990). *Science for all Americans.* New York: Oxford.

Ryan, R. M., & Deci, E. L. (2000). Self-determination theory and the facilitation of intrinsic motivation, social development and well-being. *American Psychologist* 55 (1): 68–78.

Ryan, R. M., & Stiller, J. D. (1991). The social contexts of internalization: Parent and teacher influences on autonomy, motivation, achievement and learning. In M. Maeher & P. Pintrich (Eds.), *Advances in motivation and achievement.* Greenwich, CT: JAI Press (pp. 115–149).

Sacarin, L. (1997). *Tomatoes effect: A unique listening training or auditory integration method.* Retrieved June 1, 2001, from http://home.pacifier.com/~learnging/

Sadker, M., & Sadker, D. (1994). *Failing at fairness: How schools cheat girls.* New York: Simon & Schuster.

Sallis, J. F., Simons-Morton, B. G., Stone, E. J., Corbin, C. B., Epstein, L. H., Faucette, N., Iannotti, R. J., Killen, J. D., Klesges, R. C., Petray, C. K., Rowland, T. W., & Tayler, W. C. (1992). Determinants of physical activity and interventions in youth. *Medicine and Science in Sports and Exercise* 24: 248–257.

Sanford, J. P., & Evertson, C. M. (1985). *Classroom management in a low SES junior high.* Austin, TX: Research and Development Center for Teacher Education, University of Texas at Austin.

Santor, D. A., Messervey, D., & Kusumakar, V. (2000). Measuring

peer pressure, popularity, and conformity in adolescent boys and girls: Predicting school performance, sexual attitudes, and substance abuse. *Journal of Youth and Adolescence* 29 (2): 163–182.

Saracho, O. N. (2003). Matching teachers' and students' cognitive styles. *Early Child Development and Care* 173 (2–3): 161–173.

Schell, V. J. (1982). Learning partners: Reading and mathematics. *Reading Teacher* 35 (5): 544–548.

Schnotz, W., Vosniado, S., & Carretero, M. (Eds.). (1999). *New perspectives on conceptual change.* Oxford: Elsevier.

Schoenbach, R., Greenleaf, C., Cziko, C., & Hurwitz, L. (1999). *Reading for understanding: A guide to improving reading in middle and high school classrooms.* San Francisco: Jossey-Bass.

Schoenstein, R. (1995). The new school on the block. *Executive Educator* 17 (8): 18–21.

Schofield, J. W., & Sagar, H. A. (1977). Peer interaction in an integrated middle school. *Sociomenty* 40 (2): 130–138.

Schommer, M., & Dunnell, P. (1997). Epistemological beliefs of gifted high school students. *Roeper Review* 19 (3): 153–156.

Schön, D. A. (1983). *The reflective practitioner.* New York: Basic Books.

Schriver, K. A. (1989). Evaluating text quality: The continuum from text-focused to reader-focused methods. *IEEE Transactions on Professional Communication* 32 (4): 238–255.

Schubert, M., & Melnick, S. (1997). *The arts in curriculum integration.* Paper presented at the annual meeting of the Eastern Educational Research Association, Hilton Head, SC. (ERIC Document Reproduction Service No. ED424151)

Schunk, D. H. (1996). *Learning theories: An education perspective.* Englewood Cliffs, NJ: Merrill.

Schurr, S. (2000). *How to improve discussion and questioning practices: Tools and techniques.* (Eric Document Reproduction Service No. ED453196)

Schurr, S., Thomason, J. T., Thompson, M., & Lounsbury, J. H. (1995). *Teaching at the middle level: A professional's handbook.* Lexington, MA: D. C. Heath.

Schwarts, B., & Resiberg, D. (1991). *Learning and memory.* New York: Norton.

Schwebel, A., & Cherlin, D. (1972). Physical and social distancing in teacher-pupil relationships. *Journal of Educational Psychology 63:* 543–550.

Scriven, M., & Paul, R. (1992). *Critical thinking defined.* Handout given at the Critical Thinking Conference, Atlanta, GA.

Scudder, D. F. (2001). *Class size reduction: A review of the literature* (Research Watch, E&R Report). (Eric Document Reproduction Service No. ED466478)

Sebart, M., & Krek, J. (2002). *Should grades be a motivation for learning?* (ERIC Document Reproduction Service No. ED470664)

Sedlak, M., Wheeler, C., Pullin, D., & Cusick, P. (1986). *Selling students short: Classroom bargain and academic reform in the American high school.* New York: Teachers College Press.

Seidel, L. E., & England, E. M. (1999). Gregorc's cognitive styles: College students' preferences for teaching methods and testing techniques. *Perceptual and Motor Skills 83* (3): 859–857.

Selinker, L. (1974). Interlanguage. In J. C. Richards (Ed.), *Error analysis: Perspectives on second language acquisition* (pp. 31–54). London: Longman.

Sewall G. T. (1983) *Necessary lesson: Decline and renewal in American schools.* New York: Free Press.

Shamos, M. H. (1995). *The myth of scientific literacy.* New Brunswick, NJ: Rutgers University Press.

Sharan, S. (1980). Cooperative learning in teams: Recent methods and effects on achievement, attitudes, and ethnic relations. *Review of Educational Research 50:* 241–272.

Shuell, T. (1996). Teaching and learning in a classroom context. In D. Berliner & R. Calfee (Eds.), *Handbook of educational psychology* (pp. 726–764). New York: Simon & Schuster.

Shulman, L. (1986). Those who understand: Knowledge growth in teaching. *Educational Researcher 15* (2): 4–14.

Shulman, L. (1987). Knowledge and teaching: Foundations of the new reform. *Harvard Educational Review 5*(1): 122.

Shulman, L. S. (1974). The psychology of school subjects: A premature obituary? *Journal of Research in Science Teaching 11* (4): 319–339.

Shulman, L. S. (1992). Merging content knowledge and pedagogy: An interview with Lee Shulman. *Journal of Staff Development 13* (1): 14–16.

Shulman L. S., & Quinlan, K. M. (1996). The comparative psychology of school subjects. In D. C. Berliner & R. C. Calfee (Eds.), *Handbook of educational psychology* (pp. 399–422). New York: Macmillan Library References USA.

Siegel, M., & Fonzi, J. (1995). The practice of reading in an inquiry-oriented mathematics class. *Reading Research Quarterly, 30*(4): 632–673. (ERIC Document Reproduction Service No. EJ511631)

Silver, E. A. (1998). *Improving mathematics in middle school: Lessons from TIMSS and related research.* Washington, DC: Department of Education.

Silver, H. F., Strong, R. W., & Perini, M. J. (2000). *So each may learn: Integrating learning styles and multiple intelligences.* Alexandria, VA: Association for Supervision and Curriculum Development.

Silverman, S., Kulinna, P., & Crull, G. (1995). Skill-related task structures, explicitness, and accountability: Relationships with student achievement. *Research Quarterly of Exercise and Sport 66:* 32–40.

Simon, S. (1988). *Getting unstuck.* New York: Warner Books.

Simonds, C., & Cooper, P. (2001). Communication and gender in the classroom. In D. Borisoff & L. Arliss (Eds.), *Women and men communicating: Challenges and changes* (2nd ed., pp. 232–253). Fort Worth, TX: Harcourt.

Simpson, M. K. (1986). A teacher's gift: Oral reading and the reading-response journal. *Journal of Reading 30* (1): 45–50.

Skinner, B. F. (1954). The science of learning and the art of teaching. *Harvard Educational Review 24:* 86–89.

Slamecka, N. J. & Graf, P. (1978). The generation effect: Delineation of a phenomenon. *Journal of Experimental Psychology: Human Learning & Memory* (4): 592–604

Slater, J. K. (1990). *Middle grades reform in California: Current and expected attainment of recommendations in "Caught in the Middle"* (Interim Evaluation: Technical Report 1). (ERIC Document Reproduction Service No. ED340088)

Slavin, R. (1984). *Cooperative learning student teams.* West Haven, CT: NEA Professional Library.

Slavin, R. (1997). *Educational psychology: Theory and practice* (5th ed.). Needham Heights, MA: Allyn & Bacon.

Slavin, R. E. (1990a). Achievement effects of ability grouping in secondary schools: A best-evidence synthesis. *Review of Educational Research 60* (3): 471–499.

Slavin, R. E. (1990b). *Cooperative learning: Theory, research and practice.* Englewood Cliffs, NJ: Prentice-Hall.

Smith, B. (2000). Quantity matters: Annual instructional time in an urban school system. *Educational Administration Quarterly 36* (5): 652–682.

Smith, J., & Karr-Kidwell, P. (2000). *The interdisciplinary curriculum: A literary review and a manual for administrators and teachers.* (ERIC Document Reproduction Service No. ED443172)

Smith, J. K., Smith, L. F., & De Lisi, R. (2001). *Natural classroom assessment: Designing seamless instruction and assessment* (Experts in Assessment Series). (ERIC Document Reproduction Service No. ED447093)

Smith, K. A. (2000). Going deeper: Formal small-group learning in large classes. *New Directions for Teaching and Learning 81:* 25–46.

364   **References**

Smith, N. (1999). *Student and teacher perceptions of a single-sex middle school learning environment.* (ERIC Document Reproduction Service No. ED434055)

Smith, P. (2002). A reflection on reflection. *Primary Voices K–6* 10 (4): 31–34.

Smutny, J. F. (2003). *Differentiated instruction* (Fastback). (ERIC Document Reproduction Service No. ED477301)

Smylie, M. A. (1988). The enhancement function of staff development: Organizational and psychological antecedents to individual teacher change. *American Education Research Journal* 25 (1): 1–30.

Snow, C. R. (1974). *The two cultures: A second look.* Cambridge: Cambridge University Press.

Snowman, J., & Biehler, R. (2003). *Psychology applied to teaching* (10th ed.). Boston: Houghton Mifflin.

Sommer, R. (1977). Classroom layout. *Theory into Practice* 16 (3): 174–175.

Sommers, C. H. (2000). *The war against boys.* New York: Simon & Schuster.

Sparkes, A. C., & Templin, T. J. (1992). Life histories and physical education teachers: Exploring the meanings of marginality. In A. C. Sparkes (Ed.), *Research in physical education and sport: Exploring alternative visions* (pp. 118–145). London: Falmer Press.

Sperling, M. (1996). Revisiting the writing-speaking connection. Challenges for research on writing and writing instruction. *Review of Educational Research* 66 (1): 53–86.

Spillane, J. P., & Zeuli, J. S. (1999). Reform and teaching: Exploring patterns of practice in the context of national and state mathematics reforms. *Educational Evaluation and Policy Analysis* 21 (1): 1–27.

Spoehr, K. T., & Spoehr, L. W. (1994). Learning to think historically. *Educational Psychologist* 29: 71–77.

Squire, J. R., & Applebee, R. K. (1968). *High school English instruction today.* New York: Appleton-Century-Crofts.

Stahl, R. J. (1980). *Improving the effectiveness of your questions: Some A, B, C's of questioning.* Paper presented at annual meeting of the National Council for Social Studies, New Orleans, LA. (ERIC Document Reproduction Service No. ED198052)

Stanley, A., & Gifford, L. J. (1998). *The feasibility of 4X4 block scheduling in secondary schools: A review of the literature.* Paper presented at the annual meeting of the Mid-South Educational Research Association (27th, New Orleans, LA). (ERIC Document Reproduction Service No. ED429333)

Staton, A. Q., & Hunt, S. L. (1992). Teacher socialization: Review and conceptualization. *Communication Education* 41 (2): 109–137.

Stein, M. K., Smith, M. S., Hennigsen, M. A., & Silver, E. A. (2000). *Implementing standards-based mathematics instruction: A casebook for professional development.* New York: Teachers College Press.

Stephens, E. C., & Brown, J. E. (2000). *A handbook of content literacy strategies: 75 practical reading and writing ideas.* Norwood, MA: Christopher-Gordon.

Stevenson, H., & Stigler, J. (1992). *The learning gap: Why our schools are failing and what we can learn from Japanese and Chinese education.* New York: Summit Books.

Stewart, L., Cooper P., & Stewart, A. (2003). *Communication and gender.* Boston: Allyn & Bacon.

Stiggins, R. J. (2004). Assessment crisis: The absence of assessment for learning. *Phi Delta Kappan OnLine.* Retrieved May 14, 2004, from **http://www.pdkintl.org/kappan/k0206sti.htm**

Stigler, J., & Hiebert, J. (1999). *The teaching gap: Best ideas from the world's teachers for improving education in the classroom.* New York: The Free Press.

Stigler, J. W., & Hiebert, J. (1997). Understanding and improving classroom mathematics instruction: An overview of the TIMSS video study. *Phi Delta Kappan* 79 (1): 14–21.

Stodolsky, S. S. (1988). *The subject matters: Classroom activity in math and social studies.* Chicago: University of Chicago Press.

Stone, C. A. (1993). What is missing in the metaphor of scaffolding. In E. A. Forman, N. Minick, & C. A. Stone (Eds.), *Contest for learning: Sociocultural dynamics in children's development* (pp. 169–183). Oxford: Oxford University Press.

Stone, R. (2002a). *Best practices for high school classrooms: What award-winning secondary teachers do.* (ERIC Document Reproduction Service No. ED457163)

Stone, R. (2002b). *What! Another new mandate? What award-winning teachers do when school rules change.* (ERIC Document Reproduction Service No. ED471195)

Street, C. (2003). Pre-service teachers' attitudes about writing and learning to teach writing: Implications for teacher educators. *Teacher Education Quarterly,* 30 (3): 33–50.

Streitmatter, J. (1994). *Toward gender equity in the classroom: Everyday teachers' beliefs and practices.* Albany, NY: State University Press.

Strickland, K., & Strickland, J. (2002). *Engaged in learning: Teaching English, 6–12.* Portsmouth, NH: Heinemann.

Strife, K. A. (2004). Community, the missing element of school reform. Why schools should be more like congregations than banks. *American Journal of Education* (110): 215–232.

Strother, D. (1987). Practical applications of research on listening. *Phi Delta Kappan* 59 (4): 625–628.

Stuart v. School District No. 1 of the Village of Kalamazoo, 30 Mich. 69 (1874).

Suchman, J. (1977). Heuristic learning and science education. *Journal of Research in Science Teaching* 14 (3): 263–272.

Sunstein, B. S., & Lovell, J. H. (Eds.). (2000). *The portfolio standard: How students can show us what they know and are able to do.* Portsmouth, NH: Heinemann.

Swain, M. (1995). Three functions of output in second language learning.

In G. Cook & B. Sedhofer (Eds.), *Principles and practice in applied linguistics: Studies in honor of H. G. Widowson* (pp. 125–144). Oxford: Oxford University Press.

Swick, K. (1991). *Teacher-parent partnerships to enhance school success in early childhood education.* Washington, DC: National Education Association.

Symcox, L. (2002). Whose history? The struggle for national standards in American classrooms. (ERIC Reproduction Document Service No. ED477893)

Taba, H., Durkin, M., Fraenkel, J., & McNaughton, A. (1971). *A teacher's handbook to elementary social studies* (2nd ed.). Reading, MA: Addison-Wesley.

Taggart, A. (1985). Fitness-direct instruction. *Journal of Teaching in Physical Education* 4: 143–150.

Tannehill, D., Romar, J. E., O'Sullivan, M., England, K., & Rosenberg, D. (1994). Attitudes toward physical education: Their impact on how physical education teachers make sense of their work. *Journal of Teaching in Physical Education* 13: 406–420.

Tannehill, D., & Zakrajsek, D. (1993). Student attitudes toward physical education: A multicultural study. *Journal of Teaching in Physical Education* 13: 78–84.

Tanner, J. M. (1961). *Education and physical growth.* London: University of London.

Taricani, Ellen. (2000). *Influences of concept mapping and learning styles on learning.* (ERIC Reproduction Document Service No. ED455819)

Taylor, B. A., & Fraser, B. J. (2003). *The influence of classroom environment on high school students' mathematics anxiety.* (ERIC Reproduction Document Service No. ED476644)

Taylor, John F. (1979). *Encouragement vs. praise.* Unpublished manuscript, cited by Dreikurs (see Dreikurs, 1998).

Teal, T. (2003). *Strategies to enhance vocabulary development.* (ERIC Reproduction Document Service No. ED479128)

Tennyson, R., & Cocchiarella, M. (1986). An empirically based instructional design theory for teaching concepts. *Review of Educational Research* 56: 40–71.

Texas Education Agency. (2000). *Promoting vocabulary development: Components of effective vocabulary instruction* (Texas Reading Initiative). (ERIC Reproduction Document Service No. ED453515)

Tharp, R. G. (1997). *From at-risk to excellence: Research, theory and principles for practice.* Santa Cruz, CA: Center for Research on Education, Diversity and Excellence.

Thompson, S. J. (1986). Teaching metaphoric language: An instructional strategy. *Journal of Reading* 30: 105–109.

Thorndike, E. L. (1922). *The psychology of arithmetic.* New York: Macmillan.

Tiberius, R. G. (1999). *Small group teaching: A trouble-shooting guide.* London: Kogan Page.

Tierney, D. S. (1991). The social studies teacher as analogist. *Social Science Record* 28: 53–57.

Tobin, K. (1987). The role of wait time in higher cognitive level learning. *Review of Educational Research* 57: 69–95.

Tobin, K., & Capie, W. (1980). The effects of teacher wait time and questioning quality on middle school science achievement. *Journal of Research in Science Teaching* 17. (ERIC Document Reproduction Service No. ED469475)

Tomlinson, C. (1999). *The differentiated classroom: Responding to the needs of all learners.* Alexandria VA: Association for Supervision and Curriculum Development. (ERIC Document Reproduction Service No. ED429944)

Tomlinson, C. (2001). *How to differentiate instruction in mixed-ability classrooms* (2nd ed.). Alexandria, VA: Association for Supervision and Curriculum Development. (ERIC Document Reproduction Service No. 451902)

Toplak, M. E., & Stanovich, K. E. (2002). The domain specificity and generality of disjunctive reasoning: Searching for a generalizable critical thinking skill. *Journal of Educational Psychology* 94 (1): 197–209.

Totusek, P. F., & Staton-Spicer, A. Q. (1982). Classroom seating preference as a function of student personality. *Journal of Experimental Education* 50 (3): 159–163.

Tracy, B. (1993). *Maximum achievement.* New York: Simon & Schuster.

Travers, K. J., & Westbury, I. (Eds.). (1989). *The IEA study of mathematics 1: Analysis of mathematics curricula.* Oxford, England: Pergamon.

Treasure, D. C., & Roberts, G. C. (1995). Applications of atonement goals theory to physical Education: Implications for enhancing motivation. *Quest* 47: 475–489.

Trumbull, E., Rothstein-Fisch, C., Greenfield, P. M., & Quiroz, B. (2001). *Bridging cultures between home and school: A guide for teachers—with a special focus on immigrant Latino families.* Mahwah, NJ: Lawrence Erlbaum.

Tubbs, S. L., & Moss, S. (1994). *Human communication.* New York: McGraw-Hill.

Turanli, A. S., &Yildirim, A. (1999). *A comparative assessment of classroom management of a high control and low control teacher through student perceptions and class observations.* (ERIC Document Reproduction Service No. ED441765)

Tyson-Bernstein, H. (1988). *A conspiracy of good intentions.* Washington, DC: Council for Basic Education.

Uguroglu, M., & Walberg, H. (1979). Motivation and achievement: A quantitative synthesis. *American Education Research Journal* 16 (4): 375–389.

U.S. Department of Education. (2000). *Twenty-second annual report to Congress on the implementation of the Individuals with Disabilities Act.* Washington, DC: U.S. Government Printing Office.

Vacca, R. T., & Vacca, J. L. (2001). *Content area reading: Literacy and learning across the curriculum* (7th ed.). Boston: Allyn & Bacon.

Van Camp, S. (1993). *The role of physical activity and prevention in health care reform in the United States.* Paper presented at the meeting of the members of the House Ways and Means Subcommittee on Health, Washington, DC.

VanPatten, B., & Cadierno, T. (1993). Input processing and second language acquisition: A role for instruction. *Modern Language Journal* 77: 45–57.

Van Patten, J. (2002). *Hi stakes testing polarization or accountability.* (ERIC Document Reproduction Service No. ED464151)

Vars, G. F. (1996). The effects of interdisciplinary curriculum and Instruction. In P. S. Hlebowitsch & W. G. Wraga (Eds.), *Annual review of research for school leaders, Part II. Transcending traditional subject matter lines: Interdisciplinary curriculum and instruction* (pp. 147–164). Reston, VA: National Association of Secondary School Principals; and New York: Scholastic Press.

Vatterott, C. (1995). Student-focused instruction: Balancing limits with freedom. *Middle School Journal* 27 (11): 28–38.

Vaughn, K. (2000). Music and mathematics: Modest support of the oft-claimed relationship. *Journal of Aesthetic Education* 34 (3–4): 149–166.

Voelkl, K. (1993). Achievement and expectations among African-American students. *Journal of Research and Development in Education* 27 (1): 42–55.

Vygotsky, L. S. (1978). *Mind in society: The development of higher psychological processes.* Cambridge, MA: Harvard University Press.

Vygotsky, L. S. (1986). *Thought and language.* Cambridge, MA: MIT Press.

Walberg, H. J. (1991). Productive teaching and instruction: Assessing the knowledge base. In H. C. Waxman & H. J. Walberg (Eds.), *Effective Teaching Current Research.* Berkeley, CA: McDutchin Publishing Co.

Waller, W. (1932). *The sociology of teaching.* New York: John Wiley and Sons.

Waller, W. (1961). *The sociology of teaching.* New York: Russell & Russell.

Wang, M. C., Haertel, G. D., & Walberg, H. J. (1995). *Educational resilience: An emergent construct.* Paper presented at the annual meeting of the American Educational Research Association, San Francisco, CA.

Wang, X., Wang T., & Ye, R. (2002). *Usage of instructional materials in high schools: Analyses of NELS data.* (ERIC Document Reproduction Service No. ED467793)

Waxman, H. C., Gray, J. P., & Padron, Y. (2003). *Review of research on educational resilience.* (ERIC Document Reproduction Service No. ED479477)

Weaver, L., & Padron, Y. (1997). *Mainstream classroom teachers' observations of ESL teachers' instruction.* Paper presented at the annual meeting of the American Educational Research Association, Chicago.

Weidner, H. Z. (2001). *Classrooms as "places, spaces" for communion.* (ERIC Document Reproduction Service No. ED471393)

Weilbacher, G. (2002). Is curriculum integration an endangered species? *Middle School Journal* 33 (2): 18–27.

Wenglinsky, Harold. (1997). *When money matters: How educational expenditures improve student performance and how they don't.* Princeton, NJ: Educational Testing Service, Policy Information Center.

Werner, W. (2000). Reading authorship into texts. *Theory and Research in Social Education* 28 (2): 193–219.

WestEd. (2001). *Making time count.* Policy Brief. San Francisco: WestEd. Retrieved April 24, 2004, from **http://web.wested.org/online_pubs/making_time_count.pdf**

Whelan, M. (1992). History and the social studies: A response to the critics. *Theory and Research in Social Education* 20 (1): 2–16.

Whelan, M. S. (2000). *But they spit, scratch and swear! The do's and don'ts of behavior guidance for school-age children.* Minneapolis, MN: Aha Process, Inc.

Whimbey, A., & Lockhead, J. (1980). *Problem solving and comprehension.* Philadelphia: Franklin Institute Press.

White, L. (1989). *Universal grammar and second language acquisition.*

Amsterdam and Philadelphia, PA: John Benjamin.

White, R., & Gunstone, R. (1989). Metalearning and conceptual change. *International Journal of Science Education* (11): 577–586.

Why Johnny can't write. (1975, December, 8). *Newsweek.*

Wilhelm, J. D. (1997). *"You gotta BE the book": Teaching engaged and reflective reading with adolescents.* New York: Teachers College Press.

Wilke, R. L. (2003). *The first days of class: A practical guide for the beginning teacher.* (ERIC Document Reproduction Service No. ED473256)

Will, G. (2004, March 11). Whose child shall be left behind? *Tampa Tribune,* p. 19.

William, D., & Black, P. (1996). Meanings and consequences: A basis for distinguishing formative and summative functions of assessment. *British Educational Research Journal* 22: 537–548.

Willingham, D. T. (2003a). *Cognition: The thinking animal.* Upper Saddle River, NJ: Prentice-Hall.

Willingham, D. T. (2003b). Students remember what they think. *American Educator* 27 (3): 37–41.

Wilson, J. (1997, November). *Beyond the basics: Assessing students' metacognition.* Paper presented at the annual meeting of the Hong Kong Education Research Association, Hong Kong. (ERIC Document Reproduction Service No. ED415244)

Wilson, S., & Floden, R. (2003). *Creating effective teachers: Concise answers for hard questions. An addendum to the report Teacher Preparation Research: Current Knowledge, Gaps, and Recommendations.* (ERIC Document Reproduction Service No. ED476366)

Wilson, V. (2002). *Can thinking skills be taught? A paper for discussion. Appendix 3: Starter Paper.* (ERIC Document Reproduction Service No. ED458097)

Winfield, L. F., & Manning, J. B. (1992). Countering parochialism in teacher candidates. In E. Dilwroth (Ed.), *Diversity in teacher education:*

New expectations (pp. 181–214). San Francisco: Jossey-Bass.

Wingert, P. (2004, March). Gates foundation: Now, to high school. *Newsweek,* p. 12.

Witkin, H. A., & Donald, R. G. (1981). *Cognitive styles, essence and origins: Field dependence and field independence.* New York: International Universities Press.

Wood, A. T., & Anderson, C. H. (2001). *The case study method: Critical thinking enhanced by effective teacher questioning skills.* (ERIC Document Reproduction Service No. ED455221)

Wood, D., Bruner, J., & Ross, G. (1976). The role of tutoring in problem solving. *Journal of Child Psychology and Psychiatry* 17: 89–100.

Wood, K. D., & Dickinson, T. S. (Eds.). (2000). *Promoting literacy in grades 4–9: A handbook for teach-ers and administrators.* Boston: Allyn & Bacon.

Wright, I. (2002). *Is that right? Critical thinking and the social world of the young learner.* Toronto, Canada: Pippin Publishing.

Wulf, K. M. (1977). Relationship of assigned classroom seating area to achievement variables. *Educational Research Quarterly* 2 (2): 56–62.

Wycoff, V. L. (1973). The effects of stimulus variation on learning from lecture. *Journal of Experimental Education* 41: 85–90.

Yopp, R. H., & Yopp, H. K. (2000). Sharing informational text with young children. *The Reading Teacher* 53: 410–423.

Yorks, P., & Follo, E. (1993). *Engagement rates during thematic and traditional instruction.* (ERIC Document Reproduction Service No. ED363412)

Yuruk, N., Ozdemir, O., & Beeth, M. E. (2003). *The role of metacognition in facilitating conceptual change.* (ERIC Document Reproduction Service No. ED477315)

Zellermayer, M. (1989). The study of teachers' written feedback to students' writing: Changes in theoretical considerations and the expansion of research contexts. *Instructional Science* 18 (2): 145–165.

Zill, N. (1992). *Trends in family life and children's school performance.* Washington, DC: Child Trends, Inc. (ERIC Document Reproduction Service No. ED378257)

Zimmerman, J. (2001). How much does time affect learning? *Principal* 80 (3): 6–11.

Credits

Index

Note: Locators with *t* indicate tables; locators with *f* indicate figures.